1973

T2-CSE-258

The Effects of tel-
evision advertis-
ing on children

The Effects
of Television
Advertising
on Children

The Effects
of Television
Advertising
on Children

Review and Recommendations

Richard P. Adler
Gerald S. Lesser
Laurene Krasny Meringoff
Thomas S. Robertson
John R. Rossiter
Scott Ward

with
Bernard Z. Friedlander
Leslie Isler
Ronald J. Faber
David B. Pillemer

LexingtonBooks
D.C. Heath and Company
Lexington, Massachusetts
Toronto

Library of Congress Cataloging in Publication Data

Main entry under title:
The Effects of television advertising on children.

Bibliography:
Includes index.
1. Television advertising and children. I. Adler, Richard.
HQ784.T4E35   791.45'01'3   78-24714
ISBN 0-669-02814-2

Third printing, January 1982

Published simultaneously in Canada

Printed in the United States of America

International Standard Book Number: 0-669-02814-2

Library of Congress Catalog Card Number: 78-24714

Contents

List of Figures
and Tables

Preface

This book began with a project supported by the National Science Foundation to review the existing research on the effects of television advertising on children and identify topics needing further research. Richard P. Adler served as the project's principal investigator; Bernard Z. Friedlander, Gerald S. Lesser, Laurene Krasny Meringoff, Thomas S. Robertson, John R. Rossiter, and Scott Ward were senior investigators. The report produced by that project was published in 1977 by the U.S. Government Printing Office.

The present volume is based on that report, but it has been extensively revised and updated to take account of new research findings and recent policy developments, such as the Federal Trade Commission rulemaking on children's television advertising, which began in 1978. Every chapter in this volume has been revised, and several have been substantially expanded. One chapter from the report, on the portrayal of violence and unsafe acts in commercials, has been omitted. Both the key studies in appendix A and the bibliography contain new entries.

One other change from the earlier report is that the authors of the individual literature-review chapters have been identified in this edition. However, the first and last chapters remain unsigned because they reflect the views of all the authors.

Acknowledgments

We wish to express our appreciation to the following:

To the National Science Foundation for its support for the preparation of the report on which this volume is based, and to NSF program officers Charles Brownstein, Rolland Johnson, and Allen Shinn for their interest, encouragement, and advice throughout the project.

To the members of the project's advisory committee: Seymour Banks; Peggy Charren; Walter J. Clayton, Jr.; John A. Dimling, Jr.; Mary Gardiner Jones; Ithiel de Sola Pool; Eli A. Rubinstein; Alberta Siegel; Eddie Smarden; and Lawrence Zacharias. In addition to meeting with the authors as a group on several occasions, the members of our advisory board contributed individually by reviewing and commenting on drafts of the initial report. Although not responsible for the contents of our report, they did play a significant role in its development.

To our colleague, Bernard Z. Friedlander of the University of Hartford, who served as one of the project's senior investigators. He wrote a preliminary version of the final project proposal and was responsible for compiling a roster of researchers interested in children's television advertising issues, published separately. As a participant in project meetings, he also helped define the issues that served as the framework for our review.

To the Children's Advertising Review Unit of the Council of Better Business Bureaus, Inc., for its assistance in compiling our bibliography.

To the staffs of our respective institutions, without whose help our project could not have been completed. We are also grateful to those individuals, too numerous to acknowledge individually, who took the time to respond to the questionnaire used in formulating our list of issues.

1 Introduction

This book reviews the existing research on the effects of television advertising on children and recommends a plan for future research. It is not an effort to reach a definitive verdict about those effects, since academic research on this issue remains relatively limited and there is not enough information currently available to permit such a judgment. However, this book provides a comprehensive review of the present state of knowledge about television advertising and children.

Concern about television's impact on children is largely based on the fact that most American children spend a great deal of time watching television: The average child under 12 spends approximately 27 hours per week watching television (Nielsen 1979), and the vast majority of all children watch some television every day (Lyle and Hoffman 1972a). The average high school graduate will have spent some 22,000 hours in front of the set and may have been exposed to as many as 350,000 commercial messages.

Because of its massive presence in children's lives, television is believed to be a major vehicle for acculturation to society's values. Public concern has understandably focused on the possible negative impact of the medium. The most prominent issue has been the controversy over the effects of television violence, which led to the Surgeon General's study (1972).

The 1970s have seen a marked increase in public and governmental interest in the effects of television on children in other areas as well. For example, in 1971, in response to a petition from Action for Children's Television (ACT), the Federal Communications Commission undertook a broad inquiry into children's television. In 1978, the Federal Trade Commission launched a major rulemaking concerned with children's advertising.

Perhaps the major result of these inquiries has been a general acceptance of the principle that children are a special television audience deserving special attention and protection. How this principle should be applied in terms of specific issues is much less clear. However, policymakers in both government and industry have begun looking to empirical findings about children's responses to television programming and advertising as a means for making more informed decisions about policies and practices.

Children's Television Advertising:
Background to the Controversy

The issue of the effects of television advertising on children is not new. It has a history dating at least from the early 1960s, when broadcasters first adopted guidelines for toy advertising to children. Since then, the issue has taken many forms, but it seems to be based upon four fundamental concerns:

1. Children are exposed to advertising for products or categories of products (such as drugs and heavily sugared foods) that may be hazardous if misused.
2. Any advertising directed at children is in fact "bad" because it exploits their vulnerability.
3. Specific techniques used in television advertising may be deceptive or misleading to children, who lack the skills to evaluate them properly.
4. Long-term, cumulative exposure to television advertising may have adverse consequences on the development of children's values, attitudes, and behavior.

The first concern, relating to the safety of advertised products, will not be treated as such in this book, since it is a direct effect not of advertising, but of the product itself. However, we will consider the role of advertising in relation to children's attitudes toward and consumption of two categories of advertised products—foods and nonprescription drugs. The second concern, that any advertising to children is in and of itself "bad," is primarily an ethical issue not amenable to empirical research. However, the extent to which children's perceptions of and responses to television advertising differ from those of adults (and how children's perceptions and responses vary by age) is a subject which has been addressed by research.

The third concern, about specific practices, has been the subject of most of the existing research and represents the largest portion of the literature reviewed in this book. The fourth concern, about long-term effects, is the broadest of issues amenable to research, since it relates to the very existence of a medium which advertises directly to children. Research may eventually be able to document the long-range developmental consequences of television advertising, but such research will require a scale, duration, and complexity greater than that of most research undertaken to date.

The major participants in the debate over televised advertising to children can be categorized into three groups which are involved in policymaking on children's advertising. The positions and actions taken by these three groups to a large degree define the context in which specific issues are raised and resolved, as well as the contribution to be made by empirical research. These groups are industry, government, and consumer-interest organizations.

Industry

The private, corporate side of children's television advertising breaks down into three subgroups. First, the advertisers who manufacture and market products and/or services intended, at least in part, for child consumers. These advertisers generally conduct a great deal of market research—both in-house or by research suppliers—in order to pretest their products and advertising strategies with potential consumers. Second, the advertising agencies which are responsible for developing creative strategies for promoting a client's products or services to young consumers or to their parents (the usual purchasers). The advertising agencies often conduct market research for their clients. Third, the broadcasters (networks, their affiliates, and independent stations) who sell air time to children's advertisers within programs that attract young viewers. Because, unlike other mass media, the airwaves are a limited public resource, access and control of broadcast channels are restricted by federal agency licensing.

Over the years, these three groups have developed self-regulatory codes relating to advertising to children. Broadcasters have adopted standards for children's advertising through the "Television Code" of the National Association of Broadcasters (NAB).[1] The guidelines pertaining to children's advertising are periodically updated and expanded. The NAB code prohibits certain products (for example, drugs) from being advertised directly to children, lists certain presentational techniques that may or may not be used in commercials, and sets time limits for advertising during children's programming. Alleged code violations are reviewed by the NAB's Television Code Authority, which may order that an ad be modified or discontinued by its members. The Code Authority also acts as a mandatory preclearance unit for all toy commercials and those offering a toy premium. In addition, each network reviews commercials (and programs) submitted for airing, evaluating them on the basis of the NAB guidelines and of legal policies and regulations.

Advertisers and advertising agencies have also established a system of self-regulation through the Council of Better Business Bureaus, Inc. The Council's National Advertising Division (NAD) has responsibility for monitoring ads and acting on complaints received from the public. In the spring of 1974, a Children's Advertising Review Unit was set up within the NAD, with a specific mandate to review problems concerned with advertising to children. In June 1975, the Children's Advertising Review Unit issued a set of "Children's Advertising Guidelines" whose stated purpose is "to ensure that advertising directed to children is truthful, accurate, and fair to children's perceptions." The provisions of the NAD guidelines are similar, though not identical to the NAB code. (See Appendix B for relevant sections of both codes.)

Federal Government

Congressional legislation has delegated most of the responsibility for regulation of broadcast advertising to two agencies. First, the Federal Communications Commission, in the Communications Act of 1934, was given the authority to regulate broadcasting "consistent with the public interest, convenience, and necessity." The FCC thereby acquired broad discretionary powers, circumscribed by relatively few specifically articulated guidelines, and the responsibility for developing specific standards for broadcast regulation and policy-making. It has authority not only to oversee technical aspects of licensing, but also to monitor industry behavior and to perform quasi-legislative functions (hold hearings and make rules). Its power derives from its authority to grant, renew, or deny licenses to television stations and to levy fines for certain violations.

The Federal Trade Commission, established in 1914, is the agency with principal responsibility for the regulation of interstate commerce. Since 1938, the FTC has been empowered to protect the consumer interest, as well as private competition, by means of prohibiting "false advertisements" and preventing "unfair or deceptive acts or practices." The commission has the power to act on commercials on a case-by-case basis, as well as to issue broad Trade Rules and Regulations which can restrict or require certain advertising practices. For the most part, the FTC has dealt with children's advertising by evaluating individual commercials. From 1974 to 1977, the commission considered, and finally decided against, adopting restrictions on the use of premium offers in children's television advertising. In 1978, the commission launched a major rulemaking to consider regulations restricting TV advertising directed to young children and children's advertising for sugared foods.

Historically, both commissions have demonstrated a reluctance to impose specific regulations on advertisers and broadcasters, preferring to allow industry to regulate itself.[2] However, the threat of government action has tended to stimulate industry reforms, and the commissions sometimes hold hearings in order to focus attention and generate debate on specific issues. Congress (especially through the Communications Subcommittees of the House and Senate) has intermittently performed a similar function.[3]

Consumer-Interest Organizations

The public has remained relatively uninformed and unorganized in expressing its concern regarding the uses and abuses of television advertising for children. Some organizations, such as the Consumers Union, provide the public with objective evaluations of advertised products; and several advocacy groups have concentrated specifically on the issues of children's television advertising—most notably ACT, in Boston, and the Council on Children, Media and Merchandising (CCMM), in Washington. These groups pursue reform through a variety of methods, including testimony at government hearings, publications, conferences, and research sponsorship. They have also attempted to force governmental action by filing petitions with the regulatory commissions and the courts.

Relations between industry, government, and the consumer-interest groups have often been contentious. ACT and CCMM charge that industry efforts toward self-regulation are more concerned with public relations than with the actual prevention of harm. Industry spokespersons, in turn, assert that consumer groups are self-appointed advocates who do not accurately reflect the concerns of most parents. Industry also tends to regard much government intervention as unwarranted, while consumer advocates perceive the government as timid and overly concerned with industry well-being.[4]

The Role of Research

As indicated earlier, the amount of publicly available research on the effects of televised advertising on children is still limited. The largest body of existing research is undoubtedly that conducted by advertisers in testing the effectiveness of individual commercials and advertising campaigns. This research typically consists of studies employing small samples of children to determine the comprehensibility and persuasiveness of commercials. These studies are almost always kept confidential because of "an unwillingness to share private data with competitors and a general view that such research is of little interest to the research community" (Griffin 1976). Griffin also suggests that "often the scope of the research is so small and specialized that no great enlightenment would result from publication." However, studies of children's perceptions of and responses to specific commercials can yield important data, and one of our principal recommendations is for a program of research along these lines.

Academic research on children's television advertising is much less extensive. Although the bibliography in this book cites several hundred references that have some bearing on our topic, only a fraction of these are studies that deal specifically with children and television advertising. Many citations pertain to more general issues and a number of the entries refer to speeches and testimony rather than empirical research. In addition, many of the empirical studies are small-scale, and there has been little replication of findings.

When the research proposed here has been carried out, a more definitive verdict about the effects of television advertising can be reached. However, even then, no final answers will be possible, for the following reasons: First, although the short-term effects of individual television advertisements or of small numbers of advertisements can be readily studied, such research does not encompass what is most at issue—the question of whether there are any long-term, aggregate effects upon children of either particular types of commercials or the whole volume of television advertising. Understanding the effects of advertising as an institution is simply beyond current research procedures. Although we have recommended that research be designed to study advertising at this level, we expect that current ignorance about the *en masse* effects of televised advertising will continue for some years to come.

In regard to any long-term effects of children's exposure to particular categories of television advertising or to specific features of commercials, the necessary research methods may be more within reach. Several longitudinal studies have been designed to measure the various aspects of child development. However, longitudinal research has not yet been sufficiently sophisticated to separate the effects of television advertising from other influences upon the child, including family, peers, and school. Nor is there adequate research to identify the *interactions* between these other influences and television advertising. Yet, it is precisely these long-term effects of television advertising, in the full context of the child's life, that are of the greatest concern.

Finally, since we are concerned here with research intended to be "policy relevant," we should also consider the limitations of research from the perspectives of the advertiser and the regulator.

When an advertiser looks to research to assess the effectiveness of advertising, well-established research procedures can be followed. But public concern about advertising is not, of course, to establish that advertising can benefit sales, but rather that advertising may mislead, confuse, or produce harmful effects. When advertisers look to research to demonstrate the absence of these effects, our procedures can never be fully convincing: Research can never prove the *absence* of an effect.

From the regulator's point of view, it is important to recognize that policy decisions are seldom based solely on research evidence, no matter how well planned and conducted that research may be. Research findings are typically only one element among the several factors that determine advertising policies and practices with regard to children. Ethical, legal, economic, and political forces will inevitably continue to operate and influence policy.

Despite these caveats, we believe that research can help establish an empirical basis for more rational and more effective policymaking. Indeed, the results of research have already had impact on policymaking; for example, in the formulation of the NAD's guidelines for advertising to children, and in the FTC's rulemaking concerning children's television advertising.

Defining the Issues

We began this chapter by attempting to identify a set of issues that would serve as a framework for the review of existing research. Several problems made this selection process difficult. One fundamental difficulty is that the various issues raised in the debate are often rooted in personal values. Some critics feel that any advertising directed at children is unfair and unacceptable, while some defenders of the system feel that any regulation of advertising practices is an abridgement of rights in our basically free-enterprise economy. Given such extreme points of view, objective discussion of any specific issues is difficult indeed. Beyond a very few basic points of agreement—for example, all would agree that children should not be harmed or exploited—critics and defenders of advertising share very little common ground in the controversy.

Another problem is that the issues which have been advanced by various individuals or groups involved in the debate have frequently been stated incompletely or too broadly, alleging an effect without a specific cause, or a cause without a specific effect. For example, the charges that advertising leads to "materialistic values," or that "animation in children's advertising is misleading," would be difficult to test empirically or to remedy with a realistic policy for corrective action. The charge that animation is misleading neither specifies what aspects of animation are misleading, nor how the children are misled. Similarly, it would be difficult to recommend action on the charge of materialistic values without a realistic and objective understanding of this concept, a knowledge that advertising in fact fosters the development of such attitudes, and a widespread agreement that such attitudes are detrimental to children and/or to society. One cannot realistically propose a corrective device without understanding causal factors, and one cannot evaluate a charge that a practice is "bad" without specific indications of the alleged consequences of the practice.

These problems indicated the need for a more precise specification of issues, as well as for a more adequate theoretical and empirical base for the investigation of these issues. Thus, we followed three distinct steps in our effort to define the issues more precisely and objectively: (1) we conducted an initial literature review; (2) we then surveyed interested parties in the controversy for their views of the issues; and only then did we (3) develop a framework of issues that seemed to us most meaningful and investigable.

The initial literature review was undertaken in order to help develop a tentative list of issues of concern to all interested parties. We then asked a group of advertisers and advertising agencies, politicians, regulators, industry associations, consumer groups, and academics to evaluate this list of issues. Forty-five responses were received out of the approximately 125 questionnaires mailed. Few entirely new issues were suggested in these responses; rather, most respondents urged us to modify the wording of the issues we posed, or to broaden or narrow them. Some advertisers, for example, urged us to consider more of the "positive" results of advertising on young people; some urged us to review the constitutionality of regulations of advertising practices affecting children. On the other hand, some consumerists urged us to focus on the nutritional characteristics of advertised food products prior to the question of the effects of advertising itself. Many of the responses from academics suggested topics for research which also raised policy issues.

Following these preliminary activities, we were prepared to synthesize the results and specify the framework of issues which would become the focus for the project. We agreed on five points which were useful in this synthesis:

1. We would distinguish between issues arising from advertising in general and issues related to the specific products advertised. We decided *not* to make judgments about the quality of advertised products, since these questions were beyond the scope of the project and outside the specific expertise of the project staff.

2. The issues to be considered would encompass *all* advertising to which substantial numbers of children are exposed, not just those commercials specifically intended for children and broadcast within the context of children's programming:

3. While many of the issues pertain to alleged negative effects, we would attempt, where possible, to identify issues pertaining to potentially positive or beneficial effects of television advertising.

4. Although some of the alleged negative practices in advertising occur relatively infrequently, we decided that since they do occur or have occurred, they should be included in the analysis.

5. Because we believed that the issues should be practical, we decided that the final set of issues would be more productively stated mainly in terms of advertising characteristics or practices which on the basis of research results could be corrected or modified. Thus, our main criterion in selecting these issues was *utility*: Is some action suggested by the empirical knowledge relating to the issue? Does empirical information suggest some change or some continuation in a practice? For example, one cannot readily alter the television viewing patterns of children from different socioeconomic family backgrounds, although such differences may exist and may affect their responses to advertising. One can, however, modify, eliminate, or leave unchanged certain advertising practices, such as the use of "host selling," on the basis of empirical evidence of this practice's effects on children.

Given these considerations, we derived the following list of issues.[5] The first six deal with the effects of particular practices or categories of television advertising; the final three issues are concerned with the cumulative exposure of children to television advertising and with some potential mediating factors on the effects of this exposure:

1. Children's ability to distinguish television commercials from program materials.
2. The influence of format and audiovisual techniques on children's perceptions of commercial messages.
3. Source effects and self-concept appeals in children's television advertising.

4. The effects of premium offers in children's television advertising.
5. The impact on children of proprietary medicine advertising.
6. The effects on children of television food advertising.
7. The effects of volume and repetition of television commercials.
8. The impact of television advertising on consumer socialization.
9. Television advertising and parent-child relations.

The FTC Children's Advertising Rulemaking

In April 1978, the FTC announced it was undertaking a rulemaking proceeding "to consider certain restrictions regarding television advertising directed to children" (Federal Trade Commission 1978). The rulemaking was based on petitions from Action for Children's Television and the Center for Science in the Public Interest (CSPI), as well as a 346-page report prepared by the staff of the FTC's Division of Advertising Practices. While the ACT and CSPI petitions focused on commercials for sugared products, the staff report added the issue of whether any advertising should be allowed to young children.

Specifically, the staff report recommended that the commission should consider adopting a rule which would:

1. Ban all televised advertising for any product which is directed to, or seen by, audiences composed of a significant proportion of children who are too young to understand the selling purpose of or otherwise comprehend or evaluate the advertising.
2. Ban televised advertising for sugared food products directed to, or seen by, audiences composed of a significant proportion of older children, the consumption of which products poses the most serious dental health risks.
3. Require televised advertising for sugared food products not included in Paragraph (2), which is directed to, or seen by, audiences composed of a significant proportion of older children, to be balanced by nutritional and/or health disclosures funded by advertisers.

In addition to considering these staff proposals, the FTC indicated it wished to consider four other, less drastic remedies:

1. Affirmative disclosures located in the body of advertisements for highly cariogenic products directed to children.
2. Affirmative disclosures and nutritional information contained in separate advertisements, funded by advertisers of highly cariogenic products advertised to children.
3. Limitations upon particular advertising messages used and/or techniques used to advertise to very young children, or to advertise highly cariogenic products to all children.

4. Limitations upon the number and frequency of advertisements directed
    at very young children; limitations upon the number and frequency of all
    advertisements of highly cariogenic products directed at all children.

Finally, the commission listed fifteen "general questions and issues" related
to these proposals, and invited comment on them from all interested parties.
The broadness of these issues as well as the far-reaching nature of the remedies
under consideration by the FTC make this the most comprehensive inquiry to
date into children's television advertising and its effects.

The list of issues discussed in this volume was completed before the rulemaking was launched. (In fact, the FTC staff report utilized the previous edition
of our review in discussing research evidence.) However, most of the major
issues being considered by the FTC can be found among our list of issues: The
question of whether children "understand the selling purpose" of advertising
is discussed in chapter 3, Children's Ability to Distinguish Television Programs
from Commercial Material, while chapter 8 reviews the evidence pertaining to
the effects on children of television food advertising. Other chapters deal with
research related to the effect of various advertising techniques, the ability of
children to understand required disclosures, and the effects of the volume and
repetition of commercial messages.

Organization of This Book

Reviews of the research relevant to each of the nine issues follow in chapters 3
through 11. In each of these chapters, we briefly introduce the *issue* and then
review the current and proposed *regulations* regarding that issue. The intent is to
determine to what extent existing regulations and industry codes address the
issue. A third section in most of the chapters assesses the *incidence* of the advertising practices or characteristics in question. Here we rely on data from
available content analyses. The body of each chapter then reviews and evaluates
the empirical *research evidence* relating to the practice or characteristic. Finally,
each chapter summarizes the evidence and offers *recommendations* for future
research pertinent to that issue.

A preliminary chapter, "Children's Television Viewing Patterns," summarizes the available data on how much television children watch, when they
watch, and what they watch. The final chapter summarizes the research evidence in two different ways, then presents our overall recommendations for
future research. The research is summarized first in terms of the nine key issues,
then in terms of what the evidence tells us about the stimulus properties of
children's television advertising, the possible outcomes of children's exposure to
advertising, and the role of various mediating variables in influencing these
outcomes. In our recommendations, we have attempted to spell out research

projects in detail, but have rather indicated the major directions we believe should be pursued in order to resolve the most important unanswered questions about the effects of television advertising on children. Some of our suggestions follow existing lines of research; others propose new directions. Because the need for additional research is great, we hope readers will give careful attention to these recommendations.

The back matter of this volume includes two appendixes and a comprehensive bibliography. Appendix A consists of detailed technical evaluations of twenty-six key studies specifically concerned with the effects of television advertising on children. These studies are reviewed in terms of their objectives, child samples, methods, statistical tests, and results. This appendix is intended as a technical supplement to the literature reviews in the main body of the report. Appendix B contains the self-regulatory codes and guidelines pertaining to children's television advertising developed by the NAB and NAD. The bibliography includes all research studies cited in the text, as well as important policy statements, theoretical articles and books, reports of key hearings, and relevant secondary references.

Notes

1. Not all television stations are members of the NAB. As of February 1, 1979, 473 of the 728 commercial stations on the air were NAB code subscribers. These 473 did, however, include most of the larger stations. The three national networks also subscribe to the NAB code.

2. For a useful, if partisan, review of government action (and inaction) in this area, see the statement by Robert Choate in *Broadcast Advertising and Children*, Subcommittee on Communications, U.S. House of Representatives (Government Printing Office, 1976), no. 94-53. *Reluctant Regulators* by Barry Cole and Mal Oettinger (Addison-Wesley, 1978) contains a knowledgeable account of the FCC's response to the controversy over children's television.

3. On the other hand, from time to time, Congress has acted to retard regulatory action. In 1978, for example, the House Appropriations Committee voted to prohibit the FTC from spending any of its 1979 appropriation to pass a rule restricting children's advertising. This amendment was dropped in a conference with the Senate, but was regarded as an expression of criticism of the commission's intentions.

4. For a comparative study of attitudes of representatives from each of these groups (and a sample of "public" opinion), see Atkin and Culley (1975). Results of this study are summarized in Chapter 11.

5. A tenth issue, violence and unsafe acts in children's television commercials, included in the original report, (Adler et al., 1977) has been omitted here because of limitations of space. The issue of the impact of televised violence on

children, is of great importance, of course. However, research and reviews of research on the topic are widely available, and the issue was judged less central to concerns about children's *advertising* than the other issues under review.

2 Background: Children's Television Viewing Patterns

Richard P. Adler and
Ronald J. Faber

Knowledge of children's television viewing patterns is relevant in several ways to a consideration of the effects of television advertising on children. For example, data on children's total viewing time can be used to estimate their total exposure to television advertising. Information on the times that children watch television and the programs they favor is useful in determining the kinds of commercials children are likely to see. In this background chapter, we will review the available evidence on the following specific questions:

At what age do children begin watching television?

How much television do children watch?

How much television advertising are children exposed to?

When to children watch television?

What kinds of programs do they prefer?

What is the relationship between children's viewing patterns and the industry codes governing advertising to children?

Three important points should be noted at the outset. First, in the context of this book, "children" are conventionally defined as youngsters between the ages of 2 and 12. Within such a wide age range, there are great differences, of course. The viewing habits and preferences of a 3- or 4-year-old are different from those of a 6-year-old, and vastly different from those of a 10-year-old. Unfortunately, these differences are often ignored in discussions of "children's television." Whenever possible, we will take account of these age differences in our discussion.

Second, there is no single, wholly satisfactory source of data on children's television viewing patterns. There are many different ways to collect such data, and each is likely to produce different results. For example, Schramm, Lyle, and Parker (1961) compared four separate measures of the amount of weekend television viewing by a group of twenty-four children: (1) a child's general estimate; (2) an unsupervised diary kept by each child; (3) a surreptitious measurement by older sublings; and (4) an interview in which the investigators aided the child's recall of programs watched. These four methods yielded estimates which varied by as much as 20 percent. An additional problem with most scientific studies of children's television viewing is that they are usually based on small samples taken over limited periods of time and are therefore difficult to generalize.

Third, most of the studies of children's viewing patterns lack a precise definition of "television viewing." The term can be used to encompass a broad variety of behaviors, ranging from rapt involvement to mere presence in a room in which a television set is operating. The latter extreme probably should be (but is not always) excluded from the definition of television viewing; but even within the "normal" range of viewing, research studies have established that quite different levels of involvement can be included. For example, both surveys and observations have demonstrated that children's viewing is often accompanied by other activities, such as talking, eating, and playing (Lyle and Hoffman 1972a; Murray 1972); and laboratory studies have shown considerable variations in children's visual attention to the screen, even when watching television is their only activity (Ward 1972b; Wartella and Ettema 1974).

In light of these limitations, the statistics cited in this chapter must be regarded as *gross* measures of children's viewing time and not as precise records of moment-to-moment attention by the children studied. Much of the data in this chapter come from the A.C. Nielsen Company, which compiles the best known and most detailed statistics on national television audiences.[1] There are both important advantages and disadvantages to these Nielsen data. Some of the advantages are: (1) The data are based on a relatively large and representative national sample (approximately 3,600 families); (2) The Nielsen Company has been measuring television audiences since 1950 and therefore provides a valuable historical picture of viewing patterns; and (3) The Nielsen Company analyzes the television audience on the basis of age and therefore provides viewing data specifically on children, as well as on teenagers and adults.

The disadvantage of the Nielsen data is that the company's purposes are not scientific; therefore: (1) most of the data are proprietary and not publicly available; (2) the collection and presentation of the data are primarily shaped by the needs of Nielsen's principal clients—broadcasters and advertisers—not by the priorities of scientific research; and (3) the company subdivides its child audience into two categories only—children 2 to 5 years of age and children 6 to 11. Thus, differences in viewing patterns within these age brackets cannot be determined from the Nielsen data. Because of these disadvantages, we have supplemented the Nielsen data, whenever possible, with data from other sources.

At What Age Do Children Begin Watching Television?

Little attention has been given to when and how very young children begin watching television. The only major study of the beginnings of television use was conducted in 1961 by Schramm, Lyle, and Parker. They found that 14 percent of the children studied made "regular use of the medium" by age 2. Over one-third did so by age 3, over two-thirds by age 4, and over 90 percent by age 6 (see table 2-1).

Although more recent data are not available, it seems likely that with the increased ownership of television sets since 1961,[2] and with the advent of programming intended specifically for preschoolers (such as "Sesame Street"), more children are becoming regular viewers at a very early age. Even on the basis of these dated figures, we can conclude that a majority of children are watching television regularly before the age of 4.

How Much Television Do Children Watch?

Childrens' viewing patterns vary considerably from individual to individual, as well as from day to day and week to week for the same individual. Nevertheless, some general patterns can be discerned. According to Nielsen data from November 1978, children 2 to 5 years old watched television an average of 28 hours and 38 minutes per week, or slightly more than 4 hours per day. Older children, ages 6 to 11, watched an average of 26 hours and 4 minutes each week, or more than 3½ hours per day. By comparison, the average weekly viewing time for all persons was 28 hours and 53 minutes per week. Teenagers, working women, and men under 55 watched less than children; nonworking women over 18 and men over 55 watched more than children.

The data indicate that children's viewing hours vary somewhat from year to year, but a gradual upward trend in the 1966-1978 period can be seen (see table 2-2). Earlier, Lyle and Hoffman (1972a) estimated that children's average daily viewing time had increased approximately one hour per day in the twenty-

Table 2-1
Percent of Children Using Television at Different Ages

Age	Percent Using Television
2	14
3	37
4	65
5	82
6	91
7	94
8	95
9	96

Source: Schramm, Lyle, and Parker (1961).

Table 2-2
Children's Average Daily Viewing Time (1966-1978)
(hours)

	2-5-Year Olds	6-11-Year-Olds
November 1966	3:14	2:59
November-December 1968[a]	3:28	4:01
November 1970	3:40	3:11
November 1972	3:54	3:39
November 1974	3:45	3:26
November 1975	3:47	3:41
November 1977	3:56	3:29
November 1978	4:05	3:43

Source: A.C. Nielsen.

[a]1968 data came from a six-week measurement period (November 1-December 12); four-week periods were used in the other years.

year period from 1952 to 1972. These averages do not reflect individual variations in viewing patterns within age groups. For example, among sixth graders interviewed by Lyle and Hoffman, 25 percent reported watching 5½ hours or more of television on a given day, while another 25 percent reported watching no television at all.

A number of studies have attempted to determine the factors that influence individual differences in the amount of television viewed by children. A relationship has been found, for instance, between higher viewing times and lower parental socioeconomic status (Schramm, Lyle, and Parker 1961; McIntyre and Teevan 1972). Viewing differences have also been correlated with intelligence, ethnic background, and level of social adjustment. However, most of these differences are not dramatic and have been found primarily among older children and adolescents. Moreover, research has indicated substantial reductions of these differences over time (Comstock, et al. 1978).

Allowing for individual differences, we can safely conclude that the average child over the past decade has watched 3 to 4 hours of television per day. Schramm, Lyle, and Parker's description of the role of the medium in children's lives in 1961 is still appropriate today:

> Throughout the preschool years, television time far exceeds other media time; in fact, it usually exceeds the total of all other media time. . . . Two-thirds of all children are already television viewers before they have much experience with movies. Even at the end of 10 years, when they are making some use of all media, television is the only one they are using day after day. At age 10, three-fourths of all children, as we discovered, will be likely to be watching television on any given

day. This is more than twice the percentage for any other medium at that age.

To How Much Television Advertising Are Children Exposed?

Some of the issues we deal with in this book concern the long-term cumulative effects of television advertising on children. Thus, we have tried to derive a rough estimate of the average child's yearly exposure to television advertising. Our computations suggest that children on average are exposed to some 20,000 commercial messages each year, or slightly more than 3 hours of television advertising each week.[3] Of course, light viewers (or heavy public television viewers) would see fewer commercials, and heavy viewers might see considerably more.

These figures were reached by multiplying 365 days per year times the average number of viewing hours and the approximate number of commercials per hour. The figure for the number of viewing hours per day was based on an average of Nielsen estimates for 1977 and 1978 (see table 2-2). Since Nielsen provides separate data for 2- to 5-year-olds and 6- to 11-year-olds, we computed estimates for each of these age groups, and we accounted for noncommercial public television viewing time by reducing these estimates by 10 percent (probably a high figure, except for preschool devotees of "Sesame Street").

Reaching a fairly accurate estimate of the number of commercial messages per hour was more problematic, since regulations governing the maximum amount of "nonprogram material" per hour differ for different times of the day and also change periodically. At present, the NAB code states that nonprogram material may occupy no more than 9½ minutes per hour during prime time and weekend children's programming time,[4] no more than 12 minutes per hour during weekday children's programming, and no more than 16 minutes per hour at all other times.[5]

There were two other problems in determining the number of commercials per hour. First, the length of individual commercials varies, ranging from 15 to 60 seconds. However, since Barcus (1978) reports that 98 percent of commercials monitored in his studies were 30 seconds in length, we accepted his figure as an adequate estimate.[6] Second, not all nonprogram material is advertising. This category also includes public service announcements, promotional commercials for other television programs, and program credits in excess of 30 seconds (NAB *Code News* June 1974). Due to these variables, we chose to use conservative estimates. We have used 9½ minutes per hour of nonprogram material as a base. At 30 seconds per commercial, this would result in 19 nonprogram messages per hour. We then assumed that 10 percent of these 19 messages, or two per hour, were not commercials, leaving an average of 17 commercials per hour.

Applying these figures to our formula, we arrived at the following:

Age	Average Hrs/Day of TV Viewing (1977-1978)	Minus 10 Percent Public TV Viewing		Average Hrs/Day Comm'l TV Viewing		Average Number Comm'ls/ Hour		Days		Average Number Comm'ls Viewed/Year
2-5	4.0	−0.4	=	3.6	×	17	×	365	=	22,338
6-11	3.6	−0.4	=	3.2	×	17	×	365	=	19,856

When Do Children Watch Television?

The kinds of commercials children see depend upon the hours when they watch television. Weekend mornings and especially Saturday mornings are generally thought of as "children's television hours" and do represent heavy viewing periods for children. However, according to 1977 Nielsen data (see figure 2-1), the weekend daytime hours from 7:00 A.M. to 1:00 P.M. account for only 13 percent of the total weekly television viewing time for children 2 to 11 years old. For children under age 6, the greatest amount of weekly viewing takes place during the evening hours (Monday through Saturday, 8:00-11:00 P.M. and Sunday, 7:00-11:00 P.M.—22 percent), and on weekdays (Monday through Friday, 10:00 A.M.-4:30 P.M.—20 percent; and Monday through Friday, 4:30-7:30 P.M.—20 percent). Children 6 to 11 years old also do the largest proportion of their viewing (33 percent) during prime time, followed by the late afternoon and early evening hours (21 percent). Thus, for all children under age 12, the hours from 4:30 P.M. to 11:00 P.M., Monday through Sunday, account approximately half their average weekly viewing.

A second way of describing children's viewing is in terms of the average number of children in the television audience over the course of a day. These data, based on the 1974 Nielsen measurements (the most recent year for which detailed hour-by-hour statistics were available) are presented in figure 2-2.[7] Parts a and b represent estimates of the national child audience on Saturdays and Sundays, from 7:00 A.M. to 6:00 P.M. Part c represents the child audience on weekdays until 6:00 P.M., as well as the number of children viewing television Mondays through Sundays during the evening hours, from 6:00 to 11:30 P.M. Since evening viewing patterns differ only slightly from weekdays to weekends, they are combined here to present the audience over the course of the entire week. (Note that these graphs represent *averages* at given times, not cumulative audiences.)

In general, the number of children watching television increases rapidly during the course of the early morning hours (especially on Saturday), then decreases during the late morning and early afternoon. The number begins to increase again in mid-afternoon until about 5:30 P.M., when it falls off temporarily (probably due to children's low interest in news). The child audience then continues to rise to a peak at about 8:00 P.M. (see part c of figure 2-2).

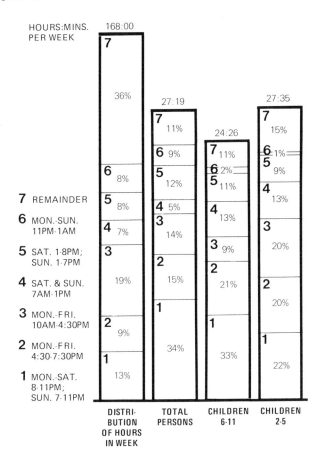

Source: Nielsen (1978).

Figure 2-1. Weekly Viewing Activity for Children, November 1977.

The size of the child audience falls off rapidly thereafter, although nearly 25 percent of all children are still watching television at 10 P.M. Even at 11 P.M., approximately 10 percent of all 6- to 11-year-olds are still counted in the television audience.

Some age differences in viewing patterns are noted in figure 2-3, which presents the viewing patterns for children aged 2 to 5 and 6 to 11 years.[8] While the graphs in the two figures are roughly similar in shape, the weekday morning audience of older children is much smaller because of school attendance. By contrast, the portion of older children in the audience during prime-time hours is significantly greater (peaking at slightly more than 50 percent of all 6- to 11-year-olds at 8:00 P.M.). Similar breakdowns were not available

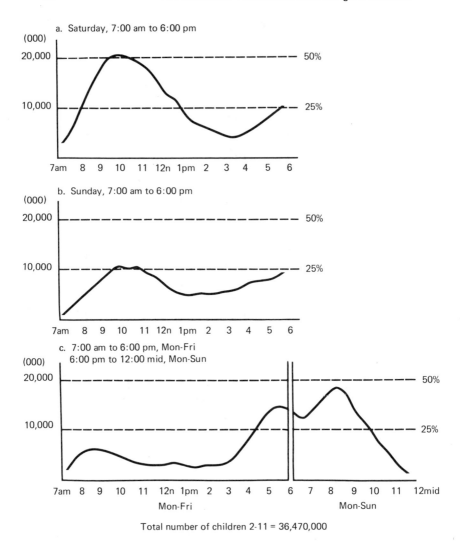

Source: 1973 Nielsen data, from Katzman (1976).

Figure 2-2. Average Number Children Watching Television, by Hour.

for weekend daytime viewing, but smaller age-related differences would be expected, since school attendance or bedtime patterns are not factors at these times.

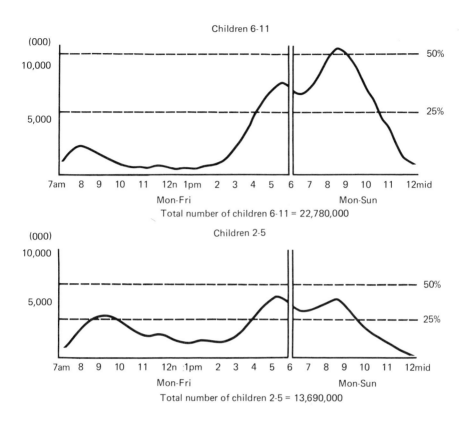

Source: 1973 Nielsen data, from Katzman (1976).

Figure 2-3. Child Viewing Audience by Age.

What Kinds of Television Programs do Children Favor?

The kinds of commercials children see are determined not only by the hours when they watch television, but also by the specific programs they watch. As with other aspects of children's television viewing, their extremely diverse program preferences are related to age. Schramm, Lyle, and Parker (1961) reported that the favorite programs of preschoolers are predominantly those designed specifically for children: "The programs have animals, animated characters, or puppets as their chief characters—are all in story form, are full

of action (often slapstick), and often have a heavy component of laughter."
By the time children are midway through elementary school, their preferences
have broadened to include child-oriented adventure and variety programs,
situation comedies, and westerns. By the time children leave elementary school,
their preferences encompass most categories of programming watched by adults.

These findings were confirmed in a study by Lyle and Hoffman (1972b),
who reported on the favorite television programs of preschool children (3-, 4-,
and 5-year-olds). See table 2-3. Even within the three-year age span, some
striking changes were revealed by the study. For example, 30 percent of 3-year-
olds reported "Sesame Street" as their favorite program, whereas only 12
percent of the 5-year-olds expressed this preference. Conversely, situation
comedies were not considered favorites by any 3-year-olds, but 12 percent of
the 5-year-olds chose the situation comedies.

Evidence on the viewing preferences for older children comes from a study
in which a national probability sample of 6- to 7-year-olds and 8- to 10-year-
olds were asked to name the programs they had watched most recently (Gene
Reilly, 1974). Table 2-4 shows the percentage of each group that named a
particular show.

We can see that by age 6 or 7, children are watching a broad variety of
programs. This is confirmed by Nielsen estimates (1976) of the number of child
viewers for various kinds of prime-time programming. Nielsen divided prime-time
programming into five categories, with the estimated average child audience
for each type of program. The figures for the period from October to December
1975 are: situation comedy, 5.22 million; general drama, 3.68 million; variety,
3.38 million; feature film, 2.83 million; and suspense and mystery drama, 2.46
million. Although these are large numbers, the most popular programs among
these genres draw substantially greater numbers of children. For example, table
2-5 lists the child audience estimates by Nielsen for the fifteen shows most
watched by children in 1973. It is interesting to note that only three of these

Table 2-3
Television Program Preferences of Preschool Children

Program or Type	Percent of 3-, 4-, 5-Year-Olds
"Flintstones"	26
"Sesame Street" (noncommercial)	16
General cartoons	12
Violent cartoons	11
Mickey Mouse-type cartoons	5
Situation comedies	5
Family situation comedies	4

Source: Lyle and Hoffman (1972b).

Table 2-4
Favorite Programs of School-Age Children

Type of Program	Percent of 6-7-Year-Olds	Percent of 8-10-Year-Olds
Situation comedies	51[a]	58
Cartoons	45	40
Other children's shows	33	31
Adventure shows	17	33
Game shows	16	25
Children's educational shows	19	7
Science fiction shows	10	9
Westerns	10	10
Movies	5	15

Source: Reilly (1974).

[a]Percentages add up to more than 100 because of frequent multiple responses.

shows ("The New Scooby Doo Movie," "Flintstones Comedy Hour," and "Josie and the Pussycats") were seen on weekend mornings. The remainder were all prime-time evening programs.[9]

Industry Codes and Children's Viewing Patterns

Other chapters of this book will consider specific advertising practices by the NAB and NAD codes. Here we will be concerned only with the relationship between the preceding evidence about children's viewing patterns and how these codes define "children's television."

According to the NAB "Children's Television Advertising Guidelines" (effective September 1, 1976), the guidelines are meant to apply to

> advertising of products designed primarily for children, or to advertising which is telecast during programs designed primarily for children or within station breaks between such consecutive programs, designed primarily for children.

In another section of the NAB code, dealing with time standards for children's advertising, "children's programming time" is defined as "those hours, other than prime time, in which programs initially designed primarily for children under 12 years of age are scheduled."

In an earlier version of the code (October 1973), "children's programming time" was defined more simply to apply during "that continuous period of time between the hours of 7:00 A.M. and 2:00 P.M. on Saturday and Sunday." In practice, the revised language of the 1976 code extends the applicability of the

Table 2-5
Most Popular Programs Among Children (1973)

Rank	Program	Average Number of Child Viewers (millions)	Percent of all Children	Percent of Audience that are Children
1.	"Brady Bunch"	12.08	33.1	40.2
2.	"Partridge Family"	11.73	32.2	34.3
3.	"Wonderful World of Disney"	11.02	30.2	27.5
4.	"All in the Family"	8.89	24.4	14.7
4.	"Emergency"	8.89	24.4	23.7
4.	"New Scooby Doo Movie"	8.89	24.4	70.2
4.	"The Waltons"	8.89	24.4	23.7
8.	"Adam 12"	7.47	20.5	20.7
9.	"Flintstones Comedy Hour"	7.11	19.5	60.5
9.	"Josie and the Pussycats"	7.11	19.5	68.4
9.	"Sonny and Cher"	7.11	19.5	19.6
12.	"Sanford and Son"	6.75	18.5	14.0
13.	"Room 222"	6.40	17.5	23.3
14.	"Bridget Loves Bernie"	6.04	16.6	17.4
14.	"Mary Tyler Moore"	6.04	16.6	15.5

Source: A.C. Nielsen.

guidelines very little: They now apply only to programs shown on weekend mornings and to a limited number of other programs oriented specifically to children (such as "Captain Kangaroo" and occasional afternoon children's "specials"). The guidelines do not apply to most afternoon programming nor to prime time—which are periods of substantial child viewing, as we have seen. In fact, children on average do only about 15 percent of their viewing at times when advertising is regulated by guidelines intended to protect children. Only three out of the fifteen most popular programs among children are broadcast during this so-called "children's programming time."

At first glance, the NAD guidelines seem to be broader in application. They are based not only on a program's intended audience, but on the actual composition of that audience. They are meant to apply both to "children's programs" (programs intended primarily for children) and to those "programs in which audience patterns typically contain more than 50 percent children."

In practice, however, these guidelines rarely apply outside of weekend mornings. Population statistics indicate that children between the ages of 2 and 11 comprise approximately one-sixth of the U.S. population. (As of September 1978, Nielsen estimated that there were 32.66 million children, out of a total viewing audience of 204.66 million persons, so that children of ages 2 through 11 represented 16.0 percent of the total viewing audience.) Thus, there are far fewer potential child viewers than nonchild viewers. For a program to attain an audience of 50 percent children, more than four times as many potential child viewers must watch the program for every potential adult viewer.

This means that the application of the NAD guidelines is determined at least as much by adult viewing patterns as by children's. As table 2-5 indicates, only three of the fifteen most popular shows among children in 1973 ("New Scooby Doo Movie," "Josie and the Pussycats," and "Flintstones") had audiences that were more than 50 percent children. For the three most popular shows—"Brady Bunch," "Partridge Family," and "World of Disney"—children comprised 40.2, 34.3, and 27.5 percent of the audience respectively. Moreover, according to 1975 Nielsen data, the average network weekend children's program attracted an audience of 3.94 million children, out of a total 6.73 million viewers (58.5 percent children); whereas all network programs shown from 7:30 to 9:00 P.M. attracted an average of 5.43 million children as part of a total audience of 26.28 million viewers (20.7 percent children). Thus, audiences for early evening prime-time programs contained, on average, nearly 1.5 million more children than the audiences for programs intended specifically for children. In light of these figures, it appears that "children's programming" is being defined partly by a program's popularity among children, but also partly by its *unpopularity* among adults.

As a result of these policies, children are exposed to a large amount of advertising not intended for them and not covered by regulations ostensibly intended to protect them. This includes advertising for potentially hazardous products such as nonprescription drugs, alcoholic beverages, power tools, household cleaners, and other chemical products. The critics assert that commercials designed to motivate adults to use these products may also motivate children to use them. (See chapter 7 for a review of evidence on the effects of over-the-counter drug advertising on children.)

Two counterarguments are offered to these charges. First, children are interested primarily in products appropriate to their ages (for example, toys, snack foods) and disregard commercial messages that are adult-oriented. Second, when children are a minority of the total audience (for example, during prime time), they are frequently watching television in the company of adults, who can correct any potential misunderstandings of adult-oriented advertising.

Summary and Conclusions

Watching television is a nearly universal experience for children growing up today in this country. Most children begin watching television at an early age. After age 2, the majority of children watch some television daily and average between three and four hours per day through age 11. This volume of television viewing means that a child will be exposed to some 20,000 commercial messages each year, or approximately three hours of television advertising per week.

We have seen that some children are likely to be watching television at any time of they day or night, but that their viewing is heaviest during prime-time evening hours and late afternoons (more than half of viewing by children aged 2 to 11). The weekend daytime "children's hours" represent less than one-fifth of children's total weekly viewing. We have also seen that very young children tend to prefer specifically child-oriented programs, but that their tastes rapidly broaden to include virtually the entire spectrum of program types. Thus, by the time children leave elementary school, their program preferences are likely to be closer to those of adults than those of preschool siblings.

On the whole, knowledge of children's viewing patterns is fairly extensive, especially in comparison with other areas reviewed in this book. One topic deserving further research attention is the influence of factors in the background and environment of children which might determine individual viewing patterns. Another important issue: Should "children's television" be defined for regulatory purposes as programs intended specifically for children, or should the definition include any program watched by a substantial number of children? If the latter, how should the term *substantial* be defined?[10] We have seen that most of children's television viewing, and therefore the commericals they are exposed to, occurs at times other than those covered by children's advertising guidelines.

Most of the research (and virtually all of the laboratory studies) conducted to date on the effects of television advertising on children have been concerned with child-oriented commercials. Research is needed that will examine such questions as: Do children discriminate in any significant ways between programming or advertising intended for children and that intended for adults? How much attention do children give to adult-oriented commercials? How do they respond to them? Is there a potential for children to misunderstand commercial messages addressed to adults? Is a child's reception of adult advertising affected by the presence or absence of adults? Some of these questions are touched upon in other chapters of this book.

Notes

1. Both A.C. Nielsen and a second company, Arbitron, provide data on the viewing audiences for local stations. These statistics are important for determining the audiences for nonnetwork syndicated programming and for examining possible regional variations in viewing patterns. However, in this chapter, we are concerned with children's viewing patterns on the national level.

2. Television set ownership in U.S. households increased from 90 percent at the end of 1961 to 98 percent at the end of 1978. Even more dramatic has been the increase in homes containing two or more TV sets: from just 14 percent at the end of 1961 to 48 percent at the end of 1978.

3. These estimates are close to those made by others. For example, Robert Choate, in testimony before the House Subcommittee on Communica-

tions (1975c) stated that "the average child sees over 22,000 commercials each year." Lewis Engman, ex-chairman of the FTC, estimated that the average high school graduate will have seen 350,000 commercial messages (1973). That figure, divided by 16 years, gives an average of 21,875 commercials per year.

4. Children's programming time is defined as "those hours other than prime time in which programs initially designed for children under 12 years of age are scheduled" (NAB *Code News* June 1974). ABC has announced its intention to reduce commercial time on weekend children's programming from 9½ minutes to 7½ minutes per hour by January 1981. This action should result in a modest reduction in children's average cumulative exposure to commercials.

5. According to Barcus (1978), monitoring of weekend and weekday afternoon children's programming indicated that the actual time devoted to nonprogram material exceeded these limits on some stations.

6. Barcus' studies were confined to child-directed commercials during children's programming. However, 30 seconds has also become the standard length for most adult-oriented commercials.

7. In a letter to the author (April 10, 1979), William Behanna of A.C. Nielsen indicated that, based on a review of 1978 data, "a very similar set of charts would result if current data were used." However, he noted that by 1978, the total number of 2- to 11-year-old children in the U.S. population had declined to 33.07 million compared to 36.47 million in 1973.

8. These figures are in terms of both absolute numbers and of percentages of children in each age bracket. Since there are approximately 9 million more 6- to 11-year-olds than 2- to 5-year-olds, the percentages provide more direct comparisons.

9. A more recent but less detailed listing of most popular programs suggests that the predominance of prime time programs among children has increased. As of the fall of 1978, the fifteen top ranking programs among children under 12 (and the percentage of all children in television households watching them) were:

1.	"Happy Days"	33.7
2.	"Laverne and Shirley"	31.3
3.	"Mork and Mindy"	30.9
4.	"What's Happening"	25.4
5.	"Wonderful World/Disney"	25.3
6.	"Battlestar Galactica"	24.1
7.	"Incredible Hulk"	23.5
8.	"Three's Company"	22.1
9.	"Eight is Enough"	21.4
10.	"Little House on the Prairie"	20.0

11. "Wonder Woman"   19.5
12. "CHIPs"   19.4
13. "Love Boat"   18.0
14. "Donny and Marie"   16.9
15. "Charlie's Angels"   15.5

All were prime-time programs. For the top three programs—"Happy Days," "Laverne and Shirley," and "Mork and Mindy"—children comprised, respectively, 24.0, 31.7, and 22.8 percent of the total audience.

10. The consumer advisors to the FTC's 1974 Children's Television Advertising Project proposed two categories of advertising affecting children, each with its own set of regulations: (1) A "children's commercial" would be defined as "a commercial in or near a program . . . for which children comprise over 50 percent of the audience"; and (2) a "family commercial" would be defined as "a commercial in or near a program for which children comprise over 20 percent but not more than 50 percent of the audience" (Consumer Advisors, 1974). According to these standards, seven out of the twelve prime-time programs most popular with children in 1973 (table 2-3) would have been classsified as "family programming." The three most popular programs with children in 1978 would also have been so classified.

3 Children's Ability to Distinguish Television Commercials from Program Material

Laurene Krasny Meringoff
and *Gerald S. Lesser*

In its 1974 inquiry into children's programming and advertising practices, the FCC called attention to the Federal Communications Act requirement that all advertisements on radio and television indicate clearly that they are paid for and by whom:

> The rationale behind this provision is, in part, that an advertiser would have an unfair advantage over listeners if they could not differentiate between the program and the commercial message and were, therefore, unable to take its paid status into consideration in assessing the message. (FCC 1974)

In considering the question of fairness to young viewers of television advertising, the commission was concerned with two different but related kinds of viewer comprehension. The first involves the ability of a viewer simply to perceive commercials as distinct and separate material from the adjacent programming; the second deals with the viewer's understanding of the selling purpose of television commercials. For adult viewers, we can generally assume that perception of a television advertisement is accompanied by an understanding of its promotional purpose. The same assumption cannot be made when the viewers are children. That is, some children may be able to correctly identify a television message as a commercial and still not comprehend its purpose.

We must consider two aspects of comprehension when questioning whether a child's inability to make accurate distinctions between commercial and program material may provide the advertiser with an unfair advantage. First, do children perceive commercial messages to be distinct and different from program content? What conditions act to blur children's perception of the separation between commercial advertisements and program content? To the extent that children do *not* spontaneously separate commercial and program content, what can be done to assist them in making the distinction? Second, to the extent that children *do* distinguish commercials from program content, are they able to assign different intentions to the two? Specifically, do children identify the selling of a product as the intention of a commercial, and do they distinguish this intention from the intention of program content? Finally, to the extent that children perceive commercials to be distinct from programs and are able to understand the sales intention of the commercials, does this awareness act as a mediator between commercial messages and their resulting persuasive effects?

Current and Proposed Regulations

In the course of its 1974 inquiry, the FCC reported that children, especially young children, apparently have considerable difficulty distinguishing commercial from program matter. The FCC referred to research evidence which found that children do not begin to understand the selling intent of commercials until they have started grade school.[1] On the basis of the information the commission had gathered, it concluded that:

> If advertisements are to be directed to children, then basic fairness requires that at least a clear separation be maintained between the program content and the commercial message so as to aid the child in developing an ability to distinguish between the two.

The commission suggested that either an announcement or some form of visual segment might be used before and after each commercial interruption.[2] Following discussion that same year with the commission's chairman and staff, the NAB amended its advertising code in 1975 to require that: "Commercials, whether live, film or tape, within programs initially designed primarily for children under 12 years of age shall be clearly separated from program material by an appropriate device." The specific form that this separation "device" should assume was not specified by the NAB beyond the indication that the sole use of a "fade to black" would not be adequate.

In its 1978 "Report on Television Advertising to Children," the FTC staff argued that much more far reaching action might be needed. Among the remedies proposed, they recommended that the commission consider banning

> ... all televised advertising for any product which is directed to, or seen by, audiences composed of a significant proportion of children who are too young to understand the selling purpose of, or otherwise comprehend or evaluate, the advertising.

This recommendation follows from the conclusion that television advertising directed to children too young to understand the selling purpose of commercials is inherently unfair and deceptive. In a footnote, the staff explained that in its report, " 'young children' refers to children below the age of eight."

In March 1979, the NAB adopted a series of more detailed guidelines on the use of separators. The new standards, which took effect September 10, 1979, require the following:

1. During children's programming, a separator device must be inserted before a commercial which says, in both video and audio, "We (or name of program) will return after these messages."
2. The device must remain on the screen at least five seconds but not more than ten seconds.
3. "Artwork, animation, still or motion pictures (or) title cards" may be used in the separators. If a program character is depicted, it must be an "incidental still shot" that does not detract from the intent of the separator device.
4. The identification logo of the network or station may be included in the separator, providing that it does not detract.
5. An announcer, either on-screen or voice-over, may deliver the separator message, so long as he or she is not connected with the program.
6. A device must be inserted on returning from the commercial to the program, using language such as, "We now return to (name of the program)."

In the report on its 1974 inquiry, the FCC also identified a specific advertising practice—the use of program characters to promote products ("host selling")—which, in its opinion, was unfair to children. Two problematic effects of host selling were pointed out by the FCC: (1) the program and the commercial become interwoven, hereby hindering the distinction between them; and (2) the sales technique takes advantage of the trust which children place in program characters. The commission expressed the belief that ". . .the use of a program host, or other program personality, to promote products in the program in which he appears is (not) a practice which is consistent with licensees' obligations to operate in the public interest.[3]

In 1975, both the NAB and the NAD incorporated a restriction on host selling into their codes for children's advertising:

> No children's program personality or cartoon character shall be utilized to deliver commercial messages within or adjacent to the programs in which such a personality or cartoon character regularly appears. This provision shall also apply to lead-ins to commercials when such lead-ins contain sell copy or imply endorsement of the product by program personalities or cartoon characters. (NAB)

> Program personalities or program characters (live or animated) on children's programs should not be used to promote products, premiums, or services in or adjacent to any program where the personality or characters appear. (NAD)

However, neither organization has made any formal attempt to address the question of children's comprehension of the different intentions of advertising and programming. Clearly, this issue and its resolution are far more complex and difficult than the physical separation of commercials and programs. The FCC acknowledged this problem in its public remarks during the 1974 inquiry: "We recognize that this (the maintenance of 'at least a clear separation') may be an incomplete solution to the problem. . . . The broadcast of an announcement and/or visual device can only aid children in identifying commercials."

The responsibility for providing a separation device between commercials and programming intended specifically for children has been assumed by the individual broadcaster. Each of the three networks has designed its own non-program "bumpers" to serve this function during children's programming: During the 1978-79 season, ABC preceded commercials with a five-second animated logo, "All-Star Saturday," such as ". . .show will continue in a moment"; CBS inserted a network logo or program visual with a voice-over audio, ". . .show will return right after these messages," "and now back to the show," before and after each set of commercials; and NBC briefly displayed a program title card on the screen accompanied by an announcement like "stay tuned." Television stations owned by Post-Newsweek have been experimenting with a format which clusters commercials at the beginning and end of each children's show, preceded in each case by the following voice-over notification:[4]

> Post-Newsweek stations do not place commercials within children's programs. It is our policy to cluster commercials at the opening and closing of each program, so there will not be any confusion between the sales message and the entertainment portions of the program. We hope you like this approach to children's programming and would enjoy hearing your comments.

Later in this chapter we will examine the question of whether the various devices currently in use actually achieve their intended effect of providing children with a clearly distinguishable separation between advertisement and program content.

With regard to the ban on host selling, the broadcasters have again assumed primary responsibility for interpreting and carrying out the code provisions. The network or station sells advertisers the opportunity to have a commercial run during a specific program on a given date. Then the broadcasters themselves put together the actual sequence of commercials in each of the commercial groups ("pods"), and must separate commercials featuring children's program hosts and characters from the programs in which these hosts or characters appear.

Research Evidence

Perception of Commercials as Distinct from Programs

In a pilot study conducted by Blatt, Spencer, and Ward (1972), twenty children ranging in age from 5 to 12 years, were exposed to a videotape of typical

Saturday morning programming and commercials and then interviewed the following data about what they had viewed. The authors found that although the children in all age groups could identify the term *commercials,* the younger (kindergarten) children exhibited some confusion about the concept and judged the relationship between commercials and programs on the basis either of affect ("commercials are more funny") or of coincidental reasoning ("commercials are shorter than programs").

Subsequent research extended and confirmed the findings of this exploratory effort (Ward, Reale, and Levinson 1972; Ward and Wackman 1973b). Personal in-home interviews were administered to a sample of sixty-seven children, ranging in age from 5 to 12 years. Children's responses to the direct question, "What is the difference between a TV program and a TV commercial?" revealed clear differences between younger (5- to 8-years-old) and older (9- to 12-years-old) children in the degree of verbalized discrimination between programs and commercials. Younger children generally exhibited a low level of differentiation, often based on recognition of different perceptual cues, ("commercials are short and programs are long"). In contrast, most of the older children's responses indicated a high level of differentiation, based upon some understanding of the meaning of the message ("programs are supposed to entertain," "commercials try to sell things").

These findings consistently demonstrate a positive relationship between children's age and their ability to describe the difference between commercial and program material. More specifically, the younger children (ages 5 to 8 years) either expressed confusion about the differences or used superficial perceptual or affective cues as the basis for the distinction. This evidence appears to have been influential in the FCC's 1974 recommendation to licensees that special measures be taken to ensure an adequate separation between television advertisements and programs directed to all children.

All of these studies were based solely on children's verbal responses to abstract questions and not on other measures of their ability to discriminate between program and commercial material in an actual viewing situation.

In an attempt to overcome this reliance on verbal response measures, Gianinno and Zuckerman (1977) provided (n = 64) four-, seven-, and ten-year-old children with photographs of animated characters from either programs or food commercials and asked them to simply recognize or identify these characters in response to various instructions, as well as to verbalize their understanding of what commercials are and how they differ from programs.[5]

Consistent with earlier findings, the younger children exhibited little ability to articulate either what a commercial was or how it differed from a program. However, even four-year olds could recognize and, to a lesser extent, identify who these characters were and could correctly match the commercial characters with the name of the specific product that they "show you" on television. Interestingly, these youngest children were less able to make these character-product associations when asked the more general question of which character was in a commercial.

These findings do not directly address the question of whether children distinguish commercials from programs; however, they do indicate that children as young as age 4 can distinguish between animated characters on the basis of whether they appear in programs or commercials, and can link those from (food) commercials to their respective products.

A number of other studies monitored children's attention patterns in an ongoing viewing situation. In one early attempt to examine attention patterns prior to and during commercial messages, mothers of 5- to 12-year-old children were trained to observe and record information about their children's normal viewing behavior (Ward, Levinson, and Wackman 1972). Analysis of these data indicated a tendency for the children to exhibit a drop in attention when a commercial was shown, compared with their attention to the prior programming. In addition, the children's attention generally continued to decline during later commercials, both within a series of commercials and over the course of the program. However, the smallest decreases in attention occurred among the youngest (5- to 7-year-olds) viewers; that is, they displayed higher levels and more stable patterns of attention to both commercials and programs than the older children.

The researchers speculated that this greater stability in younger children's attention patterns across both program and commercial materials may be evidence of the difficulty they have in discriminating between the two. The researchers therefore inferred that the lower levels and greater differentiation in older children's attention to commercials indicate their greater awareness of and immunity to television advertising.[6] The increase among older children in comments about the commercials (as opposed to the advertised products) and the more negative content of these comments was interpreted as further evidence of these children's greater appreciation of the nature of commercials.

In a subsequent experimental study of children's attention to television commercials, the investigators adopted another point of view, hypothesizing that younger children are likely to display *more* differential attention to television material to the extent that the material varies in its visual and auditory complexity (Wartella and Ettema 1974). They based their hypothesis on the premise that the younger and more "perceptually bound" the children, the greater the influence of perceptual, rather than cognitive, attributes of stimuli on their attention patterns. Twelve commercials of varying visual and auditory complexity were interspersed, in three blocks or "pods," throughout a television program shown to 120 children aged 3 to 8.[7] The criteria and methods used to record the degree of children's attention were the same as those employed in the earlier study by Ward et al. (1972). As the investigators expected, the youngest (3- to 4-years old) viewers showed the greatest differences in their attention to high versus low complexity commercials and were generally less stable in their level of attention from one observation to the next. Commercials rated high in auditory complexity were given more attention by the children than those rated low in this quality, regardless of the visual complexity rating.

As in the Ward, Levinson, and Wackman (1972) study, the researchers interpreted the tendency of the children to change their level of attention during the shifts between program and commercial material as an indication of the children's awareness of the differences between them. However, we cannot conclude, on the basis of this evidence alone, that differences in attention level to programming and adjacent advertising are attributable to the children's recognition of the distinctive nature of the two. The Wartella and Ettema findings suggest only that the degree of attention paid to television material may be a function of the material's specific audiovisual features, quite apart from whether children perceive the material as a commercial or a program.

Another study of the relationship between perceptual features of television stimuli and children's attentional behavior measured preschool children's visual attention to varied television material coded for the presence or absence of particular characteristics (Levin and Anderson 1976). The researchers found that specific features of the material, such as lively music and active motion, as well as more generalized visual and auditory changes, enhanced the children's attention to the screen. Although these findings were based on children's responses to program material, rather than to advertising, it is plausible to expect that similar changes in attention might occur as a consequence of the abrupt perceptual changes in transitions between programming and commercial messages. However, the relative influence of perceptual and cognitive factors on children's attention patterns remains a moot point until children's ability to distinguish program and commercial content is directly measured. Specifically, the effectiveness of current network separation devices needs to be subjected to testing.

Effects of Clustered Commercial Formats

Some research has been conducted on children's responses to clustered versus dispersed commercial formats (Atkin 1975b; Duffy and Rossiter 1975). Atkin randomly assigned 500 preschool through fifth grade children to view seven commercials that were either dispersed throughout a cartoon program or clustered before or following the show. The results indicated that overall attention to the commercials was significantly higher in the clustered presentation. However, no significant differences were found in the children's recall of the commercials or expressed preferences for advertised products.

When Duffy and Rossiter exposed first and fourth grade classes to the two commercial formats (the clustered commercials were preceded by a voice-over notification), the researchers reported that the first graders watching the clustered version paid significantly more attention to the commercials than the fourth grade children. Among the fourth graders, the dispersed format produced significantly higher attention patterns.[8] As in the Atkin study, however, the two formats made no significant difference in recall of advertised brand named by either age-group.[9] (Children at both grade levels tended to verbalize a preference for the clustered commercial treatment, although approximately 40 percent of the first graders either could not verbalize a clear differentiation or were unable to offer a reasoned preference between the two formats.)

In neither study was children's ability to discriminate between commercials and program material directly assessed. However, Duffy and Rossiter inferred, on the basis of data showing first graders to be less attentive to dispersed commercials, that the clustered format did *not* aid the younger children in discriminating between the commercials and the program. Since the clustered structure contained a commercial warning announcement and the dispersed version did not, the effectiveness of the warning itself cannot be determined without testing a dispersed-plus-warning version.

Effects of Host Selling

Program hosts and characters are now prohibited from appearing in commercials within or directly adjacent to their programs. In light of this restriction, it is of interest to note a study that examined the effectiveness of a "Pebbles" cereal commercial featuring the Flintstones cartoon characters (Atkin 1975b). The children were observed to pay slightly more attention to the Flintstones cereal advertisement when it was shown in the context of a Flintstones cartoon program, rather than with a Bugs Bunny cartoon. The younger children (3- to 7-year-olds) in the study expressed significantly more desire for the cereal when the commercial appeared on the same tape as the Flintstones program. The younger children were also more likely to mistakenly recall the Flintstones characters as eating cereal in the program rather than in the commercial.

Atkin also compared children's responses to the commercial when shown within the Flintstones cartoon ("adjacent" condition) and shown outside (but along with) the program in a cluster of commercials ("nonadjacent" condition). Presentation of the advertisement in the clustered, nonadjacent condition produced both greater attention to the commercial and somewhat more expressed desire for the cereal. Children in the nonadjacent condition were also slightly less accurate about where the cereal eating took place.

As Atkin points out, the findings suggest that the nearby presence, rather than direct adjacency, of the program to the commercial may be sufficient both to increase the effectiveness of a commercial featuring the program characters and to create confusion between the two, especially for younger children.[10] As previously noted, current NAP code restrictions prohibit only direct adjacency. To the extent that the children's desire for the product was influenced by their heightened identification with the familiar program characters in the commercial, rather than by program-commercial confusion, the current industry restrictions on the *placement* of host selling commercials may be addressing only a part of the full issue.

Perception of the Intent of Commercials

In the Ward and Wackman (1973b) study cited earlier, the 5- to 12-year-olds were also questioned about the purpose of commercials ("Why are commercials shown on TV?"). Nearly one-half (47 percent) of the children verbalized low levels of understanding of the selling motives of commercials.[11] The least aware children were more likely to be younger (5 to 8 years) and to be evaluated as responding at a "lower cognitive level."[12] In discussing these findings, the researchers offered this interpretation:

> While young children may simply lack information about the nature of television advertising, or fail to comprehend this information, it may be that low cognitive-level children cannot abandon their own perspective and take the perspective of the advertiser when viewing commercials.

Robertson and Rossiter (1974a) hypothesized that the ability to recognize the persuasive intent of commercials would depend in part upon the child's making a number of prior cognitive distinctions: (1) discrimination between programming and commercials; (2) recognition of an external source (a sponsor); (3) perception of an intended audience as the target of the advertiser's message; (4) awareness of the symbolic, as opposed to realistic, nature of commercials; and (5) recall of personal experiences in which discrepancies had been discovered between products as advertised and products in actuality. Interview responses from a sample of 289 first-, third-, and fifth-grade boys offered support for this hypothesis, suggesting that those children who were capable of recognizing commercials as persuasive messages met these antecedent or perhaps concurrent criteria.

As in the Ward and Wackman study, Robertson and Rossiter found the development of persuasive-intent awareness to be positively related to age: Whereas just over half (53 percent) of first graders exhibited understanding of the selling intent of television advertisements, almost all fifth graders (99 percent) understood it. As the authors explained, "Age, as a variable, reflects not only maturational factors but also cumulative experience with commercial messages."

These two studies present complementary approaches in examining development by children of a mature concept of television advertising. Ward and Wackman's study delineates certain cognitive abilities which seem to underlie children's grasp of the nature of commercials; Robertson and Rossiter's analysis identifies a number of specific cognitive distinctions which children make when they are able to comprehend the intent of commercial messages.

Persuasive Effects of Commercials

There is consistent evidence, based on verbal reports, that younger children who do not understand the persuasive intent of commercials are more likely to perceive them as truthful messages, whereas older children who can discern persuasive intent tend to express skeptical, less accepting attitudes toward commercials (Robertson and Rossiter 1974a; Ward, Reale, and Levinson 1972; Ward and Wackman 1973b). In addition, various investigations of the influence of television advertising on children's purchase requests have revealed that younger children express higher levels of purchase requests for certain advertised products than older viewers (Atkin 1975g; Gene Reilly Group 1974; Ward and Wackman 1972; Robertson and Rossiter 1974a).

Robertson and Rossiter found, for example, that more than half (53 percent) of the first graders interviewed "wanted every toy or game they saw advertised on television," as compared with only 6 percent of the fifth grade children. Observing that older children have a better understanding of the persuasive intent of commercials, these researchers concluded that "the development of persuasive-intent attributions acts as a cognitive defense to persuasion."[13] This is not to say, of course, that commercials do not influence purchases or purchase requests. The economic realities of commercial broadcasting offer clear evidence that commercials can sell products to viewers even when their sales intent is clearly understood.

Summary and Conclusions

Children's ability to distinguish between program and commercial content has only been measured indirectly, using either verbal, pictorial or attentional measures. Studies using verbal responses to general questioning found a positive relationship between age and children's verbal ability to differentiate between programs and commercials. Younger children, particularly below ages 8 or 9, either express confusion or base their discrimination of commercials on affect or on superficial perceptual cues, such as a commercial's shorter length. Older children are able to distinguish program and commercial material on the basis of an overall understanding of each message's meaning. However, children as young as 4 (and older) exhibit high familiarity with animated characters appearing in commercials and associate these characters with the products they promote.

Studies of visual attention patterns have tended to infer discrimination of commercial and program material from observed changes in children's attention levels between program segments and adjacent commercial announcements. However, there is also evidence suggesting, alternatively, that these changes in attention are attributable to the specific audiovisual changes taking place between advertising and programming sequences. Further research is required before we can determine the relative influence of specific perceptual features of commercials and commercial breaks versus children's recognition of the distinct nature and purpose of commercials. The effectiveness of current network separation devices also remains untested.

Comparisons made between dispersed and clustered commercial formats indicate that children, and particularly younger children aged 3 to 8, are more attentive to clustered commercials and express a preference for this form of presentation. No significant differences were found between the two formats in children's acquisition of information from the commercials or in their expressed desires for the advertised products.

The single study investigating the influence of host selling revealed greater desire among younger children (below age 8) for the advertised product when the commercial presented the animated character featured in the adjacent program. On the basis of this evidence, however, it cannot be determined whether the younger children's increased product interest was due to confusion between the program and the commercial or to heightened identification with the character.

Many children, but particularly those below 8 years, neither draw upon the concept of selling intent in defining commercials, in distinguishing them from programs or in explaining their purpose, suggesting little comprehension and/or the low salience of persuasive intent as a criterial feature of advertising. Development of this understanding may depend upon children's general level of cognitive functioning as well as their ability to make a number of specific prior distinctions about the nature of commercials, beginning with the discrimination of commercials as distinct from programs.

Younger children, who appear unaware of the selling motives of television advertising, also tend to express greater belief in commercials and a higher frequency of purchase requests for certain advertised products than do older children who display understanding of the intent of commercials. These differences suggest that a more mature concept of the nature and purpose of advertising acts as a mediating influence between commercials and their effectiveness as persuasive messages.

Research evidence indicating that young children have difficulty discriminating between programming and advertising has already led to the banning of one type of host selling and to the requirement of a clear separation device at commercial breaks on children's programs. However, neither the ability of children to distinguish commercials from programs nor the effectiveness of separation devices currently used to facilitate this distinction has been directly assessed. Therefore, there is still a question as to whether younger children especially can tell the difference between programs and commercials, and whether current forms of program-commercial separation are achieving their intended purpose. Both of these questions are deserving of and amenable to further testing based on the useful groundwork provided by existing studies.

For example, the separation devices could be tested by exposing randomly assigned groups of children to a television program with standard commercial breaks using one of the separation devices. A "no device" version of the program could provide a baseline measure. Children's attention in this ongoing viewing situation would be monitored. In addition, each child might be asked to identify (by means of a simple response, such as raising one hand, pressing a button, or telling the researcher) when he or she was seeing either a commercial or a program. Alternatively, if the videotape were stopped at specific points—for example, just after the separation device—children could be asked to anticipate ("guess") what they thought was going to happen next.

In light of previous studies in which auditory stimuli were found to influence children's attention to program and commercial material, it would also be instructive to have the children perform these tasks on the basis of either visual or soundtrack content alone, as well as under conditions in which both auditory and visual information were available. Comparisons of the various testing situations should reveal the effect of each separation device auditorily and/or visually, and should also reveal the age-related ability of the children to distinguish commercials from programs, and their ability to identify or anticipate the onset of the commercials.

The specific program and commercial material to be used in such a study should be selected with care. For example, commercials for products familiar to the children may be more easily recognized as advertising. Similarly, children may associate commercials with certain frequently used audiovisual techniques, such as quick-cut editing style ("montage") or musical jingles. The reasons that the children differentiate a given commercial from a given program should be probed, in order to gain insight into the specific content or characteristics that may serve as identifying cues for children. Bearing in mind the existing research findings of consistent differences in the discriminatory abilities of younger and older children, investigations should take special care to raise these questions among preschool (ages 3 through 5) as well as among older (ages 6 through 12) children.

The particular program-commercial combinations also warrant careful consideration. For instance, do children find it more difficult to discriminate adjacent programs and commercials when both are in animated form; or when the same, or similar, characters appear in both the program and the advertisement? A given program and its adjacent advertising should be considered as a hypothetical continuum from similarity to contrast, with various points of minimal difference below which children of a particular age might not be able to make an accurate distinction between them. If information were also obtained verbally from children about their understanding of the nature and purpose of television advertising, then the specific perceptual attributes used by children of different ages to make program-commercial distinctions could be compared against their more general level of conceptualization.

How children acquire an understanding of the persuasive intent of commercials is another important line of needed research. Researchers should examine the relationship between a general understanding of the purpose of commercials and specific attributes of commercials, such as particular product claims or qualifiers. If such investigations were systematically conducted, we might develop measures which would help us to predict when a particular advertising practice would be deceptive (that is, misunderstood) for children at a given age and level of cognitive functioning. Television (or other media) curricula should also be designed to instruct children about commercials and their effectiveness evaluated for children of different ages.

Notes

1. The studies referred to by the FCC (Blatt, Spencer, and Ward 1972; Ward, Reale, and Levinson 1972) are discussed later in this chapter.

2. The FCC did not consider "clustering" of commercials at the beginning and end of a program to be necessary in providing a clear separation between advertising and program content (see later in this chapter and also chapter 9).

3. While the Commission noted that the use of program characters in commercials on programs other than the ones on which they appear might still take unfair advantage of the trust relationship between the child and the performer, it recognized that it might not be practically feasible for small stations to avoid using children's show personnel in commercial messages on other programs.

4. The effect of this clustering approach on children's ability to discriminate between commercial and program material is considered in a study conducted by Duffy and Rossiter (1975), described in the Research Evidence section of this chapter (and also Chapter 8).

5. Because the tasks were presented in a fixed sequence, the earlier administered tasks may have influenced children's responses to subsequent ones, thereby lessening the internal validity of these findings.

6. It should be noted that all children were not observed viewing the same television material; the particular shows and accompanying advertising monitored in the study reflected the preferences of each viewer.

7. The children were separated into three age-groups, and the members of each age-group were randomly assigned to view one of four versions of this program. In each version, the order of commercials within each block was rotated. However, the blocks themselves were not rotated within the program.

8. Atkin's overall finding of higher attention to clustered commercials may be partially explained by the fact that over half (57 percent) of the children included in his sample were less than 8 years old.

9. Interestingly, an inverse relation was found between visual attention and brand-name recall. On the whole, the least well-watched commercials were the best recalled. As the authors pointed out, this discrepancy suggests the importance of auditory stimuli and attention.

10. Atkins' conclusions are discussed further in chapter 5.

11. Similarly, the Gianinno and Zuckerman (1977) research shows selling intent to be a concept little or poorly used by the children, especially the younger ones, in defining a commercial, distinguishing it from a program, and as the basis for sorting pictures of commercial and program characters.

12. The researchers constructed a three-level scale of cognitive functioning based upon Piaget's theory of cognitive development. Lower cognitive-level responses were identified with Piaget's "pre-operational" stage of thought.

13. The relative appeal of advertised toys and games for first- and fifth-grade children may also be a factor. See chapter 9 for further discussion of this question.

4

The Influence of Format and Audiovisual Techniques on Children's Perceptions of Commercial Messages

Laurene Krasny Meringoff
and *Gerald S. Lesser*

Many audiovisual techniques in commercials are simply aimed at gaining and holding children's attention. Policy issues arise with regard to production techniques such as those which may tend to misrepresent the appearance of children's products or exaggerate product performance. Another issue concerns the ability of children to understand descriptions of product characteristics in commercials or the meaning of disclaimers and disclosures.

Current and Proposed Regulation

The television and advertising industries have formally acknowledged the influence of commercial formats and production techniques on children's perceptions of television advertising. The NAB (1978a), for example, offers the following statements of principle in its Guidelines for Children's TV Advertising:

> In order to reduce the possibility of misimpressions being created, all information (on the characteristics and functional aspects of a product or service) shall be presented in a straightforward manner devoid of language or production techniques which may exaggerate or distort the characteristics or functions of a product.

> In order to help assure that advertising is nonexploitative in manner, style and tone, such advertising shall avoid using exhortative language. It shall also avoid employing irritating, obtrusive or strident audio techniques or video devices such as cuts of less than one second in length, a series of fast cuts, (and) special effects of a psychedelic nature (for example, flashing colors, flashing lights, flashing supered copy, or other effects which could overglamorize or mislead).

With regard to the presentation of advertising, the NAD's children's advertising guidelines (1977) call for particular care by advertisers to assure that:

Copy, sound, and visual presentations, as well as the advertisement in its totality, do not mislead on performance characteristics such as speed, method of operation, size, color, durability, nutritional benefits, noise, etc. . . .[1]

In addition to these general statements, both industry codes include guidelines for the provision of specific kinds of information about product characteristics and functions. For example, the NAB code specifies that advertisements intended for children shall:

Provide audio disclosure when a product requires assembly.

Provide audio or video disclosure as to a product's method of operation and source of power. (The code further indicates that the sole use of a superimposed video title is not considered to be adequate.)

Provide simultaneous audio and video disclosures when items, such as batteries needed to operate a product as demonstrated in the advertising, are not included.

Avoid competitive/comparative/superiority claims about (toys and other durable) products.[2]

The NAB guidelines established for toy products contain the most explicit instructions for the production of television advertisements. Thus, in order that the "audio and video production techniques (shall) not misrepresent the appearance and performance of toys," toy advertising shall seek, for example:

To present the toy on its actual merits as a plaything. (It shall neither exaggerate nor distort play value.)

To limit any view of a toy or demonstration of its performance to that which a child is reasonably capable of reproducing.

To employ the complete and authentic sound(s) of the toy.

To confine their use of generic stock film footage, real-life counterparts of toys, fantasy and animation (in none of which either a child or toy appears) to the first one-third of the commercial.

To clearly disclose the original purchase in the body of the commercial and (by video, with audio disclosure where necessary for clarification) in the closing five seconds.

The NAB guidelines also urge that music, sound effects, volume level, tempo, and other audio techniques be used with restraint and discretion. In terms of the video portions of children's commercials, caution is advised in the use of certain video techniques (for example, camera angles, special lenses, special lighting, and dazzling visual effects). The guidelines point out that the use of such techniques becomes questionable when the appearance or performance of a toy is distorted or exaggerated.

Incidence of Specific Audiovisual Features

Several recent studies have examined the incidence of specific techniques and features in commercials directed at young audiences (Atkin 1975d; Barcus 1971a, 1975a and b, 1978; Doolittle and Pepper 1975; Winick, et al. 1973). Typically, these studies videotape a sample of commercials broadcast during Saturday morning children's programming and later analyze the material for the presence or absence of various features (for example, animation, form of product display, particular product claims or disclosures). The analysis is generally based upon a previously defined coding system.

Although this method of content analysis provides a systematic procedure for describing the frequency of particular features of advertisements, such descriptions are not comprehensive. Rather, they represent the features and techniques which the particular researcher considers interesting or important. Further, by sampling commercials aired on weekend mornings, these researchers have limited their analyses to a very small portion of the advertising to which children are usually exposed.[3] Still, these studies are useful in their descriptions of the specific stimulus properties of advertising messages directed to children.

The two most recent analyses of children's commercials (Barcus 1975a; 1978) coincide most closely with current regulations and practices and are therefore the primary sources of incidence information reported herein. In both, Barcus analyzed a sample of over 400 commercials broadcast weekend mornings on Boston stations, including the three network affiliates and two (1975a) or three (1978) independent UHF stations. However, the 1975 data was collected in April 1975, whereas the later study, conducted in October 1977, provides a sample of pre-Christmas advertising. Other studies, in particular an earlier analysis by the same author (Barcus 1971a), will serve as useful sources of comparative or supplementary descriptions in the following summary.

According to these content analyses, television advertising directed primarily at children may be characterized as follows:

1. Almost all commercials are 30 seconds in length. The percentage of broadcast time devoted to commercial messages (including both product and program promotion) has decreased since 1971 (15.9 percent in 1975 from an earlier 18.8 percent), reflecting changes in the NAB code as to the maximum amount of advertising permissible during children's programs (9½ minutes per hour as of January 1976). Interestingly, this figure rose again slightly (17.3

percent) in the fall 1977 sample (Barcus 1978). Nevertheless, there are about as many commercials per hour now as there were in 1971. Apparently, this has been accomplished by reducing the average length of the commercials.

2. The types of products and services promoted to children represent a limited range of items. During most of the year, the distribution is about as follows: cereals (25 percent); candy/sweets, for example, cookies, cakes, fruit drinks (25 percent); toys (18 percent); eating places (10 percent); and miscellaneous products, such as movies (10 percent) (Barcus 1975a). Only slight shifts in the incidence of these product categories were reported from the earlier Barcus figures; cereals, candy/sweets, and toys were the staples for both periods. During the pre-Christmas season (September to December), however, there is a substantially higher frequency (59 percent) of toy advertising (Atkin 1975d; Barcus 1978).

3. Product classes differ substantially in their mode of presentation. For example, commercials promoting toys (96 percent) and eating places are almost exclusively live-action, and candy/sweets advertisements are executed primarily (79 percent) in a live-action format.[4] In contrast, the great majority of cereal commercials (88 percent) continue to be partially or totally animated. In part, this difference in format probably reflects toy advertisers' compliance with the restrictions imposed on the use of fantasy and animation in the NAB guidelines.

4. Toy commercials usually display the product or products[5] in use, that is, they show children playing with the toy (90 percent), whereas cereal advertisements are about equally likely to use a picture of the product as they are to depict a person eating it. While differences in specific code requirements may help to explain the choice of display style, it is assumed that the way these products are presented also suits the objectives of the advertisers.[6] Toy advertisers undoubtedly find it desirable to show the toy itself in active use. Analysis of specific product claims indicate that, in toy commercials, "action/speed/power," "newness," and "fun" are among the attributes most often referred to verbally. In contrast, cereal marketers use animated "presenter" characters who promote these products on the basis of such features as their "taste/flavor" (for example, "sweetness") and "texture"; offers of premiums (25 percent) may also be used.

5. With regard to physical and temporal settings, most children's commercials occur in the present (86 percent) and take place in generalized locations outdoors (34 percent) or in or around the home (31 percent). This description of commercial settings (Barcus 1975a) is consistent with those of earlier studies (Barcus 1971a; Winick et al. 1973). The use of contemporary, local settings may in part reflect advertisers' attempts to comply with the NAB guidelines, which recommend placing toy products in settings which a child is reasonably capable of reproducing.

6. Children's commercials are heavily populated by white males. Adult

males or animated male animals tend to be the announcers or authoritative voices for products, and both men and boys outnumber females as characters (Barcus 1971a, 1975b, 1978; Doolittle and Pepper 1975; Liebert, Schuetz, and Sprafkin 1975; Verna 1975). According to the most recent figures (Barcus 1978), almost two-thirds (64 percent) of the characters are children, 24 percent are adults, and a minor 4 percent are teenagers. With the exception of those whose sex was not identifiable, about six out of ten of these characters are male. In terms of race, 90 percent of the characters (whose race was reported) are white and 8 percent are black; only 2 percent of the characters are members of other ethnic groups.[7]

7. In terms of verbal content, product brand names are repeated an average of 3.5 times per commercial (Atkin 1975d). Slogans and musical jingles are often used to present brand names or other product-related content (Atkin 1975d; Winick et al. 1973). Children's commercials also tend to provide little information about the "hard qualities" of products, such as price, size, materials, quantity, durability, and so on (Atkin 1975d; Barcus 1971a, 1975a, 1978; Winick et al. 1973). While this finding is rather general and less clearly quantified than those cited previously, the infrequency of such descriptions seems inconsistent with the NAB's general guideline stating that "the disclosure of information on the characteristics and functional aspects of a product/ service is strongly recommended."

The incidence of disclaimers or qualifiers is as follows. Overall, 45 percent of all the commercials, and almost two-thirds (64 percent) of toy advertising, use one or more types of disclaimer, for example, "batteries not included," "assembly required" and "artificially flavored." Of these, 30 percent of commercials use only a voice-over audio announcement, 5 percent use video-only disclaimers, and 17 percent present such qualifiers simultaneously in both audio and video form. When compared against Barcus' earlier studies, these figures represent an increase in the practice of providing audio and/or video disclaimers.

8. The use of special effects in children's commercials has been examined to some extent. An earlier study, for example, reported 14 percent of the advertisements to be using such "striking visual techniques" as fast-cutting or psychedelic effects and almost half (46 percent) to be using "attention-grabbing music" as part of their soundtracks (Winick et al. 1973). A subsequent study found close-ups in about 40 percent of the commercials, particularly in toy advertising, but there was minimal use of other techniques, such as accelerated or slow-motion or multiple-camera angles (Atkin 1975d).

In some cases, these and other researchers have gone on to make evaluative judgments about the extent to which the use of such techniques exaggerated a product's attributes. Winick et al. (1973) indicated that exaggerated effects were created by special visual techniques ("sparkling") in 7 percent of the commercials and by sound effects ("snap or crackle") in 2 percent of the cases.

Atkin (1975d) described product performance as being "moderately exaggerated" in about half of the Saturday morning commercials studied. Barcus (1975b, 1978) noted individual cases in which the use of particular visual techniques appeared to be potentially misleading or confusing to a young child—for example, the use of tight close-ups to display a doll, without providing a perspective by which a child could judge the doll's actual size.

Unfortunately, the usefulness of such evaluative information is limited. The absence of explicit criteria upon which these judgments were based makes their replication difficult; and, more importantly, the question of whether a particular technique exaggerates the attributes of a product needs to be tested against the perceptions of the child viewers themselves. In addition, the descriptive power of these content analyses has two major limitations.

First, some attributes of commercials, specifically those more quantitative in nature (for example, numbers and types of characters, brand name references), are amenable to objective measurements, while other less easily measured qualities may evade description. For example, the emotional tone conveyed by a particular commercial is difficult to code adequately. As Winick et al. explain, "the unique ambience of a given commercial is not likely to be captured by content analysis."

Second, features which are rare or totally absent but whose inclusion in children's commercials is appropriate or even required may be overlooked, particularly when the primary purpose of such analysis is simply to describe what current messages are like. In the studies reported here the researchers did attempt to include analyses of certain areas where there was a paucity of information about "hard product qualities," or only minimal occurrence of a specific technique (use of off-pace motion).

Research Evidence

There is little published research on children's perceptions of particular formats or audiovisual techniques in commercials. Much of the academic research interest in the effects of television advertising on children has concentrated instead on whole commercials, without considering their component features (Robertson and Rossiter 1974a; Ward, Reale, and Levinson 1972; Ward and Wackman 1973b). In contrast, although children's advertisers and ad agencies often conduct pre-broadcast research with children to test the relative effectiveness of specific strategies or presentations, the results of such in-house testing have not been published or made available to the public.

Studies of Television Programs

Most of the studies that associate television techniques with particular effects upon young viewers have examined programs rather than commercials. Considerable research is available, for example, on instructional television material and the effects of various production techniques and other format elements on children's learning patterns. Schramm (1972) has summarized the findings from many of these studies and specifies certain audiovisual techniques which seem to facilitate learning. These include: providing viewers with a subjective view (for example, a camera angle recording what the viewer would see if performing the task himself or herself); increasing the size of printed labels on the screen; and naming objects on the sound track as they are presented on the picture track.[8] On the basis of such findings, Schramm offers the general observation that "what makes the difference is usually . . . how the pictorial treatment fits the learning goal."[9]

In one of a series of evaluative studies, Friedlander and his associates measured preschool children's comprehension of specific visual and verbal elements presented in a three-minute segment of an informational television program (Friedlander, Wetstone, and Scott 1974). Although the segment was generally accepted as "age-appropriate" material, the results indicated that more than half of the thirty-one children demonstrated comprehension of less than half of the tested information. Based upon their analysis, the researchers suggest that the failures in comprehension should not necessarily be attributed only to the children's cognitive limitations; lower levels of learning also were related to the use of particular program techniques, such as the presentation of information in only one modality, either visual or auditory, rather than in both.

As final examples of research on the effects of format and audiovisual techniques in television programming, an impressive number of studies have investigated children's responses to the Children's Television Workshop (CTW) production, "Sesame Street."[10] The CTW research staff developed and sustained a systematic program of child-watching and interviewing during the planning of the program. This formative research provided the basis for later testing of the appeal and teaching value of various production techniques used in the show (for example, music, animation, puppets) (Lesser 1974; Palmer 1972).

Other researchers interested in the particular effects of television on young children have also studied "Sesame Street" programs. For example, Levin and Anderson (1976) measured 1- to 4-year-old children's visual attention to particular features of the show. By rating the presence and absence of these features in parallel to the ratings of the children's attention patterns, the investigators determined whether attention was increased or decreased during the occurrence of a specific program characteristic. For example, active movement, animation, letters and script, reverse motion, and visual changes generally tended to elevate attention. Among the auditory characteristics, attention was increased by the presence of lively music, singing, rhyming, sound effects integral to the central activity, and auditory changes in general. However, the use of other special effects (like pixilation or slow or fast motion) neither enhanced nor lowered attention significantly.

Salomon (1976) used "Sesame Street" material in an attempt to investigate the effects of particular film techniques and formats on the development of corresponding cognitive skills among children. For example, he identified the close-up as a technique which calls upon the skill of relating parts to the whole. A sample of 317 5-, 7-, and 8-year-old Israeli children were tested before and after the first broadcasting season of "Sesame Street." Salomon found that the children's knowledge of the program's content and their mastery of the selected cognitive skills were unrelated at the beginning of the broadcast season, but these two factors came to be closely interrelated among the heavy viewers of the show. The author surmises that "improvements in skill mastery came to serve the extraction of knowledge." More generally, this evidence is consistent with the notion that the ability of children to acquire and understand information from television is based upon mastery of the particular perceptual and cognitive skills called upon to extract this information from the format in which it is presented ("television literacy"). Moreover, such mastery improves with increased exposure to this kind of material.

Although there are obvious differences between instructional television programs and commercials, this program research can be usefully applied in several ways to the study of the effects of television advertising:

1. In spite of their differences in content and purpose, programs and commercials share many audiovisual characteristics. Therefore, the specific program techniques and formats that have been found to significantly influence attention and facilitate learning are probably worthy of serious investigation within the context of advertising research. As a member of the research staff at Children's Television Workshop has pointed out (Fowles, 1975a):

> We can say with great assurance that children 3 to 10 years old are learning a wide variety of facts, skills, concepts, and attitudes from "Sesame Street" and "The Electric Company." Since these programs are not very different from television commercials in their production techniques, communications strategies, and attractiveness to children it would be strange indeed if the learning stopped with a switch of a channel.

2. The research designs and measures developed and used to examine various effects of program material on children may also be appropriate methods for examining the impact of commercial messages. For example, the flexibility and economy of formative research methods used on early "Sesame Street" material may well come to suit the needs of those broadcasters and regulators who are responsible for screening advertising intended for children and for evaluating its acceptability for broadcast.

3. In the course of studying the extent to which children attend to and learn from particular programs, researchers have raised a number of far-reaching questions about "unintended" effects of this material on children. In the

summative evaluation of "Sesame Street," for instance, attempts were made to investigate viewers' attitudes toward school and relations with peers (Ball and Bogatz 1970; Bogatz and Ball 1971). Further, the workshop staff has continued to give attention to the potential teaching value of program features that the producer might think of as mere incidentals of plot and setting (Fowles, 1975a). Thus, just as Salomon's work raises questions about the kinds of "media literacy" skills which may unintentionally be called upon and developed in child viewers, a parallel set of questions can be raised about the "unintended" effects which exposure to television advertisements has on children. In fact, the issues of deception, fairness, and even safety in children's commercials may all be considered questions of effects which were "unintended" by the sponsors and advertising agencies responsible for their creation.

Studies of Advertising

A number of studies have examined children's visual *attention* to commercial messages with specific audiovisual features (Atkin 1975b; Krugman 1968; Rust and Watkins 1975; Wartella and Ettema 1974).

For example, the Wartella and Ettema study, described in chapter 3, indicated that children's attention increased with the auditory complexity of a commercial, regardless of its visual complexity. On the basis of their findings, the authors suggested that variations in the auditory complexity of commercials have a greater effect on children's attentional behavior than variations in visual complexity. In another study cited in chapter 3, Duffy and Rossiter (1975) found an unexpected inverse relationship between children's observed visual attention to the commercials and their verbal recall of the brand names advertised. Although both studies relied upon visual measures of attention, their findings suggest the need to examine children's auditory attention as well.[11]

Rust and Watkins (1975) also measured children's visual attention to a series of commercials. Eighty 6- to 9-year-old children were given the choice of watching either the television screen or a simultaneous slide show (a "distractor"). By videotaping the children as they watched the two presentations, the researchers were able to determine what percentage of the sample chose to look at each commercial on a moment-to-moment basis. Their analysis indicated that the average attention level peaked during the moments characterized by the most physical action, while low attention occurred at the more static shots.[12] Rust and Watkins followed up the viewing with a group discussion in which information was obtained from the children about their recall of and attitudes toward the commercials. The methodology employed in this study offers an example of how response measures can be usefully combined and applied in studying children's reactions to specific commercial messages.

Krugman's work (1968) is noteworthy as a final example of research on viewers' attentional responses to particular techniques and properties of television advertising. According to Krugman, a viewer's "direct response" to advertising should be measured by visual attention or looking behavior (using eye-movement recording) as well as by thinking of the subject (thoughts which came spontaneously to mind while an ad is being viewed) and by the subject's feelings (changes in pupil size as a measure of response intensity). Krugman's research on these three processes deals with television and print advertisements intended for adult audiences, but the study raises some provocative questions for those studying children's responses to advertising. For example, in analyzing the eye-movement patterns of respondents as they viewed different ads for ten seconds, he found both that the respondents who scanned more recalled more about the ads and that those ads scanned less were better recalled. Interpreting this seemingly paradoxical data, Krugman suggests that easily learned ads require less (scanning) work of the viewer than ads which do not learn easily. One may reasonably speculate, on the basis of this kind of evidence, that each advertisement presents a finite amount of information to be learned. If so, it should be possible to determine how many exposures are required to learn the information in a specific ad. This would be particularly useful in that although children are likely to see ads more than once, almost all of the research on children's learning and understanding of television has been based upon their responses to a single exposure of the material being studied.[13]

The more policy relevant issues of how particular formats contribute to or detract from accurate perception and recall of commercial content have been addressed by a small but growing number of studies.

The question of whether a particular audio and/or visual feature is perceived and remembered by children is examined in a study which attempted to determine how two different techniques for presenting a product disclaimer affected children's awareness and recall of the disclosed information (Atkin 1975b). A sample of 500 preschool and grade school children were exposed to a Mattel "Vertibird" commercial in which either a video superimposed title or a video title supplemented by an audio voice-over was used to present a disclaimer of "batteries not included." When directly asked about what is not included when the toy is purchased, children exposed to the video-plus-audio version were more than twice as likely to mention "batteries" as those viewing the video-only version (43 percent versus 18 percent.)[14] Interestingly, 75 percent of the children who viewed the audiovisual disclaimer subsequently reported having heard (as opposed to having seen) the statement, which suggests that hearing the information was more influential for these children than seeing it printed on the screen.[15]

Another study has examined the relationship between how a disclaimer is worded and comprehension (D. Liebert, et al., 1977). Two toy commercials were shown to 240 6- and 8-year-olds in one of three versions: no disclaimer, a standard disclaimer ("some assembly required"), or a modified disclaimer ("you have to put it together"). Children exposed to the standard disclaimer demonstrated no better understanding that the toy had to be put together than those who saw the same commercial with no disclaimer. This held true for the older as well as younger children. However, the children who heard the modified disclaimer showed significantly greater comprehension of its meaning. The authors conclude that this "seems to indicate that wording appropriate to young children plays a crucial part in their ability to understand the disclaimer content."

As a final example, Atkin and Gibson (1978) investigated (100) 4- to 5-year-old and 7- to 8-year-old children's responses to two commercials for presweetened cereals, each of which "briefly noted" the required disclosure that the cereal is "part of a balanced breakfast" and visualized "a glimpse" of the other components of a balanced breakfast.[16] Although two-thirds of the children reported remembering the balanced breakfast statement, further probing indicated that almost all (92 percent) the younger and half of the older children were unable to specify the components of the breakfast shown in the ads. Moreover, when asked to explain what "balanced breakfast" means, almost two-thirds (88 percent younger, 40 percent older) of the children said they didn't know. The results of these studies suggest that refinements of current code provisions on disclaimers may be needed to ensure that they achieve their intended purpose.

There has been very little in-depth probing of the question of children's *interpretation* of product information or other commercial content as it is conveyed by means of specific audiovisual techniques or formats. A noteworthy effort in this direction, however, is a pilot study in which the researchers examined children's perceptions of the meaning of specific verbal slogans and product claims taken from a Christmas toy catalog (Burrall and Rossiter 1975). The slogans and claims employed various rhetorical devices, such as questions ("Who could resist adorable Ginny?") or qualified superlatives ("the best of its kind"). A small sample of second- and fourth-grade girls with high verbal ability were shown pictures of the products, with a slogan or claim printed below each picture. Only one-third of the younger children and two-thirds of the older ones could accurately paraphrase the claim. In addition, very few of the children's interpretations of these statements included recognition of the linguistic device employed. Many children, for example, incorrectly inferred that "the best of its kind" meant "the best," instead of just "among the best." While this study deals with print-ad information as opposed to television advertising, the application of psycholinguistic analysis to the study of children's comprehension of verbal product claims suggests a productive area for future research.[17]

The *persuasiveness* of specific product claims in a particular audio and/or visual form has been investigated in a number of studies. In one study, (136) second, seventh, and eighth graders were exposed to four commercials which had come under the review of the FTC for their use of possibly deceptive product displays or "belief statements" (for example, "Wonder Bread is the best thing your mother can give you to grow fast") (Haefner, Leckenby, and Goldman 1975). Although comparisons between children's responses before and after viewing the commercials revealed no significant differences in their overall attitudes toward the advertised brands, the children showed increased acceptance of specific claims about the product contained in the commercials. Further, the younger children showed greater shifts in belief than the older children.

Another similar study was sponsored by the FTC to test whether children's exposure to a series of breakfast cereal commercials could have an adverse effect (Poulos 1975). In one of the commercials, the advertised cereal was associated with wild-growing vegetation; in another, an adult is shown picking wild berries and other plants while mentioning that each is edible. In some of the ads, the berries were actually added to the bowl of cereal. The commission was concerned with whether this advertising tended to lead children to pick and consume potentially harmful plants.

Four of these commercials were shown to a small sample of 5- to 11-year-olds after they had been tested for their beliefs about the edibility of a variety of edible and nonedible plants pictured in the colored photographs. Tested again, subsequent to their commercial viewing, the children's ratings of edibility increased the most for the plants most closely resembling those depicted in the commercials which, in this case, were nonedible. Although, as the author points out, the research needs to be extended and replicated; "the results do suggest that the cereal commercials have the capacity to lead children to engage in behavior that increases the risk to their physical being."[18]

Finally, changes in children's behavior, whether undesirable or beneficial, may well be the most compelling evidence of learning that research can provide in studying the effects of commercials. It is also probably the most difficult to document, and very few studies have assessed the *behavioral effects* of particular audiovisual techniques or modes of presentation in children's commercials.

In an attempt to use behavior as an outcome,[19] Atkin (1975b) showed a large sample of preschool and grade school children one or two versions of a commercial for a building block game. In one presentation, two children were shown constructing a tall elaborate structure with the blocks; in the other, a much more modest structure was depicted. The voice-over soundtracks accompanying these two visual presentations were also different. In the more elaborate format, for example, the viewer was encouraged to build "a sky-high tower so you can be the champion"; the modest version told viewers "it's fun . . . anyone can play Blockhead."

Based on observer ratings of the children's behavior in block play following the viewing, Atkin reported that the children exposed to the "extravagant claim" presentation were more likely to display hostile behavior, in the form of anger, verbal aggression, and/or physical aggression than those seeing the "modest claim" version (28 percent versus 18 percent). The children were also asked about the expectations they had for their own performance with the game. Overall, those children exposed to the "extravagant claim" version were somewhat more likely to estimate that they could build a higher tower than the actors on the commercial (64 percent versus 55 percent). Further analysis indicated that this greater expectation of personal performance occurred almost exclusively among the younger viewers (77 percent in the "extravagant" presentation versus 62 percent in the "modest").[20]

Summary and Conclusions

A limited amount of research has investigated the specific audiovisual properties of television advertising and their various effects on children. Several studies analyzed advertising content, documenting the incidence of particular techniques or features of commercials designed primarily for children. Production techniques and format features have been found to vary substantially according to product class, for example, almost all toy commercials use a live-action format, whereas advertising for cereals relies heavily on animation. In a few cases, these analyses have also attempted to identify the prevalence of commercial practices which are specifically required (such as positive disclosures) or restricted (as in the use of special effects) by industry codes regulating advertising to children.

It would be useful if future studies of this kind specified their descriptive categories so as to examine current industry guidelines even more closely. In the case of positive disclosures, for example, both the incidence of such disclosures ("batteries not included," "items sold separately") and their presentational forms (audio and/or video, length of time, placement) need to be documented. Such an analysis would help to inform both regulators and advertisers about the ways in which currently imposed guidelines are being followed. The usefulness of these content analyses is limited, however, especially in their absence of information about children's own perceptions of these television formats and techniques. Additional research is therefore necessary to investigate children's perceptions of particular audiovisual features of television advertising and the effects of these perceptions.

Because of the limited amount of research assessing children's responses to specific audiovisual features of commercial messages, we reviewed a number of studies that examined the effects of these features in instructional program material. These studies of programming effects have potential applications for advertising research, in terms of both their approach to problems (that is, the questions raised and the methodologies used) and their substantive findings. With regard to findings, for example, the evidence of poorer learning by children when program content was presented in only one modality (either auditory or visual) supports similar findings from a study evaluating learning of product information from different format conditions in a commercial.

Several studies have used a variety of response measures to investigate the effects of particular stimulus variables on children's attention to commercials or, in some studies, children's programs. In one study, for example, an alternative visual "distractor" was provided to approximate a natural viewing situation. Using such methods, researchers have been able to measure changes in the level of children's visual attention as they are exposed to particular audiovisual features in the televised material. These attentional studies of programs and advertising material have documented the enhanced visual attention that results from such features as active movement, animation, and lively music—all commonly used in advertising messages.

In future studies, these measures of attention could be refined and expanded. For example, eye-movement records would provide a more precise and informative measure of visual attention. In addition, findings from several different studies have indicated the need to consider auditory as well as visual factors in children's attention to and learning of television content. Other responses that deserve more careful study include the intensity of response and arousal, verbal comments, expressions of emotion, and nonverbal behavior such as imitation.

In research investigating children's learning from television advertising messages, their recall, comprehension, expressed beliefs or attitudes, and behavior subsequent to viewing specific commercials have all served as response measures. Such studies have demonstrated that children's recall of product disclaimers is influenced by the form in which they are presented. For example, a disclosure about batteries for a toy was recalled better when presented in both audio and video form, as opposed to video only, although such (audiovisual) provision of a disclosure, in itself, does not ensure children's comprehension of the information disclosed. Recall has also been enhanced when the wording of a disclosure was simplified. A study of print-ad product claims revealed that children (especially younger ones) find it difficult to accurately interpret such common linguistic devices as qualified superlatives.

Other studies have found that the content of a commercial, whether it is central or incidental to the commercial's message, may bring about shifts in children's beliefs. Similarly, the behavior of children using an advertised product has been found to vary, depending upon the way the product's performance is demonstrated in a commercial.

While the evidence from these studies is often preliminary, somewhat scattered, and still unreplicated, their findings verify that: (1) specific audiovisual features of commercials can make significant differences in children's learning; and (2) such effects on children's learning and behavior can be measured by research. Future research should further explore children's ability to accurately perceive and understand commercial information presented by means of specific copy, sound, and visual techniques. Investigators should attempt to determine, for example, whether there are specific presentational forms which are more likely to produce accurate recall and comprehension of such important information as the size and components of a product, the way a product works, and a realistic perception of its performance. This research should give special attention to the perceptions of younger children.

The *cumulative* impact of specific presentational forms in commercials also requires examination. For example, what are the effects on children of the repeated emphasis on action/performance/speed in toy products, or the repeated use of animation and fantasy in cereal commercials? What are the more long-term effects of commercial techniques and formats on children's perceptual and cognitive skills?

Notes

1. Note this guideline's attempt to consider the impression that the advertisement *in its totality* may create about the product, as opposed to concern only with individual techniques used within a commercial.

2. Such claims are disallowed "because, *even when true,* it is believed such references may make a child dissatisfied with a toy he already possesses or may receive" (italics added). This reason is particularly noteworthy in that it attempts to take into consideration other undesirable effects, beyond the creation of misimpressions about products.

3. An exception are samples of weekday afternoon commercials included in the Barcus (1975b, 1978) studies.

4. This represents a shift in format from greater use of animation (51 percent) in candy/sweets advertising appearing in 1975.

5. In a substantial number (38 percent) of the toy advertisements monitored by Barcus, at least two or more items are promoted in the same ad, either sold together or separately (1978).

6. In addition, although animation is more expensive to produce than live-action, animated commercials tend to have a longer life; that is, they do not need updating as often.

7. See chapter 5, for further discussion.

8. This finding is of particular interest in considering the effectiveness

of the various forms of positive disclosures currently used in children's commercials.

9. For a discussion of the instructional effectiveness of television (with its particular audiovisual attributes) in comparison to other media, see Schramm (1977).

10. A number of the more recent studies, including evaluations of several adaptations of *Sesame Street* in other countries, appear in the *Journal of Communications* 26 (1976): 2.

11. "It is possible to make exact numerical measurements of children's listening responses to television program soundtracks" (Friedlander and Wetstone 1974).

12. This is consistent with Levin and Anderson's (1976) finding that active movement in the "Sesame Street" material enhanced preschoolers' visual attention.

13. A few studies have compared children's responses to single versus multiple exposures to particular commercials (Atkin 1975b; Goldberg and Gorn 1974b; Gorn and Goldberg, 1977a. Also see chapter 9).

14. The greater awareness and recall reported for the audiovisual form of disclaimer offers considerable support for the guideline in the NAB code which specifies that children's advertisements shall "provide simultaneous audio and visual disclosures when items such as batteries . . . are not included."

15. As noted previously, the importance of auditory factors in children's attention to and learning from television advertising deserves further study. See Schramm (1972); Wartella and Ettema (1974); and Duffy and Rossiter (1975).

16. A single audio and video reference to the proper role of the product (for example, as "part of a balanced breakfast") may satisfy this NAB requirement; no minimum amount of time or emphasis is specified.

17. Further linguistic analysis of problematic verbal product claims can be found in a paper by Rossiter, *Cognitive Phenomena in Contemporary Advertising* (1975).

18. In contrast to the Haefner, Leckenby, and Goldman (1975) investigation of commercial messages, the messages studied by Poulos (that wild plants are edible) was not primary to the commercials. Rather, it was embedded, both visually and verbally, into the context of the primary message. For this reason, the Poulos study offers a good example of what was earlier noted as the potential (in this case, negative) teaching value of incidental messages from television material.

19. This research is noteworthy in its use of multiple response measures. These include responses observed during viewing (for example, visual attention, expressions of irritation and/or enjoyment, verbalizations) and those obtained

subsequent to viewing (like brand name recall or desire for the advertised product).

20. The use of "extravagant" toy product displays or demonstrations is specifically disallowed by the NAB's guidelines, which state that toy advertising "shall neither exaggerate nor distort play value" and shall seek "to limit any . . . demonstration of a toy's performance to that which a child is reasonably capable of reproducing."

5

Source Effects and Self-Concept Appeals in Children's Television Advertising

John R. Rossiter

Characters of various kinds—human and nonhuman, live-action or animated—appear as product presenters or product users in most children's commercials. Their association with the advertised product ranges from merely a coincidental presence in the commercial to open endorsements and testimonials. The term *source effect* refers to the impact of these characters on the television audience.

Critics of television advertising for children allege that the use of such characters in commercials creates source effects that take unfair advantage of the young viewer. The following list defines a number of these alleged negative source effects:

1. Certain types of characters in commercials, notably program personalities and cartoon characters, may contribute to children's confusion between programs and advertisements. We have termed this the *confusion effect*. This confusion effect may be heightened when the program personalities and cartoon characters appear in commercials shown within or adjacent to their own programs. We call this the *adjacency effect*.

2. Celebrities or authority figures, such as a police officer, an astronaut, or a mother, can lead children to attribute to the endorsed product qualities it does not have. We call this the *endorsement effect*. The endorsement effect may be heightened when the celebrity or authority figure openly endorses or uses the product—the *direct* endorsement effect—and may be reduced when the celebrity or authority figure merely appears in the commercial without endorsing or using the product in the *indirect* endorsement effect. The endorsement effect may also be reduced or eliminated if the celebrity or authority figure does not appear as in real life, but is either acted or animated. We call this the *fantasy effect*.

3. Certain characteristics of product presenters or users, notably their sex, race, occupation, or social behavior, can contribute to children learning social stereotypes. We call this the *social stereotype effect*.

4. Certain types of advertising appeals, usually but not always involving product presenters or users, may deleteriously affect a child's self-concept. We call this the *self-concept effect*.[1] Personal enhancement appeals, social status appeals, exaggerated or unrealistic product usage portrayals, and competitive product appeals fall into this broad category.

Current Codes

This section reviews what current NAB and NAD self-regulatory codes allow and prohibit regarding source factors and self-concept appeals in television advertising directed at children.

Confusion Effect

The NAB does not specify any potential source effects in its code. The NAD does specifically refer to potential confusion between program content and advertising content. The NAB code, identical in effect to that of the NAD, states:

> No children's program personality or cartoon character shall be utilized to deliver commercial messages within or adjacent to the programs in which such a personality or cartoon character regularly appears. This provision shall also apply to lead-ins to commercials. . . .

Note that the adjacency effect actually provides the basis for the NAB and NAD codes on program personalities and cartoon characters.

The adjacency prohibition applies only to endorsers and not to program character-related products. For example, a "Superheroes" doll could be advertised in or adjacent to a "Superheroes" cartoon program provided the "Superhero" character, Batman for instance, did not appear as an endorser. NAD added a provision to its code (revised September 1977) cautioning advertisers to "clearly differentiate between the content of the advertisement and the content of the program" in such situations. The NAB code does not cover the character-related product situation in its adjacency provision and presumably permits these products to be advertised in or adjacent to the character's program.

Endorsement Effect

The NAD code allows all types of endorsers but seems to prohibit the endorsement effect itself:

> Advertisements should not falsely imply that purchase and use of a product or service will confer upon the user the prestige, skills, or other special qualities of characters appearing in the commercial or ad. Material benefits attributed to the product or service should be inherent in the use thereof.

The NAB code, on the other hand, apparently tries to minimize the endorsement effect by placing restrictions on the type of endorser and the type of endorsement—apparently based on the assumption that some types of endorsers are more effective than others. The NAB's prohibitions[2] look simple but are, in fact, quite complicated. They are summarized in table 5-1.

Social Stereotype Effect

In its preamble, the NAB code recognizes that "advertising. . . can serve to inform children. . . of many aspects of the society and world in which they live." Social stereotypes are not explicitly mentioned. The code simply states that "Advertisements shall not portray attitudes and practices inconsistent with generally recognized social values and customs."[3]

The NAD's guidelines, section C, provide a much more detailed listing of the criteria which social portrayals in commercials should meet. In addition to social stereotyping, the NAD prohibits: unacceptable reflections of social, legal, moral, institutional or family values; disdain for parents and other sources of child guidance; undesirable living habits and manners; and poor (other than informal) use of language.

Table 5-1
NAB Restrictions on Endorsements

	Human, Real-Life	Human, Actor/Actress Portrayals	Animated
Celebrities (a famous person or character)	Indirect[a] only	Allowed[b]	Allowed
Authority figures (for example, athlete, mother, astronaut, police officer)	Indirect[a] only	Allowed[b]	Allowed
Product characters (identified with or created for the product)	Not Allowed	Not Allowed	Allowed
All others	Allowed	Allowed	Allowed

[a]"Indirect" means that this type of endorser can appear in commercials but must not verbally endorse the product nor be shown using or consuming it. This relates to the *indirect* versus *direct* endorsement effect issue. The fact that animated characters are allowed in all cases and actor/actress portrayals in some, relates to the *fantasy effect* issue.

[b]To add to the complication of the provisions, actors or actresses portraying real-life celebrities or authority figures are allowable only if the portrayal is "clearly recognizable to children as 'slice of life' " rather than as an endorsement by the actual celebrity or authority figure.

Self-Concept Effect

Various advertising practices may reflect negatively on a child's self-concept. Four of the most prevalent self-concept concerns are covered in the codes:

1. Personal enhancement appeals. Both the NAB and the NAD allow personal enhancement appeals, which promise such benefits as strength, growth, physical proficiency, and intelligence, provided they are "constructively handled" and "accurately reflect documented evidence" (to use the NAB's words) and "do not mislead" (to quote the NAD guidelines).

2. Social status appeals. Social status appeals, usually peer status appeals, and prohibited by both the NAB and the NAD. The NAB code states that:

> Appeals shall not be used which directly or by implication contend that if children have a product they are better than their peers or lacking it will not be accepted by their peers.

The NAD's provision is similarly worded and identical in effect.

3. Product usage portrayals. Product usage portrayals might presumably affect a child's self-concept if the child cannot duplicate the portrayal. The NAB and the NAD have similar codes covering usage portrayals except that the NAB refers to toys and premium offers whereas the NAD refers to all products advertised to children. Both codes prohibit exaggerated portrayals of play value or performance characteristics; usage demonstrations which "a child" (NAB) or an "average child" (NAD) is not reasonably capable of reproducing; settings and contexts which a child cannot reasonably reproduce; and portrayals of children possessing unfair or inequitable numbers of products or premiums.

4. Competitive product appeals. The NAB code is clearly against competitive product appeals, allegedly because of a potential self-concept effect. The code prohibits both overt competitive appeals (comparison advertising) and covert competitive appeals (superiority claims):

> Positive exposition of a product's own attributes are acceptable (sic). However, because of their potential to encourage dissatisfaction on a child's part, competitive/comparison/superiority claims or techniques are disallowed.

The NAD also discourages competitive appeals but allows them in cases where a "true and significant advantage may exist that can be readily understood by children." Such claims should be nondemeaning to competitors' products, should not involve comparisons with previous versions of the same product, must be adequately documented, and must not be based on a biased selection of comparative attributes. Additionally, the NAD appears to prohibit subjective superiority claims or "puffery."

Incidence

Incidence refers to the prevalence of commercial practices relating to *potential* source effects and self-concept appeals, not to the incidence of effects per se. However, to maintain continuity, the headings in this section retain the word "effect" when, more correctly, they should be "potential for effect."

Confusion Effect

Content analyses by Barcus are very helpful in that they provide evidence on program personality and cartoon endorsements as well as incidence estimates on the adjacency phenomenon. *Adjacent* endorsements (either within or contiguous to the endorser's regular program) were negligible at the most recent count in early 1975: none on weekend mornings and one percent during weekday afternoons. *Nonadjacent* endorsements were recorded at an incidence of about 6 percent (7 percent on weekends and 5 percent on weekdays). This figure probably overestimated the use of program personalities and cartoon characters since "endorsers" in the Barcus analyses included celebrities (specifically sports figures and figures in the news). However, the 6 to 7 percent incidence of endorsements by program personalities and cartoon characters is probably exceeded toward the end of each year, when toy advertising predominates. Toys based on characters from "Superheroes" and "Battlestar Galactica," for example, were heavily advertised in the 1978 pre-Christmas children's television season.

Endorsement Effect

The endorsement effect relates to the type of endorsers and the type of endorsement that each is permitted to make. Again, Barcus provides the most recent incidence data, except that his content categories do not correspond to those specified by the NAB code. An analysis of 1971 commercial content by Winick et al. (1973) is of some help in that practices which are not affected by code changes can be roughly estimated from this earlier study. From these estimated breakdowns, we can draw a number of tentative conclusions about endorsement:

1. Probably 80 percent of children's commercials employ an *on-camera presenter.*[4] In other words, only about 20 percent portray no visible source, although, of course, auditory endorsement cues are usually present.
2. The most frequent visible product presenters in commercials directed to children are *animated characters* (42 percent), followed by *anonymous*

human adult or child actors and actresses (32 percent). Cartoon program characters selling products in commercials that are *not* adjacent to their own programs account for the next largest frequency (4 percent).

3. There is a 2 percent incidence of *real-life celebrity* endorsements, even though this practice is now prohibited by the NAB code. Apparently, not all advertisers are observing this prohibition.[5]

4. Virtually all children's commercials would qualify as *direct endorsements* under the NAB's definition. Besides direct testimonials (an estimated 20 percent), there are on-camera usage/consumption portrayals (an estimated 60 percent) plus off-camera verbal statements where only the product is shown (an estimated 20 percent).[6] Although these are all different degrees of endorsement, they are all direct endorsements under the NAB code.[7]

Social Stereotype Effect

The potential for social stereotype effects lies in the presence of various social cues in commercials seen by children. The following figures are based on commercials shown for the most part during programs designed for children on weekday afternoons and weekend mornings. No data are available that reflect the incidence of social cues in other commercials that children may see.

1. Age of product presenters. Table 5-2 is based on a simple average of Barcus' weekday afternoon and weekend morning content analysis, in early 1975. If we focus only on visible age cues, and ignore the teenage incidence, it may be concluded that children, overall, see about one-and-a-half times as many adults as children in commercials directed at them. However, they see about nine times as many adults as children acting as spokespersons or endorsers.

Table 5-2
Age of Product Presenters
(percent)

	Spokespersons	*Other Characters*
Adults		
On camera	62	33
Off camera	15	
Teenagers[a]	16	6
Children	7	55

Source: Barcus (1975a, b).

[a]For some reason Barcus coded animals in this category as well. Thus, this figure represents "all others" besides adults and children.

2. Sex of product presenters. Table 5-3 is based on an average of figures in Barcus (1975a, b). Overall, children see at least three times as many males as females in commercials directed at them. For spokespersons or endorsers, the ratio is nine times as many males as females. Some interesting results on sex cues come from a content analysis of 1974 children's Saturday morning commercials by McArthur and Eisen (n.d.). Including only commercials in which human males or females appeared as central characters, these investigators found, predictably, that males were portrayed mainly in authority roles whereas females were portrayed primarily as "passive" product users. However, although many more males than females were shown (80 percent versus 20 percent), both sexes appeared equally as "reward givers" and "reward getters." As McArthur and Eisen commented, advertising may be the one media area in which women are frequently rewarded for their actions—even though the rewards are usually within the context of stereotyped "housewife" or "mother" roles.

3. Race of product presenters. Although there are no data available for the period, it is likely that, prior to the late 1960s, children's commercials were almost exclusively populated by white characters, human or animated. Although the figures may vary in reliability, it is interesting to note the trend of racial characteristics in children's commercials, as shown in table 5-4.

In the most recent content analysis (Barcus 1975a, b), with 1975 data, table 5-5 shows a much lower nonwhite incidence was obtained. The explanation for Barcus' lower figures is that his 1975 figures are based on the percentage of total *characters* rather than on a percentage of total commercials. While nonwhite characters appear in about 20 percent of children's commercials, they appear alone in only about two percent (Atkin and Heald, 1977). Typically, the practice is to add nonwhite characters to depict an integrated racial setting. Atkin and Heald's statistics of 1972-73 document this phenomenon in table 5-6.

4. Occupation of product presenters. Recent specific data on occupations depicted in children's commercials are not available. In a study using 1971 data, Winick et al. (1973) reported that occupational cues were detectable in 38

Table 5-3
Sex of Product Presenters
(*percent*)

	Spokespersons	Other Characters
Male	90	67
Female	10	33

Source: Barcus (1975a, b).

Table 5-4
Nonwhite Characters (Percent of Commercials)

Study	Data Collected	Commercials[a] in which Nonwhites Appeared
Barcus (1971)	1971	27
Winick et al. (1973)	1971	24
Atkin and Heald (1977)	1972	18
Atkin and Heald (1977)	1973	24
Doolittle and Pepper (1975)	1974	17

[a]Most of the studies focused on Saturday morning commercials.

percent of children's Saturday morning commercials and that a diversity of blue collar and white collar occupations was portrayed. Occupations shown in children's commercials are most often discussed in the context of sex cues—notably the roles played by women. Available content analyses indicate that just as women are underrepresented in children's commercials, their occupational roles are also underrepresented. The media, in general, portray women most often in domestic roles (Busby 1975), although this is diminishing according to an investigation by the National Advertising Review Board (*Advertising Age* April 21, 1975). Children's commercials almost exclusively portray women in a single role, "housewife," versus seventeen occupational roles shown for men (Busby 1975; Verna 1975). This finding may be misleading, however. The label might just as often be "mother," a role we might expect to be dominant in commercials directed at children.

5. Social behavior of product presenters. According to the Barcus studies, commercials shown during weekend mornings and weekday afternoons displayed a variety of settings for exhibiting social behavior: in or around the home (30 percent), outdoor settings (29 percent), public places (15 percent), and places of work (4 percent).[8] However, no analysis has yet attempted to evaluate whether behavior depicted in children's commercials is in accord

Table 5-5
Nonwhite Characters (Percent of All Characters)

	Weekend Mornings	Weekday Afternoons
Whites	95	92
Blacks	5	7
Other	< 0.5	< 0.5

Source: Barcus (1975a, b).

Table 5-6
Character Counts by Type of Commercial

Data Collected	Average Number of Characters in All-White Commercials	Average Number of Characters in Commercials which Contain Nonwhites
1972	3.15	4.91
1973	2.70	5.33

Source: Atkin and Heald (1977).

with "recognized" or "accepted" social values and customs, as required by the NAB and NAD codes.

Self-Concept Effect

Four types of claims were identified earlier as having a potential bearing on children's self-concepts. Barcus (1975a, b) again provides the most recent and specific incidence figures:

1. Personal enhancement appeals. Table 5-7 uses Barcus' coding categories, three of which relate quite closely to personal enhancement claims by advertisers. In all, approximately one in four children's commercials carries at least an implicit promise of personal enhancement or benefit from product consumption or use. It should be noted that *documented* claims of this type are allowed by industry codes.

2. Social status appeals. Barcus comes closest to measuring the incidence

Table 5-7
Personal Enhancement Appeals

	Incidence of Appeals (percent)
Fun/Happiness (Fun taste, fun to eat, lots of laughs, cup of happiness)	7
Health/Nutrition/Well-Being (Low fat, good for you, balanced breakfast, look thinner)	13
Action/Strength/Speed/Power (No defining examples)	6
Adventure (An adventure in every bite)	1
Total	27

Source: Barcus (1975a, b).

of social status appeals with his peer status/popularity category. The averaged incidence for this type of claim was 2 percent. A 1975 example would be the commercial in which a young girl, upon procuring a brand of fried chicken, is allowed into a boys' play club. This practice is prohibited by the NAB and NAD codes.

3. Product usage portrayals. No data are available on the extent to which children's commercials exaggerate product ownership, product performance, or play settings beyond a degree reproducible by the "average" child.

4. Competitive product appeals. Overt comparisons between competing brands or models of a product—"comparative advertising" in adult commercial terminology—are apparently negligible in children's commercials. Barcus' nearest category is entitled Comparative/Associative, but this appears to refer to similes and metaphors (for example, "tastes as good as gold"). In any case, the incidence for this category was only 1 percent.

Covert comparisons—implied superiority or uniqueness claims—were more prevalent. Uniqueness claims ("the one and only. . .") were recorded at 4 percent. Superiority claims, which almost exclusively involved subjective superlatives or "puffery" (the greatest, best, fantastic) rather than objective competitive claims (best selling), were recorded at 7 percent. Thus, the estimated total for this practice, which is prohibited by the NAB, is 11 percent.

Research Evidence

Confusion Effect

This effect alleges that the use of program personalities and cartoon characters in commercials contributes to children's confusion between program and advertising content.[9] Even by 5 or 6 years of age, approximately 25 percent of all child viewers still experience difficulty in separating programs from commercials (see chapter 1 of this book).

Does the use of program characters contribute to the confusion effect? Only one published study[10] has examined this question (Atkin 1975b). The study also attempted to test the adjacency effect, which hypothesizes that the confusion effect can be reduced or eliminated if the program characters are used "outside" rather than within or adjacent to their own programs. The NAB and NAD codes are based on the adjacency hypothesis.

Atkin's study used three test conditions. One group of children saw a commercial for "Pebbles" cereal, featuring the Flintstones characters, within a Flintstones cartoon program; we call this the adjacency group. A second group saw the same commercial and the same cartoon program but in a noncontiguous sequence—this is the nonadjacency group. A third group saw the Flintstones commercial during a Bugs Bunny cartoon program; we call this the control group.

"Confusion" was measured by asking the children whether they remembered seeing the Flintstones characters eating cereal and, if so, where. (The characters ate cereal only in the commercial, not the cartoon program.) Evidence for the confusion effect was obtained in that one-fourth of the children who recalled the Flintstones characters eating cereal thought they did so in the program. This error was most prevalent among the younger children in the sample (3- to 7-year-olds). However, the *overall* magnitude of the findings was diminished somewhat by the fact that significantly fewer children in the Flintstones program groups (compared to the control group) recalled the cereal-eating event in the first place. Since we have no measure of "spontaneous" confusion, we have to rely on "recalled" confusion (the percentage recalling the event multiplied by the percentage confused). By this weighted measure, the confusion effect results are equivocal since the confusion trends are offset by lower recall of the confusion.

Atkin's study also did not support the adjacency effect hypothesis. In fact, the *non*adjacency group experienced slightly more confusion that the adjacency group. In sum, Atkin's comparison group produced equivocal results for the confusion effect and at the same time no support for the adjacency effect.

There were other findings in the Atkin study that suggested consequences other than the confusion effect. For example, children in the Flintstones program groups paid slightly more attention to the Flintstones commercial than those in the control group; they also tended to want the advertised cereal significantly more often. These results, incidentally, were stronger in the nonadjacency group. This casts further doubt on the implicit NAB/NAD hypothesis that nonadjacent commercials of this type are less efficacious than adjacent or in-program commercials.

A 1975 study by Donohue should also be mentioned. In a survey sample of 162 6- to 9-year-old black children of low socioeconomic status in New Orleans, Donohue found that 27 percent of boys and 42 percent of girls claimed that "their favorite TV character" appears in commercials. The two favorite characters in commercials were Bugs Bunny and Fred Flintstone. However, these figures are likely to be overestimates in that (1) they do not measure the proportion of commercials in which the characters appeared (the children may have been reporting about relatively few commercials); (2) they are self-reports and thus depend on the reliability of children's memories; and (3) the sample's and the region's viewing content may be somewhat atypical in terms of NAB code-covered stations. The Barcus figures should taken as more accurate.

Endorsement Effect

The endorsement issue involves not one but three alleged effects: the direct endorsement effect, the indirect endorsement effect, and the fantasy effect.

Direct Endoresement Effect. The allegation here is that certain types of product presenters can lead children to attribute to the endorsed product qualities it does not have. The recent FTC consent order against "Spider-Man" Vitamins, for instance, states that "The use of such a hero figure . . . has the tendency and capacity to lead significant numbers of children to believe that the endorsed product has qualities and characteristics it does not have" (Federal Trade Commission Consent Order File No. 762 3054).

Endorsements by real-life celebrities and authority figures are prohibited by the NAB for commercials appearing in children's programs.[11] Ironically, the single published study dealing with this phenomenon (Atkin 1975b) seems to suggest that real-life celebrities and authority figures do not produce an endorsement effect. In this study, an astronaut character was used as a "hero figure" endorser[12] and compared with a "man in the street" endorser. Atkin's summary of the study implies that the astronaut figure was slightly *less* effective in inducing children's desire for the cookies advertised. However, careful reading of the study shows that the endorsement effect depended on whether or not the children liked astronauts. Table 5-8 shows the results when subgroup analyses were conducted. The results indicate a *negative* endorsement effect among a substantial subgroup of children and no significant positive endorsement effect among the remainder.

Most endorsements in children's commercials are by product characters, either human (such as Ronald McDonald and the Burger King) or animated (such as Fred Flintstone and Cap'n Crunch). An important but flawed study on the effects of these product characters on children was recently conducted for the Federal Trade Commission by Atkin (1979). The sample comprised 480 3- to 7-year-olds, with an even distribution by age, sex, and socioeconomic status. Several findings from this study are worth examining for relevance to the direct endorsement effect.

Table 5-8
Endorsement Effects

	Desire for the Advertised Product (percent)
Experimental group	
Children who liked astronauts "pretty much" or "very much" (60 percent of group)	32
Children who liked astronauts "not so much" (40 percent of group)	22
Control group	
"Man in street" version	29

Source: Atkin (1975b).

First, the product characters used in the study were liked by a large majority of children. (Substantial disliking was a problem with the astronaut study.) Percentages of children exhibiting positive affect toward each character were as follows: Ronald McDonald, 88 percent; Burger King, 80 percent; Fred Flintstone, 75 percent, and Cap'n Crunch, 59 percent. Next, the study attempted to establish the degree of perceived expertise and trustworthiness children attributed to these endorsers. Unfortunately, the measures for these two variables appeared to have questionable construct validity, that is, they did not necessarily measure what they were intended to measure.

"Perceived expertise" in relation to foods (Ronald McDonald and Burger King) and cereals (Fred Flintstone and Cap'n Crunch) was measured by the following question, repeated for each endorser: "Do you think that (endorser) knows which (foods or cereals) are good for kids to eat?" Response options, presented on cue cards, were "Yes," "No," and "?" (signifying "Don't know"). Most children answered "Yes": 87 percent for Ronald McDonald and Burger King, 66 percent for Fred Flintstone, and 65 percent for Cap'n Crunch. On the whole, older children (age 7) were as likely as younger children (age 3) to answer "Yes." However, the words "good for kids to eat" could have been interpreted as "good tasting."[13] Also, the children may have perceived these characters as adults (real adults in the case of the two food characters) who might well be expected to know what foods or cereals are "good" for children to eat. Whether the question measured perceived expertise on nutritional matters, as apparently intended, is thus highly questionable.

The measure of children's degree of "trust" in product characters was similarly ambiguous. Children were shown pictures of product characters along with pictures of general characters, such as a mother, a nurse, and a police officer, and asked to "Pick out the ones who want to help kids." This may measure children's perceptions of charitable or occupational roles rather than "trust." Ronald McDonald, for example, is frequently featured in promotional campaigns for charitable causes (for example, the Muscular Dystrophy Association). Nurses, who scored slightly higher than mothers, may have achieved their high rating because of the helping occupation rather than because children trust them more than mothers.

Finally, the study attempted to measure the extent to which children feel "compelled to obey" product characters by selecting the endorsed product. The primary measure of this behavioral effect of endorsement contained two parts. Children were first asked "When Ronald McDonald comes on TV, he talks about french fries and shakes. Are you supposed to eat what he tells you to eat, or can you eat whatever you want?" The question was then repeated for Burger King and the responses averaged. An average of 22 percent of the children selected the "eat what he tells" answer, with an essentially constant age trend. While this might seem relatively high even for a minority response (most said "eat whatever you want"), it should be noted that the question did not refer to the endorsed products by brand, only to "french fries and shakes." Many of the "compelled" 22 percent may have interpreted the question as asking whether they were supposed to eat french fries and shakes. The direct endorsement effect here is equivocal.

To probe the "compelled to obey" issue further, Atkin then asked 5-, 6-, and 7-year-olds (the older children in the study) whether each of the two other product characters, Fred Flintstone and Cap'n Crunch, "hopes you will eat his cereal or doesn't he care what you eat?" A further direct question asked whether the children thought each character "orders you to eat his cereal, or doesn't he care?" Averaged over the two product characters, 57 percent of the children said the characters "hope" they will eat, and 22 percent went as far as to agree that the characters "order" them to eat, their brands of cereal. But let us look at the response options: "not caring" is hardly the only alternative to "hoping" and certainly is not the only alternative to "ordering." Children may simply have avoided the "doesn't care" response, for if the character didn't care, why would he advertise the product?[14] Children may have chosen the "hopes" and "orders" answers simply as the only alternatives provided by the interviewer.

In summary, the Atkin study (1979) can only be taken as suggesting that young children attribute expertise and trust to product characters, and that these characters effectively influence young children's choice of advertised products. Much less ambiguous measures are required to accurately gauge the magnitude of the direct endorsement effect in children's commercials—although there is little doubt that it sometimes occurs.

Indirect Endorsement Effect. The NAB code does not prevent real-life celebrities or authority figures from appearing in commercials directed to children, although the code does prevent these figures from verbally endorsing the product and from being shown using or consuming it. The question is: are passive (indirect) forms of endorsement any less effective than direct endorsements and outright testimonials? Since there are no studies available that compare different degrees of directness of endorsement, we can only compare across studies.

In a pilot study using print ads, Hyams, Tanner, and Rossiter (1975) found that a black athlete endorser—an authority figure by NAB definition—produced a markedly greater liking for the endorsed product (a fictitious brand of soda) than either a black businessman endorser or a white businessman endorser. The black athlete advertisement used no direct endorsement whatsoever—only a picture of the athlete juxtaposed with a picture of the product. The endorsement effect, incidentally, was stronger among the older children in the sample (fifth graders) than the younger children (second graders). In other words, lack of social learning among younger children may actually enable them to "resist" endorsement effects. In this case, older children may be the more vulnerable age group.

Dramatic source effects have been obtained in other studies with an equally indirect product-endorser relationship. Perhaps the most straightforward illustration of the indirect endorsement effect comes from a pilot study by Iskoe (1976). In this study, Iskoe picked five pairs of similar products and randomly assigned five endorsers to them. Four of the endorsers were celebrities and some were also authority figures as defined by the NAB. The fifth was an "ordinary male." Independent ratings of children's product preference were made first. An endorser was then "attached" to each product and the products re-rated. The data in table 5-9 are paired comparison preferences in which the children were required to select one item from each pair. The sample comprised 225 children across first, third, and fifth grades, with both sexes and also race representatively included.

Several conclusions are apparent from this study. First, silent endorsement clearly works. Increases in product preference of up to 67 percent were obtained purely on the basis of a product-endorser juxtaposition. Second, although interaction effects are likely between various endorsers and products, not all endorsers are equally effective. Mohammed Ali seems much more effective than, for example, Lucille Ball who, as "Lucy," actually produced a negative effect in one instance. On the other hand, the "ordinary male" endorser was just as effective as the average of the celebrities (22.5 percent versus 19.6

Table 5-9
Influence of Endorsement on Product Preference
(*percent*)

Endorser and Product Pair	Unendorsed Preference	Endorsed Preference	Difference*
Mohammed Ali			
Frisbee	36	60	+67
Beachball	64	75	+17
President Ford			
Cookies	56	68	+21
Donuts	44	57	+30
Captain Kangaroo			
Gloves	49	55	+11
Ski cap	51	59	+16
Lucille Ball			
Doll	45	45	0
Gun	55	52	−5
Ordinary Male			
Potato chips	55	67	+22
Pretzels	45	56	+23

Source: Iskoe (1976).
*Difference = (Endorsed Preference − Unendorsed Preference ÷ 100)%

percent). This reinforces the point made in connection with Atkin's "astronaut study" earlier—endorsement effects depend on how children regard the endorser.

In sum, although no research has been done that actually compares direct with indirect endorsements, separate studies show that both can produce significant effects. It is not known whether the NAB's prohibition of direct endorsement (testimonials or overt use/consumption) reduces endorsement effects by celebrities or authority figures, but it certainly does not remove these effects.

Fantasy Effect. Implied in the NAB code is a second means of reducing or eliminating the endorsement effect—the fantasy effect. Animated characters are universally allowed as presenters; they may portray celebrities or authority figures, and may serve as specially created "product characters." Also in keeping with the fantasy idea, actors and actresses are allowed to portray celebrities and authority figures so long as their portrayals are recognizable by children as "slice of life." (Presumably this means that children see acted portrayals as being of a fantasized nature.) The NAD code does not contain any fantasy effect assumption; the NAB's current code, however, virtually depends on it.

Atkin (1979) provided some partial evidence on the fantasy effect by comparing real-life (though actor-portrayed) product characters with animated characters. Very tentative indications were that full fantasy portrayal may be less effective than partially fantasized portrayal, as predicted by the fantasy effect. For example, as noted earlier, animated product characters such as Fred Flintstone and Cap'n Crunch tended to be liked less than human product characters such as Ronald McDonald and Burger King, and perceived as less expert (although this measure has flaws). Unfortunately, Atkin did not compare the effects of the two types of fantasy characters on children's brand choice behavior.

Fantasy effects are further complicated by the difficulty of defining fantasy portrayals. Ronald McDonald and Burger King, for example, are real people— various actors. They appear in-role in public as fantastic figures. They are also real-life celebrities. How should their endorser status be classified in terms of the NAB code (see table 5-1): as real-life celebrities, as portrayed celebrities, as real-life product characters, or as portrayed product characters? These distinctions escape even experienced researchers. Atkin (1979) asked 3- to 7-year-old children whether, respectively, Ronald McDonald and Burger King was "a real person or a pretend person?" Atkin assumed that those answering "real person" could not distinguish fantasy from reality, but both answers are correct and the fantasy measure is thus not valid. The fantasy status of presenters, upon which the NAB code (but not the NAD code) depends, obviously requires further definition prior to further research.

Social Stereotype Effects

The development of socially stereotyped perceptions in children is undoubtedly a long, cumulative process. The incidence figures for social cues associated with characters in children's commercials dealt primarily with ratios: young-old, male-female, or black-white. In the general context of television viewing, it has been hypothesized that ratios of violence and the social characteristics of aggressors and victims can affect adult viewers' perceptions of society (Gerbner and Gross 1976).[15] We might expect similar effects from commercials, although it would be difficult to separate them from the effects of television programming as a whole.

We might nevertheless ask whether the social characteristics of commercials produced any short-term effects regardless of any long-term contribution to the *development* of social stereotypes. In particular, by using certain characters as presenters or product users, commercials may take advantage of *existing* social stereotypes to produce endorsement effects, that is, to imbue the product with qualities or characteristics it would not otherwise have. Thus, children may find models in commercials credible, attractive, or persuasive solely on the basis of their social characteristics, quite apart from any celebrity, authority, or other special status characteristics they may possess. There is considerable evidence that these short-term social endorsement effects exist. We will examine this evidence in terms of the most salient social cues among characters in children's commercials: age, sex, race, occupation, and social behavior.

Age Cues: Most of the concern about age cues has centered on the issue of adult versus child presenters. This issue may look like an authority figure phenomenon but, as seen in table 5-1, only particular adult roles are seen as authoritative by the NAB. Thus there is a separate adult versus child presenter issue.[16]

The overwhelming use of adult presenters suggest that adults are more effective presenters than children. But there is a qualification. A study by Robertson, Rossiter, and Brenner (1975) utilized a child endorser, a parent endorser, and a parent-plus-child endorsement. Increased ratings of affect (liking) toward the endorsed product were exactly in that order: most effective was the parent-plus-child endorsement. The difference between the child endorser and parent-plus-child endorsements was significant at the .05 level, with younger children (7- to 9-year-olds) somewhat more influenced by the parental inclusions than older children (10- to 12-year-olds). The Robertson et al. study was conducted with a mixed race, mixed sex sample. The finding of parent-child superiority was replicated in a follow-up study by Gardner (1975) with an all-white, mixed sex sample—with results significant at the .01 level. In sum, the studies indicate that adults are more effective than children as presenters, especially if they are shown *with* children as a joint endorsement.

Sex Cues: The endorsement effect question in relation to sex cues is whether males or females are more effective presenters of products in children's advertising. Empirical research on sex cues has typically employed child rather than adult models, although children are atypical as presenters (see tables 5-2 and 5-3).

The single study that has employed adult models in research on sex roles in children's television advertising was conducted in the Atkin series (1975c). In this study, Atkin was interested in the auditory sex cues provided by off-camera announcers.[17] Interestingly, only 47 percent of the children in the Atkin study correctly recalled that a woman's voice had been used in the version of the commercial using a female announcer; recall did not differ by sex of viewer. Older children were much more often correct than younger children, perhaps reflecting increasing sex-role awareness. Overall, use of a female announcer made no difference as to recall of the commercial, belief in the advertised claim, or desire to use the product. By subgroups, boys were somewhat more influenced by the female announcer, as were older children. However, there was no difference in response between the children who recalled a female voice and those who did not recall the announcer's sex correctly.

The apparent implications of this study are either that the sex of an off-camera announcer makes no difference, or that a female announcer is sufficiently novel to make her just as effective as a male announcer. But there is a third possibility. Atkin used a Bufferin commercial that was probably fairly familiar to the children. Recall of the commercial, belief in the claim ("Bufferin works faster than plain aspirin"), and desire to take the product may well have been established *prior* to the test. Thus the experiment may imply nothing more about sex cues than that boys and girls are equally likely to hear them.

A similar drawback occurred in a second study by Atkin (1975c), which used boy and girl models endorsing an established product—a Tyco race car set. Only 41 percent of the children in the girl endorser version recalled the model's[18] sex accurately; again this did not differ by sex of viewer. Female endorser effects were found *only* among those children who had perceived the female endorsement. This subgroup was much more likely than the nonperceiver subgroup to approve of girls playing with race car sets. However, their own desire for the toy was only minimally affected, with boys wanting it much more than girls, regardless of the commercial manipulation.

Less equivocal sex cue results were obtained in the Robertson et al. study (1975) and the Gardner (1975) replication. The products, fictitious brands of cereal, were unknown to the children, so previously established attitudes were not a confounding factor. Across the total sample there were no significant sex cue effects. However, subgroup analyses provided a different picture. In both studies, older boys were more influenced by male endorsers (n.s. at first grade, .05 at third, and .01 at fifth). Girls showed a similar trend in response to female endorsers, but this trend did not reach statistical significance (that is, male models were equally effective with girls). Two qualifications should be added to these results. A pilot study by Sobel and Rossiter (1975) did show a marked "own sex" trend for girls.[19] The study also included a third sex cue condition: boy-plus-girl endorsement. This turned out to be equally as effective as male-only endorsement with older boys, but not at all appealing to girls.

Taken as a whole, these studies suggest that sex cue endorsement can be effective in changing children's liking for products—quite apart from any intrinsic characteristics the product may possess—although the magnitude of the effect depends on prior sex-typing of the product. Sex cue endorsement seems to be more effective with *older* children, probably because of socially learned sex-role awareness. Finally, findings lean toward an "own sex" effect in general, but the evidence is not conclusive on this point. More research is needed concerning the possible mechanisms underlying sex differences in response to sex-role cues. Some promising work in this direction was recently reported by Reeves and Greenberg (1977) who found that boys tend to be influenced by the physical strength and activity cues exhibited by television characters in deciding which ones they most want to emulate, whereas girls tend to be influenced by physical attractiveness. Dimensional research of this type should help to clarify the complicated and often contradictory findings about the impact of sex cues in children's commercials.

Race Cues: The evidence on endorsement effects due to racial characteristics of product endorsers is also complicated. Four published studies have tested the effects of black and white endorsers with black and white child samples.[20] All show a tendency for awareness of racial cues to increase with age; young children seem little affected by racial differences.

The complication in the race cue studies lies with older (10- to 12-year-old) children. Robertson et al. (1975) found a tendency for children of this age to be influenced by an "own race" effect although this trend was not statistically significant. Gardner (1975), using a white sample only, also found no significant "own race" endorsement effect. However, Hyams, Tanner, and Rossiter (1975) found very strong "own race" effects for older children, particularly black children,[21] and Atkin (1975b) found an apparently significant "cross-race" effect for older black children, but no effect for older white children.

What should be concluded from these studies? First, it is clear that race cue endorsement effects, again independent of the product's own characteristics, can occur. Second, whether these effects occur depends critically on the prior socialization of the child. Older children seem more liable to be affected by racial cues in commercials, but *how* they are affected almost undoubtedly

depends on their own socialization experiences with regard to race. It is noteworthy, for example, that the studies cited here drew their samples from schools
with quite different interracial histories, which may account for their discrepant
findings.

Occupational Cues: As noted, occupational cues are probably present in about
40 percent of commercials intended for children. Evidence on long-term stereotyping effects attributable to commercials is almost impossible to obtain, but in
the short-term, occupational cues undoubtedly have authoritative or status-
oriented dimensions which make them a special subcategory of endorsement
effects. Note the earlier reference to the study by Hyams et al. (1975) which
demonstrated that the occupation of "athlete" in an endorser role is more
effective with children than the occupation of businessman.

However, the principal controversy surrounding occupational cues in commercials involves their interaction with sex cues. Most often the controversy
centers on the occupational stereotyping of women. Content analysts imply
that women in commercials are often stereotyped as "housewives," although
as we already commented, the women might also be designated as "mothers."
In either case, the occupations portrayed by women are clearly limited.

Although the development of social stereotypes is presumably a long
process, a very interesting experiment by Atkin (1975c) suggests that certain
stereotypes of women's occupations may be reversed, at least temporarily, in a
single trial. In this experiment, Atkin prepared three versions of a commercial
in which a 35-year-old woman was shown discussing the occupation-related
advantages of eyeglasses. In one version, the woman portrayed the role of a
judge; in another, the role of a computer programmer; and in the third, the role
of a television technician repairing a TV set. Separate groups of children saw
each version, and a fourth group, which did not see the commercial, served as a
control. The dependent effects measure consisted of a checklist of occupations suitable for women in which the roles of judge, computer programmer,
and TV technician were included. Results are shown in table 5-10.

The most dramatic result of Atkin's study was the percentage of children
accepting the role of judge as suitable for women after seeing a woman portray
the role in the commercial. The remaining results, although not statistically
significant, indicated that the other two commercials had a similar effect of
reversing the stereotype. Their smaller impact may have been due, respectively,
to less stereotyping of the computer programmer occupation and to the possibility that TV repair is seen as a low status job for persons of either sex.

The most intriguing result of this experiment was the apparent strength
of a single "learning trial" in the face of considerable previous learning. The
change effects, incidentally, were stronger among the older and presumably
more role-socialized children. A delayed follow-up measure of occupational
suitability would have been an interesting addition to the experiment.

Table 5-10
Women's Occupational Suitability

	Percent of Children who Checked this Occupation as Suitable for Women	
Occupation	Control Group	Experimental Group
Computer programmer	54	62
Judge	27	51*
TV technician	26	36

Source: Atkin (1975c).
*Significant difference (p < .05).

A second experiment along similar lines was conducted recently by O'Bryant and Corder-Bolz (1978). Subjects were 6- to 7-year-old, low income, black children, eleven girls and twelve boys, who were shown a series of commercials in which female actresses played either stereotypic (traditional female) or counterstereotypic (traditionally male) occupational roles. Changes from pre-exposure to post-exposure ratings indicated that children's knowledge of alternative female roles increased significantly, although the counterstereotypical roles were still seen as less common job alternatives for women. While, as expected, the female commercials did not lead boys to prefer traditional female occupations, the girls in the experiment did show a significantly increased preference for nontraditional (traditionally male) occupations after seeing the commercials.

It is tempting to conclude from the counterstereotyping effects in these experiments that commercials must also produce stereotyping effects, but such a conclusion is not logically warranted. However, single commercials are clearly capable of affecting children's short-term social beliefs. This is an unusual finding given that such effects were popularly supposed to result only from multiple exposures.

Social Behavior: The final subcategory of social stereotype effects concerns social behavior which, according to the NAB code, must not be portrayed as being "inconsistent with recognized social values and customs." Some types of behavior, such as violence, would be almost universally regarded as antisocial, but the classification of living habits, manners, or language is distinctly more subjective. It is not surprising, then, that no one has attempted to define the stimulus characteristics needed for an effects study on the more general forms of social behavior seen in commercials.

We might ask, however, whether the phenomenon of learning social behavior from commercials is demonstrable. Atkin (1975b) has shown that it is. In his experiment, a group of children who saw an anti-littering commercial exhibited significantly less littering behavior than a group who had not seen it.

However, in Atkin's commercial, a public service announcement, the focus was on littering, whereas the sort of behavioral effects that the NAB and NAD are concerned about would presumably be of a more incidental nature. No studies are available on children's incidental learning of routine social behaviors from commercials.

Self-Concept Effects

The four types of endorsements most likely to affect a child's self-concept have already been identified: personal enhancement appeals, social status appeals, product usage portrayals, and competitive product appeals. This section will review the available evidence on the effects of each.

Personal Enhancement Appeals: Some 27 percent of children's commercials employ appeals oriented toward personal enhancement—ranging from temporary effects such as fun and adventure, to more permanent personal states such as strength, health, or well-being (see table 5-7). Many products actually deliver such benefits, of course. The main concern of critics and regulators is not so much with these claims per se as with their documentation or proof.[22] Usually such documentation requires survey evidence demonstrating that the claimed benefit is experienced or attested to by a large majority of children.

In studies of the extent to which children believe personal enhancement claims in commercials, it is particularly important to know (1) what the claim actually stated, and (2) whether or not the claim is true before passing judgment on this type of effect. Atkin's (1979) research for the Federal Trade Commission exhibits both types of inadequacy. Children in this study were asked whether each of four product characters (listed earlier in this chapter) "tells the truth about" his product. A majority of the children answered "Yes," which the investigator interpreted to indicate young children's vulnerability to "inauthentic portrayals" and "hypothetical claims" made in commercials. But, in fact, do these characters make inauthentic or hypothetical claims about the products? This essential issue is never addressed. Atkin then posed hypothetical claims for milk shakes (that they "will make kids grow big and strong") and cereals (that they "will make kids run faster"), attributed them to specific characters and their brands of these products, and measured the extent to which children believed the claims to be true. A majority of the youngest children (3- to 5-year-olds) believed these claims. Obviously, although hypothetical, the claims, broadly considered, may be true. Unless expert in the relevant area pertaining to the claim, be it nutrition, physiology, or clinical psychology, researchers must be extremely cautious about passing judgment on personal enhancement appeals.

In sum, children undoubtedly encounter many personal enhancement claims in commercials. Many of these claims are undoubtedly effective, and many may be valid as well. No reliable nonproprietary data are available on the incidence of personal enhancement claims, their truth value, or their effects.

Social Status Appeals: Children's commercials that imply ownership of a product will lead to increased social status, or that lack of the product will have the opposite effect, are prohibited by the NAB and the NAD. While the incidence of these types of appeals is currently at a very low 2 percent, they nevertheless exist. Consequently, we may raise the issue of whether social status appeals are effective with children.

An experiment by Shaak, Annes, and Rossiter (1975) tested the effectiveness of a commercial with a social status theme. A storyboard commercial for a fictitious brand of cookies was shown to a group of second and fifth graders. The final frame of the three-frame storyboard depicted two different endings. In one version, a child is shown winning new friends by dispensing the cookies; in the control group version, the child retains only his previous friends. This simple manipulation produced an increase in affect or rated liking toward the cookies of 42 percent (significant at the .001 level). The "peer reinforcement" effect was much stronger for the fifth graders ($p < .05$) than for second graders (n.s., though directionally consistent), indicating once again that code-regulated advertising practices do not always affect only the youngest children in the audience. In fact, social status appeals would be expected to be more relevant to older children for whom peer acceptance is more important for their self-concept.

Real commercials may utilize somewhat more subtle allusions to social status.[23] For example, commercials which simply show children of the target group's age using the product may border on social status or peer status appeals.[24] However, these subtler executions probably depend more on source effects than on self-concept effects specifically.

Product Usage Portrayals: Portrayals of products being used that might potentially harm a child's self-concept include exaggerated portrayals of the product's play value or performance characteristics; usage demonstrations that are difficult for children to emulate; settings or contexts that are difficult for children to re-create; and portrayals of a child with unrealistically large numbers of products or premiums. (All of these are prohibited by industry codes.)

Atkin (1975b) tested the first and perhaps the second of these prohibited portrayals. He showed two versions of a "Blockhead" building blocks commercial—one in which a child constructs a modest tower of blocks, and another in which an extremely complicated and extravagant tower was constructed. Afterward, the children in the experiment were given the opportunity to play with an identical set of blocks. Children exposed to the extravagant usage portrayal were generally unsuccessful in building similarly complicated constructions, and during their attempts they displayed more "anger, verbal aggression and physical aggression" (28 percent) than children exposed to the modest version (18 percent). This was a statistically significant, although not large, difference.

Interestingly enough, had Atkin stopped this experiment before the behavioral stage, the implications might have been quite different. The extravagant version produced only one-half the level of brand-name recall that the modest version generated—perhaps because of a distraction effect. Also, as a measure of commercial-induced desire, children seeing the extravagant version were slightly *less* likely to state that the blocks would be fun to play with.

Nevertheless, there was slight evidence that the extravagant version generated greater expectations of successful emulation than the modest version; and Atkin's analysis would have been less equivocal if he could have shown that the subsequent behavioral effects of frustration were higher for children with greater commercial-induced expectations. This would have constituted clearer evidence of a self-concept effect. However, as Atkin noted, it could be argued alternatively that self-concept "protection" might also lead children to lie about their expectations.

Despite the difficulty of obtaining a valid measure of mediational expectations, the exaggeration effects can be regarded as having considerable face validity. It is difficult to account for children's greater frustration after seeing the extravagant version of the commercial without inferring that they were frustrated because their expectations were not attained. A broader evaluation of this experiment might criticize it as atypical: the product usage portrayal was greatly exaggerated. But once again, it is possible to offer the alternative hypothesis that slight exaggerations, if not attainable, would be even more frustrating since more children may be tempted to emulate them. This is not an easy issue to resolve without a more sophisticated experiment.

No experiments have been reported on the other code-regulated aspects of product usage portrayals. The research paradigm for each would be essentially similar, requiring some demonstration that children's self-images are involved in their appraisal of commercials which include product usage portrayals.

Competitive Product Appeals: The NAB prohibits "competitive/comparative/superiority claims or techniques" expressly because of their alleged "potential to encourage dissatisfaction on a child's part." The implication is that the child's self-concept is affected. We found it useful, as the NAD does, to distinguish *overt* competitive appeals (so called "comparative advertising" in which a direct brand comparison is made by name) and *covert* competitive appeals (indirect, anonymous comparisons in which the superiority or uniqueness of the advertised brand is implied).

Overt comparisons are extremely rare (about 1 percent) in commercials directed to children.[25] The usual fear expressed by advertisers is that a comparative commercial may give the competitive brand a "free plug." Consequently, the technique tends to be used only after careful pretesting or when the brand is relatively unknown or has a lot to gain by the comparison.

Unfortunately, the one experiment designed to test children's reactions to comparative advertisements (Atkin 1975c) examined these concerns about advertising strategy rather than the alleged "dissatisfaction effect." The experiment involved two versions of a commercial, one using a comparison strategy, the other (control treatment) mentioning only the advertised product. The results showed no differences in the children's recall of the advertised product between the two versions. However, the children's recall of the "compared" brand indicated a sizeable "free plug" effect for that product. Atkin also found that the comparative commercial did not produce an increased desire for the advertised product. The null effects on the "desire" variable are equivocal, as Atkin noted, because he used two highly familiar brands: a Hershey bar and a Nestle's bar. But again, the experiment did not examine relative dissatisfaction effects nor anything related to children's self-concepts.

It is noteworthy in the Atkin experiment that the children did not seem to have any difficulty *understanding* the comparative commercial. The NAD (in contrast with the NAB) allows comparative claims in cases in which true, understandable differences exist between the brands and in which comparisons are not based on selective inclusion of comparative attributes. Commercials meeting these criteria may well be quite informative to children in a consumer socialization sense. However, no research has been conducted on this contention, apart from the tangential finding in Atkin's experiment that the comparative commercial produced much greater learning of one of two product information dimensions.

Despite NAB prohibition, covert competitive claims of the implied superiority type are estimated to appear in about 11 percent of children's commercials. Some of these claims may be based on documentable superiority ("best selling") although others are clearly subjective opinions, ("the greatest," "fantastic").[26]

Perhaps the most prevalent type of covert competitive claim in *adult* commercials is the so-called "parity claim." Obvious examples are slogans which simply state about the brand that "it's best." This may mean *among* the best or on a par with other top brands. Less obvious examples are employed by two well known brands of toothpaste: "You can't beat—for fighting cavities" and "Only your dentist can give you a better fluoride treatment than—." Winick et al. (1973) speculate that "by five, a child can probably understand 'best,' and soon after, the meaning of 'better.'" However Wrighter (1972) points out that although the formally taught quality hierarchy is "good-better-best," advertising suggests a different hierarchy; namely, "good-best-better." It is more difficult for an advertiser to support a claim of "better" than one of "best." Therefore, in advertising, "better" tends to become the superlative.

A pilot study by Burrall and Rossiter (1975) tends to support Wrighter's position that children cannot discriminate parity claims for what they really are. The study used claims that appeared in children's Christmas toy catalogs rather than in commercials, but they are representative of the types of audio claims children may encounter in commercials. The most interesting claims involved the phrases "the best of its kind" and "two of the most delightful. . . ." The sample was deliberately slanted to reflect high verbal ability; subjects were second- and fourth-grade girls from an upper middle class suburban school. Based on the first parity claim, 30 percent of the second graders and 40 percent of the fourth graders rated the advertised item as better than similar products.[27] Figures for the second claim were 20 percent and 50 percent. It seems reasonable to hypothesize that the incidence of children who were apparently fooled by the claim would be higher in a sample of children of lower verbal ability. Also, the increased effect with age hints that children may be learning advertising's new quality hierarchy. The experiment obviously needs replication, but it is indicative of the type of effect that subtle competitive claims can have on children's evaluations of advertised products.

Whether or not such heightened evaluations affect a child's self-concept would require further demonstration: for instance, that advertising might make the child feel disappointed with presently owned products or with an advertised product, once it had been purchased.

Summary and Conclusions

Confusion Effect

Although a substantial porportion of young children experience confusion between programs and commercials, there is no evidence in support of the hypothesis that the use of program characters in commercials contributes to this confusion. The one study on this issue produced equivocal results, because the confusion measure was too delayed to be conclusive.

A true test of the confusion effect would require a more instantaneous measure of children's ability to distinguish program content from commercial content. Otherwise, it is not clear whether we are testing children's memories or their actual perceptual inability to discriminate. Inability to recall a "host" commercial could indicate an extreme lack of discrimination, or lack of attention, or lack of retention. A better measure of confusion might be a signal-stopping technique in which different subjects are stopped at random intervals and questioned about their immediate perceptions.

Future research should also examine whether live program personalities are any different from animated cartoon characters in their potential for confusion. Both types of endorsers are prohibited from selling within or adjacent to their own programs, yet different restrictions are applied to human and animated endorsers elsewhere; generally, animated characters are given much freer reign. It is not clear why this should be so.

The single study of the adjacency effect hypothesis did not support the contention that program personalities and cartoon characters are less likely to produce confusion if they do not appear in commercials placed within or adjacent to their own programs. However, the nonadjacency condition used in the experiment was confounded by an attempt to test another manipulation at the same time.

The same comments on the need for an instantaneous measure of confusion apply here, as does the need to include program personalities and cartoon characters in the research. A new study is needed which provides parameters for the adjacency phenomenon. Relevant experimental treatments for commercial placement would be: within program, contiguous to program, noncontiguous but within a short time of the program, and noncontiguous and well separated from the program. The first two treatments would correspond to the adjacency ban of the NAB, while the remaining two would test the effectiveness of the separation implicitly required in the code's provisions.

Endorsement Effect

Only two studies have tested the effects of direct, testimonial-type endorsements, although others have tested less direct endorsements in studies of source effects. The direct endorsement studies found either negative or equivocal endorsement effects. Nevertheless, secondary research leaves little doubt that positive endorsement effects can occur with the direct testimonial approach. Also, at least four studies have shown that a significant change in rated affect toward the endorsed product can occur with even a passive or "mere appearance" endorsement. It is therefore highly improbable that prohibition of direct (testimonial type) endorsements will remove endorsement effects, although it may reduce them.

The entire area of source effects research in children's advertising is badly in need of theoretical direction and improved methodology. The following are the most important points:

1. On the source or "stimulus" side, there has been little specification of the characteristics or processes by which endorsers are supposed to produce their effects. For example, the FTC consent order against Spider-Man vitamins alleged that this endorser has the tendency and capacity to take advantage of the trust relationship development between children and the program character.[28] However, source theory in social psychology[29] suggests that any one or a combination of the following factors can produce an endorsement effect:

Source Characteristic	Psychological Process
Credibility Expertness Objectivity	Internalization
Attractiveness Likeability Similarity	Identification
Power	Compliance

Thus, celebrity endorsers may represent a combination of likeability and perhaps expertise. Authority figures, on the other hand, may combine credibility and power—the latter being defined as the potential to reward or punish the message receiver and thus to control compliance with the message. With more theoretical direction, we might then be able to ascertain why certain categories of sources are or should be regulated in children's advertising.

2. Research on source effects should include an assessment of the source's characteristics—credibility, attractiveness, and power—independently of how the source is used in a commercial. The product should also be assessed independently. Only then can we judge what, and how much, a source adds to a product's intrinsic characteristics via endorsement.

3. On the effect or "response" side, most studies of source effects in children's advertising have been content to record changes in overall affect or rated liking toward the endorsed product. But these changes can only be taken as evidence of an endorsement effect if overall likeability is viewed as a product characteristic, and if the endorsement effect is interpreted to include quantitative changes in existing product characteristics and not just the addition of a qualitatively "new" characteristic. More informative evidence on endorsement effects would be obtained if we incorporated specific product attributes in the research and measured specific changes in children's beliefs about these attributes as well as the more global index of overall product likeability.

4. If the intent of the NAB provisions on indirect endorsement is to reduce rather than to remove a given source's impact, a relevant study would be to provide parameters to the direct endorsement variable by including three experimental treatments: appearance only; visual endorsement in which the endorser is seen using or consuming the product but not verbally endorsing it; and a straightforward testimonial.

The *fantasy effect* phenomenon is also in dire need of theoretical direction. The fantasy effect is probably the most important assumption in the NAB's children's presenter code and it therefore demands more than just an intuitive appraisal. Some theoretical beginnings were mentioned in the study by Winick et al. (1973) from which the following list of hypotheses was derived: (1) That children perceive cartoons and fiction as a "game" and thus fantasy presenters are perceived as giving a weaker form of endorsement than real-life presenters; (2) Or, to the contrary, that fantasy endorsements are more effective because children are less skeptical of claims made by fantasy presenters than they are of the same claims made by real-life presenters; (3) That humor or magic associated with fantasy presenters adds extra appeal to the presentation and the product; (4) That animated actions are easier for young children to comprehend than live-figure action; (5) That, in cartoon program slots, animated product presenters (not necessarily program characters) make the transition from program to commercial "minimally jarring" to young viewers (Winick et al.'s expression) and may also prevent a decline in attention; (6) That certain fantasy characters such as Fred Flintstone or Bugs Bunny are so familiar that they have lost much of their fantasy content; (7) That children's perceptions of "slice of life" portrayals be examined to see whether these indeed differ from "real-life" portrayals—for example, whether role-played authority figures are any different from actual authority figures; (8) Finally, that the source characteristics model outlined previously would seem to be equally applicable to fantasy endorser research. A theory-based approach would allow us to determine whether it is really fantasy-reality that is the relevant dimension or whether the true differences between sources lie in their credibility, attractiveness, or relative power.

One final, general remark should be made concerning the endorsement effect. No one has yet investigated the question of whether children regard an endorsement as being an attribute of the product; that is, that one of a product's characteristics is that it is "recommended by_____." This research would provide insight on children's reasoning in product and source evaluation. It would also raise the issue of whether endorsements are a "legitimate" or "fair" basis on which to promote products to children.

Social Stereotype Effect

It is almost impossible to determine whether or not commercials contribute to the formation of social stereotypes. Ratio analyses of social cue content in commercials (young-old, male-female, black-white) suggest that they at least have the potential to do so. Children's commercials are biased toward adults on the age ratio and toward males on the sex ratio. They are also somewhat biased *toward* minority groups (mainly black) on the race ratio.

If these ratios can affect children's beliefs about the real world, an extremely complex and value laden issue is raised. The issue is whether commercials should be expected to match real world ratios or whether some kind of overcompensation is justified (for example, for women or for racial minority groups). The prosocial potential of commercials in this respect is interestingly illustrated by the tendency of children's commercials not only to override the nonwhite/white ratio slightly, but to accomplish this by almost exclusively depicting integrated racial settings in children's commercials. Value judgments aside, it would be of empirical interest to know what effects such practices have.

Evidence from two studies dealing with occupational stereotypes for women,[30] raised another issue worthy of attention. Although the development of social stereotypes is undoubtedly a cumulative process, these studies indicated that at least a short-term reverse stereotyping effect could take place in a single exposure. Future research on this phenomenon should include measurement of the permanence of the effect and investigation of the possibilities for counter-stereotype portrayals for other social cue categories.

Social cues in commercials also have relevance to a previous topic, the endorsement effect. Here we are concerned not with whether social cues in commercials contribute to the learning of stereotypes, but whether previously learned stereotypes contribute to children's evaluations of products. For example, children may react to models in commercials because of the credibility, attractiveness, or power associated with their social characteristics—quite apart from any celebrity, authority, or other special status characteristics they may possess. The evidence showed that children *do* respond to social cues as a source effect: (1) Age cue research indicated that adults were generally more effective than children as presenters and still more effective if shown with children in a joint endorsement. (2) Sex cue findings were not as clear cut. Experiments employing male and female endorsers revealed a significant "own sex" effect for boys and for girls, especially among older children. Most studies have been done with child models. Given the prevalence of adults in children's commercials, a logical study would be a sex-by-age "crossed" experiment on endorsement effects. (3) Race cue endorsement findings were strong but contradictory; a critical variable appeared to be the prior racial socialization of the participating children. (4) Occupational cue research has been confined mainly to studies of the occupational stereotyping of women. Men, too, are occupationally stereotyped by children, and this is a prime area for further research. (5) Research on social behavior cues has not been pursued apart from one study of a public service announcement on littering. This neglect is partly due to the difficulty of defining what is "acceptable" social behavior beyond certain extreme examples.

A final category of needed research on the social stereotype effect should be mentioned. In the sex cue studies, it was frequently, and not too surprisingly, found that many products are sex-role stereotyped by children. This raises the possibility (for other social cues as well) that source effects may operate in reverse. That is, products shown in commercials may affect children's perceptions of the characters associated with those products. Girls who are shown playing with "male" toys, for example, may be seen as unfeminine. Again, the purpose is not to pass judgment on such portrayals but simply to alert future researchers to the bidirectional possibilities of the source effect.

Self-Concept Effect

Isolated studies have been conducted with each of four types of presentations related to self-concept appeals: personal enhancement appeals, social status appeals, product usage portrayals, and competitive product appeals. There are two faults common to the existing studies on these self-concept issues. The faults are sufficiently critical to deserve special emphasis.

First, none of the studies has included measurement of the principal variable—the child's self-concept. While some of the studies have demonstrated that personal enhancement appeals, social status appeals, and competitive product appeals are effective with children, and that product usage portrayals may be emulated, no attention has been given to any transient or permanent effects on the child's self-concept.

Second, researchers have failed to realize that, in this area and others, the choice of commercials is an important sampling problem. In many cases, extreme examples have been selected and no argument has been advanced as to why the particular commercial was chosen or why it was assumed to be a representative case. As we pointed out in the discussion, many alleged effects depend on a "parameterized" stimulus. These may not be linear parameters, so it is also possible that selection of extreme examples may actually overlook the critical range.

In terms of needed research: (1) It seems incumbent upon advertisers to document their claims of temporary benefits, such as fun and adventure, or more permanent benefits such as strength, health, and well-being. However, many subjective and therefore nonverifiable personal enhancement appeals will continue to challenge policy in this area and to pose difficult research issues. (2) Social status appeals are more relevant to older children who are more aware of the need for social acceptance. Overt social status appeals are very rare in children's commercials but it could be argued that certain endorsers carry social status connotations. Further research, therefore, should probably be directed to social status as a subcategory of the endorsement effect, rather than as a practice in its own right. (3) Product usage portrayals represent a prime example of a research area in which the previous two general faults need to be overcome. Highly exaggerated protrayals may actually discourage imitation whereas more moderate portrayals might invite it. The central research issue is again, however, whether a child's inability to emulate usage portrayals actually affects the child's self-concept. (4) Competitive product claims constitute a topic for which research is strongly recommended. Overt competitive appeals, if presented fairly and accurately, may contribute positively to children's consumer socialization. Covert competitive appeals, on the other hand, are often undetected in incidence counts since they are little understood. Moreover, when they do occur, they tend to be subtle. It is likely that competitive product appeals have more effect on children's short-term understanding of product claims than on their self-concepts as such. However, a series of misunderstandings might contribute to the development of cynicism as a possibly undesirable socialization effect.

Notes

1. The relationship of source effects to self-concept effects might be expressed in terms of "who" presents the product versus "how" it is presented. Other presentation issues are discussed in chapter 2.

2. "Children's TV Advertising." Sections I.J. and I.K. Also, "Questions and Answers," January 1, 1975.

3. Two other specific social factors are mentioned. NAB prohibits use of "realistic war atmosphere" in children's commercials and also portrayals which "suggest or recommend indiscriminate and/or immoderate use" of products such as snacks, candy, gum, and soft drinks.

4. Readers who check Barcus (1975a, b) will find a very high incidence (about 41 percent) of off-stage announcers. However, this does not preclude the additional presence of an on-camera presenter. The 80 percent figure is estimated from the older Winick et al. (1973) data, but is likely to be currently applicable since there have been no code changes affecting the practice.

5. An article in *Advertising Age*, September 13, 1976 (post-dating the September 1, 1976, NAB ban) reports that Schaper Manufacturing Co. and the Muller Jordan Herrick advertising agency will be using Alex Karras—a celebrity and, as an athlete, probably also an authority figure by NAB definitions—to promote its "Super Jocks" line of children's action toys on "children's shows, sports programs and prime time network shows." Similarly, an article in the American Marketing Association's *Marketing News*, October 8, 1976, reports that Ideal Toy Corporation planned to use the following show business and sports personalities in its 1977 children's toy commercials: Evel Knievel, Kotter, Mean Joe Greene, and Chuck Connors. The schedule included twenty-five weekend children's programs on the three major networks.

6. Estimated from figures provided by Winick et al. (1973); collected in 1971, these may be somewhat inaccurate but are the nearest available estimates.

7. In addition to sections I.J. and I.K. of the NAB's Children's TV Advertising code of September 1, 1976, see NAB's "Questions and Answers," in *Code News*, Janaury 1, 1975.

8. These figures are averaged from Barcus (1975a, b). All averages of Barcus's two reports are conservatively rounded to the nearest whole number percentage.

9. For example, a recent consent order by the FTC against Hudson

Pharmaceutical Corporation alleges that commercials which use "Spider-Man," a character who appears as "Spidey" on "The Electric Company" children's program, "has the tendency and capacity to blur for children the distinction between program content and advertising" (Federal Trade Commission Consent Order File No. 762 3054).

10. A recent study by Gianinno and Zuckerman (1977) measured children's ability to distinguish program characters from commercial characters. However, the investigators eliminated characters who had both program and commercial affiliations, and therefore did not test the confusion effect.

11. Other than the "mere appearance" possibility; see table 5-1.

12. The endorser, who was identified as "Astronaut Alan Collins," was presumably a celebrity *and* an authority figure since "astronaut" is one of the roles cited by the NAB as exemplifying an authority figure in children's advertising; see table 5-1.

13. This observation was first made by Dr. Philip A. Harding of the Office of Social Research, CBS, Inc.

14. Also observed by Dr. Harding of CBS.

15. The Gerbner and Gross research was thought to have provided reasonable proof for this hypothesis. However, their otherwise careful studies of perceived risk of violence failed to control for actual crime ratios in the immediate neighborhoods of viewers. In a recent study, Doob and Macdonald (1979) showed that the relationship between televised violence viewing and perceived risk of violence disappears when actual neighborhood risks are taken into account. Other social perceptions related to television viewing in the Gerbner and Gross studies have not been investigated from this perspective.

16. Interestingly enough, the NAB is concerned about the role of children in adult commercials. NAB apparently feels that dominant use of children in commercials ostensibly intended for adults may redefine the actual target of th commercials as being intended for children. In advertising of any product "designed for and directed to adults" a commercial is exempt from the provisions of the Children's TV Advertising Guidelines even if it is shown during or adjacent to children's programming and if "Any use of a child is limited to a real-life situation and, if the child is used as other than an incidental, background character, such use is confined to a situation in which the parent/adult-child relationship is established and the parent-adult remains the dominant character" (Children's TV Advertising, section III.2).

17. Barcus (1975a, b) found that an average of 41 percent of children's commercials use an off-stage voice, although our estimates are that only 20 percent use solely an off-stage voice with no on-stage presenter.

18. Actually models' sex: Atkin used two boys and two girls in each commercial to minimize idiosyncratic cues.

19. The term "marked trend" is used because these data were not tested for statistical significance. The magnitude of the effect, however, was greater

than the significant differences in the Robertson et al. and Gardner studies.

20. One of these studies was not sufficiently well controlled to be assessed.

21. This was the only study to include an integrated setting. Older children of both races in this sample preferred this setting least, although their response to a cross-sex setting was only slightly less negative.

22. For example, the FTC's celebrated charge against Wonder Bread advertising included the allegation that it "tends to exploit children's aspirations for rapid and healthy growth." The FTC eventually ruled in favor of Wonder Bread in regard to this portion of the complaint.

23. Although the execution seemed no less obvious than the "boy's club" commercial mentioned in the Incidence section.

24. See the previous discussion of social cues.

25. According to a recent *Marketing News* article, comparative commercials comprise about 10 percent of prime-time television advertising.

26. As Preston (1975) has observed, superiority claims may even be implied by a product's name (for example, *Wonder* Bread or *Super* blocks).

27. Prior familiarity with the advertised items was not a confounding factor. The catalog was newly issued with limited circulation and children said, with only one or two exceptions, that they had seen neither it nor the items before.

28. Note that the FTC's move is a marked departure from the previous FTC policy of allowing NAB self-regulation. Spider-Man is a program character, not a human celebrity or an authority, and as such could only be cited under NAB rules for adjacent selling and the confusion effect, not for the endorsement effect.

29. For example, Kelman 1958; McGuire 1973.

30. It seems pertinent to reiterate that a separation of the roles of "housewife" and "mother" should be made. Too often investigators fail to do this. The two roles obviously have quite different implications for children's perspectives.

The Effects of Premium Offers in Children's Television Advertising

Scott Ward

Premiums are heavily employed as a purchase incentive in certain children's product categories, notably cereals. The FTC has alleged that premiums represent an irrelevant product characteristic, that they distract children from considering legitimate product attributes, and that they multiply the difficulty of choosing between brands. Defenders of premiums argue that they may actually facilitate the choice between otherwise fairly similar brands, and that premiums constitute a legitimate product attribute since they are part of the "total product package."

Regulatory Issues

While there are no current FTC regulations on premium offers in advertising to children, in 1974 the FTC did propose a guide which would have eliminated all forms of premium offers in television advertising addressed to children under age 12. The proposed guide was later withdrawn, but it is instructive to review the issues raised by the proposed rule, the reasoning underlying the issues, and the use of research mentioned in the guide and precipitated by it.

The 1974 proposed guide would have eliminated offers of "pack-ins" (small toys or other objects included in the package), "pack-ons" (cut-outs on the side of a cereal box), reusable containers, self-liquidating premiums, and any kind of remuneration for purchase, including free gifts.

The FTC proposal attracted much criticism from advertisers who used premium offers in accordance with the restrictions of existing industry codes and guidelines. For example, the NAD code permits premium offers but stresses the need to place major emphasis in advertising on the product itself, with the premium as clearly secondary. Some industry spokesmen proposed further restrictions, in response to the proposed guide, such as limiting the time devoted to the premium offer within a commercial. For example, the Cracker Jack Division of Borden Foods proposed that only one-third or ten seconds of a commercial, whichever is less, should be used to present the premium offer.

The issues were summarized in the rationale for the FTC's proposed guide:

The very purpose of the premium advertisement is to focus the child's attention on a factor that is almost always completely irrelevant to merits of the principal product, thereby greatly increasing the likelihood that the child's response to the ad will reflect confusion.

The premium offer characteristically bears no relation to the criteria which would guide choice if the product stood alone. Instead, the premium's main purpose is to distract the buyer's attention from those attributes and to motivate purchase not on the merits of the product but in order to obtain the premium.

The injection of a premium into a buying decision cannot help but multiply the difficulties of choice. . . .Merely by adding another group of factors that compete with those already demanding the child's attention, the premium must inevitably increase the likelihood of confusion and of the purchase of an inferior product.

An industry spokesman, Dr. Seymour Banks,[1] questioned whether premiums are in fact "completely irrelevant to the merits of the principal product," as stated in the FTC's proposed guide. He cites the case of presweetened breakfast cereals, the products that include the greatest proportion of premium offers. The various brands of presweetened cereals are very similar, differing mainly in shapes and colors. Virtually all of them contain the same ingredients and nutritional content. Dr. Banks argues that a purchaser, faced with such an array of similar brands, will choose one brand on the basis of a discriminating attribute, such as the premium. He questions, then, whether premiums are, in fact, an irrelevant product attribute.

Relevance and irrelevance are not directly amenable to research. Issues about premiums that *are* open to empirical analysis seem to be:

1. To what extent do premium offers "confuse" children from regarding what is actually being sold?
2. To what extent do premium messages distract children from using other product features in making product choices? Does a premium offer "multiply the difficulties" of product or brand choice?
3. Do premium offers increase intra-family conflict?

A final research issue arises from the compromise proposed by industry groups to place time limits on the premium offers within a commercial:

4. Instead of a total ban on premium offers, would placing time limitations on the premium offer (for example, ten seconds of a total of thirty) achieve the objective of making the premium offer a secondary attribute? Would such a restriction lessen the potential of premium offers to confuse children? Would it make their choices between products relatively less difficult?[2]

Incidence of Premium Offers

In recent years, two studies have found that about 10 percent of the commercials on Saturday morning television contained premiums (Winick et al. 1973; Atkin 1974). However, the percentage of premium offers is substantially higher for specific products. Atkin found, for example, that 34 percent of all cereals advertised on Saturday morning contained a premium offer.

Precise data are not available on the prevalence of premium advertising for other kinds of products or services (such as fast food restaurants), nor are there precise data on the nature of the premium offers themselves. Some anecdotal information is available; for example, Shimp, Dyer, and Divita (1976) cite an FTC source indicating that most premium offers occur within the "last half" of commercials addressed to children.

Research Evidence

Some useful background information for the issues raised by premiums is provided in a purely descriptive survey of attitudes toward and uses of premium offers among mothers and children. Conducted by The Gene Reilly Group (1974), the national survey sample of 1,200 was divided evenly between mothers and two age groups of children (aged 7 to 9 and 10 to 12). Although the study focused on premiums designed for adults as well as for children, certain findings are relevant to this discussion:

Premiums were most often associated with cereal products by both mothers (82 percent) and children (91 percent).[3]

Eighty-two percent of children said that they would "most expect to find" premium advertising on television, rather than in other media.

Children report receiving an average of twenty premiums in the past year.

Premium use, and most positive attitudes toward premiums, occur among mothers and children in the lower socioeconomic strata.

Eighty-four percent of children who said that they recently acquired a premium said that it was obtained with the purchase of a product, rather than by sending away for it.

Children were generally satisfied with the most recent premium received; dissatisfaction was linked to "lack of quality."

Mothers preferred educational premiums and other premiums that could be used by several children or by the whole family. They cited plastic toys, toys needing assembly, and easily broken toys as premiums they did not like.

Both mothers and children reported that premiums did not influence their purchase behavior. However, the social desirability bias in such questioning makes the validity of the response questionable.

Eighty-six percent of mothers rated premiums offered to children as being only fair or poor in overall quality. They generally opposed the idea of television advertising that includes premium offers. Again, social desirability factors make the validity of the latter data questionable.

In general, one could interpret these data as demonstrating that mothers verbally express somewhat negative attitudes toward premiums and are not influenced by premiums in their purchasing. However, the sheer numbers of premiums obtained by the children in the survey suggest that actual behavior is not consistent with these negative attitudes.

Confusion and Distraction From Other Product Features

Much research in child psychology has examined children's attention to and selection of information from audio and/or visual stimuli (see chapter 3). While few studies have focused specifically on television advertising, much less televised premium advertising, the existing research helps us to understand children's information-processing, which may have relevance for their responses to premium advertising on television.

Of particular interest are the studies of children's attention patterns while viewing commercials embedded in programs in both laboratory and natural, in-home environments (Wartella and Ettema 1974; Ward and Wackman 1973b; Atkin 1974). These findings consistently show age-related decreases (from nursery school to sixth graders) in children's attention to commercials, relative to program content. Some of the data suggest that younger children show greater variance in attention patterns, perhaps reflecting their shorter attention spans. Only the Atkin study examined children's attention to commercials with and without premium offers, and no differences were found in the children's attention patterns to the two kinds of commercials. Because these studies used rather gross measures of attention, they shed little light on the characteristics of commercials which affect attention in children. They do suggest, however, that commercials have notable "drawing power" for younger children.

Other research in child psychology has some relevance to premium advertising. For example, Hagen has studied aspects of children's information-processing and finds a developmental trend in children's ability to remember relevant and irrelevant information (Maccoby and Hagen 1965; Hagen 1967; Hagen and Hall 1973). In this research, the central, relevant information was defined as that which is necessary to the performance of a task, such as identifying the position of pictures in a sequential array. Incidental, or irrelevant, information was not necessary to the completion of the task. The older children (fifth and seventh graders) in these studies remembered central information much better than younger children (first and third graders), but memory of incidental information did not change with age. These findings were interpreted by the researchers as a developmental change in attention selectivity. As children grow older they are better able to allocate their attention and to select the information necessary to completion of a task.

Pick et al. (1974) summarized this research on children's processing of central and incidental information by concluding: "Accentuating what is irrelevant often makes it more difficult to attend to and use what is relevant." This is especially true for younger children. The evidence also indicates a clear developmental improvement in the effectiveness of children's search strategies. Older children engage in more search activity than younger children, but are also better able to ignore or disregard irrelevant information.

Several other research efforts in this area clearly demonstrate that: (1) older children can use more dimensions in problem-solving than younger children; and (2) children's reinforcement experiences can play a significant role in their determination of the salience of different kinds of information (Witryol, Lowden, and Fagan 1967; Odom 1972; Odom and Corbin 1973; Odom and Guzman 1972). To the extent that these findings can be applied to questions of premium offers in television advertising, they might suggest age-related differences in children's abilities to evaluate premiums and other product features in making product choices. Moreover, children's experiences of positive and negative reinforcement in using premiums originally seen in advertising may foster, or inhibit, the responsiveness of the children to future premium offers.

Two studies have directly examined children's responses to premium offers in television commercials. They followed similar procedures, exposing children to cereal commercials embedded in programming and then immediately measuring the verbal responses of the children. Both studies also involved exposure to a single test commercial as opposed to the repetitive exposures which would occur in the course of normal television viewing.

In Rubin's (1972) study, first-, third-, and sixth-grade children were exposed to a thirty-second commercial, either with or without a premium offer. Immediately after exposure, they were asked a series of questions about the commercial: what they recalled, what they felt they were supposed to want, what they were supposed to do with the product, etc. Since some of the questions were fairly abstract, they may have been difficult for the younger children to answer—for example, "What do you think (movies, ads, commercials) are supposed to be for?" "Why do you think people make them?" Further, some caution must be used in interpreting results because of the limited verbal abilities of younger children. Nevertheless, most children did provide some answers to each question.

Data on the recall of the children were obtained from the question: "Tell me what happens in the movie you just saw?" "Anything else?" As table 6-1 indicates, only the sixth graders had reasonably high recall of the brand-name in the commercial, both with and without the premium. Only a few first graders recalled the brand-name in either condition, although almost all of them remembered that the commercial concerned cereal. The third graders were split evenly in both conditions. There was high recall of the specific premium offer, a toy car, in all age groups.

In both conditions, the product symbol was accurately recalled by a relatively high percentage of all of the children. It is interesting to note that all of the sixth graders accurately recalled the symbol in the no-premium condition, whereas only seven of the twelve mentioned a symbol in the premium condition. This suggests the possibility that the premiums distracted attention from the brand-name.

The salience of the premium offer was assessed by examining children's responses to the question: "What do you think you are supposed to want after seeing the movie?" Results appear in table 6-2. In both the premium and no-premium condition, most of the third and sixth graders exposed to the premium ad said that the commercial was trying to make them want *both* the cereal and the premium. Among first graders, there was a substantial difference

Table 6-1
Recall of Specific Commercial Elements
(*number*)

	Premium			No Premium		
	First Grade	Third Grade	Sixth Grade	First Grade	Third Grade	Sixth Grade
Brand-name						
Accurate	2	4	7	2	5	9
Cereal only	8	4	4	8	7	3
Symbol						
Accurate	8	8	7	7	9	12
Other animals	3	2	0	5	2	0
Premium						
Accurate	9	11	12	—	—	—
Other objects	2	0	0	—	—	—
n	12	12	12	12	12	12

Source: Rubin (1972). Based on responses to the open-ended question: "Tell me what happens in the movie you just saw."

Table 6-2
**What Children Think They Are Supposed to Want After Exposure
to a Commercial**
(*number*)

Supposed to want	Premium			No Premium		
	First Grade	Third Grade	Sixth Grade	First Grade	Third Grade	Sixth Grade
Cereal	1	3	5	9	8	10
Cereal (emphasized) plus premium	0	5	4	–	–	–
Premium only	4	3	3	–	–	–
Other	1	0	0	2	1	1
Don't know	6	1	0	1	3	1
n	12	12	12	12	12	12

Souce: Rubin (1972).

between the two conditions. In the no-premium condition, nine of the twelve children said the advertiser wanted them to buy cereal. But in the premium condition, only one first grader thought he was supposed to want cereal. Four of the first graders thought they were supposed to want the premium, and six of them didn't know what they were supposed to want.

These results suggest that the insertion of the premium information confused the youngest children but not the others. This appears to support the general research which indicated that the accentuation of incidental information makes it difficult for young children to attend to and use relevant information. Rubin's data must be interpreted with caution, however, for reasons beyond the small sample sizes. A major problem is that the no-premium commercial featured a conventional story-line format, while the commercial with the premium offer used a form of collage—"flashes of events and no basic story line." Moreover, it may be that even the younger children "received" information about the premium commercial, but chose to talk about the premium because it was more salient to them. It may be that the premium offer did not interfere with the transmission of information about the product, but, rather, superseded it.

In Shimp, Dyer, and Divita's (1975) study, 197 children, first to sixth graders, were presented with one of four versions of a thirty-second commercial for a hypothetical cereal product named Snappy Fruit Smacks. One version had no premium offer, the other three contained ten, fifteen, or twenty seconds of premium information. Immediately after exposure, the children were given questionnaires consisting of true/false questions about the product and premium offer. Rankings of the children's preferences for the advertised product and two alternative cereals were also obtained. Shimp et al.'s subjects were primarily older children; only 45 of the 197 children were below the age of seven. Thus, there was an underrepresentation of young children, the age group for whom there is the most concern.

The Shimp findings for recall are similar to those of the Rubin study. In all of the test situations, children below 7 years old recalled less information about the product than older children (see table 6-3). Out of fifteen true/false items used to test the children, the younger children correctly answered only slightly more items than would be expected by chance alone. The young children demonstrated the best recall in the commercial which comprised a ten-second premium offer and twenty seconds of product information. Shimp et al. assigned significance to this finding, concluding that premium advertising may enhance the attention of younger children. This conclusion appears unwarranted, however, in that the authors do not report whether these differences in recall among the experimental conditions were statistically significant. Also, Shimp et al. do not report the nature of the kinds of information the children recalled from the commercial (such as brand-name, symbol, etc.); therefore, we cannot directly compare this research to Rubin's findings.

Shimp et al. also measured the children's attitudes toward the advertised product and premium. Utilizing control and experimental groups, the Shimp study found no differences in attitudes toward the cereal product, suggesting that the premiums made the advertised product neither more nor less attractive

Table 6-3
Recall of Product Information by Timing of Premium Feature

Timing of Premium	Age below 7 years		Age 7 and older	
	Correct Responses[b]	Number of Responses	Correct Responses	Number of Responses
10/20[a]	10.09	11	11.59	39
15/15	8.17	12	10.62	37
20/10	8.70	10	10.00	38
0/30	9.50	12	10.97	38
n =		45		152

Source: Shimp, Dyer, and Divita (1975).

[a]To be read: 10 seconds of commercial devoted to premium information/20 seconds devoted to product information.

[b]Indicates the mean number of correct responses to the fifteen questions concerning product information presented in the commercials.

to the children.[4] However, there was a moderate, significant correlation (r = .20) between the attitude of the children toward the premium and their choice of a product brand. This suggests that the more children liked a premium object, the more attractive the particular brand was to them. On the other hand, very few children chose an experimental product brand against two known brands—only about 10 percent of children in each group ranked the unknown experimental product as their first choice.

Since the four groups did not differ in preference for the advertised product, the authors of the study argue that premium advertising appears to have little impact on the children's actual preference for cereal brands. However, the authors do not report (1) whether the children had a history of requesting or using either of the two known cereals in the brand choice; or (2) whether the two known cereals also advertised a premium and, if so, whether the premium was visible on the box displayed to the children in the brand-choice test. Consequently, it is difficult to determine whether the low frequency of choice of the experimental cereal can be accounted for by the commercial, the premium advertisement, or other factors.

In short, the Shimp et al. research suffers from several severe limitations in choice of subjects, measurement procedures, and data analysis. Replication of this study is needed.

Three other studies are relevant to issues concerning children's abilities to use multiple attributes in product selections. Wartella and Ettema (1974) and Atkin (1974), previously described in chapter 3, embedded commercials in half-hour programs and asked children immediately after viewing the program, to recall the commercials. Although we noted earlier that such open-ended questions may tax the verbal abilities of the younger children and consequently may fail to elicit their recall, the central findings from these two studies were nevertheless consistent: Few of the children recalled having seen specific commercials during the program. For example, in Atkin's study, only one-fourth of the subjects could recall the commercial with a premium and only 21 percent could recall the no-premium commercial. In the Wartella-Ettema study, even smaller percentages of children remembered seeing a specific commercial.

The 1974 Wartella and Ettema study also assessed specific information that children recalled. The findings indicated that the youngest children (3 to 4 years old) recalled only visual and auditory images from the commercial. For the two older age groups (5 to 6 and 7 to 8 years), there was increasing recall of claims about the product ("It tastes good," "It's good for kids"), although recall was still predominantly of images.

Studies cited earlier (Ward and Wackman 1972, 1973b) also assessed the information children remember from commercials. Children were asked to name their favorite commercial, then to describe what happens in the commercial. The data indicated a developmental progression of recall from one or two visual images for young children (first and second graders) to increasingly complex, multidimensional, and complete recall among older children (fifth and sixth graders). In Rubin's (1972) study a similar developmental trend was indicated. Young children, preschoolers, and early grade school children re-called fewer images from the commercials. As age increased, recall included more and more different kinds of information, and both the story line and purpose of the commercial became better understood.

Premium Offers and Purchase Requests

Two other studies by Atkin (1975g, f) examined the importance of premiums in children's decisionmaking, using (1) mother's reports of the nature of children's purchase requests, and (2) in-store observations of mother-child interactions. The first study was based on personal interviews with mothers of children ranging in age from 3 to 11. Of the 301 mothers interviewed, 211 stated that their children "sometimes" request specific cereals seen on TV. These mothers were asked to report the reason their children usually give for his or her cereal requests (table 6-4); 47 percent said that their children cited the premium as the basis for the request. Those mothers who did not spontaneously mention premiums were asked if premiums were ever given as the reason, and about one-third then indicated that premiums were sometimes the reason for a particular brand's request.

One may question the validity of mothers' reports of their children's attempts to influence purchases. Assuming these reports are valid, however,

Table 6-4
Mother's Reports of Child's Requests for Cereals
(*percent*)

"When your child asks for a specific cereal, what does he or she usually say . . . what reasons does he or she give for wanting it?" (If premium not a major reason offered by mother: "Does he or she ever say that he or she wants a cereal so he or she can get a premium or prize in the box?")

| | Grade | | |
	Pre-Kindergarten	First-Third	Fourth-Fifth
Premium cited originally	47	51	42
Premium cited in follow-up	35	36	40
Premium not cited	18	13	18
n =	75	81	55

Source: Atkin (1975g).

the findings do not necessarily mean that premium offers "distract" children from consideration of other features of the product. Nor do they indicate whether children examined other product features and, finding most brands indistinguishable, chose to base their preferences and requests on the premium offer. We can say, however, that Atkin's findings reflect the salience of premium offers in breakfast cereal advertising and suggest that children like premiums.

Atkin (1975f) also made in-supermarket observations. Potentially, this should be the more valid method of gathering data on this subject. Observers were placed unobtrusively around the cereal aisle of a supermarket. Listening to mother-child dialogues regarding cereal purchases, they found that 9 percent of all children's cereal requests contained an explicit mention of a premium offer.

One final study provides additional information about the considerations of children in product selection, and the relative importance of premiums (Reilly 1973a). Personal interviews were conducted with a national sample of 6- to 15-year-old children, covering a wide range of media-related topics. One series of questions concerned children's product choices: "When you see a TV commercial for a product, would you like the product more if . . . (two alternative choices)?" Table 6-5 shows the results from all the questions which offered "prizes inside the package" or "offers on or inside the package" as one of the alternatives. Particular attention should be paid to the age differences in these data. Most of the youngest children chose the premium alternative; the older children made this choice less often. Several reasons for this finding are possible: Premiums are usually designed for younger children and therefore lost their appeal for older children. Older children may also have a greater tendency to respond with what they perceive to be a more socially accepted answer based on the quality of the product itself. Finally, older children may realize that the true worth of a purchase is in the product and not the premium.

To sum up, the evidence from research both on child development and on television commercials seems clearly to indicate that the selective nature of children's attention to and information drawn from television commercials is not random and that there are specific, developmental changes which occur as children grow older. Because the research on children's attention to television commercials is so limited, the specific kinds of information that children of different ages select from advertising is not very well known. Rubin's research indicates that a product's brand-name, symbol, and type of premium are three key features recalled to varying degrees by different age children. The Rubin, Wartella-Ettema, and Ward-Wackman studies also suggest a general movement with increasing age from the recall of a few perceptual images to more complex forms of recall. A better understanding of children's information selection from commercials awaits more research.

Existing research is limited in another significant way. None has addressed

Table 6-5
Children's Preferences in Television Commercial Appeals
(*percent*)

"*When you see a TV commercial for a product, would you like the product more if it . . .*"

	Age			
	6-7	*8-10*	*11-12*	*13-14*
Number responding	145	285	240	229
Had an offer	52	40	34	31
Were nutritious	43	54	58	59
No difference	5	6	8	10
Number responding	152	288	234	228
Had a prize inside	57	51	38	29
Were nutritious	35	42	51	55
No difference	8	7	11	16
Number responding	147	280	234	231
Were natural	29	39	52	58
Had a prize inside	67	56	42	29
No difference	4	5	6	13
Number responding	145	278	236	230
Were enriched or fortified	28	45	58	62
Had a prize inside	67	52	35	26
No difference	5	3	7	12

Source: Reilly (1973a).

the question of the cumulative effects of commercial on children's selection and use of information. Yet repetitiveness would seem to be the single most pervasive feature of television commercials. The research reported in the next section, although not directly assessing the impact of repeated commercials, may provide some insights into the effects of this characteristic on children's use of information from commercials.

Intra-Family Conflicts

Does premium advertising on television stimulate children to request purchases by their parents, and do these requests, in turn, generate in-family conflict? An early study by Ward and Wackman (1972) found a small, statistically significant correlation between the frequency of purchase requests and a general measure of parent-child conflict ($r = .18, p < .05$). More specific data on this topic are provided in Atkin's (1975f) supermarket observations, which report that most mothers yield to cereal requests in the supermarket (75 percent).

However, premium-based requests were accepted somewhat less frequently (68 percent) than requests based on other reasons (80 percent).

Atkin also observed that denial of cereal requests ended in conflict more frequently when requests were based on premiums (29 percent versus only 8 percent for requests for non-premium cereals). The mothers reported that their children reacted somewhat more negatively, with anger or disappointment, when their requests were based on a premium (table 6-6). Also, mothers who received premium-based purchase requests reported a higher frequency of arguments following the denial.

Another area of intra-family conflict which has not been explored to date is sibling conflict. Atkin hints at this when he cites among the reasons the mothers used in rejecting their children's purchase requests in the supermarket that "other children in the family would fight over possession of the premium."

Table 6-6
Outcomes of Cereal Requests, by Reason Cited for Request
(percent)

	Request because of Premium[a] (n = 99)	Request for Other Reasons (n = 112)
"When your child asks for a certain cereal, do you ever tell him or her that he or she can't have it?"		
Yes	78	72
No	22	28
If yes: "does he or she react when you say no?"		
Angry	6	4
Disappointed/pouting	25	18
Doesn't bother child	33	34
Understands denial	8	9
Persistence in request	2	3
Substitute request	4	4
If yes: "When you say that he or she can't have a cereal, how often do you argue? Would you say a lot, sometimes, or never?"		
Argue a lot/sometimes	42	25
Argue never	36	47

Source: Atkin (1975g).

[a]Mothers were categorized into the "Premium" classification if they cited premiums in response to the open-ended question concerning the reasons given by the child for wanting the cereal. The "Other reasons" category included those who originally gave nonpremium reasons, even though they subsequently responded positively to the followup direct question about premium requests.

Unfortunately, Atkin does not give specific figures on the frequency of this reason.

In sum, the data concerning intra-family conflict appear to indicate that premium-based requests *do* increase conflict. However, the frequency and seriousness of these conflicts have not yet been examined.

Time-Based Restrictions

A final issue concerns whether the idea of time limitations on premium offers within television commercials would be effective to ensure that the premium would be viewed by children as a secondary feature of the product. Shimp et al.'s data, discussed earlier in this chapter, are directly relevant to this point. Children who viewed the thirty-second commercial in which half or more of the time was devoted to a premium message had a lower recall of the product information than the children who saw a message for the same product without the premium offer. However, those children who saw the commercial with a ten-second premium message actually had a higher recall of product information than the group that saw the no-premium version. This was true for both younger and older children.

As we noted, the authors argue that their findings support limitation on time (ten seconds within thirty-second commercials) which could be devoted to a premium offer for maximum recall of a commercial. However, such a conclusion seems premature. Time-limitation proposals assume that children's attention to information is proportional to the amount of time devoted to its presentation. This assumes that the features of all commercial messages are weighted equally, with the only difference being the time devoted to them. However, these assumptions run counter to much current literature on children's attention, which defines attention as a selective process which may bear no relation to the time devoted to presentation. To date, there is not sufficient information to make a judgment regarding the possible effectiveness of time limitations. Research is needed which varies the time devoted to premium offers with other presentational characteristics of television advertising.

Summary and Conclusions

It appears that the key determinant of a child's likelihood of being confused by premium messages is his or her stage of cognitive development. Rubin's data shows that younger children have the greatest difficulty in comprehending the purpose of commercials containing premium offers, and that they also have the least organized recall (Ward and Wackman's studies show the same general effects) and are very likely to confuse the purpose of premium messages. Some younger children may think the premium is the primary product. Older children, however, are much better able to distinguish the product from the premium offer. In trying to answer the questions posed at the beginning of this chapter, we must constantly distinguish the differences in children's levels of cognitive development.

Premium offers do not appear to *significantly* affect children's recall of product attributes. Stages of cognitive development are of much greater importance in this area. However, premiums sometimes do far outweigh all other product features in children's brand choices. Again, we see this more frequently in younger children.

It appears that there may be a relationship between intra-family conflict and purchase requests when premiums are involved. Data are not available to indicate whether this conflict is greater than that involved in other product requests.

On the question of time-based restrictions on premium advertising, data are inconclusive. Time proportions may be a rough guide to influencing children's attention patterns and selection of information, but more research is needed on (1) the relative efficacy of different cues in advertisements, and (2) the variations in attention and learning which may result from differences in both the timing and saliency of the content of commercials.

The limited samples, and the analytic problems of many of the studies reviewed here, might suggest that top priority should be given to expansion and partial replication of the research to date. However, the findings from the studies of premium advertising, plus basic developmental studies with children, would appear to be sufficient evidence that younger children weigh premium offers heavily in their attention to and recall of advertising. Whether such a reaction can properly be called "confusion" would seem to depend on how one defines the term. At the very least, however, the reaction may be characterized as a tendency of younger children to evaluate other features of commercials less judiciously than if these features had appeared in messages without premium offers.

Because these findings are confirmed across several studies and are consistent with what one would expect from cognitive development theory, and because findings of age-related differences do not readily lend themselves to policy alternatives, any replication and expansion of previous research along these lines should not be the top priority for future work. Rather, priority should be given to research that examines various techniques and features in television commercials that might help children evaluate and use all of the elements of product and brand information in forming judgments about advertised product. In addition, a series of instructional television messages could be designed to help children evaluate the various features of commercials in making consumer decisions.

Without some better understanding of presentational modes of children's commercials, it does not seem advisable to promote research on the effects of time allocations to premium and nonpremium content. That is, since not all elements within a thirty-second spot are equally salient to children, allocating specific times to premium and non-premium messages cannot in and of itself ensure that children will use all of the elements in making product and brand evaluations. Even if it were confirmed that children demonstrate the greatest recall of all commercial elements when ten seconds is devoted to the premium and twenty seconds devoted to other product features, an adoption of such time restrictions would not be warranted, since the presentation of commercials could be designed to accentuate premium portions and downplay the other portions of the advertisements.

In summary, because industry guidelines endorse the desirability of ensuring that premium offers are "secondary," the chief research need in this area is to identify efficacious methods of presentation to ensure that children evaluate premium offers in advertising messages, and consider them in the context of the product and the message.

Notes

1. From comments on an earlier draft of this paper by Dr. Banks, vice president of Media Research, Leo Burnett, Inc.

2. We recognize that difficult choices are not necessarily "bad." One could argue, in fact, that they are beneficial for learning. However, to the extent that choice difficulty may be related to a child's choosing a brand other than his or her ideal choice (as determined, for example, by desired features), choice difficulty may be dysfunctional.

3. As noted, both child-oriented and adult-oriented ("cents-off" coupons, glassware, etc.) premiums were referred to. Since the survey is not always clear which type of premium the mothers refer to, most data reported are from children, or from mothers when the reference is clearly to child-oriented premiums.

4. Shimp et al. do not report their data by age groups; thus, we cannot discuss age-related differences in the children's attitudes.

7 The Impact of Proprietary Medicine Advertising on Children

Thomas S. Robertson

This chapter addresses the impact of proprietary medicine advertising on children. The issues regarding children's exposure to proprietary medicine commercials have come into clearer focus within the past five years. The impetus for much of the debate can be traced to the 1975 petition of the attorneys general of fourteen states before the Federal Communications Commission and the Federal Trade Commission requesting a ban on medicine advertising on television between 6:00 A.M. and 9:00 P.M. Although the petition was rejected on the grounds (primarily) of insufficient evidence for the alleged harmful effects, the petition generated a considerable outpouring of issues, concerns, and position statements by its supporters and opponents. The thrust of the attorneys general (1975) petition was the argument that children are "particularly impressionable and susceptible to the influences of television" and that medicine commercials aim to create "receptive attitudes toward pill taking" and to "present drugs as the cure-all to the tension and problems of everyday life." The petition advocated that medicine advertising should be restricted "to an audience which is equipped to evaluate and digest sophisticated drug advertising."

The effects suggested by the attorneys general were basically threefold: (1) that medicine commercial viewing by children encourages *excessive reliance on pills*; (2) that there may be a relationship between medicine advertising and *accidental poisonings*; and (3) that such advertising may relate to longer term use of *illicit drugs*. A brief review of each of these issues follows.

Excessive Reliance on Pills

The concern underlying this issue is that children exposed to medicine commercials may develop an undue receptivity to medicines. Choate (1975c), on behalf of the Council on Children, Media and Merchandising, asserts that children who are "repeatedly exposed to OTC drug advertising—where adult role models are 'rewarded' for taking medication—are likely to learn a behavioral response from such ads and to act on that learned behavior at some future time—perhaps to their detriment." Further, alleges Choate, advertising builds an association of a "pain pill with a pleasure syndrome that makes everything go away . . . . Madison Avenue, over the airways, encourages everyone, including

111

children, to take drugs to get up, to stay awake, to stay slim, healthy and at-tractive, to eliminate minor pain or discomfort, and to go to sleep."

The logical response to such assertions, it seems, is to cite the lack of available evidence to support them. This has been the response of the Pro-prietary Association (1975), a nonprofit trade association of proprietary medi-cine manufacturers. In their comments to the FCC, they also elaborated the value of proprietary medicine advertising: "Self-medication is an accepted and essential element in the scheme of health care in this nation" and it is the consumer who must judge "whether or not the symptoms are sufficiently discomforting to warrant the use of self-medication." In addition, "while it is true that young children do not possess the requisite experience and judgment to properly evaluate OTC medicine advertising or to make judicious use of the products themselves, this same statement could be made of any advertising not specifically directed to children."

Essentially, there is a lack of empirical evidence to support the arguments advanced concerning a link between advertising and children's receptivity to drugs. However, children are exposed to medicine advertising that, in the words of the Proprietary Association, they do not have the "requisite experience and judgment to properly evaluate." Nevertheless, is this grounds for removal of such advertising from television? Would its removal be adverse to the public interest, if indeed "this advertising serves a legitimate and valuable purpose by informing viewers of both the nature of various symptoms and the availability of products to treat symptoms" (FCC 1976b)?

Accidental Poisoning

This is a rather specialized issue but let us review it briefly. It is sometimes alleged that TV medicine advertising creates a favorable aura surrounding medi-cines. Associated with this depiction is the fear that young children may be intrigued by pill taking and may be tempted to consume medicines kept in the house. Accidental poisoning may occur when children raid the aspirin or cold tablet container or mistake vitamins for candy. The seriousness of poisoning resulting from proprietary medicine consumption is connoted by the fact that medications are the leading substance accidentally ingested by children under 5 years of age (ACT 1975).

Nevertheless, the scope of these problems should perhaps be questioned. Admittedly, aspirin remains the single poisoning substance most frequently ingested by children; however, it continues "to decline both absolutely and as a percent of total ingestions by the under 5 age group" (National Clearinghouse 1974). Moreover, figures cited on medicine poisoning usually pertain to children under 5 years old, whereas the criticism levelled against television advertising involves 5- to 12-year-olds. For under 5 year olds, the real issue would seem to center more upon safety caps for bottles and parental supervision rather than television viewing habits. Furthermore, there appears to be no evidence linking accidental ingestion of poisons and television advertising.

Illicit Drug Use

Associated with the fear that medicine advertising may lead to a pill-popping society is the concern that such receptivity to pills will open the door to illicit drug use. One of the major assumptions underlying the 1975 petition by Francis X. Bellotti, Attorney General of the Commonwealth of Massachusetts (and thirteen other attorneys general), urging the FCC to "ban all drug advertisements between 6 A.M. and 9 P.M." was this hypothesized OTC/illicit drug relationship. Upon a request to clarify this relationship, Bellotti commented: "it (TV drug advertising) leads to that (drug abuse)" (Bellotti 1975a). Furthermore, quoting former FCC Commissioner, Thomas J. Houser, "America's drug companies are referred to as becoming our nation's most formidable drug pushers" (Bellotti 1975a).

The American Pharmaceutical Association (1972), in testimony before the National Commission on Marihuana and Drug Abuse, reflects a similar position. They assert that "advertising of drugs is, indeed, contributing in a significant way to the problem of drug abuse." Furthermore, they reason that: "Bombarding the young mind with the 'pill-for-every-ill' philosophy is reaping its grim harvest as these children grow into adolescence and begin seeking their kicks in their own drug world."

The Proprietary Association (1975), in response to the illicit drug issue, cited a report by Oxtoby-Smith, Inc. (1975), which it commissioned. This review of the literature found no relationship between proprietary medicine advertising and drug abuse. This is consistent with the finding of research by Hulbert (1974) and Milavsky et al. (1975-76). Milavsky et al., in fact, in research with teenagers, find a slight negative relationship between exposure to proprietary medicine advertising and use of illicit drugs. This may be explainable if teenagers who are involved with illicit drugs are less home-oriented and, therefore, see less television. However, drug advertising exposure during teenage years does not necessarily relate to prior exposure patterns and it is still possible that heavy viewing among pre-teens correlates *later* with illicit drug use as they become teenagers. Choate (1976b), for example, after hearing this evidence, reflected that "... most of the studies showed what teenagers thought about ads seen while they were teenagers; their possible use of illicit drugs obviously was teenage oriented. There was no research on how OTC drug ads exposed to sub-teenagers affect drug attitudes. No research at all."

Despite evidence suggesting the lack of a medicine advertising/illicit drug use relationship, therefore, some doubt lingers.

Current Regulation

Television advertising of proprietary medicines on "children's programs" is prohibited by the NAB code: "Nonprescription medicine, regardless of how taken or administered, shall not be advertised in or adjacent to programs initially designed primarily for children under 12 years of age." Similar provisions exist in the Children's Advertising Guidelines issued by the NAD: "Medications, drugs and supplemental vitamins (liquid or pills) should not be advertised to children." The NAB guidelines apply to programs specifically designed for children, that is, those shows which are concentrated on Saturday and Sunday mornings. Most children's viewing, however, occurs during late afternoon and early evening. The NAD guidelines pertain to advertising in children's programs and programs in which "audience patterns typically contain more than 50 percent children" or to advertising which is "clearly addressed to children 11 and under."

Incidence

Children are exposed to medicine advertising, even although such advertising is not directly aimed at them. This occurs since it is estimated that 85 percent of children's viewing is to non-children's programs (Nielsen 1975a). Choate (1976b), in testimony before the Joint FTC/FCC Hearings on Over-The-Counter Drug Advertising, estimates that children see over 1,000 medicine commercials annually. This estimate was derived using Broadcast Advertisers' Reports (a syndicated tracking service that tabulates the incidence of TV commercials by category for particular geographic markets) data and is based on a frequency count of proprietary medicine commercials appearing on the top forty programs watched by children in the sample week, October 5, 1975.

Barcus (1976), in a 1973 content analysis of television advertising, found that proprietary medicine advertising accounts for about 6 percent of total product advertising, or an average of one medicine commercial every fifty-seven minutes. The distribution of medicine commercials is such that they are more frequent on weekdays and only about one-half as frequent on Saturday and Sunday. The highest frequency is during nighttime hours when there is one medicine commercial every thirty-seven minutes. By program type, the highest frequency of medicine commercials is on quiz shows, soap operas, and news programs.

Robertson, Rossiter, and Gleason (1979) found that the average child between 8 and 12 years old is exposed to 718 proprietary medicine commercials per year. This figure was determined by matching the child's reported monthly program viewing with Broadcast Advertisers' Reports data which lists actual commercials by program for the Philadelphia metropolitan area under study.

These data were then extrapolated to the annual estimate of 718 medicine commercials.

Research Evidence

There are essentially three studies which are germane to the question of proprietary medicine advertising's effects on children plus some other studies which are indirectly relevant. The three key studies are those of Milavsky, Pekowsky, and Stipp (1975-76), Atkin (1975e), and Robertson, Rossiter, and Gleason (1979) as summarized in table 7-1.

The Milavsky Study

This study is a modified panel design consisting of five waves of interviews with teenage boys and two waves of interviews with their parents over a period of three and one-half years (May 1970 to December 1973). The focus of this study is on illicit drug use, but proprietary medicine use is also included.

The strength of the study is its measure of proprietary medicine advertising exposure based on a rigorous assessment of viewing factored by Broadcast Advertisers' Reports (BAR) data which provides actual incidence of drug commercials by program. The weakness of this study is its relatively simple conceptual framework (essentially exposure and use). Some questions also arise as to the sampling process, which is random initially but then adds multiple friends per respondent. Validity of the proprietary medicine use measure is questionable (in one wave, use of only five brands) and the measurement changes from wave to wave without reporting on reliability.

The results germane to proprietary medicines (but recognizing that this is a *teenage* sample) are: (1) There is a positive, but relatively weak, relationship between exposure to proprietary advertising and reported use of drugs ($r = .07$, $p < .05$ in one wave, and $r = .12$, $p < .001$ in a later wave using a more extensive usage measure); and (2) This relationship is accentuated (but not significantly) in homes where there are many proprietary medicines around the house but does not seem to be affected by child-initiated versus mother-initiated dispensing of the medicines.

The Atkin Study

The Atkin (1975e) study (also summarized in table 7-1) employs a broader set of measures than the NBC study. However, it is limited methodologically by its use of a convenience sample, by the measurement of medicine advertising

Table 7-1

A Comparison of Three Proprietary Medicine Advertising Studies

	Milavsky, Pekowsky, and Stipp Study (1975-76)	*Atkin Study (1975)*	*Robertson, Rossiter, and Gleason Study (1979)*
Basic Methodology	Modified multiwave panel survey	Survey	Survey
Sample	Teenage boys and parents (*n* varies by wave—822 present for at least one wave); initial random selection balanced by socio-economic status but modified by addition of friends and a later subsample which was part of another study	Fifth, sixth, and seventh graders; (*n* = 256) convenience sample; no parental interviews	Third, fifth, and seventh graders and parents (*n* = 673) School districts selected by socioeconomic status: random selection of classes by grade
Dependent Variables	Intent and usage of illicit drugs and proprietary medicines (represented by 2 headache medicines, 2 cold medicines, 1 stomach medicine and 1 sleep medicine)	Beliefs, attitudes, and usage of proprietary medicines (represented by 1 cold and 1 stomach medicine)	Beliefs, affect, intent, requests, and usage of proprietary medicines for specified symptoms (headache, cold, cough, stomach-ache)
Exposure to Proprietary Medicine Commercials	Hours of exposure to programs during last four weeks (stratified random sample) factored by amount of drug advertising on these programs	Limited report on TV viewing of prime-time and news multiplied by attention to four medicine commercials	Hours of exposure to programs during last four weeks (stratified random sample) factored by amount of drug advertising on these programs
Other Variables	Typical variables include: age, socioeconomic status, IQ, family structure	Typical variables include: age, sex, socioeconomic status, and scholastic performance	Typical variable include: age, socioeconomic status, illness experience, illness anxiety, parental medicine mediation and control, and use of medicine information sources.

exposure in a rather questionable manner, and other measurement problems based on one- or two-item scales with no assessment of reliability. Validity may also be questioned since the dependent measures are based on only cold and stomach generic remedies which may not represent proprietary medicines in general.

Atkin's results may be summarized in terms of the following advertising exposure relationships, all of which are based on sixth-order partial correlations—controlling for grade, sex, social class, scholarship, child's frequency of illness and parent's approval of medicine. All except the last correlation are significant at the .05 level.

1. Perceptions of reality. Children with high exposure to medicine advertising perceive that people are more often sick ($r = .14$) and that they more often take medicine ($r = .14$).
2. Illness concern. Children with high exposure to medicine advertising worry more about getting sick ($r = .14$).
3. Approval of medicine. The relationship between medicine advertising exposure and approval of medicine is .12.
4. Medicine efficacy. Children with high exposure are more likely to report that they feel better after taking medicine ($r = .12$).
5. Medicine use. There is a general lack of relationship between medicine advertising exposure and medicine use ($r = .03$).

In general, these results suggest that medicine advertising exposure does, to a certain extent, influence the child's conceptions of illness and medicine. These relationships tend to be accentuated (but rarely to a significant extent) among the higher scholastic performance children and among the higher social status children. Atkin does not offer any explanation as to why this might be the case. Other variables, such as age and sex of the child, parental attitudes toward medicine, and the child's frequency of illness, all show inconsistent patterns.

The Robertson Study

The Robertson, Rossiter, and Gleason (1979) study is based on interviews with children and their parents concerning the role of proprietary medicine advertising on children's beliefs, attitudes, and behavior patterns toward medicines. The sample consisted of 673 children in approximately equal numbers from third, fifth, and seventh grades. The sample includes boys and girls and a socioeconomic range from disadvantaged to upper middle class families.

The key independent variable is medicine advertising exposure and is measured in the same manner as in the Milavsky study assessing the previous month's television exposure factored by minutes of medicine commercials per program. The "effects" variables for this study include: (1) the child's belief in the efficacy of proprietary medicines, (2) affect toward taking medicine, (3) intent to take proprietary medicines when symptoms occur, (4) the child's requests to parents for medicines, and (5) the actual use of proprietary medicines. The central results from this study, recognizing the limitations of the cross-sectional survey design and the reliance on children's self report measures, are as follows:

1. Children's beliefs, attitudes, and requests for medicines are affected by the televised advertising of proprietary medicines. First order correlations (controlling for grade) between medicine advertising exposure and beliefs, attitudes, and requests are from $r = .12$ to $r = .22$. Incremental explained variance for the medicine advertising exposure variable is from .01 to .03, although advertising works in conjunction with other variables in achieving total explained variance.

2. The magnitude of effects due to the advertising of proprietary medicines to children is not dissimilar to other advertising research results involving adults. Advertising is obviously a contributory factor in consumption behavior, and an explained variance on the order of 2 percent is not uncommon. Thus, children are not unreasonably affected by the advertising of proprietary medicines, although one could make the argument that the effects are considerable given that such advertising was not directed at them in the first place.

3. The relationship between the advertising of proprietary medicines and children's use of medicines is quite limited, reflecting the dominant pattern of parental control over medicine intake. Nevertheless, the relationship does reach a higher significance level among seventh graders as these children are allowed to self-administer medicines to a limited extent. However, the more appropriate behavioral outcome in assessing medicine advertising's effects on children is requests and, as discussed, there is a significant (although moderate) relationship between advertising and requests.

4. Children who are highly anxious about illness show heightened (although still moderate) effects of televised medicine advertising. As such, they can be considered a vulnerable subgroup within the total set of children. Analysis among young children, disadvantaged children, and children who are frequently ill fails to indicate any consistent pattern of greater susceptibility to persuasion due to televised medicine advertising.

5. Parental mediation is found to be somewhat limited as measured by frequency of discussion about illness and medicine. The effect of parental mediation is to lead to more positive child beliefs and attitudes toward proprietary medicines. The inference is that such discussions, rather than building discrimination, lead to a greater salience of medicines and it may be that parents find it necessary to provide positive information about medicines in order to encourage intake under illness conditions.

6. The development of children's beliefs and attitudes toward proprietary medicines seems to occur relatively independently of parental beliefs and attitudes. Analysis within the family shows a lack of parent-child correspondence, suggesting that children develop their attitudes based on independent processing of environmental and experimental stimuli. The study, therefore, supports an "independence" model of attitude formation rather than a "correspondence" model, and attributes only limited influence to parents parallel to the limited influence attributed to advertising.

7. Results suggest the existence of a "hierarchy of effects" model leading to requests as the key behavioral variable. There exists a beliefs-attitude-intent-requests sequence such that each step is predicted mainly from the preceding step.

8. In summary, this study suggests that televised medicine advertising performs only a limited role in the formation of children's beliefs and attitudes toward medicines. In the short-run, it produces a modest increase in beliefs and attitudes. In the long-run, this increase is overshadowed by a significant decline in children's attitudes and beliefs as a function of age, and thus cognitive development and experience. The study further indicates a lack of relationship between advertising and use (which is controlled by parents) and finds no support that children abuse proprietary medicines. Usage levels are moderate and the extent to which parents allow children to self administer is relatively low.

Other Studies

Other studies are of questionable relevance to the issue of medicine advertising and children, but let us take note of them briefly. A study similar in concept to Atkin's is that of Lewis and Lewis (1974). A total of 208 children from the fifth and sixth grades of an experimental school and a public school serving a disadvantaged population were asked to watch television and to describe commercials related to health.

From the children's reports, the authors inferred that television appears to exert an influence upon the health-related beliefs and behavior of children. The results indicated in particular that: (1) personal experience and parental use increased the credibility of the advertising messages, with the lowest level of credibility occurring when neither child nor parent had tried the product, and (2) the frequency of use of advertised products and acceptance of the messages as true was highest among children from lower socioeconomic backgrounds.

The methodological problems of this study are severe. As the authors themselves note, the two schools viewed television at different times; there was no validation of actual drug use; and there was no criterion established by which to judge the "truthfulness" of commercials.

Kanter (1970) found that students in fifth, seventh, and eleventh grades reported their belief that advertising influences their feelings toward medicine. However, no evidence was obtained as to actual attitudinal effects. Many of the students also expressed the belief that other young people were potentially capable of being influenced by proprietary medicine commercials. However, drug commercials were not recalled more easily than other commercials and had a low salience to the students (they were not talked about much). The youngest children (fifth grade) were the most believing, most receptive, and least critical of drug commercials, suggesting that it is among younger people that drug commercials may have the greatest potential impact. These findings also may indicate that skepticism is a function of age and comes into play more strongly in older children—a finding generally confirmed in research by Ward (1971) and by Robertson and Rossiter (1974a).

Campbell (1975) investigated the development of concepts of illness among 264 children aged 6 to 12 as a function of their parents' concepts of illness. A development trend was evidenced whereby the maturing child's conception of illness began to resemble that held by adults. In sharp contrast, a matching of the conceptions for a particular mother-child pair failed to reveal much consensus of beliefs. This disparity, in Campbell's opinion, attests to the complexity of the transmission process whereby children develop an adult conception of illness. Illness concepts were found to be related to the child's health history as well as to age. Furthermore, sophistication of illness concepts was most evident among older children whose health had fared poorly relative to that of their parents.

Needed Research

The limitations of the existing research base suggest further research directions which would be of value in definitively assessing proprietary medicine advertising's effects on children.

1. Only limited research to date has focused on *children*. Much of the research has been with teenagers and college students.
2. Most of the existing research has dealt with illicit drugs and not with proprietary medicines.
3. A common deficiency in much of the existing literature is the failure to examine the relative importance and interaction of the various information sources, including media, advertising, parents, peers, and siblings.
4. The present research base relies on children's self-reports. An alternative would be to use parental observations, especially for behavioral variables such as requests, use, and also television exposure. A further alternative would be unobstrusive measurement of these variables.
5. A further limitation concerns the inference of causal relationships between exposure and "effects" from survey data. Strictly speaking, a controlled experiment in which one group of children is exposed to televised proprietary medicine advertising and another is unexposed would be necessary to allow unequivocal causal inference. As with television research in general, the problem of finding a matched control group unexposed to pervasive stimuli such as televised medicine advertising is formidable.

6. Related to the survey methodology limitation is the usual caveat that longitudinal surveys, such as Milavsky et al. employed, are preferable to cross-sectional surveys, such as Atkin and Robertson et al. employed, when long-term processes are at issue. Actually, however, the major need is for a longitudinal comparison of childhood medicine advertising exposure with adult proprietary medicine usage.

7. A further limitation of this research base is the failure to employ fully randomized samples. Because of this, the point estimates (means and correlations) cannot be precisely generalized to all children.

8. Most of the research focuses on potential negative effects of OTC advertising, whereas there may well be positive learning effects about medicines and their appropriate uses.

9. Substantively, the question of whether children pay attention to proprietary medicine commercials, or whether "selective perception" operates to screen out such advertising has not been addressed adequately. What factors affect attention level—age of the child, the child's health history, parents' in-home use of OTC drugs?

10. Finally, do children understand OTC commercials? What meanings do they take from the commercial? How aware are they of the product's value under specific conditions? What factors affect comprehension levels? These questions need further research.

8 The Effects of Children's Television Food Advertising

Laurene Krasny Meringoff

Children's exposure to television food advertising has been a subject of increasing concern and debate over the past ten years. Questions about the possible effects of food advertising on children have been raised by many voices.

At the federal level, the White House Conference on Food, Nutrition and Health (1970) raised the issue in its proposal to harness television in educating the public about nutrition. A number of congressional committees have held hearings on the subject, including the Senate Select Committee on Nutrition and Human Needs (1973), the House Subcommittee on Communications (1975), and the House Subcommittee on Domestic Marketing, Consumer Relations and Nutrition (1977). In addition, both the Federal Communications Commission (1974) and, in particular, the Federal Trade Commission have initiated action and responded to the issues surrounding television food advertising and children. They have reviewed specific food commercials directed to children (FTC 1975b); considered specific advertising practices (the use of premium offers in cereal ads); proposed a Trade Regulation Rule on food advertising (FTC 1974); and become involved in a children's television advertising rulemaking (FTC 1978).

At the state level, a report issued by staff members of the New York State Assembly (Mauro and Feins 1977) considered the impact of television food advertising on children of sufficient concern to warrant a series of recommended state legislative actions, including a required disclosure of added sugar (above 10 percent) in all advertisements of such products.

Consumer groups, in particular, the Council on Children, Media and Merchandising (CCMM) and Action for Children's Television (ACT), have actively criticized TV food advertising to children and have offered testimony and submitted many petitions calling for changes and reductions in current advertising. The FTC's children's television advertising rulemaking was, in large part, precipitated by petitions submitted by two such consumer groups, ACT (1977) and the Center for Science in the Public Interest (CSPI 1977).

Criticisms and Concerns about Television Food Advertising

Review of these hearings, reports, and petitions reveals a number of recurring concerns, criticisms, and underlying assumptions about the effects of television

Research conducted in revising this chapter was partly supported by a contract between the author and the Federal Trade Commission.

food advertising on children. Criticism of food advertising to children has been directed at the quality and range of food products advertised and at the methods used to present these foods in commercials.

Food Quality and Sugar Content

Of primary importance in the two petitions under review by the Federal Trade Commission is concern about the high sugar content in advertised foods. Between-meal consumption of such foods, particularly when the candy or snack product is sticky (viscous) and can be sucked or chewed over time (retentive), is alleged to promote tooth decay and to contribute to other health problems, such as obesity. In addition, such foods are reported to provide little nutritional value in proportion to calories consumed (ACT 1977; CSPI 1977).

Since the focus of this review is the effects of advertising, not products, arguments about the nutritional quality of food products and their possible consequences for children's health will not be evaluated. Admittedly, the nature of the food and the commercial message are closely intertwined. For example, advertisements cannot make substantiated nutritional claims about products with little nutritional value. As explained by a major food advertiser to children: "Advertising for products which have no specific nutritional value should not imply nutritional benefits even in the most general way. . . . Only fun, snack, taste, etc., values should be claimed" (Quaker Oats, in Senate Select Committee, 1973:5, Appendix). The issue being raised is whether such products "with no specific nutritional value" should be promoted to children at all. While these questions are serious, they must be settled by food scientists, nutritionists, federal agencies, and the food industries.

Range of Food Products

Concern has been expressed that the foods most heavily advertised to children represent a very limited range of the foods available for consumption (CCMM 1977; Jerome 1975). They consist primarily of ready-to-eat presweetened cereals, candies, and other sugared snacks. It is pointed out that: ". . .the amounts of advertising for various kinds of foods are not dictated by any overall plan for the achievement of a healthful diet, but by needs of various firms at any given moment" (Senate Select Committee 1977). As a consequence, there is concern that children's food preferences may be skewed toward whole classes of advertised products (for example, candy snacks) and away from other unadvertised products (like fruit snacks). That is, the advertising of food cannot increase overall consumption if a normal weight is to be maintained; rather, "What advertising does is to shift consumption from one category of foods to another" (Mayer 1973).

There is an inherent dilemma in this concern. On the one hand, there is the question of food advertisers' accountability: should any particular food advertiser be held responsible for the absence of television advertising for other foods? On the other hand, however, since not all foods are advertised, do children inevitably receive an incomplete, distorted picture of a balanced diet?

Food-Commercial Practices

Critics have asserted that foods are not promoted to children on the basis of their nutritional value and that food commercials tend neither to provide nutritional information nor to associate the foods being advertised with principles of good nutrition and health (CCMM 1977; Gussow 1972). Instead, advertised foods are said to be related to attributes irrelevant to their inherent food value, including sweet taste or flavors, fun, adventure, hero figures and other likeable characters, and premium offers. In so doing, it is asserted, sweetness or sugared taste is identified as a desirable characteristic of foods, both those to be eaten at breakfast and between meals. Moreover, the impression is given that eating such products is fully consistent with good health, as implied by showing happy, healthy children enjoying these products in the commercials.

"Silence" about nutrition in television food advertising has been criticized by staff of the Federal Trade Commission in their statements regarding the proposed Trade Regulation Rule on Food Advertising (FTC 1974). They argued that by emphasizing ". . . the pleasure and desirability of advertised foods wholly apart from considerations of nutrition," advertising tends to inhibit appreciation of the importance of nutrition. Arguing on behalf of the child audience in particular, it is claimed that by failing to provide an explanation as to how an advertised food fits into a balanced nutritional scheme, or the risk of tooth decay involved in eating certain foods, children could be misled as to the food value of the product, believing that consumption produces only pleasure and has no adverse effects on health (ACT 1977; CSPI 1977).

One of the questions raised in response to this criticism of food commercials is whether it is feasible to present meaningful statements to children about nutrition within the format of thirty-second announcements. Doubting the possibility, some advertisers and broadcasters have suggested that nutrition education messages instead be conveyed to children by other means or be directed to parents.

Volume and Repetition

It is claimed that these effects are enhanced by the sheer volume of food advertising directed at children (CCMM 1977) and by the repetition of messages for a given brand of product. Inasmuch as the few food categories advertised are each represented by many different brands, both the repetition of commercials within a given product class and for a particular brand may contribute to the frequent intake of these foods, especially as between-meal snacks.

Relationships with Parents and Other Adults

There is also concern that food commercials may be disruptive to relationships between children and their parents, in that conflicts may be precipitated when parents refuse children's requests for the foods they see advertised. The influence of parents and other authority figures (teachers, doctors, dentists, and so on) over children's eating may be contradicted or undermined (ACT 1973). See chapter 9 for a review of evidence concerning the impact of TV advertising in general on parent-child relations.)

Underlying Assumptions

A number of assumptions underlie and help to explain these expressed concerns. First, causal relationships exist between the food commercials children see and their knowledge about food and nutrition, their food preferences, eating habits and, ultimately, their physical health. It is generally assumed that food advertisers promoting their products to children on television are fairly successful in getting children or their parents to buy them. In fact, the mere presence of food advertising on television is believed effective in suggesting to children that these foods are appropriate and desirable to consume (CCMM 1977; Jerome 1975). The result is that "The TV advertising of food products now exerts an enormous new influence on the nation's children" (McGovern, in Senate Select Committee, 1973:3, 255).

Second, television's influence as a major source of food information is accentuated by the scarcity of systematic nutrition education either at home or in school (Mauro and Feins 1977). Third, children are in the uniquely vulnerable position of forming initial food habits which are of consequence for their current growth and nutritional status as well as for their future development. At the same time, however, they first need to be taught about good nutrition and the primary relationship between the foods they eat and their health (Mayer 1973).

In the remainder of this chapter, these concerns and the assumptions underlying them will be examined in light of the available evidence.

Current and Proposed Regulation

The following NAB and NAD guidelines currently operate for food advertisers directing their product messages to children. *General statement* on the positive role of food commercials:

> Given the importance of sound health and nutritional practices, advertisements for edibles shall be in accord with the commonly accepted principles of good eating and seek to establish the proper role of the advertised product within the framework of a balanced regimen (NAB 1978).

> Representation of food products should be made so as to encourage sound usage of the product with a view toward healthy development of the child and the development of good nutritional practices (NAD 1977).

Regarding the advertising of foods served at mealtimes:

> Advertising representing mealtime in the home should clearly and adequately depict the role of the product within the framework of a balanced diet (NAD 1977).

> Each commercial for a *breakfast-type product* shall include at least one audio reference to and one video depiction of the role of the product within the framework of a balanced regimen. (It is permissible for the video to be animated and for the audio to be delivered by an animated character. However, a video title superimposed on the screen may not by itself be used to describe a balanced regimen, as some viewers do not read yet.) (NAB 1974, 1978)

A single reference to candy and other snack foods advises:

> Commercials for products such as snacks, candies, gums and soft drinks shall not suggest or recommend indiscriminate and/or immoderate use of the product (NAB 1978).

Pertaining to overconsumption in general:

> Overconsumption of food products and beverages should be avoided, nor should it be implied that any one food provides all the nutrients in a well-designed food plan (NAD 1977).

Regarding energy claims:

> Any representation of the relationship between an edible and energy must be documented and accurately depicted (NAB 1978).

With regard to message sources in food commercials:

> Real-life authority figures/celebrities are disallowed from being shown eating the advertised food, this constituting an endorsement or testimonial situation; but cartoon characters created for and primarily associated with a specific children's food ("presenter") can be shown eating the product (NAB 1974, Code Interpretation).

However,

> . . ."product characters"—personalities live or animated who are closely associated with or identified with the product—may be used as presenters for the advertised product or service provided they do not do or say anything to mislead children as to the product or service concerned (NAD 1977).

In response to the petitions from ACT and CSPI, the Federal Trade Commission has undertaken a rulemaking proceeding which has focused on many of the issues previously identified. Specifically, the FTC is considering a rule which would: (1) ban as deceptive or unfair television advertising of highly sugared or "cariogenic" snack foods (candies) to children (under age 12) too young to understand abstract long-term health risks; and (2) require that television advertising to children under 12 years old for other sugared products (for example, presweetened cereals) be balanced by nutritional and health messages funded by the advertisers. The commission also invited comment on other, less far-reaching proposals, such as requiring affirmative nutritional or health disclosures within advertisements, limitations on the use of particular techniques, or on the number and frequency of advertisements for "highly cariogenic products directed at all children."

Numerous issues of act, law, and opinion surround the various remedies proposed, and the actual consequences of this rulemaking proceeding are difficult to anticipate.

Incidence

In this section, we will consider how much food advertising is directed to children, what range of foods is promoted to children, and what commercial practices are used to advertise food to children. Data relevant to these questions are drawn primarily from research studies which have examined the incidence of specific features in commercials appearing during children's programs (Atkin 1975b; Barcus 1975a; Winick et al. 1973).[1] The two most recent analyses

(Barcus 1975a; 1978) coincide most closely with current advertising regulations and practices and are therefore the primary sources of incidence information reported below. This information is supplemented by monitoring of network advertising on children's programming conducted by Broadcast Advertisers Report (1978b).

How Much Food Advertising is Directed at Children?

During most of the year, the majority (68 percent) of commercials aimed at children promote food products and services (Barcus 1975). Similarly, according to BAR data (1978b), collected quarterly, 62 percent of all commercials on children's programs during 1977 were for food. However, during the pre-Christmas months there is an increase in the amount of toy advertising, and food commercials then comprise about one-third of total commercial announcements (Barcus 1978). To put this into the perspective of time, note that an average of 13.4 commercial product announcements appeared per hour (in fall, 1977) on network weekend morning programming (Barcus 1978). Depending on the time of year, then, children viewing at this time may see anywhere from 4 to 9 food advertising messages per hour.

What Range of Foods is Promoted to Children?

Three product/service categories continue to account for most (70.0 percent) of the commercials for edibles promoted to children (Barcus, 1978): Sugared cereals (33.0 percent); candy bars/packaged candy (20.0 percent); and eating places (17.0 percent). (Three similar categories also accounted for more than half (52 percent) of total advertising revenues earned from children's programs in 1977: cereal, $41.6 million; candy and gum, $22.6 million; and fast-food restaurants, $10.1 million (BAR, 1978b.) Cakes/cookies (5.0 percent), sugared soft drinks (1.0 percent), puddings/ice cream/desserts (1.0 percent) and fruity drinks (0.6 percent) add another 11 percent.[2] In comparison, commercial announcements for such staples as bread (2.0 percent), meat (1.5 percent), juice (0.3 percent) and milk (0.3 percent) together comprise only 4 percent of the total. There were no commercials for fruits or vegetables.[3] Summarizing across product categories, Barcus therefore concludes that about two-thirds of food advertising directed to children is for highly sugared products.[4]

These data provide evidence that a very limited range of foods accounts for most of the television food advertising directed at child audiences. A similar distribution of foods was reported for weekend morning advertising on children's programs in April 1975 (Barcus 1975a), suggesting some stability in these patterns over time.

What Commercial Practices Are Used to Promote Foods?

Format: The format employed in commercials appearing on children's shows varies by product type (Barcus 1978). Most cereal ads (88 percent weekend, 82 percent weekdays) are totally or partially animated, whereas candies/sweets commercials use animation only occasionally (21 percent weekend, 29 percent weekday).[5] In contrast, advertisements for toys, fast-food restaurants, and the premium segments of food commercials are almost exclusively live-action.

Partially animated food commercials include those in which both animated and live-action elements are present on the screen at the same time. This is often accomplished by juxtaposing a cartoon presenter figure in a real setting; for instance, junior tiger engages a young boy in roaring at the breakfast table (Sugar Frosted Rice); Tusk, the elephant, appears with children in the kitchen (Cocoa Krispies); or the Trix rabbit is placed in a Hawaiian setting with drummer and children. Partial animation also occurs when the major product portion of the commercial is animated and then the format changes to live-action, either to present a premium offer or to display the actual product (for example, pouring milk into a bowl of Crazy Cow cereal) and/or related ingredients (for example, showing peanuts along with a package of Keebler Peanut Butter Sandwich Cookies).

Characters: "Presenters" (characters whose name or appearance embodies a feature of or is otherwise identified with the product) are commonly used in advertising foods to children. Almost all the cereals make consistent use of an animated male adult, animal, or other character in their promotional messages. So, for example, there is Sugar Frosted Rice's junior tiger, the Trix rabbit, Cap'n Crunch and, more recently, Cookie Crisp's cookie maven. Live male adults are also used as presenters, specifically in association with fast-food restaurants such as McDonald's Ronald and the Burger King king.

Most other characters in these commercials are children, especially in toy (86 percent weekend) and cereal (59 percent) ads. Commercials for candies/ sweets tend to use somewhat older characters, including both adults (47 percent weekend) and teens (9 percent weekend).

Content: On the basis of what product information or attributes are foods promoted to children? How are foods described?

Cereals. According to Barcus (1978), cereals ($n = 131$) are described primarily in terms of their taste/flavor/smell (31 percent) and texture (21 percent). Specific references to sweetness or some synonomous term (like "sugar crunchy," "frosted oats") are present in 23 percent of cereal commercials.[6] Product ingredients may also be named, such as corn or oats (30 percent). Exemplified in the context of specific cereal messages: Cookie Crisp is "different than cookies cause it's crispy in milk"; Cheerios are "crunchy, toasty, oatio's"; "Frosted Lucky Charms are magically delicious"; and "You can't get away from the crunch cause the crunch always gives you away" (Cap'n Crunch).

However, somewhat aside from these similarities in the product information provided, commercials for given brands of cereal tend to sport distinctive themes, such as size: "We've got a cereal bigger than yours. . . Homeycomb's BIGGGG!"; adventure: "There's an adventure in every bowl of Alpha-Bits"; stories of lost animals and stolen cereal boxes dramatized in commercials for Cap'n Crunch; or the feature of turning milk chocolate: "Crazy Cow, the nutritious cereal that makes chocolate milk." Specific brand names are repeated an average of 3.5 times per commercial (Atkin 1975d).

Premium offers are incorporated in 25 percent of cereal commercials, as opposed to 47 percent in 1975 (Barcus 1975a). Most (83 percent) of these segments comprise between five to fifteen seconds of thirty-second commercials.

Nutritional or health-related product information appears in 27 percent of cereal commercials (Barcus 1978). This figure apparently includes simple references to: ingredients being either natural or artificial (13 percent); fortification with vitamins or minerals (8 percent); and to such health claims as "roaring good breakfast." In addition, 95 percent of these commercials describe the cereal as "part of a balanced breakfast," as required by the NAB Code. (In comparison, prior to this Code requirement, Winick et al. (1973) found balanced meals (in 1971 ads) infrequently depicted in food commercials, whether visualized (10 percent) or suggested in the audio (6 percent). However, about two-thirds display the cereal and other breakfast components for five seconds or less. Cereals are also sometimes shown or described as a snack (24 percent).

Candies/Sweets. Commercials for candies/sweets also draw upon features of taste/flavor/smell (31 percent) and texture (22 percent). Particular references to stickiness or chewiness were documented in about one-third of the (n = 110) ads, for example, chewy caramel, chewy pieces. Ingredient names are included in about half the descriptions of these foods ("rich chocolate," "fruit chew middle," "peanuts and chocolate"). This combination of product attributes may be illustrated by the following ad for a candy bar:

> (Sung by group): $100,000 Bar, chewy chewy caramel and lots of little crunchies, with a taste so chocolately. Nestle's $100,000 Bar. (Male V-O): If you like chewy chewy caramel mixed together with the fun crunch of crispy rice and a delicious chocolately taste too. . . (group sings): This is your caramel bar, Nestle's $100,000 Bar. (Broadcast 7/22/78)

Claims regarding the long lasting (retentive) value of the candy product are made occasionally (9 percent), for instance, "the flavor lasts so long" (Bubble Yum Bubble Gum). Relatedly, the large quantity or amount of the product may also be featured (10 percent), as in "bite after bite, there's crunch after crunch."

Ads for these products tend to show the product in use (Barcus 1975a); thus, live-action formats may picture children, teens, and/or adults eating the candy being advertised in such varied settings as an amusement park, barber shop, office, city street, or beside a talking tree (Tic Tac, Hershey Bar, Starburst Fruit Chews).

Commercials for candies/sweets rarely make nutritional claims per se (3 percent). However, they may identify ingredients as either natural or artificial (21 percent), usually by superimposing the words on the screen.

Fast-Food Restaurants. These commercials tend to focus less than food product ads on particular attributes of the foods they sell; instead, they do more promotion of such features as fun/happiness (13 percent), economy/price (10 percent) and general superiority (9 percent). Their presenters usually engage in some humorous bit of adventure or activity (such as Ronald and his masked crew traveling in a space ship or posing for a photograph; or the Burger King's king performing magic tricks), which eventually brings them, along with a number of children, to the locale of the restaurant. Note the following example:

> (kids sing): The magic Burger King. He knows magic and food that's fun. (Male masked man): I doubt it. I say magic can't be done. (Kids): Who's that? (BK): Why it's the Duke of doubt, kids. He doesn't believe in anything. What do you say, kids? (Kids sing): He's the marvelous magical Burger King. (Duke): I doubt he'll do a single thing. (BK sings): I know magic and food that's fun. (Duke): I double doubt it. (Kids): He's got fun fun fun for everyone. Burger King, yeah! (One kid): No doubt about it, Duke. (Broadcast, 7/22/78)

Finally, *no direct appeals* were made to children in any of those commercials to induce their parents to purchase products being promoted.

Research Evidence

Three major questions are used to organize the empirical data on children's responses to TV food advertising:

1. What information do children acquire from food commercials (or have) about advertised foods and other aspects of ads?
2. What beliefs and inferences do children hold about food product claims and other aspects of ads as a consequence of exposure to commercials?
3. What food-related behavior—preferences, requests, purchases, and consumption—do children exhibit (or influence) as a consequence of exposure to commercials?

To some extent, this choice of categories—information, beliefs, and be-havior—reflects the way data in this area (and the social sciences in general) are reported. Additionally, the particular sequence in which these responses is discussed permits examination of a potential hierarchy in susceptibility to influence, with knowledge being the most accessible to influence and be-havior the least.

As the data permit, evidence is reported so as to address each of the issues surrounding television food advertising and children. However, there is only a loose correspondence between the issues and this organization of data. For example, findings which bear upon concerns regarding such stimulus variables as the range of foods promoted, specific commercial practices, and repetition of advertising often cut across information gains and attitudinal or behavioral change. Similarly, findings regarding effects of advertising on these kinds of responses are sometimes reported in terms of such child variables as age, race, family income level, and amount of viewing. Gaps are also pointed out when there is no research evidence which bears directly upon an issue.

Information Children Acquire from Food Commercials

Product Presenters and Characters

According to one study (Gianinno and Zuckerman 1977), children as young as 4 years old can distinguish between animated characters on the basis of whether they appear in programs or commercials and can link those from food com-mercials to their respective products. The investigators provided ($n = 64$) 4-, 7-, and 10-year-old children with photographs of animated presenter characters from either programs or food commercials and asked them to recognize or identify these characters in response to various instructions. (However, because these tasks were presented in a fixed sequence, the earlier administered tasks may have influenced children's responses to subsequent ones.) Even 4-year-olds could recognize (17 out of 20) and, to a lesser extent (8 out of 20) specify who these characters were and could correctly match the commercial character with the name of the specific product that they "show you" on television. Children's familiarity with the test characters improved with age.

With regard to overall format, however, no research was found which examined the relative effectiveness of an animated, "mixed," or live-action format in conveying "comparable" commercial information to children.

Brand-Names

Survey data indicate that children exhibit fairly high recall of brand-names for nationally advertised foods, such as ready-to-eat cereals, candy, and chewing gum (Gene Reilly Group, 1973b). The Reilly data are based upon a national sample of (over 1,000) 6- to 14-year-old children and (almost 600 of) their mothers, who responded to wide-ranging questions regarding food-related knowledge, attitudes, and behavior. When asked to name (for nineteen food product categories) either the kind of product they asked their mothers to buy or their favorite kind, 86 percent of cereal-eating children and 84 percent of candy consumers identified a specific brand. Brand-name recall increased with age.

Children have also been shown to recognize an unfamiliar brand-name following a single exposure to a commercial for this food product (Gorn and Goldberg 1978). In this experiment, a sample of (about 150) 8 to 10-year-old boys were randomly assigned to a varying number of ice cream commercials, or to no commercials, in the context of a half-hour cartoon show. With six alternative names of ice cream to choose from, almost half the ($n = 12$) children exposed to only one ad correctly identified the name of the product. Haefner et al. (1975) also found very high recall (over 90 percent) of brand-names following a single commercial viewing among second and seventh to eighth graders.

Product-Specific Attributes, Claims and Themes

Available research data on children's learning of specific attributes of foods promoted in television advertising appear somewhat fragmentary.[7] For example, there has been little systematic study of recall or understanding of such commonly promoted features as the particular tastes, flavors, or textures of advertised food. However, what data do exist usually provide positive evidence of children's ability to acquire and retain information about the specific attributes or claims made regarding advertised foods (Atkin 1975c; Gorn and Goldberg 1978; Hendon et al. 1978).

In the Gorn and Goldberg study (1978), for instance, over three-fifths of the participating 8 to 10-year-olds correctly identified the number of flavors in which the advertised ice cream was available following a single viewing of the commercial.

Children have also been shown to be responsive to comparative product claims. In another experimental study, Atkin (1975e) exposed ($n = 400$) second to third and fourth to fifth grade children to one of four versions of an experimental tape containing children's programming and advertising content. Included in this material were one of two specially produced versions of a commercial for a well-known candy bar. In one execution (one-sided), the size (big) and the nutritional attributes (eight vitamins) of the candy bar are simply described and visualized, whereas in the other (two-sided) variation these attributes are favorably compared to those of a major competitor's product (bigger, more vitamins). Children viewing the comparative vitamin

claim were significantly more likely than those presented the one-sided statement to agree that the advertised candy had lots of vitamins (53 percent versus
37 percent). Interestingly, there was only a marginal difference between groups
in perception of the candy bar's size. The author speculates that (perhaps unlike
vitamins) candy bar size claims are easily validated against experience with the
product.

Premium Offers

The impact of the inclusion of premium offers on children's learning from food
commercials has also been investigated (Rossiter 1975; Rubin 1972; Shimp et al.
1975). See chapter 6 for discussion.

Nutritional and Health-Related Information

There is some indication that children learn both specific nutritional information
about a product and more general health claims presented in television food
advertising (Atkin 1975c, 1975e). For example, in one experiment (Atkin
1975c) each of 500 3- to 10-year-old children was randomly assigned to view
one of two versions of a cereal commercial (one of a series of nine commercials
inserted in a cartoon program). One version specified four vitamins present in
the cereal and simultaneously displayed this information visually on the screen,
whereas the other version claimed the cereal was loaded with energy to help
make great swimmers and depicted a swimmer in the waves. Both presentations
mentioned that the cereal tastes good and is "good for you."

Although, overall, free recall of this information was low, children tended
to learn the content that was provided in the version they viewed. For example,
among those children exposed to the vitamin information, almost half (49 percent) reported between one to four of the vitamin names, in comparison to
22 percent of those not shown this execution (and who must have guessed).
Older children were much better able to reproduce all four vitamin names
than younger children (57 percent versus 15 percent). Only among those children presented with the energy for sports claim was any (10 percent) recall of
this information verbalized. However, about one-third of the children (29 percent in one version, 37 percent in the other) reiterated the healthful "good for
you" claim present in both of the commercials.

As previously reported, children exposed to a comparative nutritional
claim (regarding the relative number of vitamins in one candy bar as opposed
to another) were more likely to perceive the product as having lots of vitamins
than those presented the *same* vitamin information about the product but
without any comparison (Atkin 1975e). In addition to providing some evidence

of the effectiveness of comparative product claims, these data raise the question of whether children (aged 8 to 10) are able to compare two products on the basis of a given nutritional attribute.[8]

Nutritional Disclosures

There is also evidence indicating that children have difficulty remembering and understanding certain nutritional disclosures made about advertised foods, specifically, the balanced breakfast disclosure made in commercials for breakfast cereals (Atkin and Gibson 1978). In this experiment, (n = 100) 4 to 5- and 7- to 8-year-old children (low-income Mexican American and middle class white) were randomly assigned to view one of two conventional commercials for pre-sweetened cereals and were questioned both about their responses to the advertising screened and, as a control, about the cereal ad they didn't see. (However, both commercials may well have been familiar to children from previous home viewing.) According to the authors' description, each of the commercials "briefly noted" the required disclosure that the cereal is "part of a balanced breakfast" and visualized "a glimpse" of the other components of a balanced breakfast; that is, only minimal time was devoted to the presentation of this information.

Two-thirds of the children reported remembering the balanced breakfast statement. However, further probing revealed that almost all (92 percent) the younger children and half (48 percent) the older children were unable to specify the components of the breakfast shown in the ads. Moreover, when asked to explain what "balanced breakfast" means, almost two-thirds of the children said they didn't know. This lack of understanding was expressed more often by younger than older children (88 percent versus 40 percent) and by lower class Mexican Americans more than middle class whites (77 percent versus 54 percent).

General Concepts about Food Classes

Although little research has directly measured the impact of television food advertising on children's more general knowledge about foods, some related evidence may be noted here. For example, the Reilly survey (1973b) asked children to define the snack product category by listing "the kinds of things you call snacks." The children most often cited "sweets" (78 percent) such as cookies, candy, cake, and ice cream. The other foods identified as snacks were, in order of frequency: salty chip-type products, fruit, sandwiches, and milk. These data indicate that the children's concepts of what constitutes an acceptable snack usually includes those products heavily advertised to them, but do not address the issue of whether commercials are responsible for their inclusion.

Nutritional Value of Advertised Foods

Children exhibit mixed knowledge about the healthfulness of advertised foods (Atkin and Gibson 1978; Reilly 1973b). For example, when 6- to 14-year-old children (Reilly 1973b) were asked to evaluate the nutritional value of foods eaten at meals and for snacks, "sweets" (notably candy and soft drinks, both frequently promoted on television) were consistently described as being "not so good for you" in the context of mealtime foods. Interestingly, however, this evaluative distinction broke down somewhat for after school snacks, where "sweets" (cookies, ice cream, and candy) were mentioned by about one out of four children as "especially good for you or healthy." Presweetened cereals were rarely cited (4 percent) as not being nutritional. Again, however, this information cannot be attributed to children's exposure to food commercials. (Indeed, given that candy ads, for example, do not cite any negative nutritional information about their products, it would be unlikely for children to acquire such information from watching them.)

Nutritional knowledge about advertised foods appears to vary on the basis of such factors as children's age, family income, and mother's educational level (Atkin and Gibson 1978; Clancy-Hepburn et al. 1974; Sharaga 1974). When asked to compare a presweetened cereal to a nonsweetened one, for example, older (7- to 8-year-olds) and middle class children were more critical of the health consequences of consuming the presweetened variety than were younger (4- to 5-year-olds) and the lower class Mexican American youngsters (Atkin and Gibson 1978). They more often chose the plain cereal as the one that would make them "grow bigger and stronger" (62 percent versus about 40 percent); and were about twice as likely to say that the presweetened product is "bad for your teeth" (about 60 percent versus 32 percent). Goldberg et al. (1978) found upscale first graders well informed about whether sugared snacks, breakfast cereals, and varied other snack foods and breakfast foods were "good or bad for you." More generally, in the survey conducted by Sharaga (1974) among second and sixth graders and their mothers, those children of higher socioeconomic status (SES) and whose mothers had more education were reported to exhibit greater knowledge of the validity of nutritional claims made in ads. Corroborative findings were reported by Clancy-Hepburn et al. (1974) in survey research with 8- to 13-year olds.

Beliefs and Inferences Children Hold about Food Product Claims

Product Presenters and Characters

Some research has examined the kinds of beliefs and inferences children have regarding the characters appearing in food commercials and the possible influence of these beliefs on their attitudes toward the advertised products (Atkin and Gibson, 1978; Donohue, et al. in press).

In the Atkin and Gibson (1978) study, children were asked a number of questions about the specific qualities of the presenter characters used in the two cereal commercials. (However, the wording of the questions may have somewhat biased these responses toward agreement.) With regard to the Honeycomb commercial, for example, most of the 4- to 8-year-old children viewing this advertising perceived that "Big Boris" was in fact "very big" and "very strong." Note that the feature of bigness is apparently made explicit verbally, whereas the character's strength is only implied (suggested visually) by his behavior (muscle flexing, lifting a house) and indirectly by his appearance. Moreover, a substantial proportion of the children associated Boris' perceived strength with his eating the cereal and, to a lesser extent, inferred that eating the cereal would also help make them grow big and strong. Consistently, these beliefs about the characters were held more often by the younger than the older children and by lower class Mexican Americans more than middle class whites.

Questioned about Fred Flintstone and Barney Rubble, the animated characters in the Cocoa Pebbles commercial, children reported they liked these characters and, to some extent, thought they "knew very much about which cereals kids should eat." Many children even said they would want to eat the cereal because Fred and Barney liked it (an inferred endorsement). Again, a higher proportion of the younger and lower class children expressed these beliefs about the characters.

In another experiment, Donohue et al. (in press) examined children's identification with commercial characters. The investigators randomly selected (n = 82) 6- to 8-year-old children (white middle class, inner-city blacks) from their classrooms and showed them two commercials for McDonald's restaurant, one designed for adults, the other for children. Questioned about which of the standard crew of characters in the children's commercial they wanted to be like and why, Ronald was selected the most often (by about half the children) for the following kinds of reasons: like to be like him, curious appearance, having fun, and gets his way. Also asked about the perceived similarity between characters in the adult-directed commercial and their own family, the majority of children observed that the family in the commercial was happier than their own, although the black children were significantly more likely than whites to say this (75 percent versus 55 percent).

The mere association of various characters with selected products has been found to increase children's expressed preferences for these items (Iskoe 1976). In this pilot research (n = 225) children across first, third, and fifth grades were asked to rate a series of paired products (for example, cookies-donuts, doll-gun). Then an endorser was "attached" to each product and the products re-rated. (Note, however, that the stimulus was not presented in the context of a commercial.) Increases in product preference of as much as 67 percent were obtained simply by juxtaposing an endorser with a product (indirect endorsement). However, some endorser figures seemed more effective than others (for instance, Mohammed Ali produced more positive change in product preferences than Lucille Ball), again suggesting that endorsement effects depend in part on how children regard the endorser.

No studies have compared the relative influence of animated versus live characters on children's food product preferences. However, when questioned about whether they would rather see cartoon characters or real live people in a commercial, the majority (72 percent) of 6- to 7-year-olds and (62 percent) 8- to 10-year-olds said they preferred cartoon figures, whereas the preference of (51 percent) the older 11- to 12-year-old children had shifted toward live characters (Gene Reilly Group 1974).

Product Attributes, Claims, and Themes

Children's acceptance or belief of specific product claims advanced in food commercials has been documented in a number of studies (Atkin and Gibson 1978; Haefner et al. 1975; Poulos 1975).

Haefner et al. (1975) examined children's responses to four commercials (three food-related, one toy-related) against which complaints of possible deception had been reviewed by the FTC. A sample of (n = 34) second grade and (n = 78) seventh to eighth grade children were interviewed before and after their viewing of a short film in which these advertisements were embedded. (Another group of older children saw the film without commercials.) Exposure to the commercials was found to influence children's acceptance of specific product claims. For example, both younger and older children exhibited significant changes in their acceptance of the health claim made in a Wonder Bread commercial ("Wonder Bread is the best thing your mother can give you to grow fast"), with the younger children agreeing more strongly, and the older disagreeing less.[9] However, dramatic age differences were indicated: whereas the younger (second grade) children's acceptance of product claims was influenced by the three ads for which findings were reported, the Wonder Bread commercial was the only one for which the older children exhibited any shifts in beliefs. (Note, however, that most of these older seventh to eighth graders are probably beyond 12 years of age and are not technically still members of the child audience under consideration here.)

There is also at least preliminary evidence of children drawing incorrect, potentially even dangerous, inferences about foods as a consequence of seeing specific commercial content (Poulos 1975). This pilot study, commissioned by the FTC, examined children's responses to a series of commercials for Post Grape-Nuts cereal in which an adult is shown picking wild growing vegetation while remarking that it is edible and, in some cases, adding the picked berries to the bowl of cereal. The commission was concerned as to whether this advertising had the tendency or capacity to lead children to pick and consume plants which could be harmful. Four of the commercials were shown to a small sample of 5- to 11-year-olds (mean age = 6) who were interviewed before and after this screening about the edibility of various plants displayed in color photographs. The children's ratings of edibility ("good or bad to eat") for the nonedibles most closely resembling those in the commercials increased much more than their ratings for either the other nonedible or the familiar, edible plants.

There has been some attempt made to pin down or specify the bases for children's expressed liking or preference for advertised foods (Atkin 1975c, 1975d; Atkin and Gibson 1978; Gene Reilly Group 1973b, 1974).

In the Atkin study (1975c) comparing two versions of one cereal ad, one with an energy claim associated with doing well at swimming and the other naming four vitamin ingredients, there were no significant differences found between the two in children's reported desire for the product. The author concluded that the "information oriented" strategy (naming vitamins) can be at least as effective as the "conventional emotional" approach (the energy for sports claim) in achieving favorable responses from children.

A more recent experiment (Atkin and Gibson 1978), exposing (4- to 8-year-old) children to two actual cereal commercials (Cocoa Pebbles and Honeycombs), presents mixed evidence on the effectiveness of specific product claims as reasons for children's wanting the cereals. In the case of Cocoa Pebbles, the children were questioned about whether they wanted to eat the cereal on the basis of three product appeals made in the commercial: its chocolately flavor, that it would make you smile, and that Fred and Barney like it (presumably implied by their behavior). Exposure to the commercial increased the extent to which children agreed with all three claims (52 to 54 percent pre, to 62 to 76 percent post). However, the older (7 to 8 years of age) and middle class white children responded the most favorably to the chocolatey flavor, whereas the younger children and the Mexican Americans were more likely to agree with the character "endorsement" and the affective "makes you smile" claim. These latter two groups were also far more responsive to each of the appeals.

With regard to the Honeycomb advertising, there were no significant differences evident in children's reasons for wanting the cereal as a consequence of viewing the commercial. Both before and after, at least half the children (52 to 60 percent) agreed with each of the three appeals focused upon: big pieces, sticker premium, and makes you big and strong. Again, more of the younger and lower class children favored these claims; for example, 76 percent of the younger children agreed they wanted the cereal because of the premium, as opposed to 28 percent of the older children.

The differences in effectiveness observed between the two commercials may be due to such factors as differences in children's familiarity with the two ads or in the relative appeal of the advertising and/or the product. (The overall lower agreement scores for Honeycomb than for Cocoa Pebbles provides some support for the latter explanation.)

Premium Offers

A number of studies have investigated the impact of premium offers on children's food product preferences (for example, Atkin 1975f, 1975g; Atkin and Gibson 1978; Gene Reilly Group 1974; Shimp, et al. 1975). See chapter 6.

Nutrition and Health-Related Information

In several of the studies reviewed here, children have been reported to accept or express belief in claims made in food commercials about the nutritional or health-related value of the products (Atkin and Gibson 1978; Haefner et al. 1975; Poulos 1975). At the same time, however, there is some indication that the appeals currently made regarding the nutritional benefits of advertised foods may not play a primary role in determining children's attitudes toward these foods (Atkin 1975d; Gene Reilly Group 1973b, 1974).

For instance, in the Reilly study (1974), 6- to 14-year-old children were presented with a series of paired product attributes (for instance, contained a prize or was nutritious) and asked which feature would make them like the product more. Only among the older 10- to 14-year-olds did the nutritional claim override the offer of a prize, perhaps in part because of the lesser appeal of premiums among older children. When the attribute of either good taste or sweet taste was paired up with nutritious, children across ages 6 to 12 showed consistent preferences for taste over nutrition: good taste over nutritious by about 68 percent to 25 percent; and sweet taste over nutritious by a smaller margin of about 50 percent to 43 percent. Thus, ranking the 6- to 12-year-olds' preferences for the commercial appeals compared, good taste and sweet taste (and prizes among the 6- to 7-year-olds) consistently superceded nutrition and enriched/fortified, although the latter moved up to third or fourth place among the 8- to 10-year-olds. Moreover, when specifically asked how often they thought about whether a food was good for them before eating it, 32 percent responded "not too often" and another 39 percent said either "hardly ever" or "never."

When parent-child interaction regarding cereal purchases was directly observed in the supermarket (Atkin 1975d), only four (out of 516) children were reported to make any explicit reference to nutritional attributes (vitamins, minerals or general health value).

Food-Related Behavior—Preferences, Requests, Purchases, and Consumption

Influence on Food Purchases—Child Requests, Parental Yielding

There is considerable research evidence documenting children's requests for the food products promoted to them on television and parental yielding to these attempts to influence purchases (for example, Atkin 1975d; Clancy-Hepburn et al. 1974; Galst and White 1976; Gene Reilly Group 1973; Syzbillo et al. 1977; Ward and Wackman 1972).

A sample of (n = 132) middle class mothers reported that out of twenty-two product categories advertised on television, their 5- to 12-year-old children most frequently requested breakfast cereals, snack foods, and candy (and games/toys), the items most heavily promoted to children (Ward and Wackman 1972). These mothers also indicated they were the most likely to "usually" yield to their children's requests for these same products: breakfast cereals (87 percent), snack foods (63 percent), and candy (42 percent) (games/toys, 54 percent).

Further evidence that children frequently request advertised foods and are relatively successful in influencing the purchase of these products is provided by the national survey conducted among 6- to 14-year-old children and their mothers (Gene Reilly Group 1973b).[10] With regard to presweetened cereals, for example, 79 percent of the (n = 321) purchasing mothers whose children specify a favored choice indicated they normally bought that cereal. According to (n = 867) children who ever want presweetened cereal (82 percent of total sample), their mothers may either yield to their actual requests for a cereal (40 percent) or already know which one they want and simply buy it (56 percent), that is, "passive dictation." Similarly with reference to cookie purchases, 78 percent of purchasing mothers reported honoring their children's product preferences which, according to the children, most mothers (63 percent) did without having to be asked. In the case of candy bars, however, while overall parental yielding was as high (74 percent, mothers report), children said they usually had to specifically ask for them (49 percent) as opposed to having their mothers bring candy bars home without being asked to do so (30 percent).

With regard to snacking behavior, more than nine out of ten of the (8- to

14-year-old) children questioned in the Reilly survey (1973) reported having a snack every day after school. Snacking also occurs at other times of the day, though less frequently. More than 80 percent of these children claim responsibility for fixing their own snack, and this responsibility increasing with age. Snacks most often include: "sweets" (50 percent); salty chip-type products (17 percent); fruit (16 percent); and sandwiches (16 percent). Children also report spending their own snack money (an average of 35¢ per purchase) on candy, soda, chips, ice cream, and chewing gum.

Children have also been reported to influence family decisions about eating out in fast-food and other restaurants (Syzbillo et al. 1977). According to a nonrandom sample of (n = 190) New York mothers, their children provide information about restaurants (93 percent), participate in the decision of which restaurant to go to (90 percent), but not in how much money to spend (21 percent). The children were more involved in the family decisions about eating in a fast-food restaurant than in a conventional restaurant.

Children's actual requests for advertised foods have also been observed in the more naturalistic setting of the supermarket (Atkin 1975d; Galst and White 1976). The Atkin study (1975d) monitored parent-child interaction with specific regard to the selection of ready-to-eat cereals. In two-thirds of the (n = 516) families observed, 3- to 12-year-old children initiated the selection of a cereal, either by telling the parent which they wanted (demanding, 46 percent) or by asking permission to have it (requesting, 20 percent). In most cases, their attempts to influence this food purchase were successful: parents were twice as likely to approve than refuse the proposed purchase. However, one-fourth of all the interactions were reported to result in parent-child conflict, usually as a consequence of a parent's negative response to the child's initiative.

In each of the studies described so far, the children's observed requests and demands for advertised foods or restaurants may well have been influenced by prior exposure to television commercials for these products and services; however, this relationship is not established in the research.

Tying Children's Food Choices to their TV Viewing

Research is available which shows children's requests and consumption of advertised foods to be related to their exposure to television advertising (for example, Atkin 1975a, 1975f; Galst and White 1976; Sharaga 1974).

For instance, in an observational study (Galst and White 1976) in which (n = 41) 3- to 5-year-olds and their mothers were again monitored at the supermarket, children's attempts to influence purchases were correlated with the amount of television they were reportedly exposed to at home. Specifically, "those children who viewed more commercial television at home made more purchase demands at the supermarket." Furthermore, the food products most heavily advertised to children on television (presweetened cereals and candy) were also the items they asked for most often. (Almost half of the cereal and one-fourth of the candy requests made by children in this study resulted in the purchase of the requested product.) Another phase of the study provided evidence that the more reinforcing children found television commercials, as compared with the program narrative (the harder they worked to maintain the TV presentation on the screen), the more purchase requests they made at the store.

Several surveys have also documented a relationship between children's television viewing and reports of their consumption of advertised foods. For example, when a large sample of ($n = 738$) preschool to fifth grade children and some ($n = 301$) of their mothers were questioned about how often they asked for the cereals they see in commercials on TV, the frequency of children's reported requests was positively correlated with the amount of their Saturday morning TV viewing. Requests were significantly greater among heavy viewers than light viewers (41 percent of heavy viewers asked for cereals "a lot" versus 24 percent of light viewers) (Atkin 1975f). There was also reasonably high agreement between mothers and children about the level of requests.

Reported exposure to television advertising has also been found positively related to candy bar consumption in a survey conducted among ($n = 506$) somewhat older, fourth to seventh grade children (Atkin 1975a). Exposure to television advertising for candy in particular was estimated by multiplying a score for children's reported attention to and knowledge regarding candy ads with the amount of their Saturday morning viewing. Interestingly, correlations were found between exposure to candy ads and children's consumption of both heavily and infrequently advertised brands of candy bars which, according to the author, suggests that advertising effects on consumption may generalize to nonadvertised brands within the same product class. Alternatively, of course, candy-eating children may watch more television and pay greater attention to the commercials for candy.

Sharaga (1974) also found significant correlations between (second and sixth grade) children's reported television viewing time (total for three days and Saturday morning) and their preference for foods highly advertised on children's television programming; those preferred foods included specific breakfast cereals, candy and other snack foods, and fast-food restaurants.

As a final and rather distinctive example, children's perceptions of the influence of television advertising on their product preferences and of their ability to influence the purchase of advertised products, including food, have been investigated in one study (Sheikh and Moleski 1977). See chapter 10 for a discussion of this study.

That children's requests and consumption of advertised foods is actually influenced by—and not simply related to—their exposure to commercials for these foods still requires making an inference about causality beyond the data provided by these primarily descriptive or observational studies. However, in several more recent experimental studies where such causal inferences can be made, exposure to specific food commercials has significantly increased children's expressed preferences or requests for the products advertised (Atkin and Gibson 1978; Goldberg et al. 1978; Gorn and Goldberg 1978).

For example, in the earlier described Gorn and Goldberg (1978) experiment in which 8- to 10-year-old boys were exposed to a varying number of advertisements (or to no ads) for an unfamiliar brand of ice cream, commercial viewing produced a significant effect on children's expressed preference for this brand versus other ice cream. Specifically, those shown three different commercials for this brand exhibited a significantly greater preference for the product than those viewing only one. (No comparison could be made with those not shown the ad at all, since they were not asked about their preference for this new brand.)

When asked to indicate their first and second choice of a snack food from a number of alternatives (bubble gum, bag of chips, chocolate bar, or ice cream cone), there were no significant differences across groups in the children's first choice of a food. However, the children's viewing of five different commercials for this unfamiliar brand of ice cream exerted a significant influence on their second choices: 45 percent of these children specified ice cream second, as compared to between 10 to 15 percent for each of the other groups. Finally, exposure to these commercials did not significantly affect the amount of ice cream children actually consumed at the end of the session.

As the authors point out, the results of this study provide some evidence of a hierarchy of effects operating among children. A single commercial exposure resulted in significant gains in information (for example, brand-name, flavors) viewing three (varied) commercials contributed to an increase in brand preference; while only exposure to five (varied) commercials produced a shift in children's choice of a snack. Lastly, there was no evidence of advertising effects on consumption.

In another experiment, Goldberg et al. (1978) randomly assigned (n = 80) first grade children (upper middle class) to one of five conditions: nine commercials for sugared snack and breakfast foods; eighteen commercials (each of the above shown twice); eight pro-nutrition public service announcements; sixteen psa's (each of the previous set shown twice)—all of these inserted in a cartoon; or no exposure to any advertising or programming (control group). Following viewing, a series of boards were presented to the children displaying six snacks or breakfast foods. Three were more wholesome, the other three less wholesome, and one or two of each were among the foods promoted. In each case, children selected the three foods they would want.

The children who viewed the commercials tended to select more sugared foods than those who saw no messages; conversely, those exposed to the pro-nutrition psa's selected the fewest sugared foods (and therefore more of the wholesome ones, like fruits and vegetables). Thus, the children's short-term snack and breakfast food preferences tended to reflect their television exposure experience. This repetition of commercials did not further increase the number of advertised sugared foods selected, but children exposed to the repeated series of ads tended to select more of the nonadvertised sugared foods.

Summary and Conclusions

Television Food Advertising to Children Characterized

During most of the year, the majority of children's television commercials are for food products and services. The specific products promoted to children constitute a very limited range of the foods available for consumption; they consist primarily of sugared cereals, candy, and other sugared snacks, all products with high sugar content. There is also considerable advertising for eating places. The few food categories advertised are each represented by many different brands of product, and each brand's commercials may be repeated on a given day or even during the course of a single morning's viewing.

The format employed in commercials directed at children varies by product type: most cereal ads are totally or partially animated, whereas ads for candy/sweets are usually live-action. Presenter characters are commonly used in association with specific products; cereals use animated characters, and fast food restaurants use live adult males. Most other characters in these commercials are children, although adult and teenage characters also tend to appear in ads for candy/sweets.

In general, food products are not promoted to children on the basis of their nutritional value. Candy/sweets commercials rarely make nutritional claims (although they may occasionally identify ingredients as either natural or artificial); neither do they associate these foods with principles of good nutrition and health. Cereals do sometimes make reference to nutrition, such as the vitamin fortification.

The single exception to this paucity of nutritional information is the NAB-required disclosure in commercials for breakfast-type products about the role of the product within a balanced meal. The majority of cereal ads make this disclosure in five seconds or less. In contrast to cereals, candy/sweets are not to be shown eaten at a meal; instead, they are depicted as being eaten in various settings.

Advertised foods are described primarily in terms of their taste, texture, and ingredients (for instance, "sugar crunchy," or "fruit chew middle"). References to particular food attributes have also been noted: "sweetness" or similar taste claims are present in one-fourth of cereal ads; references to sticky or chewy texture appear in one-third of the commercials for candy/sweets; and claims are also occasionally made in these ads about the long lasting value of the candy product. Other, less inherently food-related product attributes, such as brand-name, musical jingles, dramatic themes (fun, magic, or adventure), and premium offers (for cereals) are also prominent in these commercials.

Children's Responses to Food Commercials

Information: In general, children have been found to learn the content information provided in food commercials. They exhibit high awareness of brand-names, the identity of presenter characters, and various of the other product claims or attributes featured, for example, the nature of a premium offer, the number of flavors or vitamins. An apparent exception to this tendency is the difficulty children have remembering and interpreting the balanced breakfast disclosure. This may be attributable to the nature of its presentation rather than children's inability to learn such information, however.

Regarding more general information about food, children's concepts of what constitutes an acceptable snack usually includes the foods most frequently advertised to them. Children also exhibit some knowledge about the healthfulness of advertised foods. In neither case can children's learning be directly attributed to their exposure to food commercials; however, it is plausible to expect children to include the television examples of snacks with which they become familiar in their definitions of what snacks are. In contrast, given that candy ads do not provide information about nutritional value or health consequences, children would not be able to acquire such information from watching them.

The extent of recall and understanding of commercial content varies with child variables such as family income, mother's education and, in particular, with age. Younger preschool children consistently report less recall and understanding than older school-age children of the product information provided in ads. Younger and lower class children are also much less well-informed about the nutritional value and health consequences of advertised foods than their older, middle class counterparts.

Beliefs and inferences: Children have been shown to accept or believe many of the product claims made about advertised foods. These include claims about attributes as varied as a product's size, its ability to make you smile, and general health claims. Children have also been shown to draw inferences beyond the explicit content, including mistaken inferences about what is safely edible and inferences about the personal qualities of product presenters and characters (for example, their power and happiness. They appear to base these inferences upon observation of behavior and the visual appearance of people and things.

However, the various claims learned and accepted about advertised foods do not function equivalently in shaping children's attitudes toward these foods. More specifically, good taste, sweet taste, and premium offers have been found to be more appealing than nutritional value. Thus, reported acceptance of a given product claim (such as part of a balanced breakfast) ensures neither its salience for children nor their understanding of its meaning. Although not ranked, children's attitudes toward commercial characters also tend to become associated with the respective product.

Again, the extent to which children express acceptance of claims made or implied about foods in commercials seems to vary with such child variables as family income, race, and age. In this case, the younger children exhibit greater acceptance of product claims and draw more inferences, for example about characters, than do older children. They also report greater belief in the general truthfulness of commercials.

Behavior: Children have been found to influence the purchase of the foods advertised to them. There is evidence of a tendency both for children to register their preferences for these products and for parents to honor their children's requests or previously expressed preferences when making food choices. In cases where parents deny their children's requests, conflict between parents and children sometimes ensues. Children are also reported to take responsibility for fixing their own after-school snacks, which often include sweets like cookies and candy.

Children's expressed preferences and consumption of advertised foods have been shown positively related to their exposure to television food advertising. That is, children who report higher levels of television viewing are more likely to report preferences and consumption of heavily advertised foods than do children who view less television. Those children willing to "work harder" to maintain commercials on a television monitor, as compared to programs, were also found to make more requests for these foods.

Finally, exposure to specific food commercials has produced significant increases in children's expressed preferences or requests for the products promoted, including a new brand of a familiar product like ice cream and non-advertised foods within the same product class.

Needed Research

It is unlikely that research evidence about the effects of television food advertising on children will—by itself—determine advertising policy; somewhere in the gap between where the research leaves off and policy decisions are made lie values and pragmatics. Still, such research can effectively inform policy decisions regarding advertising practices and regulation, particularly if it is designed with that as its objective.

For example, content analyses should be conducted with the specific intent of monitoring the extent to which food advertising presents information recommended or required by industry codes or government regulations. Measures could be designed to describe the ways in which nutritional disclosures or health warnings were made (How central to the action or narrative content are they? How much time or emphasis are they given aurally and/or visually?); the ways in which foods are depicted; and the reasons offered for consuming advertised foods.

However, in order to establish what information is actually conveyed to children and whether it is correctly understood, it is necessary for the children's responses themselves to be studied and evaluated.

With regard to format variables, for example, research is needed that examines the relative effectiveness of an animated, "mixed" (animated and live-action elements present on the screen simultaneously), or live-action format in conveying "comparable" food product information to children. For instance, do preschool children assign a different reality status to animated food presenter characters depending upon whether they are depicted in an animated or live setting?

In terms of informational content, there has been little research investigation of the extent to which children remember and comprehend the references to such terms as "energy," "fortification," and "artificial or natural flavor" which sometimes appear in food commercials.

Both the FTC and the NAD (Griffin 1976) have acknowledged the usefulness of research in which small samples of children are exposed to individual commercials and asked specific questions about their understanding of those messages.

More attention also needs to be paid to assessing the aggregate effects of television food advertising on children's food knowledge, beliefs, and eating habits. For example, does children's conception of what foods are appropriate and desirable to eat for meals and snacks (and when and where they should be eaten) vary systematically depending upon the amount of television advertising they are exposed to?

Does advertising affect the bases upon which children develop preferences for foods? In this regard, research would be welcome which provided children with diverse (including nonverbal) means to "describe" the foods promoted to them on television. By identifying the specific features included in children's food descriptions or assessments, it should be possible to gain a better sense of what the salient or criterial attributes of advertised foods are for children and whether they differ from those of comparable but unadvertised products.

Finally, there is the question of using advertising to provide nutritional information to young audiences:

1. Should children be exposed to a wider range of advertised food products?

2. Should advertisers include more nutritional information to provide children with the opportunity to learn about nutrition as one factor among several in their food choices?
3. Given the influence of parent-child interaction on food selection, should food and nutrition-related television messages be directed to children *and* to parents?

Lesser (1974) describes some of the research steps necessary to design and produce nutritionally informative television material for children. First, children's existing knowledge and understanding of good nutritional patterns should be determined. On that basis, the areas of "nutritional illiteracy" most in need of correction can be identified. Then, as educational materials are developed, they must be tested with children to determine whether they hold their attention, are understood, and produce desired as well as unintended changes in behavior. Pilot materials can be revised on the basis of this feedback. Finally, any program of nutritional education must evaluate its long-term effectiveness for representative members of the intended audience.

Notes

1. Winick et al. (1973) analyzed food commercials appearing on network weekend morning children's shows in the 1971 fall season. Atkin (1975d) compared network advertising on two comparable Saturday mornings in 1972 and 1973. Conducted prior to recent industry guidelines, these earlier analyses provide useful data for assessing changes in advertising practices over the past six to seven years. In both his studies, Barcus analyzed over 400 commercials broadcast weekend mornings on Boston stations, including the three network affiliates and two (1975a) or three (1978) independent UHF stations. The 1978 study also cites data from weekday after-school programming on ten independent stations in various cities.

2. These items, plus candy bars/packaged candy, comprise the candies/sweets category referred to by Barcus in subsequent analyses.

3. Also documented in terms of volume, four product/service categories were responsible for 85 percent of the total number of food commercials on network weekend daytime programming during the first nine months of 1975 (CCMM 1977): cereals (3,832), candy and gum (1,627), cookies/crackers (841) and fast-food restaurants (782). The number of commercials for "basic foods," including meats, vegetables and dairy products yielded a combined total of four.

4. However, the foods grouped together here vary considerably in their nutritional composition. See Hershey Foods Corporation Annual Report (1977).

5. This appears to represent a decrease in the use of animation by commercials for candies/sweets from an earlier 51 percent (Barcus 1975a).

6. However, this figure may not take into account references to sweetness which are part of a cereal's name (Sugar Frosted Rice and Super Sugar Crisp).

7. In-house copy testing conducted by individual advertisers, if available, would probably supplement the published literature here.

8. Note, however, that both industry codes impose restrictions on the use of comparative claims in children's advertising.

9. This Wonder Bread commercial was, in fact, determined to be deceptive by the Federal Trade Commission.

10. Because of the size and representativeness of the Reilly sample, these findings may reasonably by generalized to the population at large.

The Effects of Volume and Repetition of Television Commercials

John R. Rossiter

This chapter reviews the research on effects of television advertising resulting from the frequency of children's exposure to commercials. We will use the term *volume* to refer to frequency of exposure to commercials in general. The term *repetition* refers to frequency of exposure to a particular commercial. Four main issues are apparent, three relating to volume and one to repetition:

1. That certain long-term effects may result from children's exposure to commercials. Alleged effects include a greater susceptibility to persuasion, development of materialistic values and, more positively, certain consumer socialization effects such as appreciation of the marketing and economic environment. Since it is hypothesized that these effects increase with cumulative exposure to television commercials as children grow older, we shall designate them as *long-term exposure effects*.

2. That certain effects may result from frequent exposure to commercials through "heavy viewing" within age groups. Susceptibility to persuasion is the most common of these alleged effects. To distinguish these more immediate effects from the previous long-term category, we shall designate them as *heavy viewing effects*.

3. That volume effects are also relevant in the short-term via the "clustering" of commercials in blocks between programs versus distributing them between and during programs. Proponents of clustering allege that it helps children to discriminate between program content and advertising content. Opponents allege that clustering lead to "clutter" and poorer individual commercial performance, which unfairly penalizes the advertisers. We shall refer to this issue as *clustering effects*.

4. That repetition of the same commercial results in stronger effects than a single exposure. Most often, the allegation is that increased susceptibility to persuasion results from such repetition but also included are other potential effects, such as "irritation." We shall refer to this issue as *repetition effects*.

Current Codes

1. *Long-term exposure effects:* The NAB has been progressively reducing the amount of nonprogram material (of which commercial content is 80 percent

or more) permissible on weekdays and weekends during programs "initially designed primarily for children." One network, ABC, plans to voluntarily reduce weekend commercial time on children's programs even further. These trends are shown in table 9-1. During adult programming, the limits are 9.5 minutes per hour during prime-time (any station-designated period of 3.5 consecutive hours between 6:00 P.M. and midnight each day) and 16 minutes per hour at all other times. The NAD has no provisions pertaining to volume of commercials; it covers specific commercial practices only.

2. *Heavy viewing effects:* The new NAB code provisions would automatically reduce children's likelihood of exposure to commercials for both heavy and light viewers—at least to the extent that they watch children's programs. This volume restriction applies to time but not to the *number* of commercials. Predictably, neither the NAB nor the NAD code prohibits "heavy viewing" per se.

3. *Clustering effects:* The NAB code allows the practice of clustering commercials in blocks between programs. In fact, the code prohibits the opposite, that is, too wide a distribution of commercials within programs. For children's programs and also prime-time programs, the number of within-program interruptions is limited to two per half-hour program or four per one-hour program. Again, this volume-related matter is not covered in the NAD provisions.

4. *Repetition effects:* As far as we can discern from the NAB code there is no limit on the number of times a particular commercial may be repeated. Nor is there a limit on how rapidly it may be repeated, apart from the restrictions on number of interruptions per hour and total nonprogram time per hour already described.

Incidence

For the sake of continuity, we will retain in this section the word "effects" in our headings. However, it should be made clear that incidence here refer merely to *potential* for effects. The effects themselves are reviewed in the research evidence section.

Table 9-1
Permissible Number of Nonprogram Minutes per Hour in Children's Programs

	1974	*1976*	*January 1981 (ABC only)*
Weekdays	16.0	12.0	12.0
Weekends	16.0	9.5	7.5

Long-term Exposure Effects

Relevant incidence figures for long-term exposure effects are tied into the question of whether or not broadcasters adhere to the NAB's restrictions on advertising volume. The indications are that, on average, broadcasters comply with these limits. Actual compliance rates are not available for the recent reduction in commercial time on children's programs. However, a survey was conducted in 1975 when the limits were 10 minutes and 12 minutes respectively (Barcus 1975a, 1975b). The average (mean) per-hour times devoted to non-program material were 9.5 minutes and 11.9 minutes respectively.[1] Barcus also noted that some stations consistently exceeded these limits slightly (usually by less than 60 seconds) and that all stations monitored exceeded them occasionally. However, since approximately 20 percent of nonprogram time is occupied by noncommercial announcements,[2] the time figures for *commercials* would almost invariably be less than 9.5 and 11.9 minutes.

Another finding in Barcus' research bears on the nature of "volume." Although the total *time* devoted to commercials in children's weekend programming declined from 19 percent in 1971 to 16 percent in 1975, the *number* of commercials was hardly reduced at all. In 1971, there was one commercial every 2.8 minutes, and in 1975, one every 2.9 minutes.[3] Thus, in 1975, children had the opportunity to see as many commercials but a lower volume of advertising time than in 1971.

A second type of incidence figure is represented by the extensive data on children's viewing patterns described in chapter 2 of this book. Note that the estimates of commercial exposure in these data should be regarded as incidence figures and not as exposure figures—unless we define exposure as "potential for exposure." The figures are based on children's viewing of programs and are not adjusted for nonviewing (plus perhaps nonhearing) of commercials. Nonviewing can be substantial, as indicated in chapter 3. As incidence figures, then, the data show that an average child between the ages of 2 and 11 is presented with about 19,000 to 20,000 commercials per year, or about 50 to 55 commercials per average viewing day.

Some supplementary statistics may be useful in placing these incidence figures in context. First of all, the Nielsen data from which the incidence figures are derived reveal a decline in viewing with age. However, the decline is slight— 3 hours 47 minutes per day for 2- to 5-year-olds down to 3 hours 41 minutes for 6- to 11-year-olds. Thus, it is unlikely that the rate of cumulative exposure to commercials declines significantly over the 2 to 11 age range. Second, it may be recalled from chapter 2 that approximately 85 percent of the commercials children are potentially exposed to are not shown during children's programs and are therefore not subject to the NAB children's code. On the other hand, it should be noted that noncode commercials are most likely to be on programs that are *co-viewed* by the child and at least one parent. The overall co-viewing incidence is estimated at 45 percent for both 2- to 5-year-olds and 6- to 11-year-olds.

Heavy Viewing Effects

The program viewing data (and, thus, potential commercial exposure data) referred to so far have been based on means or averages. As noted in chapter 2, there is considerable variation around these average figures. Although the average viewing figure is approximately 3.75 hours per day, it is likely that this ranges from about one hour or less per day for light viewers to as much as six hours per day for heavy viewers.[5] The range for potential exposure to commercials is thus about 5,400 to 32,600 per year or about 14 to 86 per day. Of course, the great majority of children will be well within these ranges, but the estimates do indicate the difference between heavy and light viewing within age groups in terms of volume incidence figures.

Clustering Effects

The normal practice is to distribute children's commercials in "pods" throughout children's programs rather than to cluster them at the beginning or end. Usually this means that a maximum of three or four commercials is presented during a single program interruption. For example, if we assume a 9.5-minute limit per hour, with all of those 9.5 minutes filled with 30-second commercials, plus the two breaks allowed during programs, a typical schedule might be 4, 3, 3, 3, 3, 3, commercials over a one-hour period.

The only stations to depart from this distributed format are, as far as we know, the four Post-Newsweek Stations (PNS).[6] On children's programs, PNS clusters the commercials between half-hour or one-hour program segments with no in-program interruptions. A typical one-hour PNS schedule would be 6, 6 (six commercials prior to a half-hour program and six at the end of the half-hour).[7] Although most unlikely, it is theoretically possible within current NAB and FCC rules that a cluster of 19 consecutive 30-second commercials could be shown.

Repetition Effects

Repetition, in terms of incidence, refers to the frequency with which a particular commercial is shown. The content analyses by Barcus (1975a, 1975b, 1976a) happened to include as appendixes the number of times particular commercials were aired during his content sampling periods. One report (Barcus

1975b) covered weekday programming between 3:00 P.M. and 6:00 P.M. on ten independent and network affiliate stations. Over the week of afternoon programs the average (median and modal) commercial was shown only once; only 4.6 percent exceeded a once-a-day rate and only 0.8 percent exceeded the twice-a-day rate, with a maximum of 14 showings of one commercial over the five-day period. Another report (Barcus 1975a) covered the period from 7:00 A.M. to 1:30 P.M. one Saturday and Sunday in April 1975 on five stations—three network affiliates and two independent stations. Over the two-day period, the median commercial was shown twice, although the modal (most frequent) figure was once; 40 percent of the commercials exceeded a once-a-day rate and 14.7 percent exceeded a twice-a-day rate, with a maximum of ten showings for one commercial over the two-day period. The third Barcus report (1976a) covered two consecutive Saturday mornings in November 1975—the peak pre-Christmas period for children's advertisers—on the three network affiliate stations. Over the two-day period the average (median and modal) commercial was shown once; 21.8 percent exceeded a once-a-day rate and 8.2 percent exceeded a twice-a-day rate, with a maximum of 17 showings, for a motion picture promotion, over the two-day (one week apart) period.[8]

However, these frequency counts covered overlapping or simultaneous programming by ten, five, and three stations respectively. A child would have to be an almost impossibly avid "channel switcher" to encounter this many repeats of a commercial. More reasonable incidence estimates for *potentially encountered repetitions* are obtained by allowing for total possible individual viewing time within the content periods and correcting them to daily rates. Based on these corrections the probable repetition rates are shown in table 9-2.

In other words, the average child is only likely to be presented with even the most frequently run commercial about twice in one day on a weekend or

Table 9-2
Potentially Encountered Commercial Repetitions

	Typical weekday afternoon (3-6 P.M.), 1975	Typical Saturday or Sunday morning, April 1975	Typical Saturday morning, November 1975
Maximum single commercial repetition assuming continuous viewing	1.4 times per day	2.0	1.8
Typical (modal) single commercial repetition rate assuming continuous viewing	0.1 times per day	0.2	0.8

seven times over a five-afternoon weekday period.[9] A few commercials, then, might be encountered about twice a day. On the other hand, the *average* commercial would be encountered only once every ten days on weekday afternoons and about once every five weekend mornings. These figures indicate that most commercials (60 to 80 percent) on children's programs would be encountered approximately once a week for as long as they are run.

Note that the preceding estimates provide no data on repetition rates encountered by children during adult or prime-time programs. They show only the estimated repetition rate for commercials appearing during program time set aside for children on weekend mornings and weekdays after school. Moreover, the data do not indicate the *total* number of times that an average child is likely to encounter a particular commercial. We can estimate daily or weekly frequency rates, but we cannot estimate total frequencies from the available data. This would require a month-by-month analysis of advertising insertion schedules (for example from *Broadcast Advertisers Reports*) and is beyond the resources of the present report.

One final repetition incidence statistic is also germane. A fairly common measure of commercial effectiveness is brand-name recall. Brand-name recall might be influenced not only by the number of times a commercial is repeated but also by the number of brand-name repetitions *within* the commercial itself. A content analysis of commercials appearing during children's programs in 1972 and 1973 (Atkin and Heald 1977) indicated that verbal (audio) repetitions of the brand name averaged 3.65 per commercial; most commercials used between two and four repetitions, only a few used one, but about one-fourth used five or more brand-name repetitions per commercial.

Research Evidence

Long-term Exposure Effects

In this section, we shall review studies which have compared children's responsiveness to television commercials across age groups. That is, we shall regard age as an index of cumulative exposure to commercials. Since the studies are cross-sectional, cumulative, age-related effects are inferred rather than longitudinally observed within the same child or group of children.[10]

Various effects have been examined as a function of age, and there are different ways in which these could be organized for discussion. We have chosen to distinguish four categories of effects: (1) *cognitive effects,* which are relevant to the question of potential deception or "deceivability"; (2) *affective effects,* which are relevant to the question of children's feelings toward commercials and toward television advertising as an institution; (3) *behavioral effects,* which are perhaps most relevant to allegations centering on children's "susceptibility to persuasion," and thus to fairness considerations; and (4) *consumer socialization effects*, which are relevant to the assessment of television advertising's contribution to children's general development as consumers.

Cognitive Effects: Three types of cognitive effects attributable to cumulative exposure to commercials have been studied. The first of these is attention. Two major studies have shown that 8- to 11-year-olds learn to pay less visual attention to commercials than 3- to 7-year-olds. This finding was originally established by Ward, Levinson, and Wackman (1972) in a natural observation setting and was replicated in laboratory settings by Atkin (1975b). However, Atkin notes that the decline in attention with age, although statistically significant, is only about two seconds less per 30-second commercial. Also, the studies monitored only visual attention whereas auditory attention is also relevant. In fact, brand-name recall, a response that could be learned entirely through auditory attention, increases about 100 percent with age (Atkin 1975b).

Of particular interest is the additional finding by Atkin that recall of message elements in commercials also increases significantly (about 50 percent) with age. Since message elements involve both visual and verbal stimuli, auditory attention alone could not account for this phenomenon. It seems likely that older children are capable of "processing" commercials faster and consequently have less need to pay much attention during subsequent exposures.[11] The attention question could be resolved with a simple experiment in which the treatments consist of new versus familiar commercials and the measures comprise auditory as well as visual attention.

From a policy standpoint, attention is not a very important response. Concern about the cognitive effects of commercials has rarely centered on how attention-getting they are. Attention is merely an assumed but necessary condition for more serious effects, such as whether children's trust in commercials, or their understanding of commercials, increases or decreases with cumulative exposure.

Children report that they trust commercials less as they see more of them. This finding holds for commercials in general and seems also to be true for specific commercials. The percentage of children who trust *all* commercials was shown to decline from 65 percent at the first grade level to 27 percent by third grade and 7 percent by fifth grade (Robertson and Rossiter 1974a). For specific commercials, Atkin (1975b) found a significant negative correlation of $r = -.51$ ($p < .001$) between the age of the child and the believability ratings of three claims in two commercials. Robertson and Rossiter (1974a) hypothesized that the decline in trust is based on children's increasing propensity to attribute "persuasive intent" to commercials. Note that the decline in trust or believability with age, or an increase in attribution of persuasive intent, does not necessarily mean that commercials are any less effective—a point which we will discuss later.

Perhaps the most important cognitive effect is children's ability to *understand* commercials as a function of cumulative experience. Rossiter (1974) and Rossiter and Robertson (1976) examined children's understanding of the conceptual basis of television commercials in terms of six variables which measured children's ability to: (1) define the difference between television commercials and television programs; (2) comprehend the existence of an external message source or sponsor; (3) perceive the existence of intended target audiences for commercial messages; (4) identify informative intent in commercials; (5) identify persuasive intent in commercials; and (6) understand their symbolic representational characteristics. Total cognitive understanding of commercials was highly correlated with age ($r = .45, p < .001$). Further analysis (Rossiter and Robertson 1976) demonstrated that age and cumulative experience accounted for 40 percent of the variance in cognitive understanding, while differences in social background accounted for only 9 percent. Using a similar but partial set of measures, Ward, Wackman, and Wartella (1975) also found a highly significant increase in children's cognitive understanding of commercials as a function of age.

One particular aspect of cognitive understanding of commercials that has received major attention is children's ability to recognize *persuasive intent*— one of the variables in the overall cognitive measure developed by Rossiter and Robertson. The Federal Trade Commission in its 1979 hearings on children's television advertising isolated persuasive intent recognition as an indicator of whether children are aware of the selling purpose of advertising and, by inference, whether it is "fair" to advertise to them if they do not show awareness of selling motives.

The age at which most children are capable of recognizing persuasive intent is in dispute. The dispute centers on the methods used to measure persuasive intent recognition. Generally, open-ended questions such as those used by Ward et al. (1972) and Robertson and Rossiter (1974a), which require the child to formulate and articulate answers, have indicated that a large proportion of young children under age 8 cannot recognize persuasive intent. Recently, however, closed-end and "nonverbal" measures, which do not depend on the articulation of an answer, have suggested that ability to recognize persuasive intent may have been substantially underestimated. This seems especially true when children are asked about the purpose of specific commercials rather than about the purpose of commercials in general, that is, when given a more concrete referent rather than an abstract one.

In a major study conducted for the Federal Trade Commission, Atkin (1979) used both open-end and closed-end questions to measure persuasive intent recognition. The children in his sample, 480 young children aged 3 to 7 from a broad range of social backgrounds, were first shown pictures (one frame) from three cereal commercials to establish a concrete context. The interviewer then said to the child: "They show these cereals on TV when kids are watching. Why do you think they show these cereals on TV?" This open-ended question required the child to formulate and articulate a response. Responses of the type "so people will buy" signified persuasive intent recognition. The interviewer then asked the child more directly: "Do they show these cereals so kids will ask for the cereal?" The child could refer to a cue card with the alternatives "Yes," "No," and "?" ("Don't know"). For this closed-end question, a "Yes" response signified persuasive intent recognition. Results by the two methods were quite different, as shown in table 9-3. The direct, closed-end question indicated an extremely high level of persuasive intent recognition among even the youngest preschool children. (It should be noted that guesses or random responses would produce a much lower level of "Yes" answers, depending on the child's intrinsic preferences for the three response alternatives.) The slightly higher level of persuasive intent recognition among *younger* children with the closed-end measure may have been partly due to a yes-saying tendency; nevertheless, the results are impressive and their contrast with the open-ended results astonishing.

It should be noted, however, that not all closed-end procedures have yielded such high levels of recognition of persuasive intent. A study by Gianinno and Zuckerman is often cited as demonstrating recognition of persuasive intent by young children whereas in fact it did not. This may have been due to the publication of a summary of the study (1977) which did not show the detailed numerical findings (unpublished). These investigators showed a sample of 4-, 7-, and 10-year-old children twenty pictures of television characters. Ten characters were from popular programs and ten were from commercials, with none appearing in both. Even the youngest children were highly accurate in telling which were the program characters and which were the commercial characters—the result most often cited. The pictures were shuffled and the children were asked to pick out the characters who "try to make you buy something." This question calls for a direct attribution of persuasive intent and is closed-end and "nonverbal" in that each child had only to pick out as many characters as he or she wished without giving a verbal answer. To prevent spuriously high scores by children selecting more than ten characters, incorrect choices were substracted from the total correct. A child who guessed or chose at random could thus

Table 9-3
Persuasive Intent Recognition

	Age					
	3	*4*	*5*	*6*	*7*	*Average (percent)*
Open-end	5	12	21	42	48	26
Closed-end	90	83	80	73	73	80

Source: Atkin (1979).

obtain a maximum score of 5 whereas a perfect score would be 10. Observed scores for the 4- and 7-year-olds were at or below chance: 3.0 and 5.2, respectively, suggesting that they could *not* reliably recognize persuasive intent. Older children, 10-year-olds, apparently could: an average of 8.9 correct versus the maximum correct score of 10. These "nonverbal" results are closely in line with the "verbal" Robertson and Rossiter (1974a) results which show a steady increase in persuasive intent recognition with age.

Measures of persuasive intent recognition are plagued with various problems which make the issue of children's ability, by age group, to understand the selling intent of commercials very difficult to resolve. "Nonverbal" or closed-end measures may avoid the articulation problem with children's *answers* but they cannot avoid the problem of children's understanding of the *questions,* which must be posed verbally. For instance, a recent study by Donohue et al. (1978) purports to show that black children have lower recognition of persuasive intent than whites but does not control for educational differences relevant to both the understanding of questions and the articulation of answers. Reliability of coding of open-ended answers, too, poses a problem. Coders should be "blind" as to the age of the child; multiple coders should be employed; and intercoder reliability should be established. The study by Robertson and Rossiter (1974a) based on Rossiter's 1974 dissertation data is the only one to meet these basic measurement criteria. Finally, the expectancies of experimenters, interviewers, or coders regarding the outcomes of the studies can also affect the results. Commercial research firms (for example, Child Research Services, Inc. 1978) tend to find considerably higher levels of persuasive intent recognition than do studies conducted by consumer advocates (for example, Atkin 1979). Strict attention to accepted scientific measurement standards for open-ended questions would probably avoid many of these differences. But open-ended questions requiring children to construct and produce answers will never be entirely satisfying and neither will closed-end or nonverbal alternatives. The issue of children's actual ability versus their measurable ability to understand commercials remains complex indeed.

In general, however, it is clear that, for the average child, cumulative exposure to commercials has a definite positive relationship to his or her cognitive understanding of what commercials are and what they are supposed to do. This effect might be due, of course, not only to experiential learning, but also, following Piaget's theory, to age-related increases in children's cognitive abilities.

Affective Effects: Apart from the question of whether children understand commercials is the question of whether children *like* television commercials, and how these "institutional" feelings change with age. An impressive body of studies has documented that children's overall affective response, or "liking," towards commercials in general declines significantly with age (James 1971; Blatt et al. 1972; Robertson and Rossiter 1974a; Ferguson 1975; Bever et al.

1975). For instance, the percentage of children who indicated that they liked *all* commercials was shown in one study to decline from 69 percent at first grade to 56 percent by third grade and 25 percent by fifth grade (Robertson and Rossiter 1974a). This affective decline seems to hold for specific commercials as well as for commercials in general. Atkin (1975b) measured children's overall liking for three specific commercials and found a negative correlation of $r = -.35$ ($p < .001$) with age. Atkin's research did turn up one contrary result. Younger children are significantly more likely to display irritation while watching commercials. However, this finding stands in minor contrast to the overwhelming negativity of children's expressed affect toward commercials as children grow older.

Behavioral Effects: An obvious question, given the increase in children's cognitive understanding of commercials with age and their increasingly negative feelings toward them, is whether commercials have any less *behavioral* impact on children as they grow older. This is not an easy question to answer. One problem is the distinction between intended behavior and actual behavior. Commercials may instill intentions or desire for an advertised product, but the execution of these intentions in most cases requires the child to make requests to parents. This obviously introduces other variables pertinent to the requesting behavior, and these other variables may have little to do with the impact of the commercials per se. Nevertheless, let us examine the evidence for both of these effects.

The evidence on intended behavior as a function of age is dependent on the nature of the research measure. An early study by Robertson and Rossiter (1974a) asked children whether they wanted *all* products they saw advertised on television. Responses indicated the expected age-related decline: 53 percent said yes at first grade, 27 percent at third grade, and only 6 percent answered affirmatively at fifth grade. However, a more moderate question used by Ward et al. (1975) asked children whether they wanted *most* things shown in television commercials. A slightly broader age range was sampled, which makes the results even more interesting: 66 percent of kindergarten children said yes, 51 percent of third graders said yes, and a marginally lower 49 percent of sixth graders said yes. Moreover, when asked whether commercials "made them want to have things," the children in the Ward et al. study exhibited an apparent *increase* in perceived motivation with age: affirmative answers by age group were kindergarten, 67 percent; third grade, 87 percent; and sixth grade, 84 percent. Consequently, the weight of evidence for a decline in advertising-induced intentions with age and cumulative exposure is slight at best.

Evidence on the ensuing behavioral effects of request frequencies is also far from clear-cut. Robertson and Rossiter (1974a) found a decrease in request frequency with age; however, the study focused on pre-Christmas television advertising in which almost half of the advertised products were toys and games—products which become less relevant as children grow older.[12] This criticism may also be applied to the frequently heard interpretation of a classic study by Ward and Wackman (1972) to the effect that children's request frequencies decline with age. Studying a wide range of products, these authors actually found only a nonsignificant tendency for request frequencies to decline with age (r = .13; an r of ± .16 would have been required for significance at the 5 percent level).

Detailed inspection of the product-by-product data in the Ward and Wackman study indicates various trends by age depending on the product in question. For example, requests for toys declined with age, but requests for bicycles increased. Requests for products which are presumably relevant to children of all ages, such as snack foods and soft drinks—both heavily advertised—did not show any age-related decline in request frequency. This nondecline effect was substantiated in a later study by Ward et al. (1975) in which requests for food products were essentially constant across age groups (X^2, n.s.), whereas requests for "child-relevant" products such as toys and games, clothing, and record albums actually increased significantly with age ($X^2, p< .01$). The earlier Ward and Wackman study (1972) is much more comprehensive in terms of product categories and should probably be favored over the Ward et al. (1975) results. Neither study, however, revealed any general decline in request frequencies as a function of age and cumulative exposure to commercials.

Before interpreting request frequencies as data on "effects," we must consider the problem referred to earlier—namely, that this type of response is under the control of factors other than advertising-induced intent. One obvious factor is the extent to which parents acquiesce to children's requests and thus reinforce this form of behavior. The Ward and Wackman study (1972) found that parental acquiescence increases with the child's age (r = .20, $p< .01$). To provide a couple of illustrative trends for products relevant to children of all ages: The percentage of mothers who said they usually yield to children's requests for snack foods was 52 percent for 5- to 7-year-olds and rose linearly to 77 percent for 11- to 12-year-olds; comparable acquiescence figures for soft drink requests were 38 percent and 54 percent. Another "extraneous variable" hypothesis might be that peer influence or other nonadvertising experiences might induce request behavior. However, Ward and Wackman's results indicated that the role of television advertising in the requesting process was relatively constant across age groups (r = −.14, n.s.). That is, television advertising did not seem to be displaced by peer influence or other factors. It therefore appears that parental acquiescence or reinforcement exerts a significant influence on children's request frequencies, and that since reinforcement increases with age, we should discount the earlier implication of a constant *advertising-induced* request level. A more accurate projection, adjusting for the effects of extraneous reinforcement, would be a slight decline in request levels. Thus, the safest conclusions from the available evidence are that the long-term exposure effect of commercials is to reduce children's intentions or desire for advertised products only slightly and to produce a correspondingly slight reduction in the frequency of advertising-induced requests to parents.

How is the slight decline in behavioral effects with age to be reconciled with the marked increase in children's cognitive understanding of commercials and with the equally marked decline in their affective feelings toward commercials? In the case of increased cognitive understanding, the most parsimonious explanation would involve abandonment of the implicit hypothesis that children who understand commercials better will be less affected by them. This hypothesis assumes that commercials are in some way "bad," that they are not supposed to persuade children to want the advertised products, or that children become poorer judges of advertised products as they grow older. All are questionable assumptions, and there is not necessarily any incompatibility in increased cognitive understanding *not* producing a decline in behavioral responsiveness.

In the case of children's increasingly negative feelings toward commercials, it is possible that children are merely learning an "institutional" response from their parents or peers. Certainly, it is the accepted thing to criticize commercials. However, this criticism may be somewhat superficial and may apply mainly to commercials *executions* rather than to the products advertised. Rossiter and Robertson (1977) have explored this and other reasons why children's attitudes toward commercials in general do not necessarily bear any relationship to their attitudes toward advertised products in particular.

In sum, long-term exposure effects (or, more conservatively, long-term exposure correlates) include a marked increase in children's cognitive understanding of television commercials, an equally marked increase in children's negative feelings toward television advertising as an institution, and only a slight decline in children's behavioral responsiveness to commercials. Note that these results imply that children do not become more susceptible to persuasion as they accumulate experience with commercials. This conclusion holds regardless of whether one chooses to attribute the slight decline in persuasibility with age to cognitive development or to experiential learning. Both factors are probably involved.

Consumer Socialization Effects: We may also question whether, in the long term, television advertising contributes to children's broader understanding of the economic environment and to the development of consumer knowledge and skills. Here, of course, it is particularly difficult to isolate the role of television commercials from other socialization forces. However, there is no doubt that television commercials play a large role—if only to initiate children's consumer behavior—at all age levels. We can therefore examine age-related trends with a fair amount of confidence that we are monitoring long-term advertising effects, albeit in a multiple influence context. (The role of television commercials can be isolated with more confidence when examining heavy and light viewer differences. See the following section.)

One effect in which television commercials are clearly implicated is children's satisfaction with choices they have made in favor of specific advertised products. Television commercials presumably generate expectations about the product and its attributes. Therefore, if children experience greater dissatisfaction with television advertised products as they grow older, it could be contended that commercials contribute negatively to children's consumer socialization.

Research findings conflict on this point. Ward, Wackman, and Wartella (1975) reported data that seemed to indicate an age-related increase in dissatisfaction from 38 percent for kindergarten children to 75 percent for sixth grade children. However, their research question was whether the children had *ever* seen something on television that, when they got the item, was not as good as they had expected. Clearly such a question provides no evidence on the incidence of dissatisfaction; it merely offers the unsurprising result that older children are more likely to have had at least one unsatisfactory experience of this kind. Robertson and Rossiter (1976c) measured aggregate satisfaction with products received as Christmas presents. They found an increase in satisfaction with age from 84 percent at first grade to 95 percent at fifth grade (significant at the .01 level). However these figures reflect satisfaction with products that were not always advertised on television (this was especially true for the older children). Thus, findings on children's satisfaction with product choices remain equivocal at this juncture.

An alternative way of assessing the impact of television advertising on children's satisfaction with product choices is to examine children's disappointment or frustration when advertising-induced requests are denied. The results of two studies suggest that, cumulatively, advertising does not increase disappointment or frustration levels. Robertson and Rossiter (1976c) found that disappointment over nonreceipt of requested items declined with age although the actual relationship was slightly curvilinear: 37 percent at first grade, 41 percent at third grade, and 25 percent at fifth grade. These findings are subject to the earlier comment regarding television advertised products which decline as a proportion of choices after third grade. The comment also applies to the study by Atkin (1975c) which found a nonsignificant correlation ($r = .04$) between age and reported "conflict and anger" over denial of requests for two products heavily advertised on television—toys and cereals. It is not clear whether disappointment declines because fewer requests for these products are made or whether children become more capable of coping with denial.

Consumer socialization effects have been measured in a more ambitious manner by Ward, Wackman, and Wartella (1975). Based on age as an index of cumulative exposure to commercials, as well as other types of experience, various consumer skills were found to increase from kindergarten to sixth grade.

Predictably, for example, the number of brands with which children were familiar was found to increase with age. This held for four product categories, two of which (soft drinks and gum) are fairly heavily advertised on television. Interestingly, children's perceptions of brand differentiation within product categories *decreased* with age. Again, this held for television advertised products (for instance, toothpaste, peanut butter). Although the authors interpreted this trend as reflecting a decrease with age in the strength of brand preference, it could also be interpreted as reflecting children's increasing recognition of "parity" status between closely competing brands—which is probably a realistic assessment of many such products.

Ward et al. (1975) also took another measure which might be affected by television advertising—awareness of multiple sources of information about new products. Ward et al.'s discussion of these data implied that children learn to use more sources of information as they grow older. However, their data actually indicated that older children rely more heavily on *television commercials* as a source of new product information. To illustrate, let us take one of the product categories, snacks, which has wide age-related appeal.[13] Table 9-4 shows what children nominated as a source of information about new snack products, with multiple responses allowed. It is hard to interpret these data simply as reflecting a more rational, multi-source search strategy as children grow older. Rather, the main trend appears to be the increase in the importance of television as a source of product information.

In any case, it is far from evident that any substantial consumer skills are attributable to children's cumulative experience with advertising. This is partly because of lack of measurement and partly because of questionable measurement. Consumer skills develop with children's cumulative experience with products. As we shall see in the next section of the discussion, there is no evidence that advertising contributes to this process other than perhaps, in quite a few cases, to initiate it.

One final consumer socialization effect centers on the allegation that cumulative exposure to television commercials leads to materialism. "Material-

Table 9-4
Sources of Product Information
(*percent*)

Information Source	Kindergarten	Third Grade	Sixth Grade
In-store observation	68	78	76
Interpersonal information	18	24	25
Mass media	32	65	71
TV's contribution	28	55	60

Source: Ward et al. (1975).

ism" is generally used to mean a preoccupation with money and possessions. For children this refers to a belief or value-orientation rather than to acquisitive behavior per se, since the latter is usually beyond a child's control. Two studies have attempted to measure materialistic orientation as a function of age (Atkin 1975c; Ward et al. 1975). Both found a significant *negative* relationship indicating that materialism apparently decreases as children grow older. Despite the convergence of findings, however, the measures of materialism in both cases are such that naive answers as well as materialistic ones could product high scores.[14]

Some evidence that materialism may be at least temporarily instigated by commercials was provided in an experiment by Goldberg and Gorn (1978). Children (ages 4 and 5) were randomly allocated to test conditions in which they did or did not see commercials for the "Ruckus Raisers Barn" (a toy) in the context of a ten-minute neutral program. The children were then shown separate pictures of two boys, with one of the boys empty-handed and the other holding the Ruckus Raisers Barn in front of him. As the experimenter showed a child the two pictures, he would say:

> I can bring one of these two boys to play with you. I can bring this boy who is not so nice and you can play with him and his Ruckus Raiser Barn, or I can bring this boy who is nice. Would you like to play with the nice boy, or would you like to play with the boy who is not-so-nice and his Ruckus Raisers Barn?

Some 70 percent of the control group (who had not seen the commercial) opted for the "nice boy," while only 35 percent of those who viewed the commercials chose the "nice boy"—the majority chose the toy. This difference was still significant (although smaller) when subjects were retested 24 hours later.

The researchers speculated that if commercials can encourage a materialistic, personal orientation which goes against common social values in the short-term, they may do so in the long-run as well. This study raises some hypotheses that bear further examination with a wider range of operational constructs, a more varied population, and most importantly, longer-term measurement of children's values. At present, the materialism issue—and especially its long-term implications—is best regarded as unresolved.

Heavy Viewing Effects

So far we have examined volume effects in terms of the average child's responses at each age level. Earlier we noted that there is considerable variation in the volume of exposure to television advertising within each age level. We now turn to a consideration of the effects of television commercials as a function of television exposure while holding age constant, to see whether the heavy viewers differ from light viewers in their responsiveness to commercials. Once again, we shall organize our analysis in terms of cognitive effects, affective effects, behavioral effects, and consumer socialization effects.

Cognitive Effects: In the previous section, we discussed three cognitive effects—attention, trust or believability, and overall cognitive understanding of commercials. It literally seems true that heavy television viewers pay more attention in total to commercials than light television viewers. This does not mean that heavy viewers necessarily pay more attention to each commercial, but simply that heavy viewing is likely to result in a greater aggregate volume of attention to commercials.

Heavy child viewers tend to place more trust in commercials than light viewers. Based on believability ratings of two commercials, Atkin (1975g) found a correlation of $r = .22$ ($p < .01$) with television exposure.[15] No corresponding finding has been reported for commercials in general, but such a finding is implied in correlations between television exposure and attitude measures which include believability or trust scales.

The third cognitive effect, children's understanding of the general concept of commercials, does not appear to vary with exposure to television commercials. Using the six-variable measure of cognitive understanding described previously, Rossiter and Robertson (1974b) found a nonsignificant correlation of $r = -.06$ with television viewing. Further analysis by the same authors (1976) indicated that exposure differences accounted for less than 4 percent of the variance in cognitive understanding compared with 40 percent for age and 9 percent for social background.

Affective Effects: Heavy viewers tend to have more favorable attitudes toward television commercials. Children's attitudes toward commercials become more negative as they grow older, but heavy viewers *within* age groups hold more positive attitudes than their peers. For example, Rossiter and Robertson (1974b) found a significant correlation of $r = .10$ ($p < .05$) between attitudes and television exposure with age held constant. (The measure of attitude in this study included trust, liking and behavioral intention scales.) Similarly, Atkin's research with specific commercials found a correlation of $r = .30$ ($p < .01$) between liking and exposure. For older children at least, it seems improbable that liking of commercials "causes" television viewing. Surely, interest in programs leads to viewing. Therefore, it is a fairly safe assumption that, for commercials, the direction of cause and effect is from exposure to attitudes.

Behavioral Effects: Heavy viewers express stronger behavioral intentions toward television advertised products. In November and December of each year, even children who are normal viewers become heavy viewers of commercials for toys and games (Barcus 1976a). A study focusing on pre-Christmas advertising by Robertson and Rossiter (1976b) found that the proportion of such toys and games in children's top-five Christmas requests increased by 5 percent over the heavy advertising period. This increase occurred at all grade levels—first, third, and fifth—a result significant at the .05 level, with no age by effect interaction.[16] Correlations between choices and various information sources indicated that exposure to toy and game commercials was the dominant causal factor.

The increase in children's behavioral intentions as a function of pre-Christmas advertising exposure was paralleled by another behavioral variable: request frequencies. Atkin (1975g) found a similarly significant correlation between television exposure and request frequencies for toys and cereals ($r = .29$, $p < .01$).[17] Both the Atkin study and the Robertson and Rossiter study focused on products of more relevance to younger children. This is not a confounding factor, however, since with heavy exposure effects, we are dealing with differences within particular age groups.

In sum, the evidence[18] from these various measures of cognitive, affective, and behavioral effects suggests that heavy viewers, in the main, respond more favorably to commercials than their light viewing peers. Heavy viewers do not seem more "persuasible"—heavy viewing is not related to cognitive understanding— but they may see more commercials to be persuaded by and thus evince more favorable attitudes and make more frequent requests than light viewers.

Consumer Socialization Effects: Earlier, we looked at children's satisfaction with advertised products as an indicator of whether exposure to commercials in volume affects their apparent ability to judge them. It was shown that satisfaction with advertised products increases with age. However, the same research study that provided the evidence for this conclusion (Robertson and Rossiter 1976c) also found that, within age groups, satisfaction was lower among those children who were above average television viewers.[19] Although the overall results were statistically significant ($p < .05$), a more detailed breakdown indicates that the heavy viewing effects were primarily located among the younger children, as shown in table 9-5.

Table 9-5
Satisfaction with Toys and Games Received at Christmas
(*percent*)

	Light Viewers	Heavy Viewers
First grade	92	76
Third grade	92	90
Fifth grade	95	93

Source: Robertson and Rossiter (1976a).

Since the measure of satisfaction asked children to state whether the products were better, the same, or worse than their expectations, it is reasonable to infer that expectations were inordinately raised among young children most heavily exposed to toy and game advertising. That is, heavy viewing first graders had the highest incidence of "disappointment" or below expectancy ratings (24 percent). The data also suggest that by third grade, heavy viewers have learned to develop more realistic expectations about products—probably due to greater experience with products as well as greater cognitive understanding of commercials. This is an example, therefore, of a volume effect which seems to apply only to a particular age group—in this case, the youngest children.

Results from the Robertson and Rossiter (1976c) study also indicated that heavy viewers experienced more disappointment over nonreceipt of advertised products ($p < .01$). Again this effect was strongest among the younger age groups, as shown in table 9-6.

A contrary result was reported by Atkin (1975g). In his study, he found a nonsignificant relationship between children's viewing levels and "conflict and anger" reported by mothers following denial of requests for toys and cereals. A likely explanation of the discrepancy in the findings is that Robertson and Rossiter focused on Christmas present requests, whereas Atkin focused on requests throughout the year. One could argue that expectations of receipt are considerably higher at Christmas time. Also, since many of the younger children's requests were made to "Santa" rather than to parents, there may have been less reluctance to admit disappointment in the Robertson and Rossiter study. A contrary possibility is that the reporters in Atkin's study (parents) may have been more reluctant to admit disappointment by their own children.

The safest conclusions from these results are that under conditions of a very high volume of advertising (like commercials for toys and games at Christmas), heavy viewers in the younger age groups are more likely to have their expectations about products raised by advertising. Accordingly, they are more likely to experience less satisfaction with products they receive and more dis-

Table 9-6
Disappointment over Nonreceipt of Requested Toys and Games
(*percent*)

	Light Viewers	Heavy viewers
First grade	30	44
Third grade	39	44
Fifth grade	24	27

Source: Robertson and Rossiter (1976a).

appointment over those they do not receive. It is not known to what extent these heavy viewing effects hold under normal volume conditions.

Turning now to the effects of heavy viewing on children's consumer knowledge and skills, we would expect that if television commercials contribute positively to this type of socialization, heavy viewers would be standouts within each age group. In their study of kindergarten, third grade and sixth grade children Ward, Wackman, and Wartella (1975) included television exposure with twenty-four other variables in an attempt to predict various consumer skills via regression analysis. Unfortunately, the investigators employed some recombinations of the original items in their survey and it is impossible to determine from their report exactly which items ended up in which particular new or "hybrid" variable. Even if we assume that the recombinations are meaningful, the results provide little evidence that frequent exposure to commercials facilitates acquisition of consumer skills by children. Sixteen skills areas were used as dependent variables and separate regressions were conducted for each of three age-groups. Of the resultant total of forty-eight regressions, television exposure appeared in sixteen of the equations as a significant predictor variable.[20] However, in half the cases, the relationships were negative, indicating that heavy exposure to commercials was associated with *poorer* acquisition of consumer skills. Moreover, there was no systematic pattern underlying the other half of the cases in which exposure showed positive relationships with consumer skills. Because of the relative failure of the television exposure variable for two-thirds of the "consumer skills" equations, and because in the remaining third it showed contradictory results, it is impossible to conclude that heavy exposure to commercials produces any consumer socialization benefits.

On the supposedly less beneficial side, let us briefly reexamine the issue of materialism. We may recall that, despite the questionable validity of the measures, both Atkin (1975g) and Ward et al. (1975) provided data suggesting that materialism decreases with age. However, holding age constant, further analysis by Atkin indicated that materialism was positively related to television exposure ($r = .10$, $p < .05$). As remarked earlier, much better instruments are required for measuring consumer values such as materialism, but the finding seems worthy of mention for future investigation.

Atkin (1975c) also reported another set of findings which cast a somewhat different light on the heavy exposure phenomenon. We noted in the previous section that children who are heavy viewers express more favorable attitudes toward commercials—trusting them more, liking them more, and being more likely to respond favorably to them. These attitudes should work both ways. It might be expected that heavy viewers should also respond more favorably toward "prosocial" commercials. Atkin tested children's reactions toward three public service announcements which advocated, respectively, use of seat belts, avoidance of littering, and emphasis on nutrition rather than sugar in foods. Heavy viewers were no more likely than light viewers to endorse the positions advocated in the commercials.

In sum, heavy viewing of commercials does not appear to result in extended benefits such as faster acquisition of consumer knowledge and skills.

Clustering Effects

Proponents of clustering children's commercials in blocks between programs argue that this practice would help children to distinguish advertising material from program material. Two studies have been conducted on clustering effects. Atkin (1975b) tested children's reactions to seven commercials in a single clustered presentation versus the same commercials distributed in four groups: once before, twice during, and once after a half-hour program. Duffy and Rossiter (1975) used a somewhat more representative format in that the cluster condition was taped from an actual Post-Newsweek children's program. Fourteen thirty-second commercials appeared around this program, six in a cluster beforehand and eight in a cluster afterward. A distributed version of the presentation was constructed by distributing the commercials in a 3, 4, 4, 3 sequence before, after, and at two logical breaks within the half-hour program, preserving the original order of the commercials.

Neither study can provide unequivocal evidence for or against the hypothesis that clustering aids program-commercial separation (see chapter 1), because neither methodology employed "in process" discrimination measures. The Duffy and Rossiter study attempted to infer discrimination based on shifts in the children's visual attention between the last two minutes of program preceding each onset of commercials and the commercials themselves. Among the youngest children in the study (first graders), the clustered format, which included an audio commercial warning, actually produced a smaller attention shift between program and commercials than the version with regular distribution. To the extent that visual attention is an indicator of discrimination, no evidence was obtained in favor of the hypothesis that clustering aids children's program-commercial discrimination ability. This finding should not be accepted as conclusive, however, in the absence of corroborating evidence from more direct measures of discrimination.

Both studies were able to provide evidence relevant to the "advertisers' hypothesis" that clustering produces poorer commercial performance. Two measures frequently used by advertisers are audience ratings—a rough, relative measure of attention—and recall scores. Atkin (1975b) found that clustering actually produced significantly greater visual attention than the normal distribution. Duffy and Rossiter (1975) found that clustering produced slightly, though not significantly, greater visual attention among first graders but significantly less attention among fourth graders.[21] Paradoxically, the result for the older children seemed to be due not so much to the commercials as to apparent irritation with the long stretch of *program* occasioned by the clustered format; perhaps older children have become used to commercial breaks. In any case, if younger children are the main subject of concern, it seems that clustering does not affect attention and may actually increase it.

The other measure of interest to advertisers is commercial recall. Adult research by Weik (1974) indicated in a laboratory study that the clustering of more than six commercials in a series leads to a significant drop in brand-name recall for commercials that follow the sixth. However this finding is contradicted by field research which indicated no differences in recall when up to eight commercials (the maximum number studied) are clustered together (Ephron 1975). The children's studies by Atkin and Duffy and Rossiter support the no-difference contention. Neither study found any difference in brand name recall for the clustered versus distributed presentations.

Ephron also presented a Gallup and Robinson field recall study which showed a deleterious effect if commercials for competing brands within the same product category appeared within thirty minutes of one another. Since the closer the two commercials were together, the weaker the recall, it appears that clustering could be detrimental for competing brands; although not for non-competing brands. Neither of the children's studies was in any way extensive enough to test this idea—an important one from the advertiser's standpoint.

Another problem in all of this recall data is that none of the studies investigated clustering effects for new commercials versus familiar ones. It is quite possible that, at the time at which the clustering effects were measured, familiar commercials could already have attained their peak recall levels from previous exposures. In this respect, the clustering manipulation, particularly in the experimental studies, might be quite superfluous since recall may actually have been attained under unclustered, or at least differently ordered conditions. A totally new commercial that appeared regularly in the middle position of an extended cluster might well have its recall performance reduced.

In sum, the evidence on clustering as a (short-term) volume phenomenon is inconclusive. Clustering does not appear to help children to discriminate between commercials and programs, but more valid measurement is needed before this primary argument in support of clustering is settled. Similarly, there seems to be little evidence to support advertisers' fears that clustering will affect the performance of individual commercials, but neither can they be put to rest since *new* commercials and competing brands have not been studied in the clustered format proposed for children's advertising.

Repetition Effects

Our final topic in the area of volume and repetition is repetition, which is defined as frequency of exposure to a single commercial rather than to commercials en masse. There are two principal allegations concerning repetition of individual commercials. One is that repetition leads to stronger persuasion effects. This is an allegation that interests advertisers as well as critics of advertising, and we can review the evidence for this contention without regard to whether stronger persuasion is valued as desirable or undesirable.

The second allegation is that repetition produces "irritation." There has been no research on repetition and irritation with children's commercials, although Greyser (1973) reported this to be a frequent complaint about commercials among adults. We shall regard irritation as being a secondary effect of repetition and one that is rather arbitrarily and subjectively defined.[22] In any case, as mentioned, there is no children's research to review. Of more interest and importance is the first allegation: the relationship between repetition and persuasion.

Incidence of repetition estimated from the Barcus data earlier suggested that the average child sees most commercials (60 to 80 percent) at a rate of about once a week, but that some may be seen as often as twice a day or more. Does rate make a difference? Secondary evidence from a review of learning research indicates that "learning proceeds at just about the same rate regardless of the interval of time that elapses between successive responses" (Hulse, Deese, and Egeth 1975). For "responses" in our case, we may substitute "attentional exposures" as the type of response relevant to commercials.[23] Pending first-hand evidence from studies of children's commercials it therefore seems extremely doubtful that differences in repetition *rate*, at the frequency that children are likely to encounter them, would make any difference in terms of learning whatever is advocated by the commercial.

A second parameter is the number of repetitions. We could not estimate from the incidence data how many times children see particular commercials. However we may guess that ten times is a fairly typical figure and that three or four times might be a minimum figure unless the commercial is backed by an extremely light media expenditure. Secondary research in learning (Hulse et al. 1975) again suggests that the number of exposures may not make much difference—at least for learning. In fact, some theorists have recently argued that the effect of repetition is not so much to increase learning as to *prevent forgetting*. That is, many of the fairly simple responses associated with children's commercials (for example, brand-names and basic brand attributes such as appearance, vitamin content, or premium offers) may be learned in just one or two trials, and the effect of further repetitions would be to ensure that the child "re-remembers" what was originally learned and might otherwise forget.

This theory has interesting implications. Besides proposing that repetition may make a child less likely to forget a brand-name, it also suggests that repetition would not be likely to change a child's attitude toward the brand, since what would be remembered would be the originally learned attitude. Thus, unless we are willing to accept an argument to the effect that brand-name recall is a sufficient definition of persuasion rather than the commonly understood definition involving a change in attitude or behavior, it is possible that repetition—or at least beyond one or two exposures—actually has no effect on persuasion. In fact, this theory fits the available data remarkably well. Adult research in a number of studies by Ray, Sawyer, and Strong (see Ray 1973) has shown that the effect of up to six repetitions of a commercial is mainly to increase brand name recall. Measures of liking and intent to purchase the product are minimally affected by repetition.

Most "laboratory" studies of children's commercials reviewed in this report have shown the test commercial only once. The exception is series of five laboratory studies by Gorn and Goldberg (1974; 1977a; 1978; Goldberg, Gorn, and Gibson 1978; and unpublished). Only one of the studies tested brand-name recall (Gorn and Goldberg, unpublished). As suggested by learning theory, repetition increased brand-name recall from one to three exposures; however, five exposures produced no further increase. All five studies tested the effects of repetition on children's attitudes or preferences. Four of the five studies found no effect beyond the first exposure. The fifth study (Gorn and Goldberg 1977a) found no repetition effect on children's attitudes toward the advertised toy but did find that three exposures led the children to work harder to obtain the toy in a post-experimental context than did a single exposure. Low income children were the subjects in this study and the authors speculated that three exposures may have been necessary to overcome these children's common real-life expectancy, confirmed by mothers, of rarely receiving advertised toys. With one possible exception, therefore, these laboratory studies suggest that repetition of commercials does not affect children's liking of or requests for the advertised product: preferences (or nonpreferences) seem to be established the first time the commercial is seen.

Another laboratory study by Atkin (1975c) produced interesting evidence on the *field* effectiveness of repetition. Approximately one hundred fourth and fifth grade children were shown a commercial for a well-known complexion remedy; half of this group saw it once, the other half twice, a few minutes apart. Another one hundred or so children from the same sample base were not shown the commercial. Atkin analyzed the results in terms of those children who reported having already seen the commercial at home, versus those for whom this was an initial exposure. Correlations with the laboratory treatment variable (shown-not shown) are depicted in table 9-7. These results indicated that the "additional" lab exposure had essentially no impact on those children who had seen the commercial before. In contrast, "first time" viewers showed significant effects.[24] A separate analysis was conducted on those who saw one versus two lab exposures of the commercial. Again, consistent with the theory, the only effect of the multiple exposure was on brand name recall.

In sum, there is little evidence that either the *rate* or *number* of repetitions affect children's tendencies to be persuaded by a commercial. Number of repetitions can affect brand-name recall, but neither attitudes nor desire for the product seem to be affected beyond one or two exposures.

Table 9-7
Effectiveness of Repetition

Effect Measure[a]	Seen Before at Home	First Encounter
Information recall	.02	.22
Believability	.02	.27
Liking of brand	−.07	.28
Intent to buy brand	−.08	.27

Source: Atkin (1975c).

[a]Atkin's longer list of effects measures is summarized here, and appropriate correlations are averaged for convenience of presentation.

Finally, there is the issue of brand-name repetition *within* a commercial. Incidence figures put this at 3.65, on average, with perhaps a quarter of all children's commercials repeating the brand name five or more times (Atkin and Heald 1977). The Duffy and Rossiter (1975) study examined the relationship between audio brand-name mentions and brand-name recall. The correlation was effectively zero ($r = 0.06$, n.s.). This could either be interpreted to mean that the recall aspect of the repetition theory does not hold for within-commercial repetition, only for separate exposures to a commercial, or that with familiar commercials, as these may have been, brand-name recall had reached a ceiling. Even if brand-name repetition were effective, brand-name recall, as an effect, would not in our view constitute sufficient evidence of persuasion. It is, of course, conceivable that brand-name repetition affects other responses such as attitudes or intentions; however, as discussed earlier, this seems unlikely. Also, repetition as a phenomenon "within" commercials has not, to our knowledge, been a really controversial issue compared with the more general phenomena of rate and number of individual commercial repetitions.

Summary and Conclusions

Long-term Exposure Effects

Perhaps the most impressive body of research on children's responses to television commercials has been that which documents the dramatic age-related increase in their cognitive understanding of the nature and purpose of commercials and the equally dramatic decline in their feelings toward TV commercials as an institution. Paradoxically, however, their behavioral responsiveness to commercials—as reflected by stated desires for advertised products and by frequency of requests to parents for these products—declines only slightly over this childhood period. The paradox involves a real contradiction only if we assume that commercials should *not* be responded to. If most commercials children see are nondeceptive and promote bona fide products, there is no reason why increased cognitive understanding should reduce children's preferences for the products advertised (nor why lack of cognitive understanding should increase them). To hold other than this view is to assume that deceptive practices and shoddy products are the rule in children's television advertising. Still, part of the paradox remains: why do children develop such negative attitudes toward advertising as they grow older?

The answer is probably just what it appears to be—the acquisition of attitudes toward advertising which are currently prevalent in society. There is no evidence that children generalize this attitude to the products promoted in children's commercials.

Still unresolved is the question of whether long-term exposure to television commercials increases children's consumer socialization. The studies in this area all suffered from either inconclusive demonstrations of the role of advertising in the socialization process and/or poor dependent measures of consumer socialization phenomena. The solution to the first limitation involves more precise "tagging" of advertised versus nonadvertised items as well as comprehensive measurement of other variables that affect consumer learning besides television advertising. The role of television advertising could then be assessed through experimental or statistical controls.

The solution to the second limitation is to develop more valid and reliable measures of consumer socialization effects. The validity problem is complex, but we could proceed well beyond the current state of measurement by excluding measures with questionable face validity. The reliability problem is simple by comparison, since it involves basic procedures of an item analysis and measurement replication (see Rossiter 1977).

A type of research that is needed mainly for theoretical reasons is longitudinal measurement of commercial exposure effects on a single child. Longitudinal measures could then be replicated with many children to provide a more generalizable picture. The predominant alternative, of course, is the reliance on cross-sectional methodology to infer longitudinal effects.

Indeed, cross-sectional research is quite satisfactory for most decisions faced by children's advertising policymakers. No one has yet mounted a convincing argument as to how or why longitudinal research would greatly improve our knowledge of advertising's effects on children. There is, in fact, little evidence in current research to suggest that longitudinal studies with individual children would yield results that are significantly different from those derived from representative figures for the "average" child at various age levels.

Heavy Viewing Effects

Heavy viewing effects are somewhat different from long-term exposure effects in that they focus on the effects of volume within age groups rather than on the cumulative volume across different age groups. Perhaps the most important conclusion in conjunction with heavy television viewing—and, by implication heavy exposure to commercials—is that such viewing does not retard children's cognitive understanding of advertising. On the other hand, heavy viewing does not accelerate it either. The evidence on cognitive understanding seems to be clearly in favor of some sort of Piagetian explanation in which development processes are dominant, and stimulus experience, beyond a minimally typical level, does not seem to matter much.

However, heavy television viewers at each age level do tend to hold more favorable attitudes toward commercials and toward products they see advertised. This is especially pronounced at younger age levels, at least until first grade, and there is some evidence that this heavy viewer difference persists at a noticeable but diminished magnitude thereafter. But we cannot conclude that this apparent tendency for heavy viewers to be persuaded somewhat more often than their lighter viewing peers has anything to do with poorer *cognitive* capacity; this simply does not differ as a function of individual viewing levels within age groups.

A possible explanation is that heavy viewers tend to see more advertised products, and more products that they like, so that their aggregate liking of commercials and aggregate total of expectations based on commercials is higher because of differential product-generated reinforcement. This explanation is supported by the supplementary finding that heavy viewers are no more favorably predisposed than light viewers toward commercials such as public service announcements which do not involve "likable" products. We must conclude from existing evidence that heavy viewers may be more often persuaded, since they see more commercials, but not that they are more easily persuaded.

Robertson and Rossiter's research has offered the best measures of children's cognitive understanding of commercials to date because they are based on a comprehensive model of cognitive criteria developed from work by Paiget and Guilford. However, further refinement and testing would be a worthwhile endeavor because so many policy decisions in children's advertising have to do with deception and, specifically, with the capacity to be deceived or misled. What we need is a valid and reliable test to establish this capacity.

The first study that should be conducted to "norm" such a test should involve girls as well as boys (the latter were the subjects of the original Robertson and Rossiter research). Other studies (for instance, Ferguson 1975) suggest that across age-groups, girls will not substantially differ from boys; consequently, the preceding conclusions did not allude to what would otherwise appear to be a deficient sampling base. However, this should be corroborated by studies in which the cognitive measures are taken with children of both sexes.

Clustering Effects

A third aspect of the volume issue is posed by the question of whether clustering children's commercials would benefit children—or perhaps penalize advertisers. The evidence on both questions is inconclusive. The separation issue is unresolved because appropriate measures of children's discriminatory ability have not been employed in studies to date. The clutter issue is unresolved because experiments on clustering have used commercials that have already been aired and whose effects (brand-name recall, brand attitudes, and so on) could have been attained prior to the clustering manipulations in the studies. A further controversy arises over the possibility that commercials for competing brands within the same product category may suffer most from the greater likelihood of juxtaposition under a clustered format.

The program-commercial discrimination issue received detailed attention in chapter 3 of this book. Recommended improvements in methodology such as the use of signal-stopping techniques are equally applicable to research on clustering which seeks to test the hypothesis that this proposed format for children's commercials offers a policy-relevant benefit. Regarding future studies on the advertisers' hypothesis that clustering is an unfair imposition on the right of individual advertisers to reach their potential audiences, we reemphasize the importance of employing commercials never seen before. Otherwise, cluster effects will be confused with previously established responses to the commercials. This research should be particularly careful to control for serial position or order effects since these are critical to the contention about clutter.

As yet untested is a corollary to the advertisers' hypothesis that commercials for competing brands are more detrimentally affected by the clustering format than commercials for noncompeting brands. This corollary introduces an area of research that goes beyond the clustering issue. Competitive brand choice has rarely been investigated with children, especially with the predominance of single-commercial samples in children's advertising research.

Repetition Effects

We can be more conclusive regarding the effects of repeated exposure to individual commercials. There seems to be little basis for concern that repetition leads to greater persuasion—unless by persuasion we mean no more than the ability to remember the brand-name mentioned in the commercial. A considerable amount of secondary research in learning theory and the available primary research indicates that neither the rate at which children encounter a commercial (that is, frequency per program or per week) nor the total number of times they encounter it, beyond the first one or two exposures, has any incremental effect on either their liking of the brand or their intention to request or buy it. The effect of repetition seems to be mainly to prevent children from forgetting their originally learned reactions to the product.

However, these conclusions about the *rate* of repetition stem from adult research. Although the theory and findings are substantial, a replication with children's commercials as the stimuli would establish whether or not the absence of a rate effect generalizes to our specific domain of interest. Conclusions about the *number* of repetitions derives from both adult and child research. Therefore, further research in this area is not a practical priority, although repetition poses a fascinating pursuit for the theoretician.

Notes

1. Computed from Barcus' data in this table 17 (1975a) and table 21 1975b).

2. For example, Barcus' weekend report recorded 79.9 percent programs, 13.1 percent commercials, 2.8 percent program promos (for a total of 15.9 percent "commercial time"), 3.2 percent noncommercial announcements, and 1.0 percent taken up by station i.d.'s, dead air, and other miscellaneous material.

3. According to Barcus' figures, a full 98 percent of commercials in children's weekend programs are now 30 seconds in duration, versus a mixture of 60-second and 30-second commercials earlier.

4. Estimated from 1975 Nielsen data by taking the percent of viewing in each viewing category (see figure 2-2) and weighting these by co-viewing levels (see chapter 10).

5. This is a range estimate; precise variance figures are not available.

6. These stations are located in Hartford, Conn.; Washington, D.C.; Jacksonville, Fla.; and Miami, Fla.

7. PNS also limits commercial time to six minutes per hour in children's programming timeslots.

8. Station i.d.'s and promotions for the stations' own programs were excluded from our tabulations.

9. These maxima could be exceeded if an advertiser were to buy a concentrated time block on a single network. Probability of exposure would still be close to these estimates, however, due to channel switching between programs.

10. The widely heard criticism of the "lack of longitudinal studies" is not as serious as it sounds. Longitudinal studies are of more theoretical than practical interest. For practical purposes such as policymaking, cross-sectional studies are quite sufficient. Reasons for this are developed later in the chapter.

11. Faster "processing" could mean better acquisition and retention of information or simply better ability to recall the information, or both.

12. Atkin (1975a) also found a decline in request frequency with age. His measure centered on toys, cereals, and two individual commercials and is almost certainly biased in the same way.

13. The two other categories in the study were toys and clothes which

probably have decreasing and increasing appeal respectively across the kinder-garten to sixth grade age spectrum.

14. Atkin (1975c) used a composite measure consisting of preference for a brand-name cereal (why this should be "materialistic" is not clear), belief that toys produce happiness, and enjoyment in showing off products. Ward et al. (1975) used an "average" of four-point ratings of agreement with three items: (1) "Do you think people would be lots happier if they had more things like color TV's and big cars?" (2) "When I grow up the most important thing is to have lots of money." (3) "Do you think that to *really* be happy when you grow up you *have* to have lots of money?" The last item appears to be redundant and might well encourage a child who gave a "non-materialistic" answer to the second item to compound it in self-justification. The reader is left to evaluate the probable validity of both of these indices of material-ism.

15. All correlations reported in this section in conjunction with Atkin's research are fourth-order partials. That is, they reflect the correlation between the variable in question and television exposure *controlling for* or partialling out the effects of the following factors: age, sex, race, and school performance (an approximate surrogate for intelligence). Atkin's television exposure measure is based on reported viewing of Saturday morning children's programs (Atkin 1975g).

16. A conservative formula was used to compute the 5 percent figure. The normal "percentage increase" interpretation would have been about 8 to 10 percent at each grade level.

17. Unfortunately the major study of children's request frequencies (Ward and Wackman 1972) did not include television exposure as a variable. These investigators did find a very high correlation between "perceived influence of commercials" and request frequencies as reported by mothers, but as the authors observed, the obvious circularity of cause and effect here renders this result spurious.

18. Most of the evidence has been correlational and therefore unable to establish a causal linkage between exposure to commercials and children's attitudes and behavior toward advertised products. Recently, however, several laboratory studies have been conducted which demonstrate the ability of com-mercials to causally influence children's attitudes and behaviors; see Resnik and Stern 1977; Gorn and Goldberg 1977a; Goldberg, Gorn, and Gibson 1978. Another experimental study, by Galst and White (1976), suggested a causal relationship between commercials and product requests but did not clearly identify *advertised* products in the requests measures.

19. Heavy and light viewers were divided at the median in this study.

20. Ward et al. (1975) tallied 21 instances in which television exposure entered the regression equation. However, inspection of their data reveals that only 16 of these involved coefficients significantly different from zero

at $F_{(24,200)}$ which are the approximately applicable degrees of freedom for their study.

21. The Ward, Levinson, and Wackman (1972) study of children's visual attention provides a field validation of the Duffy and Rossiter attention measure. Ward et al.'s study was a naturalistic survey conducted during in-home viewing; Duffy and Rossiter's study was conducted in a potentially "artificial" classroom setting. Yet, using identical rating systems, the two studies yielded highly similar attention scores (see Duffy and Rossiter 1975).

22. For example, Greyser notes that people are far more likely to complain about commercials for product categories that don't interest them and to like equally repetitive commercials for product categories that do interest them. People may also be more likely to remember commercials that irritate them despite the amount of repetition.

23. For the more theoretically inclined we should note that this conclusion applied only to operant learning and not to classical conditioning. The response of paying attention to commercials, at least beyond initial attention, is clearly a voluntary or "operant" response.

24. Estimating the degrees of freedom for these correlations at 50, with bivariate correlations an r of .27 would be significant at the .05 level.

10 The Effects of Television Advertising on Consumer Socialization

Scott Ward

Consumer socialization refers to the continuous, ongoing process by which children learn skills, knowledge, and attitudes relevant to their present and future behavior as consumers (Ward, 1974). Although there is little agreement about what skills, knowledge, and attitudes comprise consumer socialization, it is understood various agents have a role in this process—parents, peers, schools, the community, as well as television advertising.

In some form, advertising surely affects children's learning about the marketplace. Parents report that children readily learn brand-names and jingles from advertising. Research has investigated various aspects of children's learning from commercials—for example, sources of product information (Caron and Ward 1975); consumer information processing skills (Ward et al. 1977); and learning about products and premiums (Rubin 1972; Shimp et al. 1975).

But what is the nature of advertising's contribution to consumer socialization? Does advertising contribute to a broader understanding of the marketplace, and does it help to develop "good" or "effective" consumer skills during childhood and later years? Or, does advertising interfere with the development of such skills?

A prior question which must be answered is what particular skills, knowledge, and attitudes comprise "effective" or "good" consumer behavior? Also, do the long-term effects of consumer socialization supersede the short-term effects of specific advertising? In other words, if children are "misled" by individual commercials, or do not fully understand some of them, is there evidence of cumulative, long-term harm? How do we define harm? Finally, how do we compare consumer behavior for those exposed to television advertising and those not exposed, since virtually all children growing up in this country are exposed to television from an early age?

Some of these questions were addressed in the preceding chapter, in terms of the effects of children's cumulative exposure to television advertising over time. Here, we will examine the issues in terms of television advertising as one of multiple factors that play a role in the process of a child's consumer socialization. The issue has become increasingly important in recent months, since the FTC's "KidVid" rule would propose banning advertising of certain products to young children, and requiring some advertisers to include nutrition messages in their advertising. To the extent that advertising contributes to consumer

185

socialization in a "good" way, banning advertising may hinder the process; on the other hand, the effectiveness of nutrition messages as proposed in the KidVid rule certainly depend upon children's abilities to understand them.

Research Evidence

In this section, we will examine available evidence on three major policy questions relating to consumer socialization: (1) *The process*—How does consumer socialization occur? (2) *Influences on the process*—What is the role of advertising relative to other influences upon the child? (3) *The outcome*—What is the impact on adult behavior of childhood consumer-related experiences?

Outcomes of Consumer Socialization

Three studies pertaining to the impact of early experience on later behavior are examined. They illustrate the ways in which the outcomes of consumer socialization have been considered: Guest (1942, 1955) simply examined consistency in brand references between childhood and adult years; Arndt (1971) attempted to examine parental impact on older offspring; and Ward, Wackman, and Wartella (1977) defined consumer socialization outcomes in terms of the development of information-processing skills.

In one of the few longitudinal studies in consumer research, Guest interviewed subjects regarding brand loyalty and then reinterviewed them after a twelve-year interval. At the time of the original interviews (1942), the subjects (third- to twelfth-grade chidren) reported their "favorite brands." The subsequent interviews in 1954 indicated a strong degree of "brand loyalty," since about one-third of the subjects maintained their preference for earlier-named brands, even when present use, age at original interview, IQ, and socioeconomic status were controlled. However, Guest's studies suffer from the common difficulties of longitudinal studies, in that only 20 percent of the original subjects could be located and/or returned the mail reinterview questionnaire, and brand availability could not be controlled. Therefore, his data cannot be considered conclusive.

Arndt examined parental influence on offspring's consumer behavior, finding significant agreement between college students and their parents regarding favorite stores, brand loyalty, and such social characteristics as opinion leadership and innovativeness. Arndt reported that college students and their parents differed concerning their perceptions of the importance of brand differences for various products, but it is not clear whether different kinds of items were purchased by college students and their parents or whether they purchased the same items but used them differently. Arndt also reported parent-offspring similarity in "behavioral variables" (favorite stores, opinion leadership, and willingness to try new products), but these findings may correlate with other variables, since the students lived at home. Moreover, the small sample (fifty-five students and parents) does not permit generalizations to the large population of college-aged students who do not live with their parents.

Ward, Wackman, and Wartella sought to define consumer socialization in terms of the development of certain information-processing skills. They examined data from 615 mother-child pairs, including equal numbers of children in kindergarten, third, and sixth grades. "Higher" and "lower" levels of information-processing skills in the children were conceptualized by the authors according to the cognitive abilities required. For example, higher-level skills included awareness of the purpose of advertising and use of multiple and abstract features of products in brand comparisons, while lower-level skills included brand comparisons on the basis of perceptual attributes and awareness of a few sources of product information. The authors found that consumer information-processing skills were strongly related to the children's age and level of cognitive ability—an indication that such skills do indeed develop from early to later childhood. However, the relationship of television advertising to the acquisition of these skills was not at all clear or consistent (see chapter 9).

In summary, there are no firm data to demonstrate that childhood consumer experiences, including exposure to advertising, have a direct impact on later adult behavior. There have been no extensive longitudinal studies, and we do not know which early events have a lasting impact and which do not. Cross-sectional data do exist, however, to describe the average development of consumer skills during the age span of approximately 5 to 12 years.

How Consumer Socialization Occurs

Data are scant and indirect with regard to consumer socialization. Bandura (1971a) points to the importance of an imitation theory of learning for studies of consumer socialization; and some recent research provides evidence that parents expect their children to learn consumer skills through imitation rather than through directed training by parents or schools (Ward et al. 1977).

The dominant theory in studies of consumer socialization concentrates on cognitive development. A study by Ward, Wackman, and Wartella (1975) attempted to integrate ideas about cognitive development and family interaction. After reviewing research on parental influences on children, the authors identified four classes of family influences which were expected to affect consumer socialization at various stages of children's cognitive development:

1. Goals mothers have for their children's consumer learning;
2. Mothers' behavior as consumers, focusing on their use of information in consumer decisions;
3. Mother-child interaction regarding consumer decisions in both mother-initiated and child-initiated learning situations;
4. Children's opportunities for independent consumer behavior.

The specific variables included in each category are listed in table 10-1, along with the socioeconomic status of the subjects.

Different family influences affected higher- and lower-level information-processing skills, depending on the stage of cognitive development of the child. For younger children, mother-child interaction was most strongly related to

Table 10-1
Family Influences Affecting Consumer Socialization

Mother's consumer education goals
Number of money goals
Number of quality shopping goals
Number of bargain goals
Degree of opposition to children's commercials

Mother's own consumer behavior
Frequency of using contextual attributes in purchases
Frequency of using price/appearance attributes in purchases
Frequency of using advertising attributes in purchases
Relative efficiency of information use in purchases
Total information use in purchases
Number of sources consulted in major purchases
Budget planning
Budget accounting

Mother-child interaction about consumption
Frequency of negotiating purchase requests
Frequency of refusal with explanation
Frequency of not yielding to purchase requests
Frequency of discussing consumption generally
Number of comments about commercials
Flexibility in responding to purchase requests

Children's opportunities variables
Number of different sources for money
Total child income
Frequency of taking child shopping
Child power in making purchases
Frequency of exposure to television commercials

Other
Family socioeconomic status

Source: Ward, Wackman, and Wartella (1977).

consumer information-processing development, while for older children, the learning seemed to proceed more through observation and imitation of mothers' behavior as consumers.

The authors also found evidence of three ways in which parents influence consumer socialization:

1. By directly influencing the rate of cognitive development of the child, which in turn affects consumer information-processing skills;
2. By influencing the child's use of existing cognitive skills in consumer situations;
3. By directly influencing the child's performance as a consumer, regardless of cognitive abilities.

A somewhat surprising, but tentative finding is that some kindergarten children can identify the selling purposes of advertising and display other consumer-related skills beyond what would be expected from theoretical descriptions of their cognitive-stage abilities. The most important variable predicting this higher-level skill was the frequency of consumer-related parent-child interaction. If this finding is replicated, it would suggest that parents of even very young children may have a major impact on relatively advanced consumer-information processing skills.

The proposition that even young children can learn consumer skills has received some empirical support in a recent study. Moschis, Lawton, and Stampfl (1968) exposed 2- to 6-year olds who were enrolled in a preschool program, to two different educational programs. One was based on Piagetian cognitive-development theory, the other on Ausubel's learning theory.

Piaget's theory suggests that development is a series of stages following each other in a set pattern, although the child's age at any given state depends upon the individual. Children learn through active manipulation and exploration of their environment. The preschool years are generally characterized as being in the pre-operational stage of development, during which the child is assumed to be incapable of understanding logical constructs and relationships, and to have difficulty going much beyond a perceptually defined world.

Ausubel's learning theory suggests that meaningful learning occurs when the child can nonarbitrarily relate new knowledge to ideas previously learned. Learning can best be aided through the use of general ideas which provide a base for subsequent knowledge. Teaching of the abstract general idea is followed by a series of more concrete and specific learning activities.

The author's note that the usual application of Piaget's theory to early childhood education starts with the premise that learning should be geared to the child's expected state of cognitive development. This would lead one to conclude that it would be very difficult to teach consumer socialization to preschool children because they are expected to be at a pre-operational level of development. Ausubel's theory on the other hand, suggests that preschool children can be taught these abstract concepts through utilization of a sequence going from general ideas to more specific concepts and facts.

Teachers in the preschool programs in this school based their lessons closely on these two theories. They were asked to prepare a ten-day teaching unit (in line with the theoretical principles) dealing with the following concepts:

store;

product;

need recognition;

seeking for product alternatives (consumer information);

price;

money to spend;

checkout;

choice of product (choice among alternatives);

paying for products (giving checkout person enough money, transfer of ownership).

Children were tested individually before the teaching began, at the completion of the ten-day instructional unit, and again approximately a week later. The dependent measure was a shopping game, which consisted of a simulated shopping area. Children were shown the area, told what products were available, and introduced to the checkout person. Each child was given ten cents. In the pretest and the initial posttest this was ten pennies; in the second posttest, they were given a dime. The child was then asked to pick the items he or she would like to buy, take them to the cashier, and pay for them. At the completion of the game the experimenter asked the child questions about shopping.

Scores were collapsed into the following four categories based on the type of shopping task involved: (1) money to spend compared to the cost of total number of items selected, *before* purchasing transaction; (2) purchasing transaction at checkout; (3) cost per item compared to overall cost of total items selected; and (4) money to spend compared to the cost of the total number of items selected, *after* purchasing transaction. There were no significant differences between the two groups on the pretest scores. Sex was also not significant in the pretest scores.

An analysis of variance for the two posttests showed no overall sex differences and no significant differences depending upon the time of testing. The data for both groups at the two test times were therefore pooled for the remaining analysis.

There were no significant differences between the four categories of tasks for the Ausubelian group, although there were significant differences for children in the Piagetian group. Children in the latter program found the questions concerning "purchasing transaction" the most difficult and those dealing with "money to spend" the easiest. There was a significant difference between the performance of the two groups.

Children in the Ausubelian program had greater knowledge of the amount of money they could spend when presented with a dime than did children in the Piagetian program. Both groups were equally aware of the relationship between the amount of money they had to spend and the cost of the products when they were given pennies.

The purchasing transaction at the checkout required that the child know the total cost of the products selected, give the cashier the right number of pennies, and show that it was correct to keep the remaining pennies (if any). Children in the Ausubelian group scored significantly higher in both their actions at the checkout counter and on related questions than did children in the Piagetian group.

The Ausubelian group also did significantly better than the Piagetian group when the total cost of the products selected was compared to the cost of the individual items, and when asked to make a final check of the cost of items selected compared to the amount they had to spend, after the purchasing transaction.

Theories of learning, cognitive development, and family interaction all may help to increase our understanding of how consumer socialization proceeds. The limited research to date suggests that the family plays a crucial role and that the process appears to change over the course of childhood, since parents treat different-aged children differently and children's cognitive abilities change. It also appears that early parent-child interaction is a key element, followed by the increasing importance of observation and imitation in later childhood. Finally, recent results suggest even young children can be taught consumer skills.

Influences on Consumer Socialization

Several studies have attempted to assess the relative influences of family, peers, and mass media on consumer socialization. A few have used self-reports to provide estimates of family, peer, and media influences on responses to advertising (James 1971), on purchase acts (Teter 1966), and on drug attitudes and use (Kanter 1970). The general finding is that parental influence decreases, and peer influences increases, with age. Mass media influences are reported to be low and constant over later childhood and early adolescent years. However, these self-report measures of influence are of suspect validity.

Ward and Wackman (1971) examined the relative influence of parents and media on four aspects of "consumer learning" among junior and senior high school students: (1) recall of TV commercial slogans, (2) attitudes toward commercials, (3) materialistic attitudes, and (4) self-reported effects of advertising on specific purchases. They reported that learning of slogans is more a function of intelligence than of TV exposure time. However, attitudes toward advertising and materialistic attitudes were both found to be related to the reasons given by the subjects for watching commercials. Particularly important were "social utility" reasons (the motivation to watch commercials as a means of gathering information about lifestyles and behaviors associated with uses of specific consumer products).

Younger adolescents talked more with parents about specific consumption practices and acts, but such intra-family communication was operative for *all* adolescents in mediating between exposure to advertising and purchases. In a partial replication of this study, Stephens and Moore (1974) and Moore and Stephens (1974) reported findings similar to Ward and Wackman. However, in contrast to the earlier study, the researchers found only marginal differences between younger and older adolescents in parent-child communication about consumption, and also found this communication to be infrequent. This may be due to different family characteristics in their semi-rural sample (Ward and Wackman's sample was suburban).

Using self-reports, Fauman (1966) studied the relative influence of parents and peers on brand preferences and brand loyalty among 250 boys (grades ten, eleven, and twelve) from predominantly working-class families. Both peer and parental influence on brand preferences were found to decrease with children's intelligence, but were not related to media exposure time. While parental influence decreased with age, peer influence remained constant with age, suggesting that this source of influence is established by early adolescence, or about tenth grade. However, the direction of influence is not clear. If a son is correct in reporting that he and his father use the same brand, it may be that the son has influenced the father's brand preferences, rather than vice versa. Brand loyalty was found to increase with age but decrease with intelligence and with increasing media exposure.

The results with respect to intelligence are not immediately clear. Perhaps higher intelligence is related to lower respect for peers' opinions, or with increased knowledge of consumption alternatives, or perhaps, given the concurrent effects of lower intelligence and higher media exposure, certain adolescents are more easily persuaded by different brand appeals. Fauman did not explore these interesting possibilities.

Cateora (1963) analyzed teenage consumption patterns and relative influences of peers and parents on some of these patterns. Self-administered questionnaires were completed by 189 juniors and seniors in one high school in a small city. Cateora found considerable homogeneity among adolescents concerning various consumer values and goals, including attitudes toward credit and saving; attitudes toward comparison shopping; relationships among quality, quantity, and price; and attitudes toward merchants and advertising. These values were relatively independent of social class.

However, inspection of the data reveals several curvilinear relationships between social class and consumer attitudes and practices: Lower-class and upper-class students often expressed similar attitudes, but these differed from those of middle-class adolescents. Such results may indicate that different experiences may lead to expression of the same attitude. For example, regarding attitudes toward quality versus quantity in buying apparel, the responses of middle-class adolescents who said they preferred to buy one pair of good-quality shoes rather than several pairs of lesser quality shoes may reflect their having experienced this choice, whereas the same attitudes expressed by lower-class adolescents may reflect their desire to be able to make this kind of purchase selection.

It appears that the studies of consumer socialization examined here reflect the conventional wisdom that parents become less important and peers more important as children enter adolescence. However, studies have examined only a few aspects of consumer socialization, and advertising is often not even considered. More data are needed before definitive statements can be made about the relative influence of different socializing agents. In these future studies, a major problem will be to identify, measure, and compare the degrees of influence of different socialization agents. It may be less important to try to specify how much various influences affect behavior than to understand how socializing agents *combine* to affect children. We might find, for example, that television advertising provides information and a short-term stimulus for product desires, but parents mediate these outputs in their offspring over much longer periods of time. Such a possibility is considered in our next chapter, on parent-child interaction.

Summary and Conclusions

If consumer socialization is defined in terms of development of skills, attitudes, and knowledge relevant to consumer behavior, then it is probably safe to conclude that television advertising is one of many influences on the process. What is not clear from existing research is whether television advertising contributes to "effective" or "good" consumer behavior patterns; whether advertising merely provides consumer-related stimuli which provide a catalyst in the process; or whether television advertising's influences contribute to any long-range socialization effects.

Data do not exist to support the contention that long-term consumer socialization obviates short-term issues pertaining to children's comprehension of individual advertisements. In any case, if one believes that children have a right to be able to fairly evaluate advertising messages, it seems advisable to separate short-term and long-term effects, regardless of how long the effects of commercials may last. There are also no longitudinal data to assess the long-range impact of exposure to advertising during childhood. Data do support the contention that advertising contributes to some elements of "consumer learning." However, the research emphasizes the primary role of the family in mediating advertising's effects and in contributing directly to consumer socialization.

The most compelling research need is indicated by the long-term nature of consumer socialization effects. It is clear that further research is needed on the extent to which early learning affects later consumer behavior. One view is that as people get older, role changes make early learning unimportant. The other view holds that early learning remains a primary determinant of later patterns of cognition and behavior. Both of these simple views may be misleading. It may be that the question is not how much early learning experiences influence later consumer patterns, but which aspects of early learning are important and which are not.

Perhaps the most vexing problem is specifying the outcomes—just what skills, attitudes, and behaviors comprise consumer socialization, and how can these reflect something of the "quality" of consumer behavior? A promising approach may be an information-processing framework, since it focuses on such complex cognitive skills as selection and use of information relevant to purchase decisions. Such cognitive operations are fundamental to purchasing behavior and are more important and explanatory than the simple cataloging of purchases over time, or the measurement of changes in consumer attitudes.

Extremely long-term longitudinal research does not seem necessary or desirable. Rather, research could combine longitudinal and cross-sectional design features (see chapter 12). Finally, research on consumer socialization would seem to require "naturalistic" kinds of data-gathering procedures; for example, using purchase diaries followed by retrospective interviews, rather than simple surveys which rely only on verbal-report data.

11 Television Advertising and Parent-Child Relations

Thomas S. Robertson

There has been considerable concern about the effects of advertising on family relations. This concern takes several forms:

1. Consumption requests by children, particularly those attributed to advertising, may strain parent-child relations.
2. This strain may be greatest among economically disadvantaged families, who presumably must deny most requests.
3. Denial may be frustrating to both parent and child, leading to guilt and resentment.
4. Children's requests may complicate family-consumption priorities, leading to maladaptive practices, especially among the poor.

Action for Children's Television (1971b) summarizes these concerns as follows:

> In the case of children's advertising, the purpose is to use the child as a surrogate salesman to pressure the parent into buying the product. This is unfair to the child . . . to the parent . . . and can be damaging to the parent-child relationship.

Some members of the marketing community hold a contrary view, claiming that advertising can result in a positive interaction between parents and child, teaching the child intelligent habits of purchase and consumption. For example, Banks (1971b) suggests that the exchange between parents and child "may actually facilitate the child's ability to cope with the realities of independent living." These concerns are addressed by the following research questions:

1. What attitudes do parents hold toward children's advertising? How much do they resent advertising's intrusion on family interaction processes?
2. What mediation do parents exercise regarding children's viewing behavior? How much parent-child co-viewing occurs and how much do parents control the amount of television viewing by their children and the types of programs watched?
3. How much parental mediation of children's product requests occurs? What level of requests do children initiate?

4. How do parents handle children's requests? What is the incidence of parental yielding versus denial?
5. What are the outcomes of parental mediation? How much conflict or disappointment results? What learning occurs from these interactions?

Current Regulation

The purpose of advertising to children is, of course, to encourage sale of a product or, as stated by NAD (1977), ". . . to encourage trial and repeat purchase." This inevitably involves parent-child interaction of some sort, since parents are in the pivotal role of mediators between advertising influences and trial or repeat purchase.

Nevertheless, advertising on children's programs must not exhort children to pressure their parents to buy. The NAB code specifically prohibits advertising-induced pressure: "Children shall not be directed to purchase or to ask a parent or other adult to buy a product or service for them." The NAD policy is essentially the same: "Children should not be urged to ask parents or others to buy any product."

Incidence

Consistent with the NAB code, national advertisers may no longer explicitly encourage children to ask their parents to buy a product. However, even before enforcement of this code, the incidence of such direct urging was very low. Winick et al. (1973), in a 1971 content analysis of children's commercials, found that only 1.3 percent of commercials encouraged children to ask their parents to buy. Atkin and Heald (1977) in a 1972-73 content analysis reported parental urging in only 2 percent of food commercials and 1 percent of toy commercials. However, advertisers are free to encourage children to request products from parents by means other than direct exhortation.

Research Evidence

Parental Attitudes toward Children's Commercials

There are two sources of data regarding parental attitudes toward children's commercials: (1) parents' complaints about children's commercials; and (2) survey research evidence on parental attitudes toward children's commercials.

Statistics on adult complaints about advertising come from the FCC and the NAD. In 1973, the FCC received some 55,000 letters commenting on or complaining about television. Of these letters, only 34 specifically complained about children's commercials. However, in 1974 the commission received over 100,000 letters commenting on advertising practices in children's television, of which 90 percent were negative. The impetus for this outpouring of letters was the efforts of Action for Children's Television.

The second source of data on parental complaints is the NAD, which in its first year of operation (1974), logged about 125 letters from the public concerning children and advertising. On the basis of these complaints, the NAD opened six formal inquiries. The unit also opened twenty inquiries based on its own monitoring of children's commercials (Campbell 1975).

For parents to complain about advertising to children requires considerable initiative on their part, since the means of registering complaints are not widely publicized. Thus, we must assume that the frequency of registered complaints may considerably understate the actual level of concern. In contrast, it may well be that surveys of parental attitudes regarding advertising and children may considerably overstate the amount and strength of negative sentiment. When asked, parents may feel obliged to comment negatively on advertising—especially advertising to children, although such attitudes may be relatively unimportant to them.

This issue is addressed in research by Bauer and Greyser (1968). In general, they find that adults do not regard advertising as particularly salient to them. Although adults express definite opinions when asked about advertising, it is not a topic that they spontaneously discuss or feel strongly about. In terms of overall attitudes, Bauer and Greyser report that 41 percent of the public is basically favorable toward advertising, 14 percent unfavorable, 34 percent mixed, and 8 percent indifferent. About 15 percent of the sample cites advertising as needing immediate attention and change.

When parents are asked to express their opinions about advertising to children, their reported attitudes are often considerably more negative. In a study conducted on behalf of Action for Children's Television, Yankelovich (1970) found that many mothers complained about commercials, especially misrepresentation of the product, manipulation of the child, and strains on low-income families. Another survey, by Ward, Wackman, and Wartella (1977), found the following profile of responses to children's commercials among 615 parents: strongly negative (23 percent); negative (50 percent); neutral (23 percent); and positive (4 percent). These negative attitudes are most pronounced among parents of younger, kindergarten-age children, but do not seem to be associated with social class.

Adult attitudes toward children's commercials are negative, but how strongly held are they? A survey by Atkin (1975g) suggests that a majority of parents are willing to pay the price of commercial interruptions on children's programs in order to have these programs continue. Based on a sample of 301 mothers of school-age children, Atkin finds the following:

1. Most mothers are opposed to banning commercials on Saturday morning television (53 percent opposed; 28 percent in favor; 19 percent maybe or don't know).
2. TV-advertised children's products are judged to be neither a better nor a worse value than unadvertised products.
3. Only 49 percent of mothers report having seen any Saturday morning commercials.
4. Only 22 percent of mothers can cite a particular commercial that they feel is especially bad for their children.

The mothers' opinions would not seem to be based upon much direct observations, since one-half of the mothers have not seen any Saturday morning commercials. This raises the issue of salience of parental attitudes toward children's commercials.

Research by Feldman, Wolf, and Warmouth (1977) also probed attitudes of a randomly-selected sample of 150 parents of children between 2 and 12 years old. These conclusions can be drawn:

1. The average level of concern about children's commercials is not as high as "the heat of the controversy might lead one to predict."
2. Nevertheless, 65 percent of the sample felt some sort of regulation is needed.
3. There is no apparent relationship between parents' expressed dissatisfaction with commercials and their monitoring of children's television viewing.
4. Level of concern about child-directed commercials is not predictable from demographic characteristics or from family characteristics—such as family size or age of children.
5. Among the two-thirds of the sample preferring regulation, 65 percent would prefer regulation by an independent citizen's group, such as ACT; 20 percent would prefer industry self-regulation; 10 percent would prefer government regulation; and 5 percent would prefer an electronic device that could be attached to the television set.

Thus, parents seem to wish to abdicate the responsibility for regulation of censorship to other sources. However, as the authors note, the phenomenon is more complex since parents have multiple goals for their children, including fostering responsibility, education, and exposure to different value systems. Parents may feel that the regulation of television viewing is in conflict with other socialization objectives. As Feldman, Wolf, and Warmouth conclude: "Only with an appreciation of the conflicts facing parents and an appreciation of the choices available to them can we assess what should be asked of them and what must be asked of the larger society."

Roper (1979) conducted a study of parental attitudes for the Television

Information Office of the NAB. The data shown in table 11-1 indicate, in general, that resistance to commercials on children's programs is much less than acceptance; that resistance declined somewhat between 1972 and 1978; and that resistance was somewhat greater among parents of the youngest children. We could dispute the wording of the questions asked as being perhaps less than neutral, as well as the validity of single question attitude scales. These results are, however, consistent with the Atkin (1975g) survey cited earlier.

Finally, Culley, Lazer, and Atkin (1976) examined attitudes toward children's commercials across a range of publics, including townspeople, advertising agency executives, Action for Children's Television spokespersons, and government (regulatory agency) personnel. The sampling in this research is far from

Table 11-1
Parental Attitudes Toward Children's Television Advertising
(*percent*)

"Now I'd like to ask you about commercials on children's television programs—and I mean all kinds of children's programs. Some people think there should be *no* commercials in any kind of children's programs because they feel children can be too easily influenced. Other people, while perhaps objecting to certain commercials, by and large see no harm in them and think children learn from some of them. How do you feel—that there should be *no* commercials on any children's programs, or that it is all right to have them?"

| | Total Sample | | People with children | | | |
| | | | Under 6 | | 6-16 | |
Response	11/72	12/78	11/72	12/78	11/72	12/78
Should be no commercials	32	28	39	36	31	27
All right to have them	60	65	58	59	64	68
Don't know/No answer	8	7	3	5	5	5

"If eliminating commercials on children's TV programs meant considerably reducing the number of children's programs, which would you favor. . ." (Asked only of those who said "Should be no commercials")

| | Total Sample | | | |
	11/72	11/74	11/76	12/78
Eliminating the commercials and considerably reducing the number of children's programs	38	35	54	50
Keeping the commercials to keep the children's programs	53	54	38	41
Don't know/no answer	9	11	8	9

Source: Roper Organization (1979), pp. 18, 19.

ideal, except for the townspeople respondents who were randomly selected. The methodology also varies in that the townspeople interviews were conducted in-person, whereas the other interviews were secured by mail. We should also be aware that the townspeople are not necessarily parents of children. Nevertheless, the comparison of attitudes among these groups is interesting, as shown in table 11-2.

Table 11-2
Attitudes of Consumer, Advertising, ACT, and Government Regulatory Agency Group Samples Toward Children's TV Advertising
(*percent agreement*)

Subject/Attitude	Consumer (n = 455)	Advertising (n = 71)	ACT (n = 51)	Government (n = 21)
TV Advertising effects on children Advertising helps develop a child's ability to make good consumer decisions	27	65	2	23
Commercials often persuade children to want things they do not really need	95	66	100	95
Television commercials lead to an increase in parent-child conflict	67	7	93	64
Television commercials often arouse anxieties and feelings of insecurity in children	51	3	75	41
Level of Regulation Television advertising to children should be more regulated than it already is	77	23	100	91
Children's television advertising requires special regulation because of the nature of the viewing audience	89	61	98	86
Advertising on children's television programs should be banned completely	32	3	89	36
Mode of Regulation Commercials to children should be regulated by advertisers themselves	54	63	14	23
Commercials to children should be regulated by the government	30	11	70	50
It is up to the parents to regulate children's television viewing behavior	93	97	81	67

Source: Culley, Lazer, and Atkin (1976).

In regard to the perceived effects of televised advertising on children, the townspeople and government samples express surprisingly similar opinions, while the advertising agency sample is considerably more positive and the ACT sample considerably more negative. In general, about one-quarter of the townspeople feel that advertising helps develop good consumer skills (item 1 in the table); about one-half feel that commercials may arouse anxieties in children (item 4); two-thirds feel that commercials increase parent-child conflict (item 3); and almost all the townspeople feel that commercials often persuade children to want things they don't need (item 2).

As to level of regulation, the townspeople favor an increase (item 5) but, as reported in other research, do not favor an outright ban on children's commercials (item 7). The ACT sample was the most regulation-oriented of all, by a substantial margin over the government sample (items 5, 6, 7). Given the regulatory alternatives, the townspeople are more inclined toward industry self-regulation than toward government regulation (items 8, 9), whereas the ACT sample places little confidence in self-regulation (item 8).

In summary, parents do appear to be concerned and to have some complaints about children's television advertising, but, for the most part, this concern is not so intense as to favor banning commercials altogether. Parents do favor increased regulation, with a preference for industry self-regulation and some sentiment for more government regulation. Parental opinions about children's commercials may not be strongly held or highly salient. Attitudes toward children's commercials obviously vary across publics, from advertising agency executives on the positive side of the spectrum to Action for Children's Television representatives on the negative side.

Parental Mediation of Television-Viewing Behavior

Here we are concerned with two main issues: the extent of parent-child co-viewing, and the level of parental control over the amount and type of programs viewed by their children. A related factor is the presence of multiple-television sets within a household and the resulting effects on family viewing patterns.

Parental control over the amount and type of programs viewed is a direct form of mediation. The presence of a parent as a viewing partner provides a further opportunity for mediation of program and adveristing content. Parents and children may exchange comments, and instruction may take place, even if it is not deliberately studied.

Co-viewing Levels: Levels of co-viewing vary by time of day, number of sets in a household, and age of the child. Nielsen data are useful in examining such co-viewing levels, since the distortions of self-reporting are avoided and the Nielsen sampling plan is well-developed.

Nielsen data (1975) reveal considerable differences in adult-child co-viewing levels by time of day, reaching a high of 70 percent for prime-time programming (7:30 to 11:00 P.M.), falling to 57 percent for weekdays (10:00 A.M. to 4:30 P.M. Monday to Friday), and showing a low of 20 percent for Saturday mornings. Unfortunately, the level of co-viewing during late afternoon (4:30 to 7:30 P.M.) weekdays, a time when children view heavily, is not reported. Nielsen data also reveal that co-viewing varies by specific program, but does not seem to have been affected by the rise in multiple set ownership from 1971 to 1975. Co-viewing is also found to be most pronounced for younger children.

Lyle and Hoffman (1972a) examined co-viewing patterns within a working-class community in a small town outside Los Angeles. There are obvious limitations to these data, including the nonrepresentativeness of the sample, reliance on child reports, and failure to examine patterns by time of day. Nevertheless, the data do reveal a broader range of co-viewing patterns, since they include siblings. The most complete data, for first graders, are as follows: watch with siblings (37 percent); watch with parents (8 percent); watch with siblings and parents (27 percent); watch with friends (8 percent); half alone, half with someone (14 percent); and mostly alone (11 percent). These data indicate that sibling co-viewing is the dominant pattern (37 percent) and that parent/children co-viewing is next most frequent (35 percent). The study also examined parental co-viewing by age and found a declining pattern as the child grows older.

Co-viewing was also studied by Bower (1973) with a national probability sample of about 1,900 households. It is subject to the same limitations of self-reporting and lack of time-segment breakdowns, and the data do not isolate the incident of child-only viewing, since the questions all refer to joint viewing patterns. However, Bower found that in multi-set households, sibling co-viewing is the predominant pattern (in 43 percent of cases), followed by husband-wife viewing (33 percent), entire family viewing (12 percent), and parent-child viewing (7 percent). For single-set households, the most common joint viewing pattern is the entire family (55 percent) followed by husband-wife (17 percent), sibling (13 percent), and parent-child (13 percent). Mother-child co-viewing is more common among blacks (20 percent of co-viewing) than whites (8 percent) and is slightly more common among white collar families (10 percent of co-viewing) than among blue collar families (7 percent). Bower also found that when mothers and children view together, the mothers determines the program in 37 percent of the cases, the child in 33 percent of the cases. In 27 percent of the cases a joint decision is made. The potential benefit of family viewing is interaction between parents and children about programs and commercials leading to learning. Corder-Bolz and O'Bryant (1978) have demonstrated that intervention by a significant adult "can greatly influence what a young child learns from programs. . . ." Unfortunately, however, as Greenberg et al. (1972) have concluded, television viewing is generally not accompanied by any significant family interaction directed toward the medium or its content.

Similarly, Ward, Wackman and Wartella (1977) find a very low incidence of discussion of TV commercials (p. 128).

Parental Control: Regarding parental restrictions of television viewing, Bower reports definite rules about children's viewing among 46 percent of college-educated parents and 25 percent of parents with a grade-school education. Surprisingly, the amount of viewing control is not related to children's age (see table 11-3). However, the *type* of viewing control does differ according to age. For example, parents of older children are more likely to forbid watching certain programs whereas parents of younger children are more likely to change the channel when they considered a program to be objectionable. Children from higher-education households have some influence upon which program the family is to watch, but children in households with less education more often

Table 11-3
Parental Control of Viewing
(*percent*)

	Age of Child		
	4-6 *(n = 197)*	*7-9* *(n = 217)*	*10-12* *(n = 189)*
Rules about Viewing Time			
Restrict Amount of Viewing			
Often	30	39	34
Occasionally	27	25	27
Never	43	36	39
Set special hours			
Often	41	48	46
Occasionally	26	18	22
Never	32	34	32
Rules about Program Content			
Decide on Programs			
Often	45	37	46
Occasionally	28	35	38
Never	27	27	11
Change channel when program is objectionable			
Often	40	27	30
Occasionally	30	36	40
Never	31	29	31
Forbid watching certain programs			
Often	39	39	52
Occasionally	27	29	22
Never	35	32	25

Source: Bower (1973).

decide program selection. In these latter households watching television is more likely to be encouraged to occupy the child's time—the "pacifier" role.

Further research by Mohr (1978), concerning parental guidance of children's Saturday morning viewing behavior, shows a very low incidence of advice —either positive or negative—about programs. In fact, only 8 percent of parents reported offering advice to the children in the sample (9 to 15 years old). Interestingly also, about 70 percent of parents reported never having seen the programs aired on Saturday mornings.

Consensus of Parent-Child Reports: There are two problems in evaluating research on television viewing patterns. The first is that television use is often accompanied by a variety of other activities, such as eating, reading, and studying (see Bechtel et al. 1972; Lyle and Hoffman 1972a). Thus, the term *viewing* can take on a variety of different interpretations, and consensus as to what constitutes parent-child co-viewing becomes problematic. For example, does joint viewing occur if a parent is in the same room but engaged in another activity? The second problem is discrepancies between parents and children in their descriptions of viewing patterns. Greenberg et al. (1972) found a significant lack of agreement between reporting by mothers and children on rules regarding television viewing. There was best agreement on the frequency of parents being present, good consensus on the amount of viewing with friends, but a relative lack of consensus as to the level of viewing by children alone.

Research by Rossiter and Robertson (1975) examined 253 mother-child dyads regarding television control and found that parents claimed less total viewing, more co-viewing, stricter control, and greater parent-child interaction than their children reported. Examining social class, the study found that upper-class parents consistently seem to give the more socially desirable response. Therefor, actual parental control by better-educated parents may be as low as that among the poorly educated, and we cannot necessarily accept the Bower data, since his figures are based only on parental reporting.

Mediation of Buying Behavior: Request Levels

Children act as consumers in several ways. Wells (1965) posits the following: (1) by making personal purchases—spending small amounts of money on their own; (2) by making direct requests at home; (3) by making direct requests in the store; and (4) by "passive dictation" (parents buying what they know their children willingly consume and avoiding what they resist consuming). Our concern here is primarily with request rather than independent purchases by children, since our focus is on direct parent-child interaction regarding consumption. This section examines the *incidence* of request; to parents; the next section focuses on the *process* of parental mediation.

In general, the research evidence indicates that the incidence of children's in-family purchase requests varies with the age of the child and the product category. There is also some tendency for social class to relate to the incidence of purchase requests.

Age of Child: On balance the research evidence indicates that requests decrease somewhat among older children (Wells 1965; Atkin 1975a; Ward and Wackman 1972; Caron and Ward 1975; Robertson and Rossiter 1976b; Clancy-Hepburn et al. 1974; and Robertson, Rossiter, and Gleason 1979). This may be due to a number of factors, including the child's increasing sophistication in dealing with parents in more indirect ways. The relationship between age and requests is not particularly strong, however, and is mediated by the product category involved (Ward, Wackman, and Wartella 1977). Furthermore, the relationship may even be curvilinear with lower requests among very young children and among older children (Galst and White 1976).

Product Category: Children are more likely to make requests for products which are frequently consumed by them, such as breakfast cereals, or of particular interest to them, such as toys. This is intuitively obvious but has been substantiated in a number of studies, including Wells (1965), Galst and White (1976), Ward and Wackman (1972), and Ward, Wackman, and Wartella (1977).

Social Class: There is mixed evidence concerning the relationship between social class and request levels. Some studies have shown a somewhat positive link (Atkin 1975a; Caron and Ward 1975; Wells and LoSciuto 1966). A study by Robertson and Rossiter (1977) has shown a negative link whereas recent research by Robertson, Rossiter and Gleason (1978) has shown the absence of a relationship.

It is, of course, difficult to demonstrate a cause-and-effect relationship in regard to the role of television advertising in encouraging purchase requests to parents. Nevertheless, there is evidence suggesting that television advertising's impact, relative to other information sources, can be fairly great under certain conditions.

Caron and Ward (1975), in a study of 84 third- and fifth-grade child-mother pairs, report that children cite television as the source of Christmas-gift requests in 27 percent of the cases, followed closely by friends in 26 percent of the cases. Television advertising as an information source was also found to increase in importance with the age of the child. In another assessment of television advertising's impact on Christmas-present requests, Robertson and Rossiter (1976a) found it to be the dominant information source among a sample of 289 first-, third-, and fifth-graders. This study also examined the "magnitude" of advertising effects by assessing the proportion of toy and game requests versus requests for other generally nonadvertised presents during the period of concentrated toy and game advertising preceding Christmas. During this pre-Christmas period, there was an approximate 5 percent increase in the proportion of toy and game requests across all grade levels. Furthermore, heavy viewers were significantly more likely to request advertised toys and games than light viewers.

Two exploratory studies by Clancy-Hepburn et al. (1974), of 50 and 55 children in grades 3 through 6, indicate a significant correlation between the number of requests made for food products and the amount of Saturday morning television viewing. However, the author cautions that "this could be a function of age." A positive correlation was also found between the child's attitudes toward advertising and the number of requests made. Galst and White (1976), have also reported a positive relationship between television viewing and purchase requests.

Atkin (1975g) assessed children's self-reports of request preferences among 738 children, from preschoolers to fifth-graders. Parallel data were also derived from 301 mothers of these children. Consistent with our earlier discussion, Atkin finds that the younger children are considerably more likely than the other children to report requesting cereals and toys after seeing commercials. Requests for cereals and toys appear to be roughly equal. In general, there is a reasonably strong consensus between mothers and children about the level of requests.

As reported in table 11-4, requests are significantly greater among heavy

Table 11-4
Advertising-Initiated Requests
(*percent*)

	Light Viewers (n = 444)	Heavy Viewers (n = 294)
"Many of the TV commercials are for toys— things like dolls and racing cars. After you see these toys on TV, how much do you ask your mother to buy them for you?"		
A Lot	16	40
Sometimes	64	46
Never	20	14
"After you see commercials for breakfast cereals on TV, how much do you ask your mother to buy the cereal for you?"		
A Lot	24	41
Sometimes	50	39
Never	26	20

Source: Atkin (1975g).

viewers of Saturday morning television than among light viewers. The correlation between viewing and requests is +.41, and drops to +.29 when age, sex, race, and scholastic performance are controlled. Atkin also correlates the amount of children's viewing, based on a combined mother-child measure, with requests for specific products, reporting a +.28 correlation between viewing and advertising-simulated cereal request, and a +.17 correlation for toy requests. Again, when age, sex, race, and school performance are controlled, the correlations fall somewhat, to +.22 for cereals and +.10 for toys. In summary, Atkin concludes: "There is a clear pattern of evidence showing that Saturday morning television advertising has an important influence on children's asking for ceral and toy products."

Television advertising, therefore, in an important information source for child-oriented products, primarily foods and toys. Such advertising encourages requests to parents, especially among younger children. Interestingly, this raises the question of the relationship between advertising and requests for non-child-oriented products. In research on the impact of proprietary medicine advertising on children, Robertson, Rossiter, and Gleason (1978) find a positive first-order correlation (controlling for grade) of .22 (.01 significance) between advertising and requests to parents. Thus, children are to some extent affected even by advertising which is not directed at them.

Process of Parental Mediation: Yielding/Denial

What are the levels of yielding or denial when children initiate purchase requests? In general, yielding varies by product category and seems to increase with the age of the child. The relationship between social class and yielding is inconsistent across studies. There is some preliminary evidence that parental attitudes toward television and advertising may be related to yielding levels.

Product Category: Yielding seems to depend on the product and whether it is primarily for the child's consumption. For example, Ward and Wackman (1972) report yielding levels of 87 percent for cereals, 63 percent for snack foods, 54 percent for games and toys, 42 percent for candy, 39 percent for toothpaste, 16 percent for shampoo, and 7 percent for pet food—all based on the report of mothers from middle-class families.

In an observational study of 516 families, Atkin (1975f) found that 62 percent of parents yield to the child's cereal "request" or "demand." In another observational study, Wells and LoScuito (1966) reported that parents acquiesce to 69 percent of the children's requests for cereal and 57 percent of requests for candy. Galst and White (1976) found in a supermarket observation study that parents yielded to 45 percent of children's requests.

Berey and Pollary (1968) also examined the relations between mothers and children in the purchase of ready-to-eat cereals. They found that the mother is a strong "gatekeeper" in children's selections, a finding that seems contrary to the Ward and Wackman and Atkin reports that parents acquiesce to most purchase requests by children for breakfast cereals. However, the Berey and Pollay data must be regarded as highly preliminary due to the limited sample size and measurement procedures.

Examining yielding patterns for toys, Caron and Ward (1975) found that parents yield to 31 percent of children's requests. Robertson and Rossiter (1976b) found that parents yield to 43 percent of children's Christmas-gift requests.

Thus, yielding levels seem substantial for child-relevant products. For cereals, the available research indicates parental yielding to roughly two-thirds of requests. Further research, however, should document yielding levels according to price and other relevant variables.

Age of Child: Positive associations between the child's age and parental yielding levels have been found in research by Ward and Wackman (1972), Atkin (1975a), Wells (1965), and Ward, Wackman, and Wartella (1977). Other research, however, failed to find this relationship, including that of Caron and Ward (1975), and Berey and Pollay (1968). The latter conclude that the mother's purchases of cereals are independent of the child's age, as well as the number of siblings, the mother's outside employment, and the number of trips to the store by the child.

The strength of the relationship between age of child and parental yielding may logically vary as a function of yet unspecified variables, such as social class and family structure. Berey and Pollary, for example, found that highly child-centered mothers yield less often to cereal requests, prompting these authors to speculate that ". . . given her overriding concern for the child's well-being, she tends to ignore the child and to purchase what she thinks will do the child the most good." (Berey and Pollay do not, however, examine the amount of conflict created by such overruling of child preferences.) According the presence of an age/yielding relationship, Wells (1965) offers an interesting hypothesis, "Older children are more selective and more circumspect . . . especially when the product is one they are going to consume themselves."

Social Class: Mixed results are obtained across studies when social class is related to yielding (Atkin 1975a; Caron and Ward 1975; Lyle and Hoffman 1972a; Ward and Wackman 1972; Ward, Wackman, and Wartella 1977; Wells and LoSciuto 1966). On balance, however, the weight of the evidence favors the hypothesis of a positive relationship between the two. However, it may well be that social class is not a particularly meaningful or robust variable in this context.

Parental Knowledge and Attitudes: Research on adolescents by Ward and Robertson (1970) suggests that television advertising may complement intra-family communication about consumption. Commercials sometimes do provoke family communications. Ward and Robertson found that adolescents in families with high levels of communication about consumption are more favorable toward advertising, and are more materialistic in orientation. Preliminary research by Clancy-Hepburn et al. (1974) further supports the interaction between parental attitudes and children's attitudes—in this case, toward food advertising. Children whose mothers have a good understanding of the validity of nutritional claims express significantly lower preferences and fewer requests for advertised foods and report lower consumption of these products. Furthermore, mothers with good understanding of advertising claims tend to yield less to children's requests for snack foods.

Thus, parental yielding may be a function of product, age of the child, social class level, and parental knowledge and attitudes. These few relationships certainly do not fully explain yielding or denial. Other variables, especially family interaction style, are undoubtedly involved, and multivariate analysis is badly needed to understand their relative impact.

Outcomes of Parental Mediation: Learning/Conflict

Parental mediation of children's purchase requests is both an opportunity for parental instruction regarding consumption and a source of possible conflict. Most existing research on children and advertising has focused on intrafamily conflict and disappointment. Almost no studies focus on possible positive learning outcomes.

Conflict: In research cited previously, Robertson and Rossiter (1976c) probed children's disappointment upon not receiving Christmas-present requests. Disappointment, measured two weeks after Christmas, is not as high as might be anticipated. Parents refused 57 percent of children's requests, and only 35 percent of the children indicated disappointment after denial. Of course, higher levels of disappointment might have been observed if measures were taken immediately after denial. Disappointment was most pronounced among younger children, children with high television exposure and, contrary to expectation, among children from homes with a high level of parent-child interaction. Regarding this last finding, the authors suggest that children from these homes may feel more let down if they have discussed presents but did not receive them.

Sheikh and Moleski (1977) measured the responses from children after a hypothetical request for a televised item was refused. Children were presented with a story in which the main character was quite similar to the real child. The main character watched a television program including commercials and then requested a toy he had seen advertised. When parents refused the request, the children felt the outcomes would occur: unpleasant affect (33.3 percent), acceptance (23.2 percent), aggression (22.7 percent), persistence (16.0 percent), and irrelevant responses (4.8 percent).

Atkin (1975g) focuses more on parent-child arguments and anger than on disappointment. One-sixth of the children report arguing with their mothers "a lot" and another one-third arguing "sometimes" after denial of toy requests. One-fifth of the children become angry "a lot" about toy denials, and two-fifths become angry "sometimes." For denials of cereal requests, the degree of argument and anger is basically similar but somewhat lower.

Atkin reports a tendency for arguments and anger to increase as children grow older, and a slight correlation between Saturday morning television exposure and a combined conflict/anger index. However, based on path analysis, Atkin concludes that television exposure has no direct link on conflict/anger, but works indirectly through increasing the frequency of children's product requests. In parallel interviews with mothers of these children, Atkin finds that mothers detect disappointment in 21 percent of cereal denials and 29 percent of toy denials. Overt anger is reported in 5 percent of cereal denials and 10 percent of toy denials. The correlation between television exposure and anger is .11 for cereals and .18 for toys.

In another study based on unobtrusive in-store observations, Atkin (1975f) recorded conflict and disappointment over parental denials of cereal requests. In the instances of denial, conflict occurred in 65 percent of the cases and unhappiness resulted 48 percent of the time. There is some tendency for conflict and unhappiness to be highest among 6- to 8-year olds. Atkin notes that "conflict is seldom intense or persistent. Displays of child anger or sadness are also short-lived in most cases." This research does not attempt to relate levels of conflict and disappointment to television advertising exposure.

However, an experimental study by Goldberg and Gorn (1978) assessed the extent to which exposure to a TV commercial for a toy affects a child's feelings toward a parent who denies a request for the advertised toy as well as the level of disappointment on non-receipt of the toy. A sample of 166 4- to 5-year-old children were randomly allocated to control and experimental groups. Children in the experimental groups ($n = 112$) viewed commercials for a toy (labeled "Ruckus Raisers Barn") in the context of a ten-minute neutral program. A control group ($n = 54$) viewed the program without any commercials.

Following exposure to the commercials and/or program material, children were shown pictures of the same boy either happily embracing his father or walking glumly away from him. The experimenter then asked: "I know a boy whose daddy didn't get him the Ruckus Raisers Barn; when his daddy didn't give him the Ruckus Raisers Barn do you think he wanted to play with his daddy like this . . . or do you think he wanted to go away from his daddy like this . . .?" While about three-fifths of the control group thought the boy would "still want to play with his daddy," only about two-fifths of those in the experimental groups thought so. The responses remained consistent twenty-four hours later. While some of the comparisons with the control group were not quite significant, the evidence appears to suggest that, at least in this experimental setting, exposure to TV commercials for toys can contribute directly to negative feelings on the part of the child toward a parent.

In order to examine the relationship between the child's level of disappointment upon nonreceipt of a toy and exposure to the commercial, each child was shown a picture of a boy watching television, with only the back of his head visible in the picture. The experimenter then asked: "You see this boy; he didn't get the Ruckus Raisers Barn, so he went to watch television instead. Do you think he was sad that he didn't get the Ruckus Raisers Barn, or do you think he was still happy because he could watch television?" Close to two-thirds of the control group thought the boy was "still happy" compared to about one-third of those in the experimental groups who gave the same response (twenty-four hours later the responses were slightly but not significantly close to those of the control group). It thus appears that direct exposure to a TV commercial for a toy increased the likelihood that children would consider failure to receive the toy as inducing "sadness." This approach to measuring the direct relationship between exposure to television commercials and various emotional and social outcomes would appear worthy of replication and generalization.

Learning: Children's requests provide an opportunity for parental teaching about consumption. This focus, however, has not been pursued in research. It would seem, for example, that parents' responses to children's requests could help to teach the child about the realities of the marketplace—whether explicitly or implicitly. In the Atkin (1975g) survey, the most frequent reason for parental denial of toy requests was "expense" followed by "poor value." Very few parents simply said no without further explanation. (Chapter 10 gives a fuller account of this perspective.)

Summary and Conclusions

Since the foregoing analysis is based on such scattered and incomplete research, we must consider it only a source of hypothesis for future studies. These propositions seem worthy of further research:

1. Parental concern. Parental attitudes toward children's television advertising are generally negative, but are probably not very strongly held or important in their lives. Parents seem willing to pay the price of children's

advertising if the alternative were discontinuing children's programming. However, they favor increased regulation.

2. Parental mediation of viewing behavior. Levels of parent-child co-viewing vary by time of day and are lowest, as might be expected, for children's programs. Co-viewing is considerably less prevalent than children viewing alone. Viewing rules for children appear to be more common among college-educated parents. However, parents from higher social-class levels may be giving what they consider to be socially desirable responses to the questions asked in research; thus, the actual exercise of parental viewing rules needs better documentation.

3. Children's requests to parents. Purchase requests generally decrease among older children. They vary by product and are highest for products frequently consumed by children (such as cereals) or of particular interest to them (such as toys). Exposure to television advertising is found to be associated with children's request for both toys and cereals.

4. Parental yielding/denial. Yielding to children's purchase requests varies by product category, and seems to increase with the age of the child. Yielding may also be associated with parental attitudes toward television advertising.

5. Outcomes: Learning and conflict. Disappointment, conflict and even anger are found when parents deny requests. Television exposure seems linked to these outcomes. How parents teach good consumer habits when responding to child-initiated requests needs systematic study.

Of all these themes, parental mediation of the effects of television advertising is certainly one of the most important topics for future research. The existing tentative findings badly need replication. New studies must be initiated to describe the nature of parent-child exchanges about advertised products and children's purchase requests.

Describing and analyzing interactions within families is a difficult research task. Because of the distortions of self-reports, greater use should be made of direct observation and unobtrusive research methods. Studies must also observe family interactions over longer periods of time than in current studies. Parent-child relations are hardly limited to those surrounding the influence of television advertising on children's purchase requests: future studies must place family interaction about consumption into the larger context of ongoing family exchanges. Such studies of the mediation of television advertising by parent-child interactions will be among our most difficult research undertakings. They will also be among the most significant.

12 Summary of Research Findings and Recommendations for Future Research

In the preceding chapters, we have reviewed the research findings relevant to the nine key issues selected as the framework for this book. In this chapter, we first summarize these findings in terms of these key issues, then offer a second summary which examines the research in terms of what it tells us about the stimulus properties of children's television advertising, the possible outcomes of children's exposure to advertising, and the role of mediating variables in affecting these outcomes. This alternative perspective is intended as a bridge to our overall recommendations for future research which appear at the end of this chapter.

Summary of Key Issues

Distinguishing Commercials from Program Material

Issue: Two issues regarding children's comprehension of commercials have been raised: The first involves the ability of a viewer to perceive commercials as distinct and separate material from the adjacent programming; the second deals with the viewer's understanding of their selling intent. Industry self-regulators have addressed the issue of commercial-program distinction by requiring broadcasters to use "an appropriate device" to separate commercials from surrounding programs during children's program hours and by restricting the use of program characters to promote products. More recently, the FTC has emphasized the issue of children's understanding of selling intent by proposing to restrict or ban advertising to children "too young to understand the selling purpose . . . of advertising."

Evidence: Studies have shown a positive relationship between children's age and their ability to describe the difference between commercial and program material; younger children either express confusion about the difference or use superficial perceptual or affective cues as the basis for the distinction. However, children as young as 4 years exhibit high familiarity with animated characters appearing in commercials and associate these characters with the products they promote. Neither the ability of children to distinguish commercials from programs nor the separation devices currently used to facilitate this distinction has been directly assessed.

Studies have also documented a positive relationship between children's age and their expressed understanding of the selling motives of commercials. A substantial proportion of children, particularly those below age 7 or 8, do not draw upon the concept of selling intent in defining commercials, in distinguishing them from programs, or in explaining their purpose, suggesting little comprehension and/or low salience of persuasive intent as a criterial feature of advertising. Research is needed which identifies how children acquire an understanding of the persuasive intent of television.

The Influence of Format and Audiovisual Techniques

Issue: Many audiovisual techniques in commercials are used to gain and hold children's attention. However, the television and advertising industries have also acknowledged the potential influence of commercial formats and production techniques on children's perceptions of advertised products. For example, industry guidelines for children's advertising prohibit use of production techniques which may tend to exaggerate or distort the characteristics or functions of a product and require the provision of specific audio and/or video disclosures. Policy issues arise with regard to the nature of children's perceptions about advertised products and their understanding of specific disclosures.

Evidence: Analyses of commercial content have documented the incidence of particular techniques or features of commercials designed for children. For example, they have found that formats vary substantially according to product class; whereas advertising for cereals relies heavily on animation, for instance, toy advertising is restricted to live-action formats. However, the issue of how particular formats and techniques contribute to or detract from accurate perception and interpretation of commercial content has been addressed by a limited (but growing) number of studies. For example, research has indicated that children's recall and comprehension of product disclaimers is influenced by the form in which they are presented; dual audiovisual claims communicate more effectively than video alone, and simplified wording significantly increases comprehension.

In general, the research evidence verifies that specific audiovisual features of commercials can make significant differences in children's learning. However, considerably more publicly available research is needed on the short-term as well as cumulative impact of specific presentational forms of commercials. Such a program of research might facilitate more systematic policy decisions regarding acceptable commercial practices.

Source Effects and Self-Concept Appeals

Issue: Characters as well as products appear in most children's commercials. Existing policy prohibits the use of certain characters as product presenters (for example, celebrities and authority figures) and prohibits the use of program characters as presenters in commercials within or adjacent to their own programs (host selling). Other presenter characteristics, particularly race, sex, and occupation, may contribute to the development of socially stereotyped perceptions. This topic also includes self-concept appeals, which promise or imply personal benefits to children from use or ownership of the product.

Evidence: A number of studies have demonstrated that the mere appearance of a character with a product can significantly alter children's evaluation of the product with the evaluation shifting positively or negatively, depending on children's evaluation of the endorser. This raises a potential fairness issue as to whether endorsement should be regarded as a legitimate basis for promoting products to children, since endorsement is not an intrinsic product attribute. One study on the host selling issue suggested that in-program placement of a commercial containing program characters was no more effective in stimulating children's desire for the product than nonadjacent placement, but only one commercial was tested in this study and the result has limited generalizability. The broader issue of whether commercials contribute to social stereotypes remains unresolved. The potential for stereotyping is apparent from content analyses of sex and race representation in children's commercials. However, analysis of commercial content is not the same as demonstrating that actual stereotyping occurs. Several experimental studies, on the other hand, indicate that positive stereotyping may be possible, for instance, in commercials that portray women in traditionally male roles.

Self-concept appeals have not been well researched. Although certain appeals undoubtedly imply benefits to children's health or social status, none of the few studies related to this topic has actually incorporated self-concept measures.

Premium Offers

Issue: Premiums are frequently employed in commercials for certain children's products, notably cereals. The FTC has alleged that premiums are an irrelevant product characteristic; that they distract children from considering legitimate product attributes; and that they multiply the difficulty of choice between brands. Defenders argue that premiums may actually facilitate the choice between otherwise fairly similar brands, and that premiums constitute a legitimate product attribute since they are part of the "total product package."

Evidence: The allegation that premiums are an irrelevant product character-istic is a value judgment and not amenable to empirical testing. On the other hand, we can test the allegations that premiums distract children from con-sidering legitimate product attributes and that they multiply difficulty of choice between brands. Only the first of these allegations has been tested, and only on a limited basis. Results suggest that inclusion of a premium in a commercial does not seem to distract children from other product attributes (as measured by recall of the content of the commercial), nor does the premium appear to increase children's evaluation of the product. These negative results should be interpreted with caution, however, since they are based primarily on a single study in which only one commercial was tested. The issue of whether premiums increase diffi-culty of choice between brands or facilitate choice by differentiating the total product package has not been investigated.

Proprietary Medicine Advertising

Issue: Although commercials for proprietary medicines are aimed at adults, children are exposed to such advertising when viewing other than children's programming (which represents a substantial portion of their total viewing time). It has been alleged that cumulative exposure to such advertising pro-motes a tendency to rely too heavily on proprietary medicines and may con-tribute to longer term use of illicit drugs. A recent petition to the FCC, which was denied, called for the banning of all medicine advertising on television before 9:00 P.M. Opponents argued that proprietary medicine advertising is never directed to child audiences, and that this advertising in intended to pro-mote the proper use of medicines.

Evidence: A large-scale study of the impact of proprietary medicine adver-tising on children indicates that it performs a limited role in the formulation of children's beliefs and attitudes toward medicines. Televised medicine advertising exposure is associated with modest short-term increases in children's beliefs and attitudes, but this increase is overshadowed by a significant decline in children's beliefs and attitudes with age. Televised medicine advertising is found to have virtually no impact on children's usage of proprietary medicines, since usage is largely controlled by parents. A study among teenagers found no relationship between exposure to televised medicine advertising and the use of illicit drugs.

Food Advertising

Issue: Food products constitute the most prevalent category of children's television advertising. Criticism of television food advertising targeted to children has been directed both at the products themselves—their high sugar content and the limited range of foods represented—and at the methods used to present these foods. With regard to commercial practices, for example, it is alleged that promotion of foods on the basis of characteristics such as sweetness, fun, magic, and premium offers encourages children to use nutritionally irrelevant criteria in making food choices. The FTC has considered restricting or banning commercials for highly sugared products during children's programs and/or requiring the provision of nutritional and health messages.

Evidence: Empirical evidence attests to the general effectiveness of food advertising to children. Children have been found to learn the information provided in food commercials, believe the product claims made about advertised foods, draw inferences about product benefits, and influence the purchase of the foods advertised to them. In the short-term, exposure to specific food commercials has produced significant increases in children's expressed preferences for the products promoted.

Research is needed that examines the relative effectiveness of specific formats and techniques in conveying comparable food product information, and that assesses the aggregate effects of television food advertising on children's food knowledge, preferences, and eating habits. The ability of television messages to communicate nutritional information to children also deserves more research attention.

Volume and Repetition of Commercials

Issue: Critics of children's advertising are concerned about the cumulative effects of commercials on children. These concerns reduce to four discrete issues: long-term effects (with age); effects of heavy viewing (within age-groups); clustered versus distributed placement of commercials within programs; and the effects of repetition of single commercials.

Evidence: The clearest findings in research on children and advertising are that children's understanding of advertising increases with age (and thus with cumulative exposure). Heavy television viewing within age-groups seems neither to retard nor accelerate children's understanding of commercials, although it does seem to produce more favorable attitudes toward advertising and advertised products. Behavioral evidence suggests, especially when age-relevance of products is taken into account, that there is only a slight decline in children's expressed desire for advertised products and in actual requests for these items over the period of childhood—this despite the older child's increased understanding of commercials and increasingly negative attitude toward advertising generally.

Clustered advertising formats have yet to receive adequate testing, but may help younger children to distinguish between programs and commercials by sharpening separation. Clear benefits in program-commercial separation should be documented before clustering can be justified. Finally, there appears to be little cause for concern that repetition of individual commercials leads to greater persuasion beyond children's ability to remember brand-names advertised. Neither the rate at which children see a particular commercial (frequency per program or per week) nor the total number of times they encounter it (beyond the first one or two exposures) seems to have any incremental effect on either liking of the brand or intention to request or buy it. The effect of repetition seems mainly to be to prevent children from forgetting their originally learned reactions to the product. Although individual commercials may be persuasive, research to date does not indicate that aggregated exposure to commercials in volume makes children any more or less persuasible, nor that repetition of individual commercials produces other than a reminder effect.

Advertising and Consumer Socialization

Issue: Defenders of children's advertising have argued that it contributes to children's general understanding of the economic environment and, more concretely, that it contributes to the development of children's product knowledge and consumer skills. Contrary to this view is the critics' allegation that advertising fosters undesirable social values in children, with materialism most often cited as an example.

Evidence: There is no doubt that television commercials play a role in initiating children's consumer behavior at all age levels. Commercials also serve as an important information source for products that are advertised on television, ranking lower than in-store observation but higher than interpersonal sources. Whether commercials are informative in the broader sense of consumer socialization is unresolved at this point. Long-term exposure to commercials (with age) has been shown to be accompanied by increases in the number of brands known in advertised product categories and by an apparent decrease in perceived differences between brands. However, since neither of these effects was associated significantly with television viewing levels within age-groups, it is impossible to conclude that advertising along was responsible for them. Unfortunately, attempts to measure consumer skills of other than brand awareness and differentiation have involved little attention to valid and reliable measurement and have revealed mixed relationships—usually neutral but as often negative as positive—between television advertising exposure and acquisition of these skills. Attempts to measure children's values and attitudes toward consumer behavior (for example, materialism) have suffered similar measurement problems. In summary, the role of advertising in the process of consumer socialization has not been adequately documented. Better measures are required as well as sophisticated research designs capable of isolating the contribution of television commercials from other socializing forces.

Television Advertising and Parent-Child Relations

Issue: Parent-child interactions can be viewed as either a *mediator* of television advertising to children or as an *outcome* of advertising. The mediation issue is to what extent parents influence the effects of advertising on their children. The outcome issue is whether advertising places strains on the parent-child relationship through parental denial of advertising-induced purchase requests. In both cases, questions are raised about patterns of parental yielding and denial, and the extent of conflict created by request denials.

Evidence: Parents' expressed attitudes towards children's television advertising are moderately negative, but most parents do not favor abolishment of children's advertising if it would mean discontinuation of children's programming. There is evidence that parents tend to overstate the degree of control they exercise over children's TV viewing and, simultaneously, to overestimate their children's understanding of commercials. These findings suggest that relatively little mediation of children's exposure and reactions to commercials occurs in most households. Mediation is much more likely to occur when children request products which they have seen advertised. Disappointment, conflict, and anger are reported when parents deny children's purchase requests. Further research is needed to examine the persistence of these effects, and also to gauge the extent to which parents utilize these occurrences for consumer instruction.

An Alternative Summary

We now step back from an issue-oriented framework to summarize the present state of knowledge in terms of what is known about the links between the stimulus properties of advertising, the possible outcomes of children's exposure to advertising, and the role of several mediating variables in affecting these outcomes. We present this alternate perspective as a bridge to our final, overall recommendations for future research which appear at the end of this chapter.

The following list of stimulus properties, possible outcomes, and mediating variables is almost certainly incomplete, but it provides a means for identifying the most important variable and the possible links among them:

Stimulus Properties

Amount and placement of advertising
Program-commercial separation practices
Nature of products advertised to children
Commercials *not* directed at children (drugs, etc.)
Content and techniques of commercials
> Format and audiovisual techniques (animation, music, pacing, special effects, etc.)
> Characters and spokespersons
> Product claims, disclosures, and disclaimers
> Premium offers

Possible Outcomes

Intended effects of advertising
> Attention to and recall of product brands and attributes
> Desire for advertised products
> "Trial and repeat purchases" of products or purchase requests to parents

Unintended effects of advertising

Short-range
> Confusion between program and commercial materials; failure to understand selling intent of commercials.
> Failure to comprehend product attributes or disclaimers (complexity of assembly or operation, role of a food product in a "balanced diet," etc.)
> Incorrect (exaggerated) assessment of product performance or of satisfaction provided by product
> Encouragement of unsafe behavior through imitation

Mid-range
> Encouragement of "inappropriate" standards for consumer choices (sweetness or "fun" rather than nutritional value; premiums rather than product attributes, etc.)
> Promotion of parent-child communication and/or conflict
> Learning about workings of marketplace and advertising (for example, comparing advertising claims with actual product)

Long-range
> Encouragement or reinforcement of unhealthy or hazardous behavior (for instance, poor nutritional habits, drug abuse)
> Encouragement or reinforcement of social values (for example, sex role or other stereotyping, distrust or cynicism toward society, unselfishness)
> Development of consumer skills

Mediating Variables

Child's characteristics (age, cognitive development, sex, socioeconomic status, intelligence, etc.)

Child's viewing patterns—volume of exposure to advertising

Parent-child interactions (parental control of viewing, co-viewing, control of consumption)

Other sources of consumer information (for example, peers, school, stores, other TV content, other media)

Stimulus Properties

The literature provides fairly detailed and extensive descriptions of the stimulus properties of television advertising directed at children. The two principal sources of this information are self-regulatory codes and content analyses. The former, the NAB and NAD codes, specify what is and what is not permitted in advertising to children, but, of course, these guidelines are prescriptive rather than descriptive of the actual content of children's commercials. Content analyses are more analytical, typically describing a sample of commercials according to such categories as products, audiovisual techniques, characters, and frequency. However, in the process of breaking down and coding specific attributes of commercials, the researcher sometimes neglects the affective dimension of each commercial as a whole—even though this may well be the most salient aspect of a commercial's impact on viewers. Nevertheless, content analyses are useful in defining the nature of the commercials seen by children, and there will be a continuing need for periodic analyses to keep knowledge of actual practices up to date.

Possible Outcomes

The effects of television advertising on children have been investigated by both experimental and survey-type studies utilizing a wide variety of outcome measures. Most experimental studies have been based on the assumption that advertising does have some effect on children, and have therefore been generally designed to test the relative effectiveness of specific techniques (for example, rational versus emotional appeals, standard versus modified disclaimers, premium offer versus no premium offer). Because of the specificity of these studies and the widespread use of nonstandard measures, their results can be generalized only to a limited degree. In addition, most experimental studies have focused on short-term effects which may diminish or disappear over time.

By contrast, broader survey-type studies have attempted to assess the impact of advertising on actual attitudes and behavior. However, the results obtained from surveys raise the question of the validity of self-reported data and do not permit inferences to be drawn about cause and effect. In addition, the existing survey-type studies do not always examine their results in terms of specific measures of children's exposure to television advertising.

With these qualifications in mind, we can nevertheless reach some conclusions about the intended and unintended effects of television advertising on children.

Intended Effects: It is clear that children pay attention to television commercials. Their level of attention seems to be dependent on several factors: attention is likely to be greater to commercials for products relevant to children and to commercials with higher levels of audio complexity or physical action. Research based on program material rather than advertising indicates that children's attention is enhanced by the presence of audio elements such as lively music, singing, rhyming, and sound effects; and visual elements as active movement, animation, and visual changes in general.

There is also considerable evidence about children's learning from commercials. A number of studies have found that children are able to recall or recognize products and product attributes after even a single exposure to a commercial. Comprehension and recall of disclaimers have been shown to increase when the disclaimer is in both audio and video tracks and when wording of the disclaimer is simplified.

The impact of advertising on children's attitudes and beliefs is of particular interest, since the most basic defining characteristic of advertising is its persuasive intent. The existing evidence indicates that advertising is at least moderately successful in creating positive attitudes toward a product and in stimulating requests for the product. In several surveys, a large majority of both children and mothers reported that the children asked for toy and food items advertised on television. Laboratory studies have found modest correlations between children's exposure to specific commercials and increased short-term desire for the products advertised. While repeated exposure to the same commercial (or different commercials for the same product) produced increased levels of recall, it did not lead to greater liking of or desire for the product. Evidence on the effectiveness of specific commercial techniques—such as the presence of product endorsers or premium offers—has been reviewed in the issue-by-issue summary.

Unintended Effects: It may be assumed that advertisers do not set out to confuse or mislead children, nor to promote unhealthy or socially undesirable behavior. Yet critics have claimed that such outcomes may in fact result from children's advertising, and most policy concern has focused on the issue of incidental learning or other unintended effects. (A notable exception is food advertising, where intended persuasion resulting in the consumption of sugared products also seems to be at issue.)

Among the short-term issues are: the ability of children to distinguish between program and commercial material; the possibility of children being confused or misled by specific features of commercials (like premium offers); and the role of commercials in promoting conflict between children and parents as the result of parental denial of advertising-induced product requests. In addition, the issue of the impact of adult-oriented advertising (for example, for nonprescription drugs) is almost entirely an issue of unintended effects, since these messages concern products presumably not of interest to children. Evidence on these issues has also been reviewed in the issue-by-issue summary.

In regard to the possible longer-range cumulative consequences of children's television advertising, most of the questions concern the influence of advertising on children's development of consumer skills, their formation of attitudinal and behavioral patterns in drug and food usage, and their development of broader social attitudes. On these issues, the research conducted to date offers relatively little guidance. Thus, although a body of research is available on the process of children's consumer socialization, little of it focuses explicitly on the contribution of television advertising. Whether television aids this process or conflicts with it remains to be determined.

Research on nonprescription drug advertising suggests that children's exposure to this advertising has little cumulative influence on their attitudes toward nonprescription medicines, their actual use of OTC drugs, or use of illicit drugs. Knowledge of the long-term effects of children's exposure to food advertising is very limited, but the available evidence suggests that children's conceptions of what constitutes appropriate breakfast and snack food as well as actual consumption patterns may be influenced by the products children see advertised. More research on this question should be a high priority because of the policy relevance of this issue.

Mediating Variables

It is evident that many variables mediate or influence the relationship between the stimulus properties of advertising and the outcomes which are observed. These mediating variables include sources of product information other than television commercials, children's experiences with advertising, and the extent to which parents interpret this experience for the child. Most studies to date have focused on television advertising and have been devoid of the family content, although researchers are increasingly taking a broader perspective and including more potential mediating variables in their studies.

The mediating variable that emerges most clearly in nearly every study is *age* (which is actually a surrogate index of more complex underlying processes including the child's cognitive development and experiential learning). For example, existing research indicates that, compared to older children, younger children are: more likely to believe claims they hear in commercials; less likely to recall specific features and information from commercials they have seen; and more likely to be confused by or fail to understand disclaimers. Perhaps most significant is the finding that young children frequently do not understand the selling intention of advertising. Taken as a whole, these studies demonstrate that children become more sophisticated in dealing with advertising as they grow older. This finding is hardly surprising in light of the considerable body of psychological literature documenting stages of child development in other areas. In fact, much of the research on age-related differences in relation to television advertising has been based on the prior work of Piaget and other child development psychologists.

While existing research firmly establishes age as an important mediating variable, the policy implications of this finding are less clear and are currently the source of heated controversy. From cross-sectional studies of different age-groups, it appears likely that young children's difficulty in understanding and assessing television advertising is primarily a short-term phenomenon, because older children do not show the same difficulty. However, from a policy standpoint, the question is whether negative effects, even in the short-term, are permissible. Thus, the Federal Trade Commission staff has argued that all television advertising directed to "children too young to understand the selling purpose of, or otherwise comprehend or evaluate, the advertising" is "inherently unfair and deceptive," and should therefore be banned (*FTC Staff Report* 1978). Industry representatives, on the other hand, have claimed that such exposure is harmless or even positive, because it provides children with trial and error learning experiences necessary for developing mature consumer skills.

Moreover, if exposure of young children to television advertising is ultimately judged to be a serious problem, several practical questions remain to be answered. One such question concerns the definition of "young children" for the purposes of policymaking. In its report, the FTC staff stated that "young children" were to be considered children "below (the) age of eight," but acknowledged that "it is difficult to identify precisely the age group that is too young to understand . . . advertising," and recommended that "comments and testimony in the (children's television advertising) rulemaking should address the appropriateness of this age definition." The FTC staff and its supporters have cited evidence to support its definition (for example, Ward et al. 1971; Ward and Wackman 1973b; Robertson and Rossiter 1974a), while industry representatives have argued that other research, using nonverbal measures, indicates that children much younger than 8 years old are able to understand the intent of advertising (Gianinno and Zuckerman 1977; Donohue, Henke, and Donohue 1978). Determining what constitutes an adequate understanding of advertising—and how this understanding should be measured—is obviously of critical importance.

Another practical question concerns how a ban on advertising to young children would operate. The FTC staff has suggested that "one possible solution would be to have the ban take effect when younger children constituted more than 'X' percent of the audience and adults constituted less than 'Y' percent." Another possible remedy suggested by the staff is "a scheme which eliminated television advertising whose 'dominant appeal' was to young children or which featured products which appeal primarily to, or were purchased primarily for, younger children" (*FTC Staff Report* 1978). In its Notice of Proposed Rule-making, the Federal Trade Commission itself asked for comment on possible alternatives to an outright ban, including "limitations upon particular advertising messages used and/or techniques used to advertise to very young children" and "limitation upon the number and frequency of advertisements directed at very young children" (Federal Trade Commission 1978).

At a minimum, then, it is clear that treating all children aged 2 to 12 as a homogeneous group (as is the case with most current policy) masks important, perhaps crucial differences. It is also clear that age is an essential mediating variable to be included in all future policy-related research on the effects of television advertising on children.

A second important mediating variable is the influence of parents. As recipients of children's purchase requests, parents directly mediate much of their children's consumer behavior. The existing research on this topic has focused primarily on parental compliance with or denial of children's purchase requests. Little attention has been given to the possibility that positive learning is provided, or can be provided, by these interactions. Also, parents (especially mothers) play key roles in controlling their children's television viewing, and there is some evidence of a discrepancy between mothers' reports of the degree of this control and the level of control reported by their children. This finding suggests the need for further study of how parents actually monitor and regulate children's viewing.

Recommendations for Future Research

Empirical research, no matter how extensive and well conducted, will inevitably remain but one element in determining children's television advertising policies. Ethical, legal, economic, and political considerations will continue to demand attention. Nevertheless, policies formulated in the absence or ignorance of research findings run the risk of being inappropriate, ineffective, or unfair. Research can guide policy by providing concrete information on the actual impact of television advertising on young viewers.

If research is to play a larger role in policymaking, several steps will be required. Policymakers must formulate their concerns as specifically as possible, so they may be subjected to empirical testing, and they must then give attention to research results when available. Researchers must be willing to undertake studies which address policy concerns more directly. In this regard, recent indications of interest in considering research findings on the part of both industry and government policymakers, and the response of researchers to that interest, are encouraging signs.

In terms of new research, we are recommending that future studies move in three directions more closely linked with ongoing policy concerns. We conceive of these as three levels of generality: (1) mid-level research to test specific hypotheses or premises on which existing or proposed regulations are based; (2) macro-level research on the role of television—and television advertising— in children's lives; and (3) micro-level research to document how children perceive actual, individual commercials. We set no priorities among these three levels; all are important and needed. Each is described briefly.

1. Mid-level research to address specific questions relevant to policy issues. Several current policy issues can be usefully addressed using existing research methods. Each of the literature review chapters contains specific suggestions for further research relevant to the issues discussed.

Such studies need not be elaborate, time consuming, nor expensive to conduct. If properly designed, they can have real impact on resolving outstanding policy issues. One methodological point should be noted, however. In previous research at this level (for example, on premiums), single commercials have often been employed to represent an entire issue, thus limiting the generalizability of the findings. The usefulness of future policy issue studies would be considerably enhanced if greater attention is given to selecting not only representative samples of children, but representative sample of commercials. In addition, the development of standard outcome measures would facilitate direct comparison of results across studies.

2. Macro-level research on the role of television and television advertising in children's lives. The research we are proposing here is intended to determine more definitively the importance of television as an influence on children in comparison with other major socializing factors, including parents, relatives, peers, school, church, and other media. There is a pressing need for studies which could help settle the prolonged controversy between those who believe television is simply an innocuous source of leisure-time entertainment, which children quickly learn to treat with a causal and healthy skepticism, and others who believe the medium has become a primary shaping force in children's lives, competing strongly with the traditional roles of parents, school, and church. The research we are proposing would not be focused on television, but rather on children and the shaping factors in their environment, *including* television and television advertising.

Such a program of research would be neither simple to organize nor inexpensive to conduct. It would undoubtedly require the extension of current research methods and the development of new techniques of measurement. Particular attention would have to be given to the validity of observational and survey measures. Despite these considerable difficulties, we believe that the effort would be justified by the importance of the results, not only to issues relevant to television and television advertising, but also to a variety of other issues related to the quality of children's lives in this country.

We are not proposing a multi-year, longitudinal study. Following the development of a group of children over an extended period of time might well produce the most revealing data, but the cost of carrying out such research, and the long delay in reporting results, make this a less attractive alternative. Rather, we envision a program of research with a relatively large and heterogeneous population of children (and other members of their families). It would employ a variety of techniques and measures to determine the relative importance of and the interactions between the sources from which children acquire the information that influences their values and attitudes and shapes their behavior. Among the project's objectives would be an examination of the role of television within the context of family experience, and an examination of family interactions within the context provided by television.

3. Micro-level research on children's perceptions of individual commercials. The research we are proposing here is at the opposite end of the spectrum from the preceding recommendation. The objective of this micro-level research would be to determine how well actual television advertisements for children comply with the NAD's admirable principle that children's commercials be "truthful, accurate, and fair to children's perceptions." This research would resemble the type of studies routinely conducted by advertising agencies in preparing commercials. It would focus on commercials as whole entities as well as on the specific techniques or component elements which were the concern of most of the academic studies reviewed in this report.

However, the research we are proposing differs from that conducted by advertising agencies in several important ways: It would be conducted systematically; it would employ randomized samples of commercials as well as of children; it would examine unintended as well as intended effects; and, of course, it would be publicly available. While the research would concentrate on commercials intended for children, it should also include adult-oriented advertisements. This research would not be costly, nor would it require elaborate facilities to conduct it.

The purpose of this research would be two-fold. First, it would allow the development of methods to identify specific commercials which are confusing or misleading to children. Second, it would lead to the accumulation of data about children's perceptions of commercials (based on children's responses to a range of actual commercials), which could be used to determine the comprehensibility and fairness of advertising for a particular product or product category or the effectiveness of a particular technique. Ultimately, it may be possible to develop a standardized instrument to test commercials prior to broadcast to ensure that they are, in fact, "truthful, accurate, and fair to children's perceptions."

Appendix A
Evaluation of
Individual Studies

David Pillemer and
Leslie Isler

This appendix is intended to provide a technical supplement to the literature reviews in the preceding chapters. It contains detailed analyses and evaluations of twenty-six empirical studies. This list of studies is by no means definitive. However, an attempt was made to include as many studies as possible which have made a distinctive contribution to the field and/or have been widely cited.

Each study is reviewed in terms of its purpose, population, sample selection procedure, sample size, outcome measures, experimental design, unit of analysis, statistical tests, results, and success.

The following studies are included:

9. Goldberg, Marvin; Gorn, G.; and Gibson, W. "TV Messages for Snacks and Breakfast Foods: Do They Influence Children's Preferences?" *Journal of Consumer Research* 5 (1978).   254

10. Howard, John A.; Hulbert, J.; and Lehmann, D.R. "An Exploratory Analysis of the Effect of Television Advertising on Children." Unpublished working paper, n.d.   257

11. Lewis, Charles E., and Lewis, M.A. "The Impact of Television Commercials on Health-Related Beliefs and Behaviors of Children." *Pediatrics* 53 (March 1974).   259

12. Liebert, Diane E.; Sprafkin, J.N.; Liebert, R.M.; and Rubinstein, E.A. "Effects of Television Commercial Disclaimers on the Product Expectations of Children." *Journal of Communication* 27 (Winter 1977).   261

13. Liefield, John P. et al. "Television Advertising and Children: An Experimental Study." Unpublished working paper, University of Guelph, Guelph, Ontario, Canada, 1974.   263

14. Milavsky, J. Ronald; Pekowsky, B.; and Stipp, H. "TV Drug Advertising and Proprietary and Illicit Drug Use Among Teenage Boys." *Public Opinion Quarterly* 39 (Winter 1975-76).   265

15. Robertson, Thomas S., and Rossiter, J.R. "Children and Commercial Persuasion: An Attribution Theory Analysis." *Journal of Consumer Research* 1 (June 1974).   267

16. Robertson, Thomas S., and Rossiter, J.R. "Short-Run Advertising Effects on Children: A Field Study." *Journal of Marketing Research* 13 (February 1976).   270

17. Robertson, Thomas S.; Rossiter, J.R.; and Gleason, T. *Television Medicine Advertising and Children*. New York: Praeger Publishers, 1979.   272

18. Rossiter, John R., and Robertson, T.S. "Children's TV Commercials: Testing the Defenses." *Journal of Communication* 24 (Autumn 1974).   276

19. Rossiter, John R., and Robertson, T.S. "Children's Television Viewing: An Examination of Parent-Child Consensus." *Sociometry* 38 (September 1975).   278

20. Rubin, Donald S. "An Exploratory Investigation of Children's Responses to Commercial Content of Television Advertising in Relation to Their Stages of Cognitive Development." Unpublished doctoral dissertation, University of Massachusetts, 1972.   280

21. Shimp, Terence A.; Dyer, R.F.; and Divita, S.F. "An Experimental Test of the Harmful Effects of Premium-Oriented Commercials on Children." *Journal of Consumer Research* 3 (June 1976).   283

22. Wackman, Daniel B.; Wartella, E.; and Ward, S. "Children's Information Processing of Television Advertising." Final Report to the National Science Foundation, 1979.   286

23. Ward, Scott, and Wackman, D. "Family and Media Influences on
    Adolescent Consumer Learning." *American Behavioral Scientist*
    14 (January–February 1971).   291
24. Ward, Scott, and Wackman, D. "Children's Information Processing
    of Television Advertising." In *New Models for Mass Communica-
    tion Research,* edited by P. Clarke. Beverly Hills: Sage
    Publications, 1973.   294
25. Ward, Scott; Wackman, D.; and Wartella, E. *How Children Learn to
    Buy: The Development of Consumer Information Processing
    Skills.* Beverly Hills: Sage Publications, 1977.   297
26. Wartella, Ellen, and Ettema, J. "A Cognitive Developmental Study
    of Children's Attention to Television Commercials." *Communica-
    tion Research* 1 (January 1974).   299

Study 1

Atkin, Charles. "Effects of Television Advertising on Children—First Year Experimental Evidence." Report #1, TV Advertising and Children Project, Michigan State University, June 1975.

Purpose: To examine the impact of various advertising practices on the knowledge, attitudes, and behavior of young children.

Population: Elementary and preschool children in the Lansing area.

Sample Selection Procedure: Five elementary schools and two preschools "were carefully selected to provide a substantial proportion of black students." Thus, they were not randomly selected. "Most" students in each school participated (parent's permission required). While the sample included subjects of all SES levels, it was "purposively skewed to over-represent children from less advantaged backgrounds."

Sample Size: n = 500.

Experimental Design: Subjects were exposed to one of the eight twenty-minute stimulus tapes containing entertainment material, advertising, and news. There were nine experimental hypotheses being tested. The basic design for investigating each of the hypotheses involved comparing half of the total subjects exposed to one version of the stimulus and the other half viewing an alternate version (while there were eight stimulus tapes, there were not eight different E treatments; rather, there were nine hypotheses for which there were two conditions).

The stimulus tapes were played to groups of four children at a time. It is unclear how these groups were formed. One of the eight stimulus tapes was randomly selected for showing to each group. One half of the subjects responded to post-viewing interviews, while the other half underwent a product selecting procedure. In addition, one half of all subjects were monitored for responses while viewing. The method for assigning subjects to these conditions is unspecified.

Outcome Measures: Coders rated the attentional and affective responses of half of the subjects during the tapes. Attention was rated on a five-point scale (amount of eye contact). Degree of enjoyment and irritation were rated on three-step scales (high, moderate, low). Verbalizations were coded according to topic and valence. Change in interest was rated on a three-point scale (increase, no change, decrease).

After viewing the tapes, half of the subjects responded to nonstandard interviews. The other half participated in a product selection and play condition. Behavioral and verbal preferences, expectations, and aggressive behaviors were recorded by an assistant.

Statistical Tests: Yes (t-tests, χ^2).

Results: This study of the impact of various advertising practices on the knowledge, attitudes and behavior of young children reports a large number of findings. Some are selected here:

1. *Premium offer strategy.* Children more often desired a breakfast food when the commercial featured a premium toy than when a premium was not mentioned; however, they were not more likely to anticipate asking their mother to buy it for them.

2. *Program characters appearing in commercials.* Those viewing a Flintstones cereal ad more often desired the product when the ad was shown in the context of a Flintstones cartoon than in a Bugs Bunny cartoon; this did not seem to be due to confusing the commercial with the content of the program, but rather a heightened identification with the program characters in the commercial.

3. *Rational message strategy.* A rational vitamin-oriented cereal ad was readily learned and equally successful in terms of recall and desire, compared to a standard emotional presentation of the cereal.

4. *Learning from public service announcements.* Those who viewed an anti-littering PSA less often exhibited littering behavior afterwards, compared to those who did not see this ad.

5. *Medicine advertising.* Children who viewed a Dristan commercial more often indicated that they would take medicine for a cold, thought pills were more effective, and perceived higher levels of illness in society, compared to those who did not see the ad.

6. *Disclaimers.* A toy commercial with an audio as well as a video super-imposed disclaimer of nonincluded batteries produced greater awareness of this qualification but created less product desire than a video-only disclaimer.

7. *Clustered versus dispersed structure of presentation.* Slightly greater levels of commercial attention, enjoyment, learning, and desire were obtained when commercials were bunched together rather than conventionally dispersed.

Success: It is difficult to determine if the treatments were generally successful, since a large number of hypotheses were tested. In general, attention to and learning from commercials were strongly related to the age of the subjects; the effects of the various treatments on learning and other behaviors is *mixed,* and depends strongly on the specific aspect of the program which is being considered.

Criticisms: The method of assigning subjects to the various measurement conditions is unclear. In addition, while stimulus tapes were randomly assigned to groups of four subjects, the method of assigning subjects to groups is unclear.

Ratings of subject responses (for example, degree of enjoyment) were based on observer judgments. It is obvious that these ratings may not accurately represent the subject's underlying condition. In addition, coder expectations may have unconsciously biased the results.

This study focused on short-term effects of TV advertising. It would be informative to conduct longer-term studies to supplement these findings.

The authors tested the significance of their findings with multiple t-tests, thus increasing the probability of a difference appearing due to chance.

Published: No.

Sponsorship: Office of Child Development.

Summary: This study tested several hypotheses concerning the effects of TV commercials on children's learning and other behaviors. Learning and attention were strongly related to the age of the subjects, while the effects of the various treatment manipulations on subject behaviors were mixed and depended on the specific hypothesis being considered. The study's major weaknesses are failure to specify how subjects were assigned to groups and measurement conditions, and the questionable validity of coder's ratings of subject behaviors.

Study 2

Atkin, Charles. "Effects of Television Advertising on Children—Second Year Experimental Evidence." Report #2, TV Advertising and Children Project, Michigan State University, June 1975.

Purpose: To test children's intentional and incidental learning from television commercials.

Population: Elementary-school students (grades 2 to 5) in Lansing and East Lansing, Michigan.

Sample Selection Procedure: While the author states that the schools represented "varying socio-economic neighborhoods," how these schools were selected is unspecified. "Almost every student" in the selected grades in each school participated in the experiment (with parents' permission).

Sample Size: n = 400.

Experimental Design: Subjects viewed one of four versions of a fifteen-minute videotape containing children's views, entertainment, and advertising content. The content of the commercials was manipulated across the four experimental tapes, to allow the testing of nine experimental questions. The students from each classroom were randomly assigned to two groups. One of the four stimulus tapes was randomly selected for showing to each group. After viewing the tape, subjects responded to a ten-page multiple choice questionnaire.

Outcome Measure: Ten page multiple-choice questionnaire (not standard).

Statistical Tests: Yes (χ^2 and correlations).

Unit of Analysis: Individuals.

Results: Many findings are reported; some are selected here.

  1. *Occupational sex roles.* The occupational role portrayed by a woman in an ordinary eyeglass advertisement was varied: one group saw her dressed as a court judge, another as a computer programmer, a third group saw her as a technician repairing TV sets, and the control group saw no eyeglass commercial. *Ss* who were exposed to a particular occupational model were more likely to select that occupation as appropriate for women.

  2. *Recreational sex roles.* The sex of children shown playing with a traditionally male-oriented racing car set was varied: one group saw two girls playing with the racing cars and the other group saw two boys. Not all *Ss* perceived the sex of the models, but those *Ss* who did perceive the actors to be girls were far more likely to feel that girls should appropriately play with racing cars and were slightly more desirous of playing with the toy themselves.

3. *Learning from public service announcements.* One group viewed a half-minute cartoon message emphasizing that sugar consumption produces cavities and may eventually cause teeth to fall out; the control group did not see this PSA. Exposed-subjects tended to believe that sugar causes cavities and makes teeth fall out, were more worried about getting cavities, and more often felt that sugar was not good for them. Viewers were slightly more likely to say that they would eat less sugar in the future.

4. *Medicine use.* The verbal script of a standard headache remedy commercial was altered to emphasize moderation in usage. Half heard conventional claims of speedy headache relief, while the others also heard the qualification that the medicine should be taken only "when you really need it" and that one shouldn't take "too many" pills for a headache. The qualified ad was just as effective in terms of brand awareness and acceptance of relief claims. There was a slight tendency for *Ss* hearing the qualified message to say that people shouldn't take pills for mild headaches and that they would personally take less pills for headache relief.

5. *Hero-figure endorsement.* In a commercial promoting a cookie product, the spokesman was dressed either in ordinary street clothes or in an astronaut uniform. The group viewing the ordinary spokesman were slightly more likely to want to eat the cookies than *Ss* exposed to the astronaut hero figure; there was no difference in the intention to ask parents to purchase the product.

6. *Comparative message strategy.* One version of a chocolate bar commercial employed a conventional "one-sided" strategy of describing only positive attributes of the product, while a "two-sided" version included comparisons with a competing brand along dimensions of size and nutrition. *Ss* in the two-sided condition were somewhat more likely to learn about the two attributes of the advertised product. Although many two-sided subjects mistakenly thought that they had seen an ad sponsored by the competing brand, they were no more likely to prefer the competitor; *Ss* receiving the one-sided message liked each candy brand about as well as the two-sided *Ss*.

7. *Message repetition.* One group saw a blemish-cream commercial once and half saw it presented twice several minutes apart on the tape. Those in the double exposure condition were more likely to remember the brand-name of the product and to worry about blemishes than those exposed once, but it did not express any greater liking for the product, intention to buy it, or belief in effectiveness.

Success: Depends upon specific hypothesis being considered.

Sponsorship: Office of Child Development.

Published: No.

Criticisms: As always, the validity of results obtained with nonstandard multiple-choice questionnaires is open to question. For this reason, the inclusion of behavioral indices would seem advisable.

The authors do not state the exact number of subjects at each age level viewing the different tape versions.

This study focused only on short-term effects. Also, the experimental setting (lack of diversions in experimental room) may have artificially heightened attention to commercials.

Summary: This study used a partially randomized design in investigating nine experimental hypotheses concerning the effects of TV advertising on children's sex-role attitudes and personal health, practices, and the persuasive impact of certain advertising message strategies and source attributes. The results differ according to the specific hypothesis under consideration. The study's major weaknesses are questionable validity of the outcome measure, and the artificiality of the test situation.

Study 3

Atkin, Charles. "Effects of Television Advertising on Children—Survey of Pre-Adolescent's Responses to Television Commercials." Report #6, TV Advertising and Children Project, Michigan State University, July 1975.

Purpose: To describe patterns of advertising exposure and evaluation in the naturalistic setting and to examine the role of commercials in late childhood socialization.

Population: Fourth through seventh graders from Michigan schools.

Sample Selection Procedure: While the author states that subjects came from "a number of schools in urban, suburban, and small town areas of Michigan," the method used to select these schools is unspecified. It is unclear if all available subjects within the chosen schools participated in the study.

Sample Size: n = 775.

Experimental Design: This study was purely descriptive. An "omnibus survey instrument" containing multiple choice and open-ended questions designed to measure children's responses to TV advertising was administered to all subjects. In addition, each questionnaire contained a supplementary set of items: 256 fifth-, sixth-, and seventh-grade students responded to a supplement containing questions about medicine, while 506 children (fourth to seventh grades) received a food and nutrition supplement. It is unclear how the supplements were assigned to subjects (but assignment apparently was not random).

Outcome Measure: Nonstandard questionnaire.

Statistical Tests: Yes (correlation coefficients).

Unit of Analysis: Individuals.

Results: Selected findings are:

1. *Advertising exposure.* Preadolescence is a period of heavy television consumption, with respondents reporting more than two hours of prime-time viewing each evening. They still view many Saturday morning programs (particularly fourth and fifth graders) and also watch teen-oriented music programs. These viewing patterns indicate that youngsters encounter a large number of commercials for a wide variety of product types. Across twenty-six specific ads, children report being moderately attentive when commercials appear.

2. *Evaluation of advertising.* Most children report being irritated by commercial interruptions; the sample is divided on the question of banning Saturday morning commercials, with younger children and those who are highly irritated tending to favor removal. Preadolescents are generally skeptical of the trustworthiness of TV ads; less than one-fourth think that commercials always

238

tell the truth. Children who disbelieve commercials tend to disbelieve authority figures such as adults and salesmen, but attention and liking of ads are not related to either form of distrust.

3. *Advertising and hygiene.* There are substantial positive associations between exposure to deodorant/mouthwash/acne cream commercials and worrying about personal hygiene, using hygiene products, perceiving the importance and societal usage of these products, and believing that the products work effectively.

4. *Medicine advertising.* Exposure to ads for headache/stomachache/sleeplessness remedies is moderately related to children's perceptions that people often become ill and rely on medicine, and to their personal concern about getting sick. Personal usage and approval of medicine is only weakly affected by advertising. There is no evidence that ads contribute to positive attitudes toward illicit drugs.

5. *Cereal advertising.* Children who watch the most cereal ads on Saturday television are much more likely to ask parents to buy cereals and to eat advertised brands; those from families with no snack rules are most strongly affected. Arguing with parents and becoming angry when requests are denied are mediated by increased request frequency. Advertising does not significantly affect beliefs of the value of sugar or the incidence of tooth cavities.

6. *Candy advertising.* Advertising has a modest impact on children's eating of advertised candy brands and quantity of candy bars consumed. There are negligible effects on beliefs about sugar and development of cavities.

7. *Advertising and nutrition.* Children most exposed to informational cereal messages stressing nutritional breakfast habits tend to recognize the importance of eating a good breakfast and to give higher nutritional ratings for the cereal, toast, and orange juice foods that are emphasized in these ads.

Success: Not applicable, since there was no treatment.

Sponsorship: Office of Child Development.

Published: No.

Criticisms: The study's major weakness is its total reliance on survey research; the degree to which questionnaire responses represent the subjects' true behavior is open to question. The author feels that "the field setting allows more confident generalization of the findings to the real world in which the children live." This study underscores the recurrent problem of choosing between controlled (and possibly artificial) experimental conditions and surveys.

The author includes specific commercials and TV shows in their indices. It is unclear how they were chosen, and it may be that these specific choices influenced the outcome, (for example, assessing reported attention to medicine commercials, a subject may attend more closely to those included in the questionnaire than to medicine commercials in general). In addition, in comparing some indices the author used a "multiplicative technique" which combined degree of attention and frequency of viewing. It is unclear why these relationships are multiplicative.

Study 4

Bever, T.G.; Smith, M.L.; Bengen, B.; and Johnson, T.G. "Young Viewers' Troubling Responses to TV Ads." *Harvard Business Review* 53 (November–December 1975).

Purpose: To examine trends in children's attitudes toward advertising during the years 5 to 12.

Population: 5- to 12-year-old children from middle- and working-class families in northern New Jersey.

Sample Selection Procedure: Unspecified.

Sample Size: There were six boys and six girls in each of four two-year interval age groups (5 to 6, 7 to 8, 9 to 10, 11 to 12) for a total of forty-eight subjects.

Experimental Design: Subjects were interviewed about morality, fantasy, economics, and TV commercials, and the responses were tabulated.

Outcome Measure: Nonstandard interviews.

Statistical Tests: None reported (although the authors state in the introduction that some were performed).

Unit of Analysis: Individuals (frequencies).

Results: The authors report in an anecdotal manner the ability of different age subjects to make judgments about fantasy, morality, and economics, and their reactions to TV advertising. Their reported results generally suggest that "children between 5 and 12 gradually learn to interrelate their understanding of fantasy, morality, and economics. This integration appears to coincide with an increased ability to deal with advertising. . . ." Children aged 5 and 6 "largely ignored advertising as being irrelevant to their lives," 7- to 9-year-olds "attempt with great difficulty and little success to integrate advertising into their lives," and at age 10, "they resolve the conflict temporarily through an overgeneralization that all advertising is misleading." Children aged 11 and 12 "resolve conflicts more satisfactorily . . . thus they can identify both the good and the bad aspects of advertising." The authors conclude by stating that "the 10-year-olds' anger towards misleading advertising as well as the 11- and 12-year-olds' increased tolerance of social hypocrisy raise serious questions about the role of TV advertising in the socialization of children." The only data supplied by the authors are two histograms which show the average number of children in each age-group who: (1) comprehend questions about morality, fantasy, and economics; and (2) are able to respond "figuratively" and/or "operationally" to advertising. Both histograms demonstrate increases with age.

Success: Not applicable (no treatment).

Published: Yes.

Sponsorship: Unspecified.

Criticisms: This study informally presents children's responses which support the authors' interpretation of their data. The reader needs more information to fairly assess the authors' conclusions.

No statistical tests are reported in this study and the method of selecting subjects for participation is unspecified.

While the authors cite the 7- to 10-year-olds' "limited operations powers" as a major reason for their problems in dealing with misleading advertising, one of the histograms indicates that approximately half of 7- to 8-year-olds were able to respond "operationally" to advertising.

Summary: This descriptive study suggested that children's sophistication with respect to their attitudes toward TV advertising increases with age. The data which are presented in support of many of the authors' contentions are informal.

Study 5

Caron, Andre, and Ward, S. "Gift Decisions by Kids and Parents." *Journal of Advertising Research* 15 (August 1975).

Purpose: To examine certain aspects of the relative influences of mass media and interpersonal sources on children's product desires and parental decision-making regarding their children's product desires.

Population: Middle- and upper-class mother-child pairs in Montreal. The children were third and fifth graders.

Sample Selection Procedure: Random.

Sample Size: Eighty-four mother-child pairs actually produced data (initial random included fifty-four third graders and fifty-two fifth graders).

Experimental Design: Four weeks before Christmas, subjects (children) were asked to write a letter to Santa, telling him what they wanted for Christmas. Children were asked where they got the idea for each gift requested. "Mothers were trained to unobtrusively record each Christmas gift request during a seven-day period and to note their verbal response (if any) to the child." A content analysis of television commercials directed to children in these age-groups was also conducted although not used in this study. Following Christmas vacation, the specific gifts which children received were noted.

Statistical Tests: Yes, but not all necessary tests were carried out (or perhaps, simply not reported).

Outcome Measures: Children's requests, mothers' notes of children's requests and their responses, and parent's buying behavior (not standard).

Unit of Analysis: Gift requests, gifts received, and individual subjects.

Type of Analysis: Descriptive and χ^2.

Results: Children requested "much the same kinds of items (to Santa, parents, or both) regardless of age or social class." Children most often cited television as the source of gift ideas, followed by friends. Older children were considerably more likely to cite TV and less likely to cite friends than younger children, and older children were more likely to cite catalogs (differences not tested statistically).

Younger children asked for more gifts than older children. However, they were less likely to receive specifically requested gifts. Middle-class children requested more gifts than upper-class children, and they requested more gifts from "Santa only." Middle-class children received more gifts, although the receipt of specifically requested gifts (conversion rate) was "very similar" in both economic groups.

242

There were significant differences (χ^2) in the types of gifts requested by children of different social classes, and there were also significant age differences. Sex differences were not significant.

Parents most often responded verbally in neutral terms (for example, "we'll see") to children's gift requests. The age and social class differences in parental verbal responses were not significant.

There were significant age, social class, and sex differences in types of gifts received. Fifty percent of the gifts received had been explicitly requested either in the letter to Santa or to the parents. The percent of specific gift requests that were fulfilled is "somewhat higher" for upper class children. Requests made both to Santa and to parents were most likely to be fulfilled. Middle-class families were more likely to yield to requests for certain types of toys, while upper-class parents were more likely to yield to requests for other types of toys.

Criticisms: This was not an experimental study. It is possible that mothers did not accurately record all of the children's gift requests and their own responses to the requests. In addition, participation in the research study may have affected parents' gift buying.

Since there was a high attrition rate, there should have been an effort to determine if those not producing data were atypical.

The authors state that older children more often cite TV as a source of product information, and that younger children are more likely to find out about products through seeing them in stores. However, their data indicate that the store is as often an information source for fifth graders as for third graders.

Sponsorship: Grants from Radio Canada and Marketing Sciences Institute.

Published: Yes.

Success: The authors did not initiate an actual program or treatment; thus it is not possible to evaluate the success of the study.

Summary: This nonexperimental study demonstrated several age and social class differences with respect to sources of gift ideas, gift requests, and gifts received, although the differences were generally not dramatic.

Study 6

Galst, Joann, and White, M. "The Unhealthy Persuader: The Reinforcing Value of Television and Children's Purchase-Influence Attempts at the Supermarket." *Child Development* 47 (December 1976).

Purpose: To examine the relationship between children's attentiveness to television commercials and their product requests, using the techniques of operant conditioning and direct observation.

Population: Children (aged 4 to 6) attending one of two affiliated Montessori nursery schools in Westchester County, New York, and their mothers.

Sample Selection Procedure: Parental permission forms were sent home with the children; follow-up phone calls were made to help obtain permission. Selection of the schools was not specified.

Sample Size: Forty-one child-mother pairs.

Outcome Measures: Proportion of available program time watched by child; proportion of available commercial time viewed by child; total number of purchase-influence attempts (PIAs); mean number of PIAs per minute in store; number of independent and parental information on child's home television viewing, based on a partial sample of the child's actual viewing for a one week period.

Experimental Design: This study was conducted in two parts. The first was designed to measure the reinforcement value of television commercials for the child, using the device described herein. The second phase of the study involved direct observation of mother-child interaction during an actual grocery shopping trip.

The television viewing segment was conducted in the nursery school. Children were taken individually to a room equipped with a television set which could be turned on for four-second intervals by pressing a button. This device was explained to the child who was told that he or she could watch as much of an oncoming program as desired. When the child did not want to view anymore, he or she was instructed to call the interviewer who would be doing some work in a curtained off section of the room. Children were given approximately two minutes of taped commercial time in which to become accustomed to using this device; these data were not analyzed. The four-second intervals which the child maintained on the screen were recorded automatically on an Esterline Angus event chart, providing a record of what the child actually watched. The device was also arranged so that the experimenter was able to monitor the beginning and end of each commercial and record it electronically, thus making a hatch mark on the child's response record. This button-pushing technique is related to psychological principles of operant conditioning. Three different half-hour television programs were used. Children watched only one program at a sitting, the order of programs was randomized, and at least one week elapsed between viewing sessions.

An observer followed the mother and child through one shopping trip in the grocery store to record purchase-influence attempts. Parents were not informed of the actual purpose of the study and the interviewer appeared to be shopping. The only request made of the mothers was that they go through all of the aisles in the store. The observer recorded the following information for each mother-child pair: total time in store; number of PIAs by the child; items requested; location of PIA; type of PIA (child instigates or child is given a choice of products by mother); method of PIA; and the success of the PIA.

PIAs were defined as attempts by the child to influence the mother's purchase by making an independent and observable request for a product (by asking, pointing at product, putting object in shopping cart or grabbing), choosing between products at mothers' request or buying an item with his or her own money.

Unit of Analysis: Individuals.

Statistical Tests: Yes (Wilcoxon matched-pairs signed-rank tests, Pearson product-moment correlations, Spearman rank correlations).

Results: The proportion of available program and commercial time viewed varied depending upon the content of the particular program or advertisement.

Children made an average of fifteen PIAs during the shopping trip. This was approximately one PIA every two minutes; twelve were independent PIAs and the other three were in response to the mother's request for a choice. Sixty-four percent of the independent requests took place in front of the item. Children's success rate on PIAs was forty-five percent.

There was a significant positive relationship between the total amount of television reinforcement time (programs and commercials) and the number of PIAs at the store, as well as a significant positive relationship between the amount of commercial reinforcement time and the number of PIAs made. Age was positively correlated with the total television ratio and the commercial ratio.

There were no significant correlations between the success of a child's PIAs and the number of requests made. Age was positively correlated with the number of independent PIAs. Age was not significantly related to the success of the child's requests.

The total number of hours of commercial television viewed at home was significantly and positively related to the number of PIAs made while shopping, although this relationship between home television viewing and number of PIAs did not exist when non-commercial television was included.

Success: If success is defined as finding a relationship between children's television viewing and their purchase influence attempts in the grocery store, the study was moderately successful when criticisms and caveats are taken into account.

Published: Yes.

Sponsorship: Not specified.

Criticisms: One problem with this study is that watching television (and pushing a button to keep the commercials and programming coming) may not be directly related to PIAs as the authors conclude. The correlations between button pushing and in-store PIAs may be related to some third variable, for example, the child's natural inquisitiveness, aggressiveness, or some general activity-level measure. It would have been preferable to have a larger sample, to include children who had not gone through the television-viewing part of the experiment at all, and compare these children with those who had gone through the exercise. The authors do not state the period of time between viewing and the store visit, making direct linkages between television commercial exposure and in-store PIAs even more difficult. Moreover, no relationships are explored between the particular advertisements children saw, and the particular products they requested in-store. This would have been a much more powerful test of advertising's *particular* influence.

A second criticism of the study is that the authors do not detail the wide *range* of products asked for in the supermarket, and the widely varying rates of "success" (presumably, mother's purchasing the product at the time the request was made). The range of products requested includes meat, fish, and poultry (27 out of 616 requests), 19 requests for fruit juices, 38 for vegetables and a total of 56 requests for dairy products. For comparison to more heavily advertised products, there were 50 requests for cereals, 37 for candy, and 10 for soda. It appears that children have a wide range of product desires, and these are by no means limited to products which are heavily advertised on television.

With respect to the second point, mothers were least likely to buy candy products (27 percent successful), and most likely to buy dairy products (61 percent successful). The data thus indicate that mothers play an active role in mediating children's product requests, but this fact is not discussed by the authors.

Other criticisms include the fact that the sample used in this study was small, and presumably homogeneous. Children enrolled in a Montessori nursery school would appear to be a self-selected sample. However, the authors suggest that lower-class children may be more influenced by television commercials than the children in this study, as children from lower-income families tend to be heavier television viewers. The authors also point out that only one measure of purchase-influence (actual requests in the supermarket) was examined in this study. They commented that children are likely to exert their influence in a number of other ways (for example, passive dictation) and places.

Summary: This study indicated that there was a positive relationship between the effort a child would exert to keep television commercials on the screen and the number of purchase influence attempts he or she made at the supermarket. The amount of commercial television viewed at home was also significantly related to the total number of PIAs they made. Older children made more total PIAs per minute in-store and more independent PIAs than younger children. Age was not related to the success of the child's request. The success of the child's attempts was also unrelated to the number of PIAs made.

Study 7

Goldberg, Marvin, and Gorn, G. "Children's Reactions to Television Advertising: An Experimental Approach." *Journal of Consumer Research* 1 (September 1974).

Purpose: To determine the extent to which TV commercials motivate children to try to obtain advertised products.

Population: Boys aged 8 to 10 years old associated with a recreation department in an English speaking upper-middle-class suburb of Montreal.

Sample Selection Procedure: Unspecified.

Sample Size: $n = 133$.

Experimental Design: Subjects were introduced to two new toys (not yet on the market). Baseline measures of attitudes toward each of the two toys were obtained on a five-point bipolar scale (apparently not standard). On another five-point bipolar scale with the first toy (CC) representing one pole and the other toy (HW) representing the other, the subjects specified which of the two toys he would rather get.

Expectancy was experimentally manipulated by the experimenter telling the children that he had only one (low expectancy), eight (moderate expectancy) or fourteen (high expectancy) CC's for the fifteen boys in each group. Subjects were told that to win the toy they would have to solve a puzzle. If they were the first, among the first eight, or the first fourteen boys (depending on level of expectancy), they would win the toy. If they quit before the winners in their group solved the puzzle they would receive HWs, but if they were still working after the winners solved the puzzle they would win nothing. HW was chosen as the alternative prize because pilot tests (unreported) indicated that the children had a slight preference for the CC. Children were asked for their perceived chances of winning on a five-point scale. Groups of children were subsequently shown a program with either zero, one, or three CC commercials inserted. After the program children rated their attitudes toward the program on a five-point scale. The pre-program measures of the desirability of the toys and the perceived probability of winning CC were readministered. Children were then reminded of the number of toys available and the perceived probability of winning was measured a third time. Children then worked in separate cubicles on a difficult experimental puzzle. When a child decided to stop he left the cubicle, and the other children were unaware of his departure. E noted the time each child worked on the puzzle. Finally, subjects rated the task's interest and difficulty on two five-point scales, and were given a set of HW for participating.

In summary, the design was a 3x3 factorial (three levels of commercial exposure and three levels of expectancy) with approximately fifteen subjects/cell.

248

Subjects were randomly assigned to cells. The dependent measures were time spent on the task and the attitudinal data.

Unit of Analysis: Individuals.

Statistical Tests: Yes; analysis of variance, analysis of covariance, and post-hoc comparisons.

Results: The manipulation of expectancy was successful in that the post-test results revealed a significant main effect. A Newman-Keuls test revealed that the perceived chances of winning the CC were higher in the high expectancy group than in the other two groups; however, the moderate and low groups were almost identical.

Prior to exposure to the commercials CC and HW were seen as approximately equally attractive. The program was viewed as fairly interesting. The puzzle was perceived as very hard and fairly interesting. There were no significant differences among treatment levels on any of these measures.

Two-way ANOVA's were performed on attitudinal and behavioral data to determine the effects of expectancy and commercial exposure. Analyses with time spent on the puzzle before quitting (persistence measure) were meaningful for those subjects who could not solve the task ($n = 122$). Thus, the subjects solving the task ($n = 11$) were excluded from all analysis. The authors performed a logarithmic transformation to normalize the time at task data. ANCOVA's on the attitudinal data were performed, covarying on pre-program scores. The covariance analysis was essential since there were substantial pre-program differences on the attitudinal measures (despite random assignment). The two attitudinal measures were attitude toward the CC and comparative attitude (CC versus HW).

There was a significant main effect on expectancy on both attitude measures. In both cases, the only significant difference occurred between subjects in the high and moderate expectancy groups (the attitudes for low expectancy groups fell in between). Thus, high expectancy of receiving the toy enhanced its value in comparison to moderate expectancy. There was also a significant expectancy effect on the amount of time spent working on the puzzle. High expectancy subjects worked significantly longer than those in the low expectancy group (with moderate expectancy in the middle). Thus, persistence behavior was related to expectancy.

There was a significant commercial exposure effect on the comparative attitude measure but not on the attitude toward the CC measure. The increases from zero to both one and three exposures on the comparative measure were significant, but there was no difference between the means in the one and three exposure groups. The number of commercials also significantly affected time worked at the tasks to win the CC. Only the difference between zero and one exposures was significant, with one commercial resulting in increased time worked at the task. (The difference between the zero and three conditions was "just below the 5 percent level of significance.")

There were no significant intereaction effects (commercial exposure x expectancy). Thus, children with low expectancy of obtaining a toy are still affected by commercials. Alternatively, the commercials did not create enough desire for a toy to eliminate the differential affects of expectancy.

Success: Although some subhypotheses were not supported (for instance, the authors predicted an interaction effect, and the predicted positive relationship between expectancy and attitude toward the product was only partially supported), the results generally supported the hypotheses that expectancy and commercial exposure affect attitudes and behavior in the predicted directions. Thus, the study should be considered successful.

Sponsorship: Canada Council Grant.

Published: Yes.

Criticisms: The experimental manipulation of expectancy was only partially successful; while the high expectancy group differed significantly from the moderate and low expectancy groups, these latter two groups had similar perceived chances of winning (expectancy). Thus, it may have been more appropriate to combine these two groups for the purposes of analysis, since differences between these two groups on the dependent variables would appear not to be caused by expectancy differences.

The exclusion of the eleven subjects who actually solved the puzzle may indicate that the brightest students were eliminated, thus limiting the generalization of the findings. In addition, excluding these subjects may have contributed to pre-program attitude differences between groups despite random assignment.

Summary: This study was well-executed. Subjects were randomly assigned to treatment combinations, and the data analysis appeared careful and appropriate. The results suggest that commercial exposure to a toy and expectancy of receiving the toy influence the child's attitude toward the toy (in comparison to another toy) and his behavior in attempting to obtain it.

Study 8

Goldberg, Marvin, and Gorn, G. "Some Unintended Consequences of TV Advertising to Children." *Journal of Consumer Research* 5 (June 1978).

Purpose: To determine the extent to which TV advertisements may (1) lead the child viewer to select material objects over more socially-oriented alternatives; (2) potentially increase parent-child conflict; and (3) may lead to a more disappointed, unhappier child.

Population: Nursery school children (4 and 5 years old) from schools in the Montreal area which tended to attract children from middle- and upper-middle-income backgrounds.

Sample Selection Procedure: Not specified.

Sample Size: n = 164.

Outcome Measures: All children were first shown a photograph of a toy ("Ruckus Raisers Barn") so that it would be visually, as well as conceptually, familiar to them. Each child was then asked a series of five questions, most of which were accompanied with photos. To examine the ability of commercials to enhance the value of the toy, relative to the value of being with peers, children were asked to choose a playmate (a "nice" child without the toy versus a "not so nice" child who has the advertised toy). They were also asked to choose between playing with the Ruckus Raisers Barn or with their friends in the sandbox.

The impact of commercials on parent-child interaction was measured by asking the children to choose between the advertised toy and one they are told their mother prefers. The children are also presented with a projective situation in which the hypothetical child's request for Ruckus Raisers is turned down. Finally, to determine if children are generally upset when they do not get a desired toy, they were asked if a boy (in a picture) who did not receive the advertised toy is sad.

Experimental Design: Children were exposed to three levels of commercials for the toy (Ruckus Raisers Barn) in the context of a neutral ten-minute program. Ruckus Raisers was selected because it is a simple toy which is familiar to all children, including those who did not see the commercials for it. Children in each school were randomly assigned to the treatment conditions.

The control group (*n* = 54) saw the program with no commercials. One experimental group (*n* = 58) viewed the program with the Ruckus Raisers commercial inserted once near the beginning of the program and once near the end. Approximately half of the subjects in this group (*n* = 28) were tested both immediately after viewing and the following day, and the other half were tested only on the second day, to determine whether the children's responses on the second day would be affected by their responses on the first day. Because there were no differences between the delayed responses on any of the dependent measures, the delayed test data (n = 58) was pooled. The second experimental group (n = 52) was exposed to the commercial on two consecutive days, twice each day, and tested both immediately after viewing and a day later.

Unit of Analysis: Individuals.

Statistical Tests: Yes (χ^2).

Results: The commercial had a significant effect on the children's preference for playing with the toy rather than with their friends. Of those exposed to the ad for one day, only 30.0 percent chose to play with their friends over the Ruckus Raisers. This percentage was virtually unchanged a day later. In the control group, however, 70.4 percent of the children opted to play with their friends.

The commercial also appeared to increase the likelihood that the children would choose the negatively described child who had the advertised toy instead of the "nice" child. Almost twice as many children in the control group chose the positively portrayed child than did children who had viewed the commercial for one day.

More children in the control group (78.7 percent) followed their mother's lead and stated that they preferred the toy she liked better. In the group that had seen the commercial for one day, however, only a little more than one-half of the children accepted their mother's judgment, regardless of whether the measure was taken immediately or after a one-day delay.

Children who had not seen the commercial were likely to say that the child whose father refused to purchase the Ruckus Raisers for him still wanted to "play with his daddy." Those who had seen the commercial were not as likely to say the child portrayed "still wanted to play with daddy." This was only significant, however, in the one exposure group under delayed test conditions. Therefore, although there is data that the commercial did affect the children's responses to this measure, the support for this hypothesis is not clear-cut.

The measure concerning children's emotional responses to not obtaining the advertised toy showed that almost two-thirds (65.2 percent) of the control group felt that the boy in the hypothetical situation was "still happy" even though he had not received the toy. Less than one-third (32.0 percent) of the group which had viewed the commercial on a single day felt that way when tested immediately after viewing. This distinction was still significant the following day (41 percent).

No significant differences on any of the dependent measures were found between children exposed to the commercial for one or two days. There was also a tendency in the data for a decrease in effects with repetition.

Success: This study supported the author's hypothesis concerning the effects of television advertising on children as measured by their preference for playing with a new toy rather than with their friends. The projective techniques employed also moderately supported the hypothesis concerning children's disappointment and negative feelings toward parents when refused the advertised product.

Published: Yes.

Sponsorship: Canada Council Grant.

Criticisms: One question was used as the sole measure to test each of the hypotheses. The measures might have been expanded so that the child's attitudes could be tapped in more than one way, as one question does not provide a basis for examining the consistency or logic of the child's answers. There is no way to determine if the child is simply giving an arbitrary answer when faced with a situation requiring a choice.

Given the artificial, laboratory testing situation, coupled with children's normal initial interest in a new toy, the results are hardly surprising. It is possible that most children would temporarily prefer to play with a new toy than with their friends, and many would even endure a "not so nice" friend to try out a new toy. Finally, it is also not very surprising that children feel another child would be disappointed at not receiving a toy. What is unfortunate about this and other laboratory studies is that the findings are often interpreted to mean something far more general and significant than the laboratory measures really suggest. For example, the fact that some children felt other children would be disappointed at not receiving the toy does not necessarily indicate that "parent-child conflict" will occur, or that some global state of disappointment among children will result if they do not receive desired toys.

Summary: This experiment attempts to examine whether exposure to a TV commercial results in unintended effects for preschool children. Findings support hypotheses presented pertaining to the child's preferences for playmates and choice of activities, reactions to parental refusal to purchase the advertised product, acceptance of parental suggestions of products and emotions when refused the advertised toy. No repetition effects were found.

Study 9

Goldberg, Marvin; Gorn, G.; and Gibson, W. "TV Messages for Snacks and Breakfast Foods: Do They Influence Children's Preferences?" *Journal of Consumer Research* 5 (1978). Another version of this study can be found as "The Effects of TV Messages for High and Low Nutritional Foods on Children's Snack and Breakfast Food Choices." *Advances in Consumer Research* 5 (1978).

Purpose: To test television's potential for influencing children's snack and breakfast food preferences.

Population: First-grade children from three upper-middle-class Northern California Bay area schools.

Sample Selection Procedure: All first-grade children in each school were asked to participate. Students were randomly assigned to treatment groups. The selection of schools was not specified.

Sample Size: n = 122.

Outcome Measures: Children's selections of snack and breakfast foods from lists containing nutritious and less nutritious options, and children's indications of whether selected foods are "good" or "bad" for them.

Experimental Design: Children viewed one of the following videotaped programs in small groups:

1. *Yogi's Gang,* a twenty-four-minute cartoon program with thirty-second commercials for the following food products: Mounds Candy Bar, Lollipop Lifesavers, Crackerjacks, Hershey Candy Bar, Blow Pops, Milky Way Candy Bar, Kool-Aid, Sugar Crisps, and Fruity Pebbles. This was a total of four and one-half minutes of ads.

2. *Yogi's Gang* plus the ads for those nine food products each repeated once so that there was a total of nine minutes of advertising.

3. *Yogi's Gang* plus eight public service announcements (PSAs) stressing the value of eating fruits, vegetables, and milk, and urging moderation in the consumption of sugared products. The total time of these PSAs was four and one-half minutes.

4. *Yogi's Gang* plus the eight PSAs each repeated once for a total of nine minutes air time.

5. A twenty-four-minute "Fat Albert" program, entitled *Junk Food.* "Fat Albert" is a humorous cartoon starring Bill Cosby, which hopes to teach children through the use of television cartoons and humor. This episode deals with the importance of eating nutritious foods.

6. The Fat Albert junk food program with the eight PSAs repeated once each for a total of nine minutes air time.

7. The Fat Albert junk food program with the nine thirty-second food commercials for a total of four and one-half minutes of advertising.

8. A control group which was exposed to no program at all.

Unit of Analysis: Individuals, foods selected by children.

Statistical Tests: Yes (ANOVA, t-tests).

Results: As an initial examination showed no significant differences between the responses of the children in the groups exposed to either four and one-half or nine minutes of commercials in the context of *Yogi's Gang,* these groups were combined for the remainder of the analysis. This was also done with the groups which had viewed *Yogi's Gang* with either four and one-half or nine minutes of PSAs.

Children who viewed the "Fat Albert" program with no commercials or PSAs selected the lowest number of the less nutritious foods. Children who viewed "Fat Albert" with *either* commercials or the PSAs selected a greater number of the nutritious foods than the children who viewed the program uninterrupted, but these differences were not statistically significant. Children who viewed "Yogi's Gang" with the PSAs selected significantly more of the less nutritious foods than did the children who had viewed *Fat Albert.* This group, however, selected significantly fewer of the less nutritious foods than did the group that had viewed *Yogi's Gang* and the commercials. The control fell between the two groups which had seen *Yogi's Gang* in the number of less nutritious foods they selected, but was not significantly different from either.

The children made very few errors on indicating if selected foods were "good" or "bad" for them, and an overall analysis of variance indicated no significant differences between the groups.

Success: If success is defined as children's snack and breakfast food choices reflecting the type of television message they viewed, this study was successful in demonstrating the effectiveness of different types of presentations. A full length program was more successful than PSAs in eliciting choice of more nutritious foods, although children who saw commercials for snack foods still selected fewer nutritious foods than those who viewed either the PSAs or the program.

Published: Yes.

Sponsorship: Not specified.

Criticisms: This study is quite well done, with the authors pointing out most of the possible weaknesses. The main weakness is the artificiality of the exposure and choice situations, which could account for the finding in that children may simply choose what they saw in programs and ads.

It would have been interesting to test the effects of both *Yogi's Gang* and *Fat Albert* with a combination of PSAs about nutrition and food commercials inserted in the programs. This would probably more closely approximate what a child might see on television at home. This would especially be true if the FTC does rule that advertisers/broadcasters must air nutritional PSAs on children's programs.

It would also be interesting to repeat this study with preschool and older elementary school children to examine developmental trends in television's potential to influence breakfast and snack food preferences.

Summary: This study found that the type of breakfast and snack foods requested by children may be a function of the type of messages they view on television. A full-length cartoon program dealing with nutrition was more effective than PSAs dealing with the same subject. Children accurately indicated which foods were "good" for them.

Study 10

Howard, John A.; Hulbert, J.; and Lehmann, D.R. "An Exploratory Analysis of the Effect of Television Advertising on Children." Unpublished working paper, n.d.

Purpose: To determine how children between the ages of 2 and 6 responded to television advertising.

Population: "Relatively well-to-do" two- to six-year-old children from rural New Hampshire and urban New Jersey.

Sample Selection Procedure: Unspecified.

Sample Size: n = 96.

Outcome Measure: Nonstandard interview.

Experimental Design: Children and mothers were interviewed.

Statistical Tests: No (frequencies are presented).

Results: The authors collected data on a large number of questions. Interesting findings will be highlighted:

1. Children almost never mentioned advertising as the important reason for buying toys or cereals.
2. TV seems to be the most important source of new-product information for cereals and toys.
3. Most mothers feel that children distinguish between commercials and programs, and most claim to discuss TV advertised products with their children.
4. Most mothers feel that TV causes their children to ask them to buy things.
5. Mothers had mixed opinions as to their feelings about the value of watching TV ads for their children.

Unit of Analysis: Individuals; or individual responses; frequencies.

Criticisms: This study was entirely descriptive. The authors make several statements which are not based on data presented.

There is a very high incidence of "no response", which weakens these findings.

The findings of this study should be interpreted cautiously, for example, the fact that children did not mention advertising as an important reason for buying products does not indicate that it has no effect on purchase requests. Advertising may influence the other reasons listed (for instance, taste, special feature).

Published: No.

Success: Not applicable.

Sponsorship: Faculty Research Fund of the Graduate School of Business, Columbia University.

Summary: This purely descriptive study presents several findings concerning TV advertising, children, and mothers. (See Results section.)

Study 11

Lewis, Charles E., and Lewis, M.A. "The Impact of Television Commercials on Health-Related Beliefs and Behaviors of Children." *Pediatrics* 53 (March 1974).

Purpose: To study the impact of health-related television messages on children.

Population: There were two populations under study: (1) University lab school students (fifth and sixth grades) presumably of middle- to upper-class and mostly white (group A); and (2) public elementary school fifth and sixth grades classified as disadvantaged and mostly nonwhite (group B).

Sample Selection Procedure: All students were asked to participate. However, only 90 percent of Group A subjects and 54 percent of group B subjects actually participated. The method of selecting the two participating schools is unclear.

Sample Size: School A: 117 (out of 130) actually completed reports. School B: 91 (out of 170) actually completed reports.

Outcome Measures: Written student responses to several questions concerning health messages they viewed on TV.

Experimental Design: Written instructions were distributed to children and parents explaining that the "assignment" was part of a social studies program and students were to complete it without assistance. The forms requested data about six messages concerning health or illness which students viewed on TV in their home. The students apparently could choose which messages to report. The students supplied information about time of viewing, nature of the program, what the message was, if they believed the message, and (if they reported on a commercial) whether or not they had ever tried the product and if their parents had ever used it. Subjects had one week to complete the assignment. This study was not experimental since the researchers did not assign subjects to groups and there was no "treatment" in the strict sense; the investigators were simply interested in the reactions of two naturally-occurring groups to one condition (watching health-related messages on TV).

Unit of Analysis: Commercial messages (advertised products) and individuals.

Statistical Tests: Yes: (χ^2) and descriptive data; no tests specified.

Results: Most of the messages viewed in both groups were commercials. There were differences (not tested statistically) in the types of commercials reported by the two groups. A higher percent of school B students believed the messages, used the product, and parents used the product. There were other specific differences with respect to these factors for various types of product. There was a statistically significant association (χ^2) between children's beliefs and parents' use of the products advertised: the child is more likely to believe if the parent uses or vice versa. The authors report that there were statistically significant positive associations between children's beliefs and their use of the products, and parent use and child use, but the analyses are not presented for these latter findings. Percentages seem to indicate that parental use was more influential with respect to children's beliefs than children's use. Students attending school A were classified as to the number of commercials they believed and were rated by their teachers as to their "critical thinking ability" (rated from 1-9). There was little apparent difference between the critical thinking ability ratings of "believers," and "in-betweeners," and "skeptics" (the authors report that no association between these variables was found—test unspecified). Finally, over 90 percent of students in both schools made inferences from their descriptions exactly as intended by the sponsors, and the viewing patterns of the two groups were similar.

Success: Not applicable, since a program or treatment was not being evaluated.

Criticisms: The authors point out three weaknesses: (1) television programs were viewed by groups A and B at different points in time (ten weeks apart). In addition, what shows (and commercials) were actually watched and reported on was not controlled; it is possible that some subjects reported only certain types of commercial messages—for example, those that they believed; (2) the data on drug taking behaviors of both children and parents are unvalidated; and (3) no attempt was made to determine what types of errors in judgment the children made (disbelieving a true message or believing a false one).

As was mentioned, the response rates were low, especially for the disadvantaged group. In addition, the authors report that certain responses were incomplete and thus were eliminated. An effort should have been made to determine if those subjects not participating were different from those included.

Published: Yes.

Sponsorship: Public Health Service.

Summary: This essentially descriptive study indicated that children generally believe TV health-related messages, and that associations exist between children's beliefs and parent's use, children's beliefs and their own use, and parent use and child use. Its major weaknesses are high attrition rate and questionable validity of data.

Study 12

Liebert, Diane E.; Sprafkin, J.N.; Liebert, R.M.; and Rubinstein, E.A. "Effects of Television Commercial Disclaimers on the Product Expectations of Children." *Journal of Communication* 27 (Winter 1977).

Purpose: To determine children's understanding of two types of disclaimers (for assembly of the product) in televised toy commercials.

Population: White kindergarten and second-grade children from middle-class, Long Island, New York public schools. The sample was half male and half female.

Sample Selection Procedure: Parental permission forms were sent home from school with the children in the appropriate grades. The selection of schools and classes within the schools was not specified.

Sample Size: n = 240.

Outcome Measures: Children's understanding that assembly was required for the game in the commercial.

Experimental Design: Children saw one of three versions of the same commercial for one of two toys. One commercial had the original disclaimer ("Some assembly required"), one had a modified disclaimer ("You have to put it together") and the third had no disclaimer. A 3 (disclaimer) x 2 (age level) x 2 (sex) factorial design was used.

Each child was shown a commercial by one experimenter and interviewed by another. The interviewer did not know which commercial the child had seen. Each child viewed the commercial individually.

Unit of Analysis: Individuals.

Statistical Tests: Yes (ANOVA).

Results: Children in the modified disclaimer groups had significantly more understanding that the game needed to be assembled than did the children in either the original or no disclaimer conditions. The last two conditions did not differ from each other. The modified disclaimer doubled the number of children who understood the message when compared to the original message.

Age differences were only found for the modified disclaimer, the original wording did not seem to have much meaning for either group of children. No significant effects were found for age or toy product differences.

Success: The study supported the hypothesis that children would understand a disclaimer using simplified language more fully than they would understand the standard disclaimer used on television toy commercials.

Published: Yes.

Sponsorship: National Advertising Division of the Council of Better Business Bureaus.

Criticisms: The child viewed the commercial outside of the context of a television program. This is an unusual situation for most children, and one which probably resulted in the child paying greater attention to the ad than he or she might otherwise have done. However, even under these conditions (that is, attention focused on the ad) most children did not understand the standard disclaimer.

The authors tested two toy products so that their findings would not be product specific. It would also have been interesting to test another disclaimer frequently used on toy and game commercials, "(parts) sold separately."

One measure (the child's verbal indication of whether he or she thought the toy needed to be assembled) was used to test the child's understanding of the disclaimer. Additional measures—perhaps of a less verbal nature—might also have been used as other ways of tapping the child's understanding of the disclaimer.

Summary: This study found that six- and eight-year-old children who heard the disclaimer "some assembly required" in a television commercial, had no more understanding that the toy needed to be put together than did children who had not heard a disclaimer. Almost double the number of children understood that the toy required assembly when the disclaimer wording was simplified to "You have to put it together." This study concludes that the disclaimer generally used on television ads is not understood by the young children at whom the commercials are aimed.

Study 13

Liefield, John P., et al. "Television Advertising and Children: An Experimental Study." Unpublished working paper, University of Guelph, Guelph, Ontario, Canada, 1974.

Purpose: To investigate the effects of TV advertisements on selected physical and verbal behavior of 5-year-old male children.

Population: Mother and son pairs from white-collar or managerial/professional families who were at least second generation, Anglo-Saxon Canadians.

Sample Selection Procedure: Fifty subjects meeting the above specifications were identified through ads in newspapers, letters to mothers of children in public school kindergarten classes, and through "personal references." Questionnaire responses allowed the investigator to eliminate those subjects who consumed the two cereals or owned the two toys to be advertised in the experiment.

Sample Size: Thirty-two mother-son pairs met the above requirements and agreed to participate, of which thirty pairs completed the experiment.

Experimental Design: Subjects were randomly assigned to two treatments. Both groups of subjects viewed cartoons. Subjects in the first group were shown four commercials advertising each of two cereals ("cereal subjects"); subjects in the second group viewed four commercials for each of two toys ("toy subjects"). After the viewing sessions, the subjects in both groups were told that they could play with some toys. Eight out of the seventeen toys were the products advertised in the commercial seen by the subjects in the second group. Observers recorded the physical and verbal behavior of the subjects for a ten-minute period, and their observations were checked by viewing video tape records. During the toy play period, the subjects exposed to toy commercials were the experimental (E) group while the children exposed to the breakfast cereal commercials made up the control (C) group.

Following the toy play session, mothers collected their sons and proceeded to a large grocery store. Each mother entered the supermarket and began shopping "normally." No more than one mother and son pair entered the breakfast cereal aisle at one time. Children's reactions to the cereals were recorded by observers dressed in clerk uniforms, and verbalizations were tape recorded (the recorder was buried in a cart full of groceries which was unobtrusively pushed by a woman shopper). In the shopping condition the subjects exposed to cereal commercials were the E subjects, while the subjects exposed to toy commercials acted as C subjects. Two days after the experiment a sample of subjects (selection procedure unspecified) was interviewed to determine if the child had developed awareness of the experiment: none of the subjects indicated such awareness.

Outcome Measures: Background information provided by mother, and observations of the child's TV watching behavior, shopping behavior, and toy playing behavior.

Statistical Tests: Yes (t-tests, z-tests).

Unit of Analysis: Individuals.

Results: There were few differences between the groups in background, TV viewing, playing, and shopping behaviors not directly related to the experimental hypotheses; thus, the groups appeared comparable. The results demonstrate that E subjects were more likely to direct their behavior toward the advertised toys. Also, E subjects in the shopping experiment showed more "approach" behavior toward the advertised cereals than C subjects (the group differences were not dramatic, however). There was no difference between the groups in purchase influence attempts. Differences in behavior between C subjects or between E subjects on two different testing days (one week apart) were interpreted as resulting from differences in background variables—however, n's were so small for these comparisons that little confidence can be placed in them.

Success: If success is defined as the E subjects approaching the advertised products more than C subjects, there was only slight indications that this occurred.

Sponsorship: Unspecified.

Published: No.

Criticisms: The authors are aware of the study's major weaknesses: small sample sizes, using multiple statistical comparisons, failure to control for differences in initial attractiveness between the E and other products, and measuring only the short-term effects of TV advertising. The authors admirably emphasize that as a result, these findings are only tentative: "These procedures were deemed justifiable given the exploratory nature of this study. They are useful for developing hypotheses for further study and for providing tentative evidence on the effects of television advertising on children."

Summary: This study suggests that TV advertising increases approach behavior of subjects toward advertised toys and cereal. Subjects were randomly assigned to treatment groups, and the investigators attempted to observe children's behavior in a natural setting (grocery store). The study's principle weaknesses are small sample size, use of multiple statistical comparisons, failure to control for the initial attractiveness of the E and other products, and measuring only short term advertising effects.

Study 14

Milavsky, J. Ronald; Pekowsky, B.; and Stipp, H. "TV Drug Advertising and Proprietary and Illicit Drug Use Among Teenage Boys." *Public Opinion Quarterly* 39 (Winter 1975-76).

Purpose: To empirically test the charge that drug advertising may be related to use of proprietary and illicit drugs.

Population: Seventh-, eighth- and ninth-grade boys in low and middle socio-economic status (SES) midwestern schools. The precise location of these schools is unspecified.

Sample Selection Procedure: Schools were apparently selected in an attempt to obtain a sample "balanced with respect to SES and grade and, among the low-SES boys, balanced by race." Target boys were randomly selected from enrollment lists. The target boys were then asked for names of up to 8 neighborhood friends, who were also recruited. Additional subjects (friends and subjects participating in a separate study) were recruited in later phases of the study.

Sample Size: There were 822 boys present for at least one phase (wave) of the study.

Experimental Design: The subjects were interviewed with questionnaires five separate times over a period of three and one-half years (May 1970 to Dec. 1973), while their parents were interviewed twice. The subject questionnaires tapped the subjects' proprietary and illicit drug use and drug advertising exposure. (Note: the authors followed an elaborate procedure for computing exposure to drug commercials from subjects' reports of TV exposure. The exposure measure tapped the amount of drug advertising the subject could have watched.) The authors made special efforts to insure that their measures were valid, and they randomly selected TV shows for inclusion in the initial (Wave I) questionnaire. The questionnaires differed across the different measurement times.

Outcome Measure: Nonstandard questionnaires.

Unit of Analysis: Individuals.

Statistical Tests: Yes (nonparametric Tau—since data is only ordinal scale).

Results: Drug advertising exposure and proprietary drug use: There is a small but significant relationship: subjects with high exposure use more proprietary drugs than those with lower exposure.

Drug advertising exposure and illicit drug use: A *negative* relationship was found between exposure and drug use: the higher the TV advertising exposure, the less are illicit drugs used. This relationship remained negative even when the amount of total TV exposure was partialed out, and was negative or not significant when low, medium, and high viewers were considered separately. The authors "searched" for subgroups in which the relationship between drug advertising exposure and illicit drug use was positive by controlling for many variables, such as age, race, IQ, SES, etc. No subgroups were found in which the relationship was positive. The negative relationship appeared in part to be a result of the fact that eventual users of illicit drugs watch less TV (and experience less exposure to drug advertising) before experimentation with drugs begins. These results suggest that "television is not a factor leading directly to illicit drug use."

Indirect links between drug advertising exposure and illicit drug use: Subjects' use of proprietary drugs was not related to use of illicit drugs. Subjects' *readiness* to take proprietary drugs was significantly related to their use of illicit drugs; however, there was no relationship between exposure to drug advertising and the subjects' *readiness* to take proprietary drugs—thus, TV was not indirectly related to use of illicit drugs.

Published: Yes.

Success: Not applicable.

Sponsorship: National Broadcasting Company.

Criticisms: There were differences in the descriptions of some drugs and the number of drugs listed between the last administered and the earlier questionnaires. As the authors point out, therefore, a certain amount of caution should be exercised in interpreting changes over time.

A fair percent of subjects responded to questions about non-existent "dummy" shows, or reported their drug use inconsistently. While the authors took precautions to insure that these errors did not bias the results, this fact is indicative of the questionable validity of survey research.

It is difficult to determine why the *n*'s for the different analyses vary.

Summary: This correlational study suggests that exposure to TV drug advertising does not directly or indirectly lead teenage boys to take illicit drugs. "On the contrary, the data indicate that it is the lighter viewer of drug advertising on TV who is more likely to use illicit drugs." Drug advertising exposure was positively related to proprietary drug use. Since the study was not experimental, causal inferences are unwarranted.

Study 15

Robertson, Thomas S., and Rossiter, J.R. "Children and Commercial Persuasion: An Attribution Theory Analysis. *Journal of Consumer Research* 1 (June 1974).

Purpose: To examine the extent to which children are capable of understanding the purposes of television commercials and the effects of such understanding on attitudes and purchase requests.

Population: First-, third-, and fifth-grade boys in five schools within the Philadelphia area Catholic school system.

Sample Selection Procedure: All of the boys in four of the schools were included (census), while in the fifth school all the boys in one class at each grade level were included. The procedure for selecting the classes included in this latter school is unspecified. In addition, the procedure for selecting the five schools is unspecified. Only two students did not participate.

Sample Size: n = 289.

Outcome Measures: Interviewers used open-ended questions adapted from Ward (1972b) "and modified in line with our conceptual framework and questionnaire pretests," thus, the measures were not standard.

Experimental Design: This was a descriptive study. Children were interviewed using open-ended questions by trained graduate students. Subject responses were coded blind by three judges, and the few cases (less than 5 percent) where the judges did not agree were eliminated from the study. Several variables were coded in this manner—for example, whether or not a child could discriminate between programs and commercials, or could recognize the intent of commercials. Parent-child interaction was based on child reports, and peer interaction was based on the child's designation by other students in the sample as a "best friend."

Unit of Analysis: Individuals.

Statistical Tests: Yes (Kendall correlation coefficients and multivariate discriminant analyses).

Results: An overview of the results suggests "increasingly sophisticated cognitions and less positive attitudinal structures" toward commercials with age (increasing grade levels).

Children's attribution of persuasive intent to commercials was significantly and positively related to age and parental education. Discriminant analysis suggested that age was the most significant factor. The child's interaction level with parents, the presence or absence of older siblings, and level of peer integration were all unrelated to the perception of persuasive intent. The only factor significantly associated with attributing assistive (helpful or informational) intent to commercials was absence of older siblings—the older or only children tend to see advertising as designed to assist.

Children who are capable of recognizing commercials as persuasive (1) can distinguish commercials from programming, (2) can recognize the existence of an external source or a commercial sponsor, (3) perceive the idea of intended audience, (4) are aware of the symbolic nature of commercials, and (5) cite instances of negative discrepancies where the product did not meet their expectations based on the commercial message (correlations between each of these five variables and recognition of persuasive intent were all significant; however, all are probably highly correlated with age). Stepwise discriminant weights suggested that symbolic perception was the primary determinant of persuasive intent recognition. Only two of the correlations between recognizing assistive intent and these five variables were significant: recognition of an external source or sponsor and perception of an intended audience.

The two intent variables (assistive and persuasive) were also related to attitudes (trust, liking, and consumption motivation). There are several significant results. Children holding assistive intent attributions tend to trust commercials more (positive correlations), whereas if they see them as persuasive they tend not to like them (negative correlation). While ability to recognize either type of intent is negatively related to consumption motivation, only the correlation between persuasive intent recognition and diminished desire for advertised products is significant. Discriminant analyses indicated that persuasive intent is the dominant factor (over assistive intent) in predicting trust, liking, and consumption motivation when both types are considered in combination.

Success: Not applicable (no treatment).

Sponsorship: Leo Burnett Inc., Mattel, Kellogg, Nestle, Management and Behavioral Science Center of the University of Pennsylvania, and National Science Foundation.

Published: Yes.

Criticisms: As the authors point out, the sample was limited to Catholic boys. Thus, the results are not generalizable to other groups. The authors mention that a pilot study in a public school found that religious differences "tended to complicate interview content and measurement," which suggests that differences between various religious groups on the measured variables may well exist.

This study is subject to all the criticisms accompanying the use of open-ended questionnaire techniques—especially the question of whether the responses accurately represent reality. The use of three judges adds confidence to the scoring of the interviews, although the subjects who were eliminated due to lack of rater agreement may have been atypical, thus further limiting the generalizability of the results.

Summary: This descriptive study suggested the following relationships: Children appear to develop increasingly sophisticated cognitions about commercials, including attribution of persuasive intent, with age. Parent education was also positively related to attribution of persuasive intent, as were five cognitive variables. Children who attributed persuasive intent to commercials, tended to like them less, trust them less, and were less likely to express a desire for the products advertised. Children who attributed assistive intent tended to like and trust the commercials, but not necessarily to express a desire for the products. Recognition of persuasive intent was dominant over recognition of assistive intent in predicting liking, trust, and commercial motivation. The study's principle weaknesses are limited generalizability of the results and the weaknesses associated with the use of a nonstandard open-ended interview format. Since the study was non-experimental, causal inferences are not justified.

Study 16

Robertson, Thomas S., and Rossiter, J.R. "Short-Run Advertising Effects on Children: A Field Study." *Journal of Marketing Research* 13, (February 1976).

Purpose: To investigate the effects of TV advertising on children's toy and game choices in a "naturalistic setting."

Population: First-, third-, and fifth-grade boys in Philadelphia area schools.

Sample Selection Procedure: The procedure for selecting schools and subjects within schools is unspecified. The study was conducted in five "diverse" Philadelphia area schools "to provide a wide range of socioeconomic backgrounds"; thus, it appears likely that the schools were not randomly selected.

Sample Size: n = 289.

Experimental Design: A two-wave survey was administered in which children were asked to nominate their five most strongly preferred Christmas present choices at two time periods: five weeks before Christmas and one week before Christmas. Children were also asked how often they had actually requested each item from their parents, and where they had seen or heard about each item mentioned.

Children's item choices were assigned to one of four categories: (1) toys and games, (2) education and craft items, (3) leisure and personal items, and (4) sports equipment. The authors then traced brand-name items in TV advertising logs; this effort revealed that only the toy and game group received "substantial" TV advertising support, while items in the other three groups were advertised only "occasionally." On this basis, the authors conclude that "any change in the proportion of toy and game requests (versus requests for items in the other categories) from the first wave, which preceded the peak of TV advertising for toys and games, and to the second wave, which followed the peak of TV advertising for toys and games, could be taken as *prima facie* evidence for TV advertising effects."

Unit of Analysis: Individual.

Statistical Tests: Yes (ANOVA, Kendall's tau).

Outcome Measure: Survey (not standard).

Results: Overall toy and game preferences increased slightly from 45 percent to 48 percent during the four-week measurement period. The pre-post choice changes were statistically significant (ANOVA). The authors state that the increase in toy and game choices may be conservative since the advertising campaign had already begun by the time of the first measurement. In addition, the mean number of toy and game category requests to parents increased from 2.2 to 2.7 during the measurement period. The correlation between TV as an information source and children's toy and game choices was 0.24 (p .001), larger than for several other sources.

Sponsorship: National Science Foundation, Leo Burnett, Inc., Mattel, Kellogg, Nestle.

Published: Yes.

Success: Not applicable.

Criticisms: The authors feel that this study demonstrates the short-term effects of TV advertising on children's toy and game choices and purchase requests. However, the study suffers from several weaknesses. First, the two different measurement times were supposed to reflect pre-peak and post-peak TV toy and game advertising efforts. However, no information as to the *differences* in percentage of commercials dealing with toys and games at the times of measurement and between measurements is provided. Second, there are many other factors besides TV advertising which may have influenced the increase in toy and game choices and purchase requests (for example, increased conversation about Christmas by peers and family, increased awareness that requests for toys were likely to be received favorably, store-front displays, etc.). The authors' assumption that "the major difference in product information input over the survey period was television advertising, which was concentrated on the toy and game category," is not supported with data.

The increase in toy and game requests was modest and not tested statistically.

Summary: This study suggests that pre-Christmas TV advertising increased children's toy and game choices and purchase requests. However, these findings must be viewed with caution.

Study 17

Robertson, Thomas S.; Rossiter, J.R.; and Gleason, T. *Televised Medicine Advertising and Children.* New York: Praeger Publishers, 1979.

Purpose: To examine the impact of proprietary medicine advertising on children.

Population: Mother-child pairs, with children in the third, fifth, and seventh grades. Socioeconomic status ranged from disadvantaged to upper-middle-class.

Sample Selection Procedure: Six school districts were initially selected by SES. Individual classes of students by grade level were selected through a random sample. Approximately half of the students were male, the other half were female.

Sample Size: 673 mother-child pairs.

Outcome Measures: Self-administered questionnaire for children; results of phone interview for mothers.

Experimental Design: Children completed questionnaires in school; phone interviews with mothers were conducted by professional interviewers. The questionnaires covered the following topics: illness behavior and conception, medicine conceptions, medicine behavior, parental mediation, and television exposure.

Unit of Analysis: Individuals, and mother-child dyads.

Statistical Tests: Yes (correlations, regression, factor analysis, ANOVA).

Results:
1. Child and parental conceptions and attitudes about illness and proprietary medicines. Children report higher frequencies of illness than do parents, although children's patterns become more similar to their parents as they get older. Children also show more anxiety about illness than parents, as measured by their concern about getting sick. They also think there is more illness in the general public than their parents do. Although differences between parents and children narrow with age about illness anxiety and perception of illness in the general population, there is still a significant difference between parents and the oldest children in this study.

Younger children have high beliefs in the efficacy of medicine, although this drops with age. Even for adults, however, this belief is still positive. Children do not seem to have a great deal of knowledge of the appropriateness of specific brands of medicine for certain ailments, and they tend to reflect their family's positive orientation toward medicines.

Children report higher intent to take medicine when sick than their parents. Children also report higher actual usage of proprietary medicines than parents.

The youngest children request medicine more often than they receive it, but for fifth and seventh graders, medicine use is greater than their requests.

The findings indicate that most parents and children discuss illness and medicine infrequently. It does not seem as if parental education about medicine is extensive. High frequency of parental medicine mediation (influencing children's knowledge and beliefs about medicine) is related to higher reported illness levels, higher illness anxiety levels, high perceptions of illness within the general population, more positive beliefs about medicine efficacy and more positive feelings about taking medicine. There is a slight negative relationship between parental medicine mediation and brand knowledge of medicine. Parental mediation level is positively associated with intent to take medicines, request frequency, and the use of proprietary medicines.

Social class seems to moderate child medicine conceptions and use. Children from higher social class families showed less illness anxiety, less positive beliefs and affect toward medicine, and less medicine-related behavior, as measured by lower intent, request frequency, and use. There is also a positive correlation between social class and brand knowledge.

Children tend to regard their parents and doctors as the most logical sources of information about medicine. Television advertising was the third most often cited source. Older children indicate slightly less use of all information sources than younger children.

There is not much relationship bewteen parents and children's conceptions about medicine. The relationship is strongest for use, which is logical since parents generally control children's use of proprietary medicines.

2. Findings regarding the impact of proprietary medicine television advertising. The average child in this study watched 4.05 hours of television per day. The authors calculate that this results in potential exposures to a yearly average of 718 commercials for proprietary medicines.

Medicine commercial exposure shows positive and significant relationships to medicine conceptions and behaviors. It is positively related to illness experience, illness anxiety, a belief in the efficacy of medicine, affect toward taking medicine, intent to take medicine, requests for medicine to parents, and use of medicine. Curiously, exposure is negatively related to brand knowledge. There is no relationship between the amount of exposure to medicine commercials and the child's perception of illness in the general population.

3. Findings regarding the effects of proprietary medicine advertising on subgroups of children. Effects of television drug advertising on the following four subgroups of children were examined: young children, low parental education children, high illness frequency children and children with high illness anxiety.

Young children are exposed to more television advertising for drugs than are older children. They show significantly more positive attitudes toward, and make more requests for proprietary medicines than older children, although there is no significant difference in use. Correlational results indicate that younger children are not more strongly influenced by television advertising for proprietary medicines than older children.

Children were considered to be from low parental education families if the head of the family had not completed high school; this group comprised 20 percent of the sample. These children had significantly more exposure to TV drug advertising than the remainder of children in the sample. However, there were no significant differences between these children and the other children in the sample in attitudes, requests, or proprietary drug use. Intent to take proprietary medicine and requests for such medicine were correlated with TV drug advertising exposure for children from low parental education families.

Children who have a higher frequency of coughs, colds, stomachaches and headaches show higher levels of proprietary medicine use than the other children in the sample. High illness children are slightly, but significantly more likely to be exposed to more TV drug advertising. With the exception of belief in the efficacy of these medicines, high illness children have significantly more favorable attitudes toward proprietary medicines and are more likely to request them if symptoms occur. TV advertising was correlated with a tendency to like taking proprietary medicines for high illness children; exposure was not related to beliefs, intentions, requests or usage for this subgroup.

The high illness anxiety group was comprised of those children in the highest scoring quartile in the illness anxiety index. Since levels of illness anxiety tended to be fairly low, children in this group were those exhibiting *moderately* high illness anxiety. High illness anxiety children are exposed to significantly more television advertising for proprietary medicines, and have significantly more favorable attitudes, more frequent requests, and higher usage levels than the other children in the study. The high illness anxiety children also showed significantly higher correlations between TV drug advertising exposure and belief in the efficacy of medicines, affect toward taking such medicines, intent and requests than did low illness anxiety children.

Factor analysis showed a lack of correspondence between parental attitudes and beliefs about proprietary medicines and children's beliefs and attitudes. The results support an independence model, suggesting that children's conception and usage of proprietary drugs cannot be primarily attributed to parental influence.

Success: Not applicable.

Sponsorship: National Science Foundation.

Published: Yes.

Criticisms: It is unclear why the particular age-levels sampled were selected, as they do not represent clearly distinct levels of development. The study also might have examined younger children and their parents, since levels of understanding and medicine-related parent-child interaction are not well understood.

In addition to the usual qualifications about self-reported data, there seems as if there might be a particular problem with reliability on those questions which ask the child about use, parental mediation, and illness experience. In these questions, the child is being asked to reflect over approximately a seven-month period to determine the number of times each of these events occurred. Although illness may be a salient enough experience for the child to remember each incidence separately, it does not seem likely that a discussion about either medicine in general, or medicine shown on TV ads specifically is something that would be remembered well enough to provide an accurate basis to report the number of times it occurred. Perhaps parental reports of their children's illnesses, requests for medicine, and actual medicine usage could have been obtained to corroborate the children's self-reports.

Summary: This survey examined the effect of proprietary medicine advertising on children. Television advertising for proprietary medicine was found to have some relationship to the child's conceptions and attitudes toward medicine and to their requests for medicine to their parents. Television advertising was not related to children's medicine use, which was found to be generally regulated by parents. Children with high levels of illness anxiety was the only subgroup for which increased effects of exposure to television drug advertising was found.

Study 18

Rossiter, John R., and Robertson, T.S. "Children's TV Commercials: Testing the Defenses." *Journal of Communication* 24 (Autumn 1974).

Purpose: To investigate "persuasion processes" in children's susceptibility to television advertising.

Population: Primary school boys (first, third, and fifth grade) from Philadelphia Catholic Schools (same as other articles by these authors).

Sample Selection Procedure: The area was selected in an effort to provide a "broad social class profile." Selection of schools and subjects within schools is unspecified.

Sample Size: n = 289.

Outcome Measure: Open-ended interviews (not standard) were used to measure each child's level of understanding of commercials (cognition) and his associated belief, affect, and motivational disposition with respect to them (attitude).

Commercial-instigated choice behavior was measured as follows: children listed Christmas present selections in early November and again in December. The measure was the proportion of toy and game requests (for which there was concentrated TV advertising) in relation to total requests. (See Study 16.)

Experimental Design: This study is part of the 1976 study (Study 16) which investigated the effects of pre-Christmas toy and game advertising. This study focuses on cognitive and attitudinal defenses with respect to commercials. Cognitive defenses were indicated by the child's level of understanding of commercials, while attitudinal defenses were indicated by his beliefs, affect, and motivational disposition toward commercials. Children were interviewed, and the interview protocols were scored anonymously with respect to the child's school and grade level by three independent coders into response dimensions developed *a priorie.* Cognitive and attitudinal defenses were related to a number of factors.

Statistical Tests: Yes (Kendall's tau).

Unit of Analysis: Individuals.

Results: Predictors of children's cognitive and attitudinal defenses to television advertising: Maturational development (age and grade) is the most significant determinant of children's cognitive and attitudinal defenses to television advertising (maturation results in a greater understanding of and a more defensive attitude toward commercials). The other correlations which follow were computed with age and grade partialled out.

276

TV exposure was unrelated to cognitive defense level, but was significantly related to the child's attitude toward commercials (heavy viewers are more favorably disposed toward TV advertising).

Children of better educated parents exhibited stronger cognitive and attitudinal defenses to commercials, although parent-child intereaction was not a significant variable. Children with no older siblings were found to be more cognitively sophisticated. Peers do not play a significant role in the child's acquisition of defenses to advertising.

Cognitive and attitudinal defense effectiveness over the peak toy and game television advertising period (the correlations between children's cognitive and attitudinal defenses and their preference levels for television advertised toys and games, both before and after the peak of the toy and game TV ad period, were computed separately by grade level): Children's cognitive and attitudinal defenses are strongest at the beginning of the peak ad period, but are "neutralized" at its conclusion (children with strong defenses to commercials selected fewer TV promoted toys and games on the pre-measure than children with weaker defenses; however, on the post-measure, defenses are generally ineffective predictors of preference). This is a result of increased TV item preference among children with the initially strongest defenses. The cognitive defenses of the 5th graders appeared to be most resistant to advertising.

There is a shift in importance from attitudinal defense to cognitive defense with increasing grade level (cognitive defenses are minimally important for first graders, as are attitudinal defenses for fifth graders).

Success: Not applicable.

Sponsorship: Leo Burnett, Inc., Mattel, Kellogg, Nestle, National Science Foundation.

Published: Yes.

Criticisms: The authors attribute effects to the concentrated toy and game TV advertising during the pre-Christmas weeks. However, the authors do not provide information about the level of such advertising at the two measurement times. In addition, there were no controls to insure that TV advertising, and not some other factor, was responsible for the "neutralization" of cognitive and attitudinal defenses with respect to TV advertised toys and games.

Summary: This correlational study suggests that maturation is the most significant determinant of children's defenses to TV commercials; TV exposure was significantly related to attitudinal defenses to commercials. There is some evidence that defenses were effective at the pre-peak measurement time, but were less effective at post-peak; the cognitive defenses of fifth graders were most resistant to the effects of concentrated advertising. There was a shift from attitudinal to cognitive defenses with age. The study lacks sufficient controls to confidently attribute deterioration of defenses to concentrated TV advertising.

Study 19

Rossiter, John R., and Robertson, T.S. "Children's Television Viewing: An Examination of Parent-Child Consensus." *Sociometry* 38 (September 1975).

Purpose: To compare parent and child reports with respect to TV viewing and television advertising influence, and to examine response patterns in relation to children's ages and parental social class.

Population: First-, third-, and fifth-grade boys from Philadelphia area Catholic schools.

Sample Selection Procedure: How schools and subjects within schools were selected are unspecified in this article. However, this sample appears to be identical to the one used in Robertson and Rossiter (1974), in which all of the boys in four of the schools were included, and all the boys in one class at each grade level in the fifth school were included. The method of selecting schools and the classes in the fifth school is unspecified in the 1974 article. Interviews were completed with the mothers in 87 percent of the cases, thus eliminating 13 percent of the subjects from this study.

Sample Size: n = 253 mother-child dyads.

Experimental Design: This study was essentially correlational in nature. Children's responses were obtained through personal interviews at school by trained graduate students. Parents responses were obtained through telephone interviews conducted by the same interviewing team.

Specific Outcome Measures: Parent and child reports with respect to two sets of variables were obtained. The first set (television exposure, viewing supervision, co-viewing, and parent-child interaction) assessed parentally imposed television controls with closed-end questions. The second set (persuasive intent recognition, liking, believability, motivation) assessed the perceived susceptibility of children to TV commercials with closed end-questions for parents, and open-end questions for children. The response sets for all of the variables were trichotomized either by utilizing closed-end questions with three categories, inspecting the total response distribution for each variable and dividing the responses on this basis, or by coding open-ended responses into three categories.

Statistical Tests: Yes (parametric and nonparametric).

Unit of Analysis: Individuals.

Results: Only two of the television control measures and two of the commercial susceptibility measures show significant parent-child correlations (Pearson r). The TV control variables producing a significant (positive) correlation between parents and children were television exposure and parent-child interaction. The commercial susceptibility variables producing significant (positive) correlations were persuasive intent recognition and believability. The reported r's for all of the variables are low (all under 0.18).

χ^2 analyses for aggregate response similarity indicated that parents and children respond differently; parent and child response distributions were significantly different for all but one (believability) of the response variables. Parents reported exerting more viewing supervision than the children reported experiencing. In addition, parents appeared to underestimate their children's commercial susceptibility.

An analysis of parent and child consensus by grade level indicated that the age variable can not account for the parent-child reporting discrepancy. Analysis of parent and child responses by parent's education and occupation indicated that parents report stronger social-class effects than their children: "The added bias by social class means that the sound practices of more enlightened parents may not be as prevalent as they appear" (p. 21).

Success: Not applicable.

Sponsorship: Leo Burnett, Inc., Mattel, Kellogg, Nestle, Management and Behavioral Science Center of the University of Pennsylvania, and National Science Foundation.

Published: Yes.

Criticisms: The principle criticism of this study concerns the questionable validity of parent and child reports without observation of children's actual viewing patterns, etc. Also, it is difficult to determine if parents' and children's responses are equivalent. For example, when both a child and parent report that the child "likes" commercials (or report differently), it is questionable whether the concept of "likes commercials" means the same thing for children and adults.

Summary: This correlational study suggests that parents' and children's perceptions of TV control exerted by parents' and children's susceptibility to commercials may differ.

Study 20

Rubin, Donald S. "An Exploratory Investigation of Children's Responses to Commercial Content of Television Advertising in Relation to Their Stages of Cognitive Development." Unpublished doctoral dissertation, University of Massachusetts, 1972.

Purpose: To explore TV advertising viewing as it affects the "consumer learning process" of the child.

Population: First, third, and sixth graders attending Bondsville Elementary School within the Palmer School district in western Massachusetts.

Sample Selection Procedure: Not random. The youngest subjects (and subjects not repeating a grade level) at each grade level were selected.

Sample Size: n = 72.

Experimental Design: The experiment tested for the effect of six experimental conditions. The six levels were determined by three levels of cognitive development (the three grade levels) and two formats of commercial content. Subjects were randomly assigned to the two commercial content formats (twelve subjects per cell, six male, six female). Subjects viewed two different versions of a new breakfast cereal commercial—one version was product-oriented, while the other emphasized a toy racing car premium which comes in the cereal box. The commercials had not been previously viewed by subjects. The outcome measure was recall of selected elements of the commercials and understanding of the commercial message, as measured by a flexible questionnaire interview, designed for this study. Subjects were interviewed immediately following the presentation of the commercial.

Outcome Measure: Flexible questionnaire interview, designed for this study.

Statistical Tests: Yes (χ^2).

Unit of Analysis: Individual.

Results: There was a significant association between the specific elements recalled and stages of development: older children were more able to recall detailed information. The recall of specific elements was independent of level of commercial content presentation. The amount of elements recalled was significantly related to stages of development (older subjects recalled more information) and to the form of commercial presentation (children viewing the premium-oriented commercial recalled more elements). The action sequence recall of the subjects was significantly associated with developmental stage (trend toward sequence recall with increasing age), and with commercial content presentation (improved sequence recall with product-oriented commercial). The child's understanding of the use of the product was independent of his or her developmental levels (although there was a trend toward increased understanding with age), but was related to commercial content (children viewing the product-oriented commercial were more often classified in the "understanding" category). There was a relationship between awareness that they were viewing a commercial and stage of cognitive development (increased awareness with age), while children's awareness was independent of commercial content presentation. Understanding of why commercials are shown (selling aspects) was related to stage of development (increased understanding with age), but this variable was not related to commercial content presentation. Similar findings existed for the child's understanding of why commercials are made. There was a relationship between the child's understanding of "what is supposed to be wanted" and stage of development (older understand better) and also with commercial content presentation (product children more often answered "cereal" while premium children mentioned the premium). The reasons subjects gave as to why they were supposed to want the product were related to developmental level and commercial content presentation (older and product presentation subjects were more aware of buying motive).

The author presents additional analyses concerning results using aided recall and breaking down the stage of development comparisons into comparing two consecutive stages of development (instead of analyses involving all three levels). These results will not be presented here.

Success: If "success" is arbitrarily defined as the existence of a relationship between children's ability to recall and understand commercial messages and stages of development or form of commercial content presentation, the study was generally successful for stage of development but mixed for commercial content presentation.

Sponsorship: Unspecified.

Published: No.

Criticisms: Differences (for example, use of animation) other than premium presentation existed between the two commercial versions which may have influenced children's responses.

Coding of responses into categories, such as level of recall of action sequences, appeared to depend somewhat on the coders judgment and thus may reflect an unconscious bias in the direction of the experimental expectations, especially if the ages or commercial content data were available while coding.

In classifying subjects as to their understanding of the use of the product, responses about the premium were classified as reflecting lower-level understanding. However, the child may view the premium as part of the product; failure to comment on the product does not necessarily indicate a lack of understanding of its use.

While the author refers to grade levels as "stages of cognitive development," "age" would be a more accurate label for that variable.

This study is subject to the usual qualifications accompanying the use of flexible questionnaire interview techniques with children.

Summary: This study indicated that there is generally an association between children's ability to recall and understand commercial messages and their cognitive level (determined by age), and that at times commercial content presentation (product versus premium emphasis) is related to children's responses, but to a lesser extent than stage of development. Subjects were randomly assigned to types of commercial presentation. The study's principal weaknesses are differences between commercial types other than premium emphasis, possible bias due to using flexible interview techniques, and possible coding biases.

Study 21

Shimp, Terence A.; Dyer, R.F.; and Divita, S.F. "An Experimental Test of the Harmful Effects of Premium-Oriented Commercials on Children." *Journal of Consumer Research* 3 (June 1976).

Purpose: To empirically test the Federal Trade Commission's position that television advertising of premium offers to children are harmful and should be discontinued. Two specific research questions were investigated: (1) Does the inclusion of a premium portion in a TV commercial distract the child's attention from merits of the principal product?, and (2) Is the necessary effect of the premium offer to cause children to purchase or want to purchase the advertised product?

Population: First- to sixth-grade children attending a Washington, D.C., suburban parochial school which volunteered to participate in the study.

Sample Selection Procedure: The school volunteered to participate; it is unclear if all of its students actually participated.

Sample Size: n = 197.

Experimental Design: TV commercials were constructed for a hypothetical cereal product. Four versions of a thirty-second TV commercial were prepared: a control commercial which only presented information concerning the cereal and three experimental ads which included both premium and product information. The three experimental ads differed only as to the length of time devoted to premium presentation (ten, fifteen, or twenty seconds). The premium object was a football team patch. Subjects were presented with a five-minute cartoon, the thirty-second commercial, and a one-minute announcement about pet care.

Students within the four groups (viewing different commercial versions) were matched on age and sex and "balanced" on "cognitive ability" (memory and verbal comprehension measures). Subjects were randomly assigned to the control condition, but it is unclear whether subjects were randomly assigned to the different E treatments.

Immediately post-exposure, subjects' recall of specific features of the commercial and attitudes towards the product and the premium were measured. In addition, a "simulated purchase setting" was used to test the children's cereal preference (the advertised product versus two well-known brands).

Outcome Measures:

1. Recall. Subjects completed a pencil-and-paper multiple choice test (yes, no, not sure). There were fifteen "product" questions. In addition, E subjects answered an additional eleven premium-oriented questions.

2. Attitude. Children selected one of five faces (ranging from an extreme smiling face to an extreme frowning face) corresponding to their feelings about the premium and the experimental product.

3. Brand choice preferences. The child selected the cereal he or she would most and second most prefer from three cereals (E brand and two others).

Unit of Analysis: Individuals.

Statistical Tests: Yes.

Results: The first set of findings pertain to the hypothesis that including premium offers distracts the child from relevant information about the quality of the product.

A two-way ANOVA (cognitive level by length of commercial time devoted to presenting information about premium) demonstrated significant main effects. (The authors arbitrarily labelled children less than 8 years "preoperational" and children eight or older "concrete-operational.") Higher cognitive level subjects exhibited greater recall of product information than lower cognitive level subjects. Scheffe's *post-hoc* comparisons indicated that the "ten-second premium" E group had significantly higher product recall than the other two E groups. However, the performance of the C group was not significantly different from the E groups: "children exposed to a product/premium ad did not have significantly less product recall than the product version only subjects" (p. 18).

A two-way ANOVA (cognitive development x treatment) was performed on the amount of product recall (this was taken to be a measure of distraction). The treatment differences were again significant in the same fashion as in the previous analysis. However, the cognitive development factor was not significant.

The E groups' accuracy in recalling product information was compared to their premium recall accuracy using t-tests for differences between proportions. These results suggest that as the length of premium presentation increases, the proportion of accurate product information recall decreases and premium recall increases. Even when equal time is devoted to product and premium information, subjects were able to more accurately recall premium information. (It should be noted, however, that premium recall decreased from the fifteen-second to the twenty-second premium presentation.)

The second set of findings pertain to the hypothesis that the premium presentations will influence subject reactions to the product.

The E groups' responses to the "happy face" attitude measures toward the premium and the advertised product were correlated (Pearson). The correlations for both sex-groups were positive, they were quite small and nonsignificant. Thus, "it appears that greater liking of a premium object does not necessarily create greater liking of the product containing the premium" (p. 24). In addition, the C group actually displayed a *more* favorable attitude toward the advertised product than the E subjects (t-test comparing mean attitudes) even though the E subjects were very favorably disposed to the premium.

In the brand choice experiment, the majority of subjects chose the experimental product as their least preferred cereal. While there is a tendency for subjects to become more favorable to the experimental product as the proportion of time devoted to presenting the premium increases, the results (χ^2) were not statistically significant. Correlations between the respondents' brand choice preferences for the experimental product with their attitudes toward it were significant, as were the correlations between attitudes toward the premium object and preferences for the experimental product. Although the latter correlation is modest, it suggests that "the more a premium is liked, the more appealing is the advertised product containing the premium" (p. 28).

Sponsorship: The School of Government and Business Administration, George Washington University.

Published: Yes.

Success: If "success" is arbitrarily defined as the different treatments differentially affecting subject's recall of relevant commercial information and, brand-choice preferences, the support is mixed, and appears to lean toward the "not successful" conclusion.

Criticisms: The authors' decision to divide the sample according to age (less than 8 years versus 8 or older) and to claim that this division corresponds to "level of cognitive development" is questionable. The fact that two variables are correlated (in this case age and cognitive level) is not sufficient reason to substitute one for the other. It would have been more accurate to refer to the variable as "age."

It is possible that in selecting brand preferences, the child responded according to his or her desire for the product, but that in an *actual purchase situation,* he would purchase the product one time to obtain the premium.

The authors compute Pearson correlations when one of the variables is the five "face values." While these data are ordinal, they may not be interval scale and thus a nonparametric analysis may have been more appropriate. In addition, the t-tests computed for differences between proportions of correct product and premium recall should have been for correlated samples; whether or not this is the case is unspecified.

Summary: The results indicate that product recall accuracy may decline as greater proportions of commercial time are devoted to presenting premiums. However, it does not appear that devoting relatively short periods of time to premium presentations distracts from the child's product recall ability. In addition, liking a premium object does not necessarily insure that children will desire the product containing the premium. The study was experimental, with subjects randomly assigned at least to the control condition. The use of the "cognitive level" label appears inappropriate, and the use of certain statistical procedures is questionable.

Study 22

Wackman, Daniel B.; Wartella, E.; and Ward, S. "Children's Information Processing of Television Advertising." Final Report to the National Science Foundation, 1979.

Purpose: To examine how children perceive, evaluate, and use information in television advertising, through three integrated but separate studies, using recognition and recall measures.

Population: Kindergarten and third-grade children in the greater Boston area; a suburban area near Columbus, Ohio; and a suburb of Minneapolis-St. Paul, Minnesota. The Boston children represented a wide range of socioeconomic backgrounds; the Ohio and Minnesota children were from middle- and upper-middle SES backgrounds.

Sample Selection Procedure: Boston: children receiving parental permission participated; selection of the schools not specified. Ohio: all kindergarten and third-grade children attending three schools received parent permission slips; those returning the forms were interviewed. Selection of schools not specified. Minnesota: all kindergarteners in a single school participated. Selection of third graders and of the school not specified.

Sample Size: Boston: $n = 425$. Ohio: $n = 298$. Minnesota: $n = 209$. (Combined total for three studies: $n = 932$).

Outcome Measures: The same basic measures were used in all three parts of the study. All children in Boston, half the children in Ohio, and the Minnesota kindergarteners responded to interviews containing both recall and recognition questions about the commercials they had viewed (representational processes). Recognition questions were both verbal and visual. Questions dealt with product information, commercial elements, and inferences children could draw from the ads. Additionally, children made a choice between the two advertised brands.

The other half of the Ohio students and the Minnesota third graders responded to interviews designed to examine children's choice strategies (information use). The measure manipulated two aspects of product information: attribute preference and amount of an attribute in a given candy. Both attributes and amount were visually differentiated. Children were shown cards representing candies with various amounts and combinations of the attributes. They were told a hypothetical friend's preference for the attributes and asked which of two or three candies that friend would prefer. Children responded to eight sets of choices; the first was a "warm-up."

Experimental Design: All parts of the study used the same stimulus commercials. Commercials for two fictitious candy and two fictitious game products were

286

produced specifically for the project. The candies were two different brands of the same product; the games differed considerably in complexity.

Boston: Conditions varied on the type of commercial appeal (product information versus social acceptability) and repetition of ads (high = three times per day, low = once per day). Design was counterbalanced to provide data on appeal effects holding repetition constant, repetition effects holding appeal constant, and interactions between the two effects. This yielded twelve conditions, with one kindergarten and one third-grade class comprising each condition. Children viewed cartoons with commercials inserted for three consecutive days. Each child was individually interviewed about either the two candy or the two game commercials on the two days following viewing.

Ohio: Commercials varied on appeal and the presentation mode—audio only, audiovisual, and visual only. Only the candy commercials were used in this study. The twelve conditions differed on how the commercials were presented. All conditions included a commercial for each candy product, one product information appeal and one social acceptability appeal and one of the following combinations of presentation mode: audio versus audiovisual, visual versus audiovisual, and audio versus visual. Children were released from class in groups of five to seven to view the videotapes. After viewing, half the children received representational process interviews, and half received information use interviews.

Minnesota: Two of the kindergarten classes were presented with a training program about advertising; the other two classes served as a control group. Objectives of the training program were to teach children that commercials were designed to persuade people to buy things and to teach the types of information children could get from an ad. Sub-objectives included distinguishing between commercials and other TV material and recognizing four types of commercial appeals. Children received approximately 3½ hours of training over a two-week period, then were tested ten to thirteen days after training. Children viewed videotapes in small groups. Each child saw ads for two candy and two game products. One product in each category was a product information appeal, the other was a social acceptability appeal. After viewing, each child was interviewed individually about either the candy or game commercials. Except for omission of training, procedure was the same for children in the control group. Minnesota third graders were individually interviewed to examine choice strategies.

Unit of Analysis: Individuals.

Statistical Tests: Yes (t-tests, χ^2).

Results: In all conditions and in all three locations, children performed significantly better on recognition than on recall measures.

Boston: Third graders consistently scored higher than kindergarteners for both products on recall and recognition measures. Kindergarteners showed higher beliefs in the benefits of the candies than the third graders. Repetition of the candy commercials did not have a systematic effect on either recall or recognition. For the game products, repetition had no effect on product element information for children at either age. However, third graders did show greater recall and recognition of commercial elements under the high repetition condition. This was particularly true for the simpler game. Type of appeal had no consistent significant effect for recall or recognition of either product.

Repetition had no effect on kindergarteners choice of brands, but third graders were significantly more likely to select the brand for which there had been high levels of advertising repetition. Type of appeal had no effect on children's brand choice.

The reasons children cited for choosing a specific brand were also examined. A substantially larger percentage of third graders relied upon product features for the basis of their candy choices than kindergarteners. The younger children tended to cite general affect reasons. For the games, about the same percentages of third graders and kindergarteners mentioned concrete product features. Third graders were approximately four times more likely to mention abstract features as the younger children, and a greater percentage of kindergarteners were unable to provide any reasons for their game choice.

Ohio: Third graders showed better recall and recognition of the product elements and better recall of commercial elements for both commercials. There were no significant age differences in recognition of commercial elements. Kindergarteners attributed more health and social benefits to the products than did the third graders.

There was no main effect of type of appeal on product element retention or perceived benefits. For kindergarteners, presentation mode had a significant effect only for recall measures in the product information condition: audiovisual and visual only were equivalent and far superior to audio only. For third graders, mode was statistically significant in only one condition.

Kindergarteners were equally likely to choose the audiovisually advertised brand or the other brand. Third graders were slightly more likely to choose the audiovisually advertised brand, but this was not statistically significant. Appeal had no effect on brand choices.

All the reasons children gave for selecting a particular answer were examined, creating three scales: product features, general affect, and other responses. There were essentially no differences between age groups in the use of these three response categories in making candy choices.

Minnesota: Testing of the training program took place during the program itself, after a ten- to thirteen-day delay, and eight months later. Children's scores were not as high after eight months as when tested ten to thirteen days after training, but they still showed significantly higher levels of understanding than the control (no training) group. The program was most successful in teaching the persuasive intent of commercials and recognition of different types of content, less successful in teaching recognition of different types of commercial appeals.

For the candy commercials, children in the training program showed higher levels of product elements knowledge for product information commercials; there were no differences between experimental and control groups for social acceptability ads. Children in the experimental condition showed higher levels of product element recognition in two of the four game conditions. There were no significant differences in children's recognition of commercial elements; scores for these scales were extremely low, with children in six of eight groups scoring lower than chance. Type of commercial appeal had no effect on brand choice for children in either experimental or control group.

Children were significantly more likely to give reasons for their game choice than their candy choice. Game-choice children were significantly more likely to use an affect reason for their choice than the candy-choice children. About one-fourth of the children in both the game and candy-choice situations cited product features as reasons for their choice. There was no difference between the experimental and control group kindergarteners in their use of product features in making product choices.

Results from the choice strategy measure indicated that a significantly larger percentage of third graders than kindergarteners were classified as "strategy users" (that is, they had a highly consistent choice pattern). The percentage of children at both grade levels using a strategy, however, was quite high: 93 percent of third graders and 83 percent of kindergarteners. A majority of kindergarteners used an amount strategy, involving no attribute information. Approximately one-fourth of the third graders used a strategy involving attributes ordered by preference; only one kindergartener used this type of strategy.

Success: The project was successful in demonstrating the effectiveness of recognition versus recall measures as a means of measuring children's understanding and retention of information from commercials. The training program showed that young children can successfully be taught about ads. Support for other hypotheses was mixed.

Sponsorship: National Science Foundation.

Published: No.

Criticisms: The similarity of the two candy products resulted in confusion of the brands for many children. This caused problems with measuring children's retention of product information and commercial elements. The authors indicate that it might have been better to show children ads for only one brand of candy. The games were quite distinct but one was so complex, it seemed that many of the younger children may not have understood or been interested in it. Thus, it might have been better if two simple but distinct games had been used.

Summary: This study examined children's information processing of television advertising through the use of recall and recognition measures and choice strategies in three separate but integrated studies. Recognition was significantly more effective than recall in examining children's retention of both product information and commercial elements. A training program to teach kindergarteners about ads was successful. Results on effects of types of appeal, repetition of commercials, and mode of presentation were mixed. Third graders were found to be more likely than kindergarteners to use a choice strategy, although the percentage of children in both grade levels was high. Kindergarteners tended to use much simpler choice strategies than did the older children.

Study 23

Ward, Scott, and Wackman, D. "Family and Media Influences on Adolescent Consumer Learning." *American Behavioral Scientist* 14 (January–February, 1971).

Purpose: To investigate the development of consumer learning in adolescents.

Population: Eight- through twelfth-graders in the Prince Georges County, Maryland, school district.

Sample Selection Procedure: Classrooms in twelve schools were randomly selected. The twelve schools were not randomly selected (for instance, Black schools refused to participate).

Sample Size: $n = 1,094$.

Experimental Design: This study is descriptive. The subjects completed self-administered questionnaires.

Outcome Measures: The four criterion variables were: recall of commercial content, attitudes toward TV advertising, materialistic attitudes, and self-reported effects of commercials on buying behavior. These and other variables were measured by the questionnaire responses except: SES (measured by Duncan socioeconomic index) and IQ (measured by "track" in school).

Statistical Tests: Yes, for some analyses.

Unit of Analysis: Individuals.

Results: Subjects were divided into two age-groups for the analyses, eighth- and ninth-graders versus tenth-, eleventh-, and twelfth-graders. Comparisons between the age-groups indicate no significant differences on the four learning criteria: recall, attitudes, materialism, and buying behavior. There were significant (test unspecified) age differences on almost all of the "communication" variables: younger subjects watch more TV, talk more with their parents about consumption, and are more likely to watch commercials for "social utility" and "communication utility" reasons. According to the authors, "Their results suggest that although younger and older adolescents may be at the same level in terms of consumer learning, the processes of learning may differ for the two age groups."

Correlations (product-moment) among the criterion variables for both younger and older adolescents are "nearly all essentially zero," indicating that "several criteria of consumer learning . . . are quite independent of each other."

The investigators conducted "step-up" regression analyses to study differences in "consumer learning processes" across age-groups. Each criterion variable was predicted by three sets of independent variables (demographic, communication, and reasons for watching TV commercials). The authors discuss those independent variables which when added to the regression equation increased the proportion of variance accounted for by at least 1 percent. Intelligence was the major predictor of TV recall for older and younger subjects. Two variables—social utility reasons for viewing commercials and time spent watching TV—account for much of the younger group variance in attitudes toward TV advertising. In contrast, three different variables—vicarious consumption reasons for viewing commercials, family communication about consumption, and SES—accounted for much of the variance for older subjects. Social utility and vicarious consumption are major predictors of materialism for both age groups. However, the amount of money the adolescent has available is a predictor for younger subjects, while IQ was a predictor for older subjects. Three variables are important predictors of the effects of TV advertising on buying behavior for both age groups: family communication about consumption, social utility reasons for viewing TV commercials, and exposure to magazines. In addition, communicatory utility reasons for viewing commercials is also a predictor for younger subjects. According to the authors, these results suggest that "simple exposure to advertising is not a sufficient condition for buying behavior . . . other variables involving the processing of information about consumption intervene between exposure to the commercial and purchase."

Success: Not applicable

Sponsorship: National Institute of Mental Health, and the Marketing Science Institute.

Published: Yes.

Criticisms: Since the study was not experimental, it is not possible to make inferences about "directionality" of relationships between variables, or "causality." Thus, the authors' claims that certain independent variables which predict the criterion variables are involved in the "learning process" for the criterion variables are not justified. For example, it is possible that consumer learning as indicated by attitudes toward TV advertising influences the amount of time spent watching TV, and not the reverse.

This study is subject to the usual qualifications associated with obtaining data with self-administered questionnaires.

Summary: This descriptive study suggests that older and younger adolescents do not differ with respect to consumer learning (as measured by the four criterion variables), but that the factors influencing the learning processes may differ across age groups. Particularly interesting was the fact that several factors were better predictors of the effects of TV advertising on buying behavior than TV exposure; in fact, there is small but negative relationship between TV exposure and effects of TV advertising on buying behavior. While this finding is not discussed by the authors, it would seem to warrant further investigation.

Study 24

Ward, Scott, and Wackman, D. "Children's Information Processing of Television Advertising." In *New Models for Mass Communication Research*, edited by P. Clarke. Beverly Hills: Sage, 1973.

Purpose: To examine two aspects of children's information processing of TV commercials—selection of information and cognitive processing of information.

Population: Children of mothers participating in Boston area service clubs.

Sample Selection Procedure: A random sample of the service clubs was initially contacted. From each of these clubs, "approximately" equal numbers of mothers of 5- to 12-year-olds were randomly selected. Of 108 mothers initially contacted, 90 agreed to participate. The final sample, for which all of the collected data are available, numbered 67.

Sample Size: $n = 67$.

Outcome Measures: Children's information processing was investigated through direct interviews with the children. The interview transcripts were coded by two research assistants. Children's selection of information was examined through training mothers to code their children's attentional behavior while watching TV. Mothers completed viewing logs which indicated when the child was likely to be watching TV. Specific times for observation were sampled from these logs. Every tenth commercial sequence that the child watched was coded and included in the study.

Experimental Design: This study was completely descriptive.

Statistical Tests: Yes. (χ^2) for information processing data, but not for selection of information data.

Unit of Analysis: Individuals and individual responses.

Results:

Information processing of commercials. Most 5- to 8-year-olds exhibited a low-level understanding of what a commercial is, while the majority of 9- to 12-year-olds exhibited a medium-level understanding (significant χ^2 age by level of awareness).

Most 5- to 8-year-olds exhibited low level differentiation between commercials and programs, whereas three-fourths of the 9- to 12-year-olds exhibited high level differentiation (significant χ^2). For both of these variables (commercial understanding and program-commercial differentiation) low-level responses indicated a reliance on perceptual cues, while higher-level responses indicated a greater understanding of the meaning of the message.

The sample was divided into three "cognitive levels": low (children who gave low-level responses to both questions), medium (children who gave a medium- or high-level response to the commercial understanding question and a high-level response to the program-commercial differentiation question), and high (the performance characterizing these subjects is unspecified). These classifications were related to the subjects' ages.

Children's awareness of the purpose of commercials was shown to increase with cognitive level. A similar result was demonstrated for the relationship between complexity of recall of liked and disliked commercials and cognitive level. The reasons given for liking or disliking commercials differed somewhat across cognitive levels; in particular, a third of low- and medium-level children based their feelings toward the commercial on their response to the product advertised, compared to only 5 percent of high-level children. Lower cognitive level children are more likely to perceive commercials as truthful, to judge the commercial's truthfulness on a perceptual (as opposed to a reality-testing) basis, and to give trusting responses (not aware of the selling motive) when asked why commercials do or don't tell the truth.

Children's Selection of Information. Attention to commercials decreased from the first to later commercials in a sequence; lower cognitive level subjects showed the smallest decrease in attention from the program to the first commercial, while the high-level children showed the greatest differentiation between attention to the program and the first commercial. Low cognitive level children also demonstrated the most stability in their attentional behavior toward commercials appearing at the beginning or end versus the middle of a program, or at different viewing times. Children's attention to commercials was related to the types of products advertised; however, the low-level subjects did not appear to demonstrate greater stability across different product types than the higher-level subjects.

Success: Not applicable.

Sponsorship: National Institute of Mental Health, The Marketing Science Institute, and the American Association of Advertising Agencies.

Published: Yes.

Criticisms: A large proportion of the subjects initially contacted were not included in the final analysis. An attempt should have been made to determine if these subjects were atypical.

It is unclear if the coders of the information processing interviews were aware of the subjects' ages. If this were the case, the ratings of subject responses may have been unintentionally biased. Also, one may question the accuracy and comparability of the mothers' codings of their children's viewing patterns (e.g. mothers of children of different levels may have differed in their coding behaviors).

The authors neglect to specify the criteria for a "high cognitive level" classification.

Summary: This descriptive study indicated that "children's information selection and processing is influenced by their cognitive development" (p. 143). Lower cognitive level children tended to focus on perceptual features of commercials, while higher-level subjects focused on more abstract features. In addition, lower-level children were more likely to trust commercials than higher level children. The attentional patterns of the lower-level children were stable across different conditions, while the higher-level subjects showed more differentiation in their attentional behavior. The study's principle weakness is the possibility of bias in the coding of subject responses.

Study 25

Ward, Scott; Wackman, D.; and Wartella, E. *How Children Learn to Buy: The Development of Consumer Information-Processing Skills.* Beverly Hills: Sage Publications, 1977.

Purpose: To investigate children's acquisition of buying skills.

Population: Kindergarteners, third-, and sixth-graders in Boston (Somerville area) and Minneapolis-St. Paul (Mounds View area). The Boston subjects were from a predominantly working-class community, while the Minneapolis subjects were from middle-class suburbs.

Sample Selection Procedure: It is unclear if all available schools were included; the authors randomly sampled subjects from the participating schools, but the response rates were far below 100 percent (55 percent in Boston, 87 percent in Minneapolis).

Sample Size: 615 child-mother pairs (301 in Boston, 314 in Minneapolis). The sample was divided almost equally among grades, cities, sexes, and SES levels.

Experimental Design: This study was descriptive. Children and mothers were interviewed for one hour each. In addition, mothers completed a self-administered questionnaire. Children's responses to open-ended questions were coded as to "theoretical categories of interest."

Outcome Measures: Nonstandard interviews and parent questionnaires (see Tables Variables).

Unit of Analysis: Individuals and individual responses (an individual may respond more than once on certain items).

Statistical Tests: Yes (χ^2, correlations, multiple regression).

Results: The major independent variable in this study is the child's grade in school; sex and SES differences are also considered. There are many results reported in this book-length study; thus, they will not be reported in detail here. The following summary comments describe the general findings:

    1. Children's consumer information processing. "There are consistent age-related changes in the kinds of information children attend to, select, and use to describe and conceptualize the consumer environment. This change appears to reflect basic developmental growth in children's cognitive capabilities toward increased awareness and use of more abstract, functional kinds of information in consumer information processing."

2. Children's money use and purchase requests. "Children's money use skills (for example, saving) increase as children grow older"; however, the authors did not find age-related changes in nonskilled money use (for example, frequency of *purchase requests*) except for "child relevant products."

3. The family context of children's consumer socialization. "The family context for consumer learning varies in rather consistent ways for different SES levels" (in particular, interaction with the child about consumption increases as the mother's social status increases, while lower-status parents appear to give their children more opportunities to operate as independent consumers). . . . Also, "The family context for consumer socialization differs substantially for children of different ages. . ." (for instance, mothers of older children are more likely to negotiate with their child about purchases, and to provide them with greater opportunities for independence as consumer).

4. The relationship between the family context and children's consumer behavior. In regression analyses with all age groups combined, "age was the best predictor for nearly all child behavior variables and the family support variables did not increase explanatory power to any major extent. In the subsequent analyses for the three separate grade levels, family context variables did increase our explanatory power, but the importance of specific support variables changed, between kindergarten and third grade. In particular, mother-child interaction variables were consistently important for the development of kindergarteners' consumer skills. On the other hand, mothers' own consumer behavior appeared to be consistently important for older children's skill development."

5. Additional findings. The relationship between exposure to commercials and children's consumer learning is mixed and of rather limited importance. Also, exposure to commercials "does not appear to motivate children consistently toward increased spending or asking for products."

Success: Not applicable (no treatment).

Sponsorship: Office of Child Development, Marketing Sciences Institute, and the Educational Foundation of the American Association of Advertising Agencies.

Published: Yes.

Criticisms: This study is based solely on survey data, and thus is subject to the usual qualifications accompanying survey research.

Summary: This descriptive study presents several relationships between children's consumer behavior, family context, and level of cognitive development. (See summaries in Results section.)

Study 26

Wartella, Ellen, and Ettema, J. "A Cognitive Developmental Study of Children's Attention to Television Commercials." *Communication Research 1* (January 1974).

Purpose: To test the relationship between stimulus complexity of television commercials (with content controlled) and children's attention to the stimuli.

Population: Nursery school, kindergarten, and second-grade students in an upper-middle-class suburban St. Paul, Minnesota, school.

Sample Selection Procedure: Unspecified.

Sample Size: n = 120 (40 at each grade level).

Specific Treatment: Subjects were free to watch (or not watch) a television show (situation comedy). The original commercials were deleted and commercials manipulated in terms of stimulus complexity were inserted. Twelve commercials were used, grouped in three blocks: (1) irrelevant commercials, composed of four commercials concerning products of low relevance for children, (2) three relevant commercials concerning foods, and (3) five relevant commercials also concerning foods. The commercials varied as to visual and auditory complexity, as rated by a measure developed by Watt and Krull (1972). Four versions of the program were used, with the commercials rotated within the blocks so that each appeared as the first commercial in the block in one version (except for one of the block three commercials). Blocks were not rotated within the program.

Experimental Design: Within each of the three age levels, ten children were randomly assigned to view each of the four versions of the program. Subjects viewed the program in pairs. Since blocks were not rotated, commercial content was not used as an independent variable (due to possible fatigue factors).

Outcome Measures: Attention was measured by a scheme devised by Ward, Levinson, and Wackman (1972). Attention was coded as full, partial, or none at given observation intervals. Full attention indicated that the child was in a viewing position with eyes on the screen; partial attention indicated that the child was in a viewing position with eyes off the screen, or "apparently not listening," or verbally or physically reacting to the television content; no attention indicated that the child was not in a viewing position and eyes were not on the screen. Interobserver reliability on a subsample of subjects was 90.6 percent.

Unit of Analysis: Individuals.

Statistical Tests: Yes (ANOVA).

Results: Analysis employed the observations of only the first two blocks. The authors predicated that differences in stimulus complexity of the commercials should produce differences in attention with the most complex commercial (high on both visual and auditory) receiving the most attention and the least complex (low-low) receiving least. It was also predicted that this difference should decrease with age. An attention score (the subject's average attention across all observations during a single commercial) for each subject on each commercial was computed. The attention scores were analyzed by a two-way ANOVA (age by stimulus complexity) with repeated measures on the 1st factor. A separate analysis was computed for each of the two blocks. For the irrelevant product block, both main effects were significant, while the age x stimulus complexity interaction was not significant. A comparison (not statistically tested) of the means indicated that kindergarteners had the highest mean attention and nursery schoolers the lowest mean attention, and that attention was highest for the high-visual/high auditory commercial and lowest for the high visual/low auditory commercial. The interaction was in the predicted directions (although not significant): the difference in attention to the high-high (h-h) and low-low (l-l) is greatest for nursery schoolers, smallest for second graders. For the relevant product block, both main effects and the age x stimulus complexity interaction were significant. Attention to these commercials was not ordered according to stimulus complexity (l-visual, h-auditory highest, l-l lowest). As predicted, the (h-h) – (l-l) difference is largest for the youngest group. The authors note that the fact that the irrelevant block came first may have influenced the insignificant interaction for that block, since the subjects may have been adjusting to the environment during that period.

Further analyses were undertaken with an attention change measure, which is the sum of the changes in attention from one observation to the next for twelve observations marking transitions from commercials to programs and *vice versa*. A one-way ANOVA for age was significant. Nursery school children appeared to change the most in their attention from observation to observation. The authors feel that this finding supports the hypothesis that younger children are more sensitive to shifts from program to commercial and vice versa. Further data analyses demonstrated that, for the irrelevant block, mean attention scores of all children were higher for high-auditory than low-auditory commercials. This suggests that variation in auditory complexity may be more important than variation in visual complexity (differences not tested statistically). In addition, high auditory commercials exhibit more movement toward full attention than low auditory commercials, and the decline in attention for the former is generally more gradual.

Success: The treatment effects partially supported the author's hypothesis of the effects of stimulus complexity on children's attention.

Criticisms: The authors point out two weaknesses of the study: (1) the older subjects had a uniformly high attention mean, which may have produced a ceiling effect depressing the different scores of these children—thus, "the issue of whether or not the influence of perceptual attributes declines with age remains open to debate," and (2) stimulus complexity only accounted for 2 percent of the variances in attention. Thus, the absolute effect of this variable (while significant) was small. The attention measure appeared to be more sensitive to the child's visual reactions than his auditory reactions. For example, a child who was not in a viewing position and whose eyes were not on the screen would be rated "no attention" although he could have been listening quite attentively.

The block 2 commercials differed in length—this fact may have had an effect on children's attention scores in addition to complexity. Also, the commercials within blocks differed in specific content (for example, Burger King versus Gatorade) which may have influenced attention to them—children's familiarity or interest in the products apparently was not controlled. It would seem to be more effective to create different versions (with different complexity levels) of one commercial and to present the different versions to different groups of subjects.

The authors do not state why the third block data (representing intermediate ratings of complexity) were not reported. It would be informative to know if finer gradations of complexity did not demonstrate a significant effect on attention.

It would have been informative to test the specific contrasts within factors with a *post hoc* test or, better yet, to have built planned contrasts into the analysis. This would have been possible since the authors had a priori hypotheses about the outcome.

Sponsorship: Office of Child Development.

Published: Yes.

Summary: This study suggests that the stimulus complexity of commercials and age are related to children's attention, and that the effects of differences in stimulus complexity on attention decrease with age. The study's principle weaknesses are a possible ceiling effect for the older subjects, the fact that stimulus complexity only accounted for a small percent of the variance in attention, and the potential biasing effects of differences in length and specific content of commercials within blocks.

Appendix B
Industry Codes and Guidelines for Children's Television Advertising, Set Forth by the National Association of Broadcasters and the National Advertising Division, Council of Better Business Bureaus, Inc.

Children's Television Advertising Guidelines

National Association of Broadcasters

Children, especially preschoolers, are highly dependent on the guidance and direction of the adult world around them—television included—for their individual development. Since children, especially when unsupervised by adults, may not in all situations be able to discern the credibility of what they watch, they pose an ethical responsibility for others to protect them from their own potential susceptibilities. However, broadcasters believe that advertising of products or services normally used by children can serve to inform children not only of the attributes of products/services but also of many aspects of the society and world in which they live. Everyone involved in the creation, production and presentation of such advertising to children has a responsibility to assure that such material avoids being exploitative of or inappropriate to a child's still developing cognitive abilities and sense of value.

Recognizing these special considerations the NAB Code Authority issues these Children's Television Advertising Guidelines designed to assist manufacturers. their agencies, and broadcasters in the preparation and evaluation of television commercials.

Except where hereinafter stated, or where advertising has been granted an exemption under the application of III. Adult Interpretation, these guidelines apply to advertising of products designed primarily for children, or to advertising designed primarily for children or to advertising which is telecast during programs designed primarily for children or within station breaks between such consecutive programs, designed primarily for children.

In addition to the following special guidelines, all such advertising is subject to review, where applicable, under the standards contained in the Television Code.

1. General

A. Documentation adequate to support the truthfulness and accuracy of all claims and representations contained in the audio or video of the advertisement must be made available upon request to broadcasters and/or the Code Authority.

Second edition, April 1977.
Copyright 1977, The Code Authority, National Association of Broadcasters. Reprinted with permission.

B.   The disclosure of information on the characteristics and functional aspects of a product/service is strongly encouraged. This includes, where applicable, relevant ingredient and nutritional information. In order to reduce the possibility of misimpressions being created, all such information shall be presented in a straightforward manner devoid of language or production techniques which may exaggerate or distort the characteristics or functions of the product.

C.   Television advertisements shall not include presumptions that a product or service requiring material investment can be had for the asking. Children shall not be directed to purchase or to ask a parent or other adult to buy a product or service for them.

D.   In order to help assure that advertising is non-exploitative in manner, style and tone, such advertising shall avoid using exhortative language. It shall also avoid employing irritating, obtrusive or strident audio techniques or video devices such as cuts of less than one second in length, a series of fast cuts, special effects of a psychedelic nature (e.g., flashing colors, flashing lights, flashing supered copy, or other effects which could overglamorize or mislead).

E.   Any representation of a child's concept of himself/herself or of his/her relationship to others must be constructively handled. When self-concept claims are employed, the role of the product/service in affecting such promised benefits as strength, growth, physical prowess and growing up must accurately reflect documented evidence.

F.   Advertisements shall not portray attitudes and practices inconsistent with generally recognized social values and customs.

G.   Appeals shall not be used which directly or by implication contend that if children have a product they are better than their peers or lacking it will not be accepted by their peers.

H.   Material shall not be used which can reasonably be expected to frighten children or provoke anxiety, nor shall material be used which contains a portrayal of or appeal to violent, dangerous or otherwise anti-social behavior.

I.   Advertisements and products advertised shall be consistent with generally recognized standards of safety. Advertisements shall not include demonstrations of any product in a manner that encourages harmful use of dramatizations of actions inconsistent with generally recognized standards of safety.

J.   The use of real-life authority figures/celebrities as product presenters shall not include their personal testimonials or endorsements.

K.   Persons who are recognized as being identified, specifically or generically, with an advertised product's counterpart in real-life may not be used as spokespeople or endorsers. This prohibition also applies to actors representing such persons.

L. Nonprescription medications and supplemental vitamin products, regardless of how taken or administered, shall not be advertised in or adjacent to programs initially designed primarily for children under 12 years of age. (This prohibition does not apply to products which have been vitamin enriched or fortified in accordance with accepted nutritional principles.)

M. Advertisements shall not include dramatizations of any product in a realistic war atmosphere.

N. Over simplification or minimization of price such as "only" or "just" shall not be used.

Price may be employed in advertising only if it can be supported as the usual and customary price in a substantial number of retail outlets in the given trade area or areas where the advertising is scheduled.

O. Advertisements shall include audio and video disclosure when items such as batteries needed to operate a product as demonstrated in the advertising are not included.

P. Positive exposition of a product's own attributes are acceptable. However, because of their potential to encourage dissatisfaction on a child's part, competitive/comparison/superiority claims or techniques are disallowed.

Q. Advertising shall positively and clearly disclose a product's method of operation and source of power, where applicable.

R. Advertising shall disclose when a product requires assembly. There shall be no demonstration which creates the impression that a product comes fully assembled when such is not the case.

II. Products/Special Categories

A. Toys

In addition to the foregoing I. General precepts the following guidelines are applicable to all television toy advertising and to other advertising designed primarily for children which emphasizes a product's play value. Excepted are those commercials primarily designed for and directed to adults.

1. Advertising shall present the toy on its actual merit as a plaything. It shall neither exaggerate nor distort play value.

2. Audio and visual production techniques shall not misrepresent the appearance and performance of toys. Any view of a toy or any demonstration of its performance shall be limited to that which a child is reasonably capable of reproducing.

3. When a toy is presented in the context of a play environment, the setting and situation shall be that which a child is reasonably capable of reproducing.

4. The use of stock film footage, real-life counterparts of toys, fantasy and animation are acceptable if: (a) they are confined to the first one third of the commercial. (b) no child or toy appears within them and, (c) the commercial as a whole conforms to the Children's Television Advertising Guidelines.

Any other use of stock film footage, real-life counterparts, fantasy, and animation and any over-glamorization (e.g., large displays, dazzling visual effects) is not permitted.

5. The original purchase must be clearly disclosed in the body of the commercial. There shall not be any implication that optional extras, additional units or items that are not available with the toy, accompany the toy's original purchase.

In the closing five seconds of the commercial the original purchase must be disclosed by video with audio disclosure where necessary for clarification.

6. Advertising shall not employ costumes and props which are not available with the toy as sold or are not reasonably accessible to the child without additional cost.

B.   Premiums and Offers

The Advertising Guidelines for Children's Premiums and Offers shall be applied to all advertising designed primarily for children which promotes premiums or offers. Excepted are those commercials which are primarily designed for and directed to adults.

1. The amount of time devoted to a premium or offer shall be a continuous segment and shall not exceed one half of the commercial or twenty seconds, whichever is less in length. If the premium/offer is related to and used with the product advertised, its incidental appearance in the product segment of the commercial will be permitted on a case-by-case basis.

2. The premium/offer shall at some time be displayed in a still visual presentation, so that it is clearly depicted.

3. In the premium/offer segment, the use of stock footage, real-life counterparts, fantasy or animation is not permitted. In order to maintain continuity, the product spokesperson may deliver a lead-in to the premium/offer segment, provided it contains no endorsement or sell copy for the premium or offer. Also for continuity, the voice-over used in the premium/offer segment may be that of the product spokesperson.

4. The number of items shown in a play situation shall not exceed two per child, or a maximum of four with two or more children, unless the possession of more by one child can be reasonably supported by the advertiser.

5. Positive disclosure of special information, such as the price or separate purchase nature of the items offered, shall be made in the audio. As deemed appropriate, supporting disclosure simultaneously in the video will be required.

6. If any conditions are attached to obtaining a "free" premium or offer, all the conditions must be clearly and conspicuously disclosed simultaneously in audio and video. The appearance of the word "free" in a video super shall not exceed in size that of the conditions disclosed.

7. Toy Advertising Guidelines and all Children's Television Advertising Guidelines shall apply where applicable to premiums and offers.

C. Food

All Children's Television Advertising Guidelines under I. General in addition to the following specific guidelines will apply to food advertising.

1. Given the importance of sound health and nutritional practices, advertisements for edibles shall be in accord with the commonly accepted principles of good eating and seek to establish the proper role of the advertised product within the framework of a balanced regimen. Any representation of the relationship between an edible and energy must be documented and accurately depicted.

2. Each commercial for breakfast-type products shall include at least one audio reference to and one video depiction of the role of the product within the framework of a balanced regimen.

3. Special, enriched foods designed to serve as a substitute for a meal may be advertised as such provided their purpose and nutritional value are featured in the advertising and supported by adequate documentation.

D. Snacks, Candy, Gum, and Soft Drinks

All Children's Television Advertising Guidelines under I. General in addition to the following guideline will apply to advertising for snacks, candy, gum and soft drinks.

1. Commercials for products such as snacks, candies, gums and soft drinks shall not suggest or recommend indiscriminate and/or immoderate use of the product.

E. Clothing

All Children's Television Advertising Guidelines, I. General, will apply to clothing advertising. In addition, where such advertising references the play value of clothing, the Toy Advertising Guidelines II. A. will also be applicable.

F. School/Educational Supplies

All Children's Television Advertising Guidelines, I. General, will apply to school/educational supply advertising. In addition, where such advertising references the play value of the product, the Toy Advertising Guidelines II. A. will also be applicable.

G. Feature Film Trailers

Feature films, other than those appropriate for a general family audience, shall not be advertised in or adjacent to programs initially designed primarily for children under 12 years of age.

III. Adult Interpretation

A. Advertising of any product covered by the foregoing categories if designed for and directed to adults, will be exempted from the application of the provisions of the Children's Television Advertising Guidelines provided:

1. The creative concept and execution of the commercial, both the audio and video, are clearly designed to appeal to adults and not primarily to children under 12.

2. Any use of a child is limited to a real-life situation and, if the child is used other than as an incidental, background character, such use is confined to a situation in which the parent/adult-child relationship is established and the parent/adult remains a principal character.

3. The broadcast schedule does not include the placing of the commercial in or adjacent to programs designed primarily for childeren.

4. The commercial complies with all applicable Television Code standards.

B. The advertising of any product designed primarily for use by adults shall be reviewed on a case-by-case basis to determine acceptability for telecast in or adjacent to programs designed primarily for children, taking into account safety and like considerations. Such advertising may be exempted from certain provisions of the Children's Television Advertising Guidelines (e.g., I-J, I-K, I-P).

Selected Sections of the NAB Television Code Relevant to Children

National Association of Broadcasters

II. Responsibility Toward Children

Brroadcasters have a special responsibility to children. Programs designed primarily for children should take into account the range of interests and needs of children from instructional and cultural material to a wide variety of entertainment material. In their totality, programs should contribute to the sound, balanced development of children to help them achieve a sense of the world at large and informed adjustments to their society.

In the course of a child's development, numerous social factors and forces, including television, affect the ability of the child to make the transition to adult society.

The child's training and experience during the formative years should include positive sets of values which will allow the child to become a responsible adult, capable of coping with the challenges of maturity.

Children should also be exposed, at the appropriate times, to a reasonable range of the realities which exist in the world sufficient to help them make the transition to adulthood.

Because children are allowed to watch programs designed primarily for adults, broadcasters should take this practice into account in the presentation of material in such programs when children may constitute a substantial segment of the audience.

All the standards set forth in this section apply to both program and commercial material designed and intended for viewing by children.

IX. Presentation of Advertising

1. Applicability of Code Standards

A. This Code establishes basic standards for all television broadcasting. The principles of acceptability and good taste within the Program Standards section govern the presentation of advertising where applicable. In addition, the Code establishes in this section special standards which apply to television advertising.

B. Commercial television broadcasters make their facilities available for the advertising of products and services and accept commercial presentations for such advertising. However, television broadcasters should, in recognition of their responsibility to the public, refuse the facilities of their stations to an advertiser where they have good reason to doubt the integrity of the advertiser, the truth of the advertising representations, or the compliance of the advertiser with the spirit and purpose of all applicable legal requirements.

C. Since advertising by television is a dynamic technique, a television broadcaster should keep under surveillance new advertising devices so that the spirit and purpose of these standards are fulfilled.

2. Sponsor identification. Identification of sponsorship must be made in all sponsored programs in accordance with the requirements of the Communications Act of 1934, as amended, and the Rules and Regulations of the Federal Communications Commission.

3. Safety considerations. Representations which disregard normal safety precautions shall be avoided.

Children shall not be represented, except under proper adult supervision, as being in contact with or demonstrating a product recognized as potentially dangerous to them.

6. Audience sensibilities; children.

A. The broadcaster and the advertiser should exercise special caution with the content and presentation of television commercials placed in or near programs designed for children. Exploitation of children should be avoided. Commercials directed to children should in no way mislead as to the product's performance and usefulness.

B. Commercials, whether live, film or tape, within programs initially designed primarily for children under 12 years of age shall be clearly separated from program material by an appropriate device.

C. Trade name identification or other merchandising practices involving the gratuitous naming of products is discouraged in programs designed primarily for children.

D. Appeals involving matters of health which should be determined by physicians should not be directed primarily to children.

E. No children's program personality or cartoon character shall be utilized to deliver commercial messages within or adjacent to the programs in which such a personality or cartoon character regularly appears. This provision shall also apply to lead-ins to commercials when such lead-ins contain sell copy or imply endorsement of the product by program personalities or cartoon characters.

XIII. Premiums and Offers

1. Full details of proposed offers should be required by the television broadcaster for investigation and approved before the first announcement of the offer is made to the public.

2. A final date for the termination of an offer should be announced as far in advance as possible.

3. Before accepting for telecast offers involving a monetary consideration, a television broadcaster should be satisfied as to the integrity of the advertiser and the advertiser's willingness to honor complaints indicating dissatisfaction with the premium by returning the monetary consideration.

4. There should be no misleading descriptions or visual representations of any premiums or gifts which would distort or enlarge their value in the minds of the viewers.

5. Assurances should be obtained from the advertiser that premiums offered are not harmful to person or property.

6. Premiums should not be approved which appeal to superstition on the basis of "luck-bearing" powers or otherwise.

XIV. Time Standards for Network-Affiliated Stations*

In order that the time for non-program material and its placement shall best serve the viewer, the following standards are set forth in accordance with sound television practice:

1. Non-Program Material Definition. Non-program material, in both prime and all other time, includes billboards, commercials and promotional announcements.

Non-program material also includes:

A. In programs of 90 minutes in length or less, credits in excess of 30 seconds per program, except in feature films, shall be counted against the allowable time for non-program material. In no event should credits exceed 40 seconds in such programs.

The 40 second limitation on credits shall not apply, however, in any situation governed by a contract entered into before October 1, 1971.

---

*For children's time standards on independent stations, see provisions XIV-2C, 3D under Time Standards for Network-Affiliated Stations.

B. In programs longer than 90 minutes, credits in excess of 50 seconds per program, except in feature films, shall be counted against the allowable time for non-program material. In no event should credits exceed 60 seconds in such programs.

Public service announcements and promotional announcements for the same program are excluded from this definition.

2. Allowable time for non-program material.

A. In prime time on network affiliated stations, non-program material shall not exceed nine minutes 30 seconds in any 60-minute period.

Prime time is a continuous period of not less than three consecutive hours per broadcast day as designated by the station between the hours of 6:00 PM and midnight.

B. In all other time, non-program material shall not exceed 16 minutes in any 60-minute period.

C. **Children's programming time.** Defined as those hours other than prime in which programs initially designed primarily for children under 12 years of age are scheduled.

Within this time period on Saturday and Sunday, non-program material shall not exceed nine minutes 30 seconds in any 60-minute period.

Within this time period on Monday through Friday, non-program material shall not exceed 12 minutes in any 60-minute period.

3. Program interruptions.

A. Definition: A program interruption is any occurrence of non-program material within the main body of the program.

B. In prime time, the number of program interruptions shall not exceed two within any 30-minute program, or four within any 60-minute program.

Programs longer than 60 minutes shall be prorated at two interruptions per half-hour.

The number of interruptions in 60-minute variety shows shall not exceed five.

C. In all other time, the number of interruptions shall not exceed four within any 30-minute program period.

D. In children's weekend programming time, as above defined in 2C., the number of program interruptions shall not exceed two within any 30-minute program or four within any 60-minute program.

E. In both prime time and all other time, the following interruption standard shall apply within programs of 15 minutes or less in length:

     5-minute program—1 interruption;
     10-minute program—2 interruptions;
     15-minute program—2 interruptions.

F. News, weather, sports and special events programs are exempt from the interruption standard because of the nature of such programs.

4. Consecutive announcements. No more than four non-program material announcements shall be scheduled consecutively within programs, and no more than three non-program material announcements shall be scheduled consecutively during station breaks. The consecutive non-program material limitation shall not apply to a single sponsor who wishes to further reduce the number of interruptions in the program.

Guidelines for the Use of Separator Devices

National Association of Broadcasters

Television Code standard IX-6-B requires that commercials, whether live, film or tape, within programs initially designed primarily for children under 12 years of age shall be clearly separated from program material by an appropriate device.

The purpose of the separator device is to help children or re-enforce children's ability to differentiate between program and nonprogram material.

The Television Code Board is of the opinion that guidelines would further advance the purpose of Television Code standard IX-6-B. Toward that end, the Board issues the following separator device guides to assist Code subscribers in their preparation and use of such devices:

1. At the end of any program segment (including, if appropriate, titles and credits shown at the beginning of a program), a separator device shall be used to delineate the program material from the non-program material that follows. The separator device shall contain the following language in both audio and video:

> We will return after these messages or (Name of program) will return after these messages.

2. Artwork, animation, still or motion pictures, title cards, etc. may be used in the separator device provided that if such a separator includes the depiction of a program character, such depiction shall be limited to an incidental still shot of the character used in a manner that does not detract from the basis intent of the separator device.

3. The identification logo of the station or network may appear in the video portion of the separator device provided it does not detract from the basic intent of the separator device.

4. The separator device shall be kept on-screen at least five seconds, but no longer than 10 seconds.

5. An announcer, either on-screen or voice-over, may deliver the language of the separator device, provided he or she is not involved in the program in

Code News 12 (May 1979). Copyright 1979, The Code Authority, National Association of Broadcasters, Reprinted with permission.

an on-air or otherwise identifiable capacity, and does not appear in a setting associated with the program. The video separator language is also required in such situations.

6. A video and/or audio device shall be used to create a separation between a non-program material element and the program which follows it. Language such as, "Now back to the program" or "We now return to (name of program)" could be used to signify the transaction. [These guides become effective September 1, 1979.]

Children's Advertising Guidelines

Children's Advertising Review Unit, National Advertising Division, Council of Better Business Bureaus, Inc.

Preamble

These guidelines have been developed for the use of advertisers and advertising agencies and for the self-regulatory mechanism which they have established, the National Advertising Division, to help ensure that advertising directed to children is truthful, accurate and fair to children's perceptions.

Because trends in advertising are continually changing and because research and study are constantly shedding new light on children's development and understanding of advertising, these Guidelines have been revised and will continue to be revised periodically as circumstances dictate.

In this second revision, modifications have been made in sections D (Presentation) and E (Promotion by Program Characters etc.). Specifically, subsections D-3, 6, and 10 have been added and subsections D-8 (formerly D-6) and D-9 (formerly D-7) and E-1, 2 have been expanded. In addition, word changes, which clarify the text, have been made in several places.

Principles

Five basic Principles underlie these Guidelines for advertising directed to children:

I. Advertisers should always take into account the level of knowledge, sophistication and maturity of the audience to which their message is primarily directed. Since younger children have a limited capability for evaluating the credibility of what they watch, they place a special responsibility upon advertisers to protect them from their own susceptibilities.

II. Realizing that children are imaginative and that make-believe play constitutes an important part of the growing up process, advertisers should exercise care not to exploit that imaginative quality of children. Unreason-

Revised September 1977. Reprinted with permission, Council of Better Business Bureaus, Inc.

able expectations of product quality or performance should not be stimulated either directly or indirectly by advertising.

III. Recognizing that advertising may play an important part in educating the child, information should be communicated in a truthful and accurate manner with full recognition by the advertiser that the child may learn practices from advertising which can affect his or her health and well-being.

IV. Advertisers are urged to capitalize on the potential of advertising to influence social behavior by developing advertising that, wherever possible, addresses itself to social standards generally regarded as positive and beneficial, such as friendship, kindness, honesty, justice, generosity and respect for others.

V. Although many influences affect a child's personal and social development, it remains the prime responsibility of the parents to provide guidance for children. Advertisers should contribute to this parent-child relationship in a constructive manner.

A. Interpretation

Advertisers are reminded that the interpretation of these Guidelines should conform to and implement the Principles stated above. The intent in all cases should be to deal fairly and honestly with children, fulfilling the spirit as well as the letter of the Guidelines. Each individual commercial or advertisement should be considered in that context. Differences in the nature of broadcast media and print media should be taken into account. The Guidelines should not be regarded as prescribing rigid or inflexible rules which may deprive children and advertisers of the benefits of innovations and new approaches.

B. Scope

The clauses in these Guidelines embrace advertising designed to appeal to children eleven years of age and under. This includes children's advertising which is broadcast in children's programs and programs in which audience patterns typically contain more than 50% children. Commercials appearing in shows in which children are a substantial audience segment, but less than 50%, will be regarded as subject to these Guidelines only when they are clearly addressed to children eleven and under. Print advertising is subject to these Guidelines when it is primarily directed to or primarily read by children.

C. Social Values

Advertising should emphasize positive social and moral values and enrich the dignity of human life, and should avoid portrayals of violence, appeals to fear, or prejudice of any kind. To this end:

1. Advertisements should never portray as desirable any practices which are generally considered unacceptable from the standpoint of social, legal, moral, institutional or family values. Social stereotyping which is demeaning or derogatory to any group should be avoided.

2. Advertisements should not reflect disdain for parents or parental judgment, nor reflect unfavorably on other generally recognized sources of child guidance.

3. Advertisements should never portray undesirable living habits. Advertising should convey respect for others and the world in which the child lives. Civility and good manners should be encouraged.

4. Advertisements should encourage good use of language. This does not preclude informal usage.

5. Advertisements should avoid the contention that, by possessing a product, a child will be more accepted by his peers, or by lacking it, he or she will be less accepted by his peers.

6. Advertisements should avoid the implication that a parent or adult who purchases a given product or service for a child is better or more generous than one who does not.

7. Advertisements should not falsely imply that purchase and use of a product will confer upon the user the prestige, skills, or other special qualities of characters appearing in the commercial or ad. Material benefits attributed to the product or service should be inherent in the use thereof.

D. Presentation

Children have vivid imaginations. Use of imagination enables a child to project himself beyond his immediate capacities and reach for his future potential. Advertisers should, therefore, always respect a child's imagination. The use of imaginative situations appropriate to the audience concerned is an acceptable and normal communications practice. Implicit in the foregoing is the concept that fantasy, including animation, is an appropriate form of communication to any audience, including the very young. However, the use of special situations and fantasy in advertising should not suggest unattainable expectations of performance. To achieve this, presentations should not exploit the child's difficulty in distinguishing between the real and the fanciful. Therefore:

1. Copy, sound and visual presentations—as well as the advertisement in its totality—should not mislead (a) on performance characteristics such as speed, method of operation, size, color, durability, nutritional benefits, noise, etc.;

(b) on perceived benefits such as the acquisition of strength, popularity, growth, proficiency, intelligence and the like; or (c) on the expectation of price range or cost of the product.

2. The advertisement should clearly establish what is included in the original purchase of a product. When items are to be purchased separately, the fact should be disclosed in a way that is clear to the child audience primarily addressed. Advertising for all products sold unassembled should indicate that assembly is required. If any other product is essential in order to use the advertised product—such as batteries—this should be disclosed.

3. In general, information which requires disclosure for legal or other reasons should be in language understandable by the child audience to which the advertisement is addressed. In television advertising, audio as well as video disclosure is encouraged. In all media, disclaimers, when used, should be clearly worded, legible, and prominent.

4. A clearly depicted presentation of the complete advertised product should be shown in the advertisement. Where appropriate to help identify the product, the package may also be depicted, provided it does not mislead as to product characteristics, content, or the price range to be expected.

5. Advertising demonstrations should show the use of a product or premium in a way that can be duplicated by the child for whom the product is intended.

6. An effort should be made to establish the size of a product clearly and adequately. This is of particular importance when size claims are being used, such as "giant sized," "monster size," etc.

7. Representation of food products should be made so as to encourage sound usage of the product with a view toward healthy development of the child and the development of good nutritional practices. Advertisements representing mealtime in the home should clearly and adequately depict the role of the product within the framework of a balanced diet. Over-consumption of food products and beverages should be avoided, nor should it be implied that any one food provides all the nutrients contained in a well-designed daily food plan.

8. To ensure truthful and accurate representations of playthings in television advertisements, they should be shown in normal play environments and situations, except when the number of products to be featured exceeds what would reasonably be owned by the child or children shown in the play situation.

9. Should a whole line of toys or more toys than might reasonably be owned by the average child be featured, in a television advertisement, limbo settings (which are defined as non-representational settings with a plain background) or in-store settings are suggested. These settings might provide a better context for fair demonstration of such products to children. When representing

large lines of products (in print or television) special care should be taken to ensure that the child will understand the separate purchase requirements.

10. When toys or any other product can be purchased either individually or as a collection of related items, price representation, if any, should clearly indicate to the child that the cost of the collection is greater than the cost of the individual item.

E. Promotion by Program Character, Editorial Character or Personal Endorsement

It is recognized that very young children may not fully recognize differences between editorial and program content and advertising content. Hence, endorsement by characters on the programs or in the editorial content of a publication may confuse children. Therefore:

1. Program personalities or characters, either live or animated, on children's programs should not be used to promote products, premiums or services in or adjacent to any program(s) in which the personality or character appears. Similarly, when a product resembling the program personality or character is advertised within a program in which the person or character appears, care should be taken to clearly differentiate between the content of the advertisement and the content of the program.

2. In print media, characters and personalities associated with the editorial content of a publication should not be used to promote products, premiums or services in the same publication. Nor should elements from the editorial content be used in such a way as to prevent the child from readily distinguishing the advertisement from the editorial content.

3. Subject to paragraph (1) of the section, "product characters"—personalities live or animated who are closely associated with or identified with the product—may be used as presenters for the advertised product or service, provided they do not do or say anything to mislead children as to the product or service concerned.

4. Nationally known persons may not be used to attribute a characteristic or quality to a product (including a premium) unless they are generally recognized as qualified to speak on the subject. All personal endorsements should reflect the real experience and beliefs of the endorser.

F. Comparative Claims

It is recognized that advertising which compares the advertised product to another product may be difficult for children to understand and evaluate and may therefore be misunderstood. Therefore, advertisers are urged to present products on their merits without reference to competition.

In the event that a true and significant advantage may exist in a product which can be readily understood by children, this advantage should be clearly explained. If advertisers do develop comparative advertising to children this should be done with the following cautions in mind:

1. Comparative statements should be informational and not demeaning to other products or to previous versions of the same product.

2. Comparative statements should not suggest that the advertised product is superior to another in individual attributes or overall characteristics unless such statements can be documented.

3. Comparative statements implying overall superiority should be avoided when such statements are based on attributes in which the advertised product excels, and where the competitor's product excels in other attributes not mentioned.

4. Comparative price statements should be based on the usual and customary price paid in a substantial number of sales in the trade area where the advertising is carried. Price comparisons should be understandable to the average child for whom the product is intended.

G. Pressure to Purchase

The purpose of advertising to children is to encourage trial and repeat purchases. However, children are not as prepared to make independent decisions—or contribute to family decisions—as are adults. Accordingly, to avoid undue pressure to purchase:

1. Children should not be urged to ask parents or others to buy any products.

2. Products which by their very nature are not primarily intended for use by children should not employ advertising directed to children; nor should such products be promoted by premiums or other means directly to children.

3. All price representations should be clearly and concisely set forth in a manner so as not to exert undue pressure to purchase, and price minimizations such as "only" or "just" should not be used in any advertising directed to children.

H. Safety

For the child, imitation, exploration and experimentation are important facets of the learning process. The various media can enhance this process, as can advertising in each of the media which the child encounters. Recognizing this, advertisers should guide their advertising to contribute to the establishment of safe and sound habits in children. Moreover, children, and occasionally parents, may not be cognizant of hazards that may exist through use or abuse of products. Therefore:

1. Advertisements should not portray adults or children in any unsafe acts, situations or conditions or in acts which are harmful to others.

2. Advertisements should avoid demonstrations or portrayals that encourage miuse, or dangerous or inappropriate use of the product which is inconsistent with generally accepted standards of safety.

3. Medications, drugs and supplemental vitamins (liquid or pills) should not be advertised to children.

I. Claim Substantiation

In accordance with the basic principle of dealing fairly and honestly with children:

1. Advertising to children should not claim or imply any product or performance characteristics which are not supportable by factual data or research which conforms to sound professional practices.

2. Puffery (identified as "flattering publicity" or "extravagant commendation") is not acceptable support for an objective product claim. Advertising claims which might be construed as literally true must be literally true.

J. Additional Guidelines for Premium Advertising

The use of premiums in advertising has potential to enhance the appeal of a product to a child. Special attention should, therefore, be paid to the use of premiums in advertising. To guard against premiums exploiting the children's immaturity:

1. Care should be taken that the child's attention is focused primarily on the product rather than the premium. Therefore, major emphasis should be given to the product and its benefits. Emphasis on the premium should be clearly secondary.

2. It is recognized that limitation of the time devoted to a premium offer within a commercial may not be sufficient to ensure primary attention to the product offer. Therefore, advertisers are urged to weigh all factors, including time, to ensure that the product message is primary.

3. When a premium offer is used, the conditions of the offer should be stated simply, in terms which a child can understand. Every effort should be made to communicate socalled "mandatory" statements and disclaimers in terms which will be understood by a child audience.

Bibliography

Abel, John D. "Television and Children: A Selective Bibliography of Use and Effects." *Journal of Broadcasting* 13 (Winter 1969-70).

Action for Children's Television. Brief II, Toys advertised deceptively. A filing to the Federal Communications Commission, December 11, 1970.

_____. Petition to prohibit advertisements for children's vitamins on children's and family television programs. Petition to the Federal Trade Commission, November 10, 1971a.

_____. General comments on television advertising to children. Testimony before the Federal Trade Commission, November 10, 1971b.

_____. Testimony before the U.S. Senate Select Committee on Nutrition and Human Needs, March 6, 1973.

_____. Petition to promulgate a rule prohibiting the advertising of vitamins on children's and family television programs. Petition to the Federal Trade Commission, October 1975.

_____. Petition to promulgate a rule prohibiting the advertising of candy to children on television. Petition to the Federal Trade Commission, April 1977.

Adler, Richard P. "Policy Relevant and Irrelevant Research on the Effects of Television Advertising on Children." Paper presented to the American Psychological Association annual conference, San Francisco, August 1977.

_____. "Research on Children's Television Advertising Policy." In Herbert S. Dordick, ed. *Proceedings of the Sixth Annual Telecommunications Policy Research Conference*. Lexington, Mass.: Lexington Books, D.C. Heath, 1979: pp. 161-168.

Adler, Richard P.; Friedlander, Bernard Z.; Lesser, Gerald S.; Meringoff, Laurene; Robertson, Thomas S.; Rossiter, John R.; and Ward, Scott. *Research on the Effects of Television Advertising on Children: A Review of the Literature and Recommendations for Future Research*. Washington, D.C.: U.S. Government Printing Office, 1977.

Advertising Age. " '68 Teen Spending Hits $20 Billion Rand Bureau Says." (March 10, 1969): 39.

_____. "Psychologist Urges Moratorium on TV Ads for Kids." (November 15, 1971): 88.

_____. "TV's Effect on Kids Unknown, FTC is Told." (November 15, 1971): 1, 92.

_____. "Many Gripe at Proposed Ban on Premiums; Quaker Likes It." (June 10, 1974): 1.

_____. "See Fast Showdown on Engman's Call for Premium Ad Ban." (June 10, 1974): 1.

_____. "Engman Softens Demand for Children's Premium Ad Ban." (June 24, 1974): 1.

_____. "Advertising Portraying or Directed Toward Women." (April 21, 1975): 72-76.

_____. "Proposal to Ban Premium Ads Imperiled by New Research Data." (May 19, 1975): 1.

_____. "Shaper Line of Action Toys Readied for Fall." (September 13, 1976): 54.

_____. "Report by FTC's Staff Recommends Major Strictures on Children's TV Ads." (February 27, 1978): 1.

_____. "Kids TV Ad Battle Opens; Industry Groups Hopeful." (March 6, 1978): 1.

Aldous, Joan, and McLeod, Jack M. "Commentaries on Ward 'Consumer Socialization.'" *Journal of Consumer Research* 1 (September 1974).

Ambrosino, Lillian. "Do Children Believe in TV?" *Children Today* 1, 6 (1972): 18.

American Pharmacuetical Association. Statement to the National Commission on Marihauna and Drug Abuse, Washington, D.C., July 17, 1972.

Anderson, Daniel R.; Levin, Stephen R.; and Pugzles Lorch, Elizabeth. "The Effects of TV Program Pacing on the Behavior of Pre-School Children." *AV Communications Review* 25 (Summer 1977): 159-166.

Anderson, Kristin; Comstock, George; and Dennis, Nancy. "Priorities and Recommendations." *Journal of Communication* 26 (Spring 1976): 98-107.

Arndt, Johan. "A Research Note on Intergenerational Overlap of Selected Consumer Variables." *Markeds Kommunikasion*, 1971.

Associates for Research in Behavior, Inc. "The Effects of Child-Directed Television Advertising on Children: An Analysis of the Charges and a Conceptualization." Consumer Research Institute, Inc., Washington, D.C., September 1972.

Association of National Advertisers. "Children's Television Advertising Guidelines." Adopted May 31, 1972.

Atkin, Charles. "The Impact of Premium Offers in Children's Television Commercials." Department of Communications, Michigan State University, 1974.

_____. "Children's Social Learning from Television: Research Evidence on Observational Modeling of Product Consumption." Presented at conference of Association for Consumer Research, Cincinnati, 1975a.

_____. "Effects of Television Advertising on Children—First Year Experimental Evidence." Report #1, Michigan State University, June 1975b.

_____. "Effects of Television Advertising on Children—Second Year Experimental Evidence." Report #2, Michigan State University, June 1975c.

_____. "Effects of Television Advertising on Children—Content Analysis of Children's Television Commercials." Report #5, Michigan State University, June 1975d.

_____. "Effects of Television Advertising on Children—Survey of Pre-Adolescent's Responses to Television Commercials." Report #6, Michigan State University, July 1975e.

_____. "Effects of Television Advertising on Children—Parent-Child Communication in Supermarket Breakfast Selection." Report #7, Michigan State University, October 1975f.

_____. "Effects of Television Advertising on Children—Survey of Children's and Mother's Responses to Television Commercials." Report #8, Michigan State University, December 1975g.

_____. "Children's Advertising Rulemaking Comment: A Study of Children and TV Advertising." Presented at the Federal Trade Commission Hearings on Children's TV Advertising, San Francisco, January 1979.

Atkin, Charles, and Culley, J. "Effects of Television Advertising on Children—Attitudes of Industry Executives, Government Officials, and Consumer Critics towards Children's Advertising." Report #4, Michigan State University, June 1975.

Atkin, Charles, and Gibson, Wendy. "Children's Responses to Cereal Commercials." Report to Public Advocates, Inc., 1978.

Atkin, Charles, and Heald, Gary. "The Content of Children's Toy and Food Commercials." *Journal of Communication* 27 (Winter 1977): 107-144.

Atkin, Charles; Murray, J.P.; and Naymen, O.B. eds. "Television and Social Behavior: An Annotated Bibliography of Research Focusing on Television's Impact on Children." National Institute of Mental Health, Washington, D.C., 1971.

Atkin, Charles; and Reinhold, Charles. "The Impact of Television Advertising on Children." Paper presented to the Advertising Division, Association for Education in Journalism, August 1972.

Attorneys General. Petition of the Attorneys General to Promulgate a Rule Restricting the Advertising of Over-the-Counter-Drugs. Presented before the Federal Trade Commission, August 1975.

Baer, Donald M. "Laboratory Control of Thumbsucking by Withdrawal and Representation of Reinforcement." *Journal of the Experimental Analysis of Behavior* 5 (1962): 525-528.

Ball, Samuel, and Bogatz, Gerry Ann. *The First Year of Sesame Street: An Evaluation*. Princeton, N.J.: Educational Testing Service, 1970.

Bandura, Albert. "Influence of Models' Reinforcement Contingencies on the Acquisition of Imitative Responses." *Journal of Personality and Social Psychology* 1 (1965): 585-589.

_____. *Social Learning Theory*. Morristown, N.J.: General Learning Press, 1971a.

_____. "Modeling Influences on Children." Testimony to the Federal Trade Commission, November 1971b.

_____. *Aggression: A Social Learning Analysis* (Englewood Cliffs, N.J.: Prentice-Hall, 1973).

Bandura, Albert; Ross, D.; and Ross, S.A. "Imitation of Film-Mediated Aggressive Models." *Journal of Abnormal and Social Psychology* 66 (1963a): 3-11.

Bandura, Albert; Ross, D. and Ross, S.A. "Vicarious Reinforcement and Imitative Learning." *Journal of Abnormal and Social Psychology* 67 (1963b): 601-607.

Bandura, Albert, and Walters, R.H. *Social Learning and Personality Development.* New York: Rinehart and Winston, 1963.

Banks, Seymour. *Summary of Research on Child Development and the Effect of Mass Media on Television Advertising on Children.* Chicago: Leo Burnett Co., 1971a.

_____. Statement in Behalf of Joint ANA-AAAA Committee before the Federal Trade Commission. October 28, 1971b.

_____. "Children and Television." Remarks at the 15th Annual Conference of the American Advertising Federation, Washington, D.C., January, 1973a.

_____. Remarks prepared for the Seminar on Consumer Socialization of Children, Chicago, January 11, 1973b.

_____. "Advertising and Children." Talk presented to the AMA Public Interest Workshop, Washington, D.C., May 1973c.

_____. Statement to the Federal Communications Commission, Washington, D.C., 1973d.

_____. "Advertising and Children." In S. F. Divita, ed., *Advertising and the Public Interest.* Chicago: American Marketing Association, 1974.

_____. Remarks to the NAB National Conference on Children's Television, Washington, D.C., June 3, 1975a.

_____. "Public Policy on Ads to Children." *Journal of Advertising Research* 15 (August 1975b): 7-12.

_____. "The Policy Issues Involved in a Discussion of Children's Commercials." Paper presented at the American Psychological Association, Chicago, August 30, 1975c.

_____. "Review of Literature on Children's Influence in Family Purchase Decisions." Unpublished paper, Leo Burnett, U.S.A., Chicago, 1978.

Barcus, F. Earle. "Advertising in the Sunday Comics." *Journalism Quarterly* 39 (Spring 1962): 196-202.

_____. *Saturday Children's Television.* Newton, Mass.: Action for Children's Television, July 1971a.

_____. "Description of Children's Television Advertising." Statement before the Federal Trade Commission hearings on modern advertising practices, November 10, 1971b.

_____. "Concerned Parents Speak Out on Children's Television." Newton, Mass.: Action for Children's Television, March 1973.

_____. *Weekend Commercial Children's Television.* Newton, Mass.: Action for

Children's Television, October 1975a.

_____. *Television in the Afternoon Hours.* Newton, Mass.: Action for Children's Television, October 1975b.

_____. *Pre-Christmas Advertising to Children.* Newton, Mass.: Action for Children's Television, September 1976a.

_____. "Over-the-Counter and Proprietary Drug Advertising on Television." in Ronald E. Ostman, ed., *Communication Research and Drug Education*, vol. 3. Beverly Hills: Sage Publications, 1976b, pp. 89-111.

_____. *Commercial Children's Television on Weekends and Weekday Afternoons: A Content Analysis of Children's Programming and Advertising Broadcast in October 1977.* Newton, Mass.: Action for Children's Television, 1978.

Barry, Thomas E. "64 of 65 Mothers Say TV Ads Influence Children." *Pediatric News* (February 1976).

_____. "Race as a Dimension in Children's TV Advertising: The Need for More Research." *Journal of Advertising* 6 (Summer 1977): 5-10.

_____. "The Effect of a Modified Disclaimer on Inner-City vs. Suburban Children." Unpublished paper, 1978.

Barry, Thomas E., and Hansen, R.W. "How Race Affects Children's TV Commercials." *Journal of Advertising Research* 13 (October 1973): 63-67.

Bauer, Raymond A., and Greyser, Stephen A. *Advertising in America: The Consumer View.* Boston: Harvard Business School, 1968.

Bechtel, Robert B.; Achelpohl, Clark; and Akers, Roger. "Correlates Between Observed Behavior and Questionnaire Responses on Television Viewing." In Eli Rubinstein et al., eds., *Television and Social Behavior*, vol. 4. Washington, D.C.: U.S. Government Printing Office, 1972, pp. 274-344.

Bellotti, Francis X. Statement Before the Subcommittee on Communications, Hearings of the Committee on Interstate and Foreign Commerce. Washington, D.C.: House of Representatives, July, 1975a, Serial No. 94-53.

_____. Petition before the F.C.C. of the Attorneys General of Massachusetts, Alaska, Colorado, Delaware, Hawaii, Illinois, Maryland, Nebraska, New Hampshire, North Carolina, Maine, Pennsylvania, Rhode Island, and Wyoming to promulgate a rule restricting the advertising of over-the-counter drugs, July 1975b.

Berry, Lewis A., and Pollay, R.W. "The Influencing Role of the Child in Family Decision-Making." *Journal of Marketing Research* 5 (February 19, 1968): 70-72.

Berkowitz, Leonard. *Aggression: A Social Psychological Analysis.* New York: McGraw-Hill, 1962.

_____. *The Development of Motives and Values in the Child* New York: Basic Books, Inc., 1964.

Beuf, Ann H. "Television Commercials as Socializing Agents." In J. Kernan, ed., *Advances in Consumer Research*, vol. III. Proceedings of the Association for Consumer Research, 1975.

Bever, T.G.; Smith, M.L.; Bengen, B.; and Johnson, T.G. "Young Viewers Troubling Response to TV Ads." *Harvard Business Review* 53 (November-December 1975): 119-21.

Birch, Leann Lipps. "Dimensions of Preschool Children's Food Preferences." Paper presented at the Society for Nutrition Education Annual Meeting, 1978.

Bjorklund, Gail. "An Exploratory Study of Toddlers' Satisfaction with Their Toy-Environments." Unpublished paper, 1978.

Blatt, Joan; Spencer, L.; and Ward, S. "A Cognitive Developmental Study of Children's Reactions to Television Advertising." In Eli A. Rubinstein et al., eds. *Television and Social Behavior*, vol. 4. Washington D.C.: U.S. Government Printing Office, 1972, pp. 452-467.

Bluestone, Stephen L. "Inquiry into Modern Advertising Practices." Statement before the Federal Trade Commission, November 12, 1971.

Bogatz, Gerry Ann, and Ball, Samuel. *The Second Year of Sesame Street: A Continuing Evaluation*, vols. 1 & 2. Princeton, N.J.: Educational Testing Service, 1971.

Bond, E.L., Jr. "New Young and Rubicam Study shows Pragmatic Youth." *Advertising Age* 35 (April 13, 1964): 8.

Bower, Robert T. *Television and the Public*. New York: Holt, Rinehart and Winston, Inc., 1973.

Brazelton, T. Berry. "Children and Television." Unpublished talk.

Breckenridge, M.E. "Food Attitudes of 5-12 Year Old Children." *Journal of the American Dietetic Association* 35 (1955).

Breen, Miles P., and Powell, J.T. "The Relation Between Attractiveness and Credibility of Television Commercials as Perceived by Children—A Replication." Paper presented to Central State Speech Association, Minneapolis, 1973.

Brim, Orville G., Jr., and Wheeler, S. *Socialization After Childhood: Two Essays*. New York: John Wiley & Sons, Inc., 1966.

Broadcast Advertisers Reports. *Daypart Sales Force Report.* New York: BAR, 1975, 1978a.

_____. *Network TV Service.* New York: BAR, 1978b.

Broadcasting. "Television for Children.: There's More than May Meet the Eye." (November 20, 1972): 33.

Broadcasting Yearbook, 1979. Washington, D.C.: Broadcasting Publications, Inc., 1979. Series of annual volumes.

Brodbeck, A.J. "The Mass-Media as a Socializing Agency." Paper presented at the American Psychological Association Symposium on Children and the Mass-Media, San Francisco, 1955.

Bronfenbrenner, Urie. "Developmental Research, Public Policy and the Ecology of Childhood." *Child Development* 45 (1974): 1-5.

Brown, Ann L. "Recognition, Reconstruction and Recall of Narrative Sequences by Pre-operational Children." *Child Development* 46 (1975): 156-166.

Brumbaugh, Florence N. "What Effect Does TV Advertising Have on Children?" In Constance Carr, ed., *Children and TV*. Washington, D.C.: Association for Childhood Education International, 1954.

Bryant, Jennings, Jr. "Formative Research in Advertising." Paper presented for Children's Television Workshop, 1972.

Buck, Ross. "Nonverbal Communication of Affect in Children." *Journal of Personality and Social Psychology* 31 (1975): 644-53.

Bureau of Advertising, American Newspaper Publishers Assn. "The Adult Toy Buyer: A Further Exploration of How Parents and Non-Parents Buy Toys." American Newspaper Publishers Association, September, 1967.

Burr, Pat, and Burr, Richard M. "Product Recognition and Premium Appeal." *Journal of Communication* 27 (Winter 1977): 115-117.

Burrall, Sarah, and Rossiter, John R. "Perceived Meaning of Product Claims in F.A.O. Schwartz Toy Catalog Advertising." Paper presented to the Conference on Culture and Communications, Temple University, March 1975.

Busby, Linda J. "Sex-Role Research in the Mass Media." *Journal of Communication* 25 (Autumn 1975): 107-131.

Cagley, James W. "Advertising Preference Testing in Middle Childhood." Paper presented at Southwest Social Science Association, March 1973.

_____. "Children's Preferences of Selected Print Appeals." *Journal of Advertising* 3, no. 4 (1974): 34-39.

Calder, Bobby J.; Robertson, Tom; and Rossiter, John. "Children's Consumer Information Processing." *Communications Research* 2 (July 1975): 307-316.

Campbell, John D. "Illness Is a Point of View: The Development of Children's Concepts of Illness." *Child Development* 46 (March 1974): 92-100.

Campbell, Roland P. Statement on the Self-Regulation of Children's Advertising. Presented to the Subcommittee on Communications of the Committee on Interstate and Foreign Commerce, U.S. House of Representatives, July 15, 1975.

Canadian Advertising Advisory Board. "The Child's World and Television Advertising." (November 1971).

Canadian Association of Broadcasters. "Broadcast Code for Advertising to Children." (October 1971), revised 1973.

Canadian Broadcasting League. "Quebec Code for Ads to Children." *Telenation* 1 (January 1973).

_____. "A Brief to the Parlaimentary Standing Committee on Broadcasting, Film, and Assistance to the Arts." (June 4, 1973).

Capon, Noel., and Kuhn, Deanna. "The Development of Consumer Information Processing Strategies." Unpublished working paper, 1978.

Caron, Andre H. "The Effects of Advertising on Children." Le Publicite—Club de Montreal, Inc., Montreal, 1971.

Caron, Andre, and Ward, S. "Gift Decisions by Kids and Parents." *Journal of Advertising Research* 15 (August 1975): 12-50.

Cateora, Philip R. "Teenagers as Consumer-Buyers." Chapter 6 in *An Analysis of the Teen-Age Market,* Studies in Marketing No. 7, Bureau of Business Research. Austin: University of Texas, 1963, pp. 86-103.

Center for Science in the Public Interest. Petition for a Rule to Regulate Advertising of Sugared Food Products on Children's Television. Petition to Federal Trade Commission, April 1977.

Chaffee, Steven H., and McLeod, J.M. "Adolescent Television Use in the Family Context." In E.A. Rubinstein et al., eds., *Television and Social Behavior,* vol. 4. Washington, D.C.: Government Printing Office, 1972, pp. 149-172.

Charren, Peggy. "Roundtable 5: Children's TV." Group discussion attended by Peggy Charren, Bill Claggett, George Heinemann, Jack Jacobson, Gerald Thain, Seymour Banks. *Media Decisions* (August 1973).

_____ . Testimony before the House Communications Subcommittee, July 14, 1975.

Cheles-Miller, Pamela. "Reactions to Marital Roles in Commercials." *Journal of Advertising Research* 15 (August 1975): 45-49.

Children's Advertising Review Unit. *See* National Advertising Division.

Child Research Service, Inc. "Study of 5 and 6 Year Olds Who Are Knowledgeable About the Purpose of Commercials." CRS # 5597, Child Research Service, Inc., New York, February 1978.

Choate, Robert B. Testimony before the Subcommittee on the Consumer Committee of Commerce, U.S. Senate, July 23, 1970.

_____ . "Researchers Air Views on Kids' Ads." *Advertising Age* (November 15, 1971): 86-87.

_____ . "The Sugar-Coated Children's Hour." *The Nation* (January 31, 1972a).

_____ . "Proposed Public Television Code Authority for Advertising Edibles, Beverages, Pills and Other Internally Consumed Products." Presented to the Code Authority, National Association of Broadcasters, 1972b.

_____ . "The Selling of the Child: The Role of Motivational Research Houses in Children's TV Advertising." Statement before the Consumer Subcommittee of the Committee on Commerce, U.S. Senate, New York City, July 23, 1973a.

_____ . "The Eleventh Commandment: Thou Shalt Not Covet My Child's Purse." Council on Children, Media, and Merchandising, Washington, D.C., 1973b.

_____ . Petition of the Council on Children, Media and Merchandising to issue a trade regulation rule governing the private regulation of children's television advertising. Filed before the Federal Trade Commission, Washington, D.C., March 1975a.

_____ . Petition for the Council on Children, Media and Merchandising for reconsideration and redrafting of Amendments to Television License

Renewal Form on Child Related Topics and for Extension and Equalization of Restraints on Television Advertising to Children. Before the Federal Communications Commission, March 1975b.

_____ . Statement presented at Hearings before the Subcommittee on Communications of the Committee on Interstate and Foreign Commerce, House of Representatives (Serial No. 94-53). Washington, D.C.: Government Printing Office, 1975c.

_____ . Testimony to the Federal Trade Commission in the matter of trade regulation rule on food/nutritional advertising, October 1976a.

_____ . Testimony before the FTC/FCC OTC Drug Advertising to Children Panel, Washington, D.C., May 21, 1976b.

Choate, Robert B., and Debevoise, N. Presentation to the Child Development Consultants of the Council of Better Business Bureaus, Inc., January 1975.

Clancy, K.J. "One Nutritionist's View of Food Advertising: The Proposed TRR's of the FTC." Talk presented at American Marketing Association Educator's Conference, August 1975.

Clancy, K.J., and Sharaga, S. "Some Effects of Television Advertising on Children's Nutrition Attitude, Nutrition Knowledge and Eating Habits." Paper presented at the meeting of the Society for Nutrition Education, Boston, August 1974.

Clancy, K.J.; Sharaga, S.; Hickey, A.; Nevill, G.; Goldbert, H.; and Bibby, B. "The Effects of Television Advertising on Children's Food Habits." Cornell University, in progress.

Clancy-Hepburn, Katherine; Hichey, A.A.; and Neville, G. "Children's Behavior Responses to TV Food Advertisements." *Journal of Nutrition Education* 6 (July-Sept. 1974): 93-96.

Clausen, John A. *Socialization and Society.* Boston: Little, Brown, and Co., 1968.

Collins, W. Andrew. "The Developing Child as a Viewer." *Journal of Communication* 25 (Autumn 1975): 35-44.

Collins, W. Andrew, and Hooten, C.A. "Relative Effects of Communication and Message on Opinion Change by Children and Adolescents." Unpublished paper, Institute of Child Development, University of Minnesota, 1975.

Comstock, George. "Effects of Television on Children: What is the Evidence?" Paper presented at Telecommunication Policy Research Conference, Airlie, Virginia, April 1975a.

_____ . *Television and Human Behavior: The Key Studies.* Santa Monica, Calif.: Rand Corporation, June 1975b.

_____ . "Television and the Teacher." Working paper, Santa Monica, Calif.: The Rand Corporation, 1976.

_____ . "Paradoxes in the Role of Mass Media in Citizen Education." S.I. Newhouse School of Public Communications, Syracuse University, October 1977.

Comstock, George; Chaffee, Steven; Katzman, Natan; McCombs, Maxwell; and Roberts, Donald. *Television and Human Behavior*. New York: Columbia University Press, 1978.

Comstock, George, and Fisher, M. *Television and Human Behavior: A Guide to the Pertinent Scientific Literature*. Santa Monica, Calif.: Rand Corporation, June 1975.

Comstock, George, and Lindsey, G. *Television and Human Behavior: The Research Horizon, Future and Present*. Santa Monica, Calif.: Rand Corporation, June 1975.

Condry, J. "Psychologist Urges Moratorium on TV Ads for Kids." *Advertising Age* (November 15, 1971).

Congressional Research Service, Library of Congress. *The Role of the Federal Government in Nutrition Education*. Study prepared for the House Subcommittee on Domestic Marketing, Consumer Relations and Nutrition. Washington, D.C.: U.S. Government Printing Office, 1977.

Consumer Advisors to Children's Television Advertising Project. "Proposed additions and alterations to present code standards governing television advertising to children." Memo to Federal Trade Commission Chairman Lewis Engman, January 14, 1974.

Cook, Carolyn; Eiler, Doyle; and Kaminaka, Elizabeth. "How Much Nutrition Education in Grades K-6?" *Journal of Nutrition Education* 9, no. 3 (1977): 131-135.

Cooper, Barbara, and Philp, Murray. "Evaluation of Nutrition Education in Everyday Teaching Environment." *Journal of Nutrition Education* 6, no. 3 (1974).

Corder-Bolz, Charles R., and O'Bryant, Shirley. "Teacher vs. Program." *Journal of Communication* 28 (Winter 1978): 97-103.

Cosmas, Stephen C., and Yannaopoulos, Niki. "Advertising Directed to Children: A Look at the Mother's Point of View." Virginia Polytechnic Institute and State University, Blacksburg, Virginia (Working Paper No. 125), May 1978.

Costley, Gary E. "Novel Approaches to Nutrition Education." Remarks before the 1973 Newspaper Food Editor Conference.

Coulson, John S. "Buying Decisions Within the Family and the Consumer-Brand Relationship." In J.W. Newman, ed., *On Knowing the Consumer*. New York: John Wiley and Sons, Inc., 1966.

Council on Children, Media and Merchandising. Comments before the Federal Communications Commission, September 25, 1975.

_____. *Edible TV: Your Child and Food Commercials*. Washington, D.C.: U.S. Government Printing Office, 1977.

Culley, James D. "Perceptions of Children's Television Advertising: An Empirical Investigation of the Beliefs and Attitudes of Consumer, Industry, and Government Respondents." Preliminary report, Bureau of Economic and Business Research, January 1975.

Culley, James D.; Lazer, William; and Atkin, C.K. "The Experts Look at Children's Television." *Journal of Broadcasting* 20 (Winter 1976): 3-21.

Cuozzo, Peter F. "An Inquiry into the Image of Food and Food Habits as Presented by Television Food Commercials." Unpublished masters thesis, Annenberg School of Communications, University of Pennsylvania, 1971.

Danzinger, K. "Children's Earliest Conceptions of Economic Relationships (Australia)." *Journal of Social Psychology* 47 (1958): 231-240.

Deering, B.J., and Jacoby, J. "The Effects of 'Alternative Relationships' and 'Relative Resources' on Consumer Decisions Between Mother and Child." In *Proceedings of the 2nd Annual Conference of the Association for Consumer Research.* College Park, Md.: Association for Consumer Research, 1971, pp. 135-142.

Diamond, Steven L. "Consumer Education: Perspectives on the State of the Art." Unpublished paper, Harvard Graduate School of Business Administration, May 23, 1972.

Dickins, Dorothy, and Gerguson, U. "Practices and Attitudes of Rural White Children and Parents Concerning Money." Mississippi Agricultural Experiment Station, Technical Bulletin #43, State College, Mississippi, June 1957.

Dickins, Dorothy, and Johnston, A. "Children's Influence on Family Food Purchase Decision." Mississippi Agricultural Experiment Station, Bulletin #671, State College, Mississippi, 1963, p. 15.

Disson, Stephen. "The Effects of Television Advertising on a Child's Eating Habits and Control Over the Family Food Purchase." Unpublished manuscript, University of Pennsylvania, 1974.

Donohue, Thomas R. "Effects of Commercials on Black Children." *Journal of Advertising Research* 15 (December 1975): 41-47.

Donohue, Thomas R.; Henke, Lucy L.; and Donohue, William A. "Non-Verbal Assessment of Children's Understanding of Television Commercial Intent and Program Market Segmentation." Unpublished paper, October 1978.

Donohue, Thomas R.; Meyer, Timothy P.; and Henke, Lucy L. "Black and White Children: Perceptions of TV Commercials." *Journal of Marketing Research* 42 (October 1978): 34-40.

Donohue, Thomas R.; Meyer, Timothy P.; and Henke, Lucy L. "Learning about Television Commercials: The Impact of Instructional Units on Children's Perceptions of Motive and Intent." *A V Communication Review,* in press.

Doob, Anthony N., and Macdonald, Glenn E. "Television Viewing and Fear of Victimization: Is the Relationship Causal?" *Journal of Personality and Social Psychology* 37 (February 1979): 170-179.

Doolittle, John, and Pepper, Robert. "Children's TV Ad Content: 1974." *Journal of Broadcasting* 19 (Spring 1975): 131-142.

Duffy, John, and Rossiter, John R. "The Hartford Experiment: Children's Reactions to TV Commercials in Blocks at the Beginning and the End of the Program." Paper presented at the 1975 Conference on Culture and Communications, Philadelphia, Temple University, March 1975.

Dunsing, Marilyn. "Spending Money of Adolescents." *Journal of Home Economics* 52 (1960): 756-759.

Editor and Publisher. "Teenage Spenders Rely on Ads in Newspapers." (January 22, 1966): 17.

Elias, Marilyn. "How to Win Friends and Influence Kids on Television." *Human Behavior* (April, 1974): 16-23.

Eliot, Thomas. "Money and the Child's Own Standard of Living." *Journal of Home Economics* 24 (1932): 1-9.

Engman, Lewis. Address before Young Lawyer's Section of American Bar Association, August 1973.

_____ . Address before the 1974 Annual Convention, American Advertising Federation, Washington, D.C., June 3, 1974.

_____ . Statement before the Subcommittee on Communications, Committee on Interstate Commerce, House of Representatives, United States Congress, July 16, 1975.

Ephron, Erwin. "How (and How Not) to Solve TV Clutter." *Advertising Age* 46 (April 21, 1975): 57-58.

Eppright, E., and Swanson, P. "Distribution of Nutrients Among Meals and Snacks of Iowa School Children." *Journal of the American Dietetic Association* 31 (1955): 256.

Erickson, E. *Childhood and Society.* New York: Norton, 1950.

Faber, Ronald, and Ward, S. "Validation of Mother-Child Purchase Influence Frequency Reports by the Multitrait-Multimethod Matrix." Marketing Science Institute Technical Report, April 1975.

Fauman, Bruce C. "Determinants of Adolescents' Brand Preferences." Unpublished thesis, Sloan School of Management, M.I.T., June 1966.

Federal Communications Commission. *Federal Communications Commission Annual Report,* 1973.

_____ . "Children's Television Programs—Report and Policy Statement." *Federal Register* 39 (November 6, 1974).

_____ . "Public Notice: February 23, 1976." (a)

_____ . "Request for Ban on Television Drug Ads Denied." *News Report,* No. 14747, Washington, D.C., December 10, 1976b.

Federal Register. Vol. 39, no. 134 (July 11, 1974): 25505-25510.

Federal Trade Commission. "FTC Explores Children and Advertising." *Broadcast Advertising* (November 15, 1971).

_____ . "Food Advertising: Proposed Trade Regulation Rule and Staff Statement." *Federal Register* 39, 218 (1974).

_____ . "Final Notice Regarding Food Advertising Proposed Trade Regulation Rule." *Federal Register* 41, no. 42 (1975a).

_____ . *In the Matter of General Foods Corporation. Complaint; Decision and Order.* Docket No. C-2733 (1975b).

_____ . "Hudson Pharmaceutical Corp." FTC Consent Order File No. 762 3054, Washington, D.C. 1976.

_____ . "Children's Advertising: Proposed Trade Regulation Rulemaking and Public Hearings." *Federal Register* 43, no. 82 (1978): 17967-17972.

Federal Trade Commission News Summary. Vol. 3, no. 24 (1978).

Federal Trade Commission Staff Report on Television Advertising to Children. Washington, D.C.: Federal Trade Commission, 1978.

Feldman, Shel, and Wolf, Abraham. "What's Wrong with Children's Commercials." *Journal of Advertising Research* 14 (February 1974): 39-43.

Feldman, Shel; Wolf, Abraham; and Warmouth, Doris. "Parental Concern about Child-Directed Commercials." *Journal of Communication* 27 (Winter 1977): 125-137.

Ferguson, Clara P. "An Investigation of Preadolscent Children's Attitudes Toward Television Commercials." Unpublished dissertation, North Texas State University, August 1973.

_____ . "Preadolescent Children's Attitudes Toward Television Commercials." Bureau of Business Research, The University of Texas, Austin, 1975.

Feshbach, Norma; Jordan, Tricia; and Dillman, Arline. "The Nutritional Graphic Preliminary Investigation." Submitted by the Council on Children, Media and Merchandising to the Federal Trade Commission, Washington, D.C., October 1976.

Feshbach, Norma; Jordan, T.S.; Dillman, A.S.; Choate, R.; Feshbach, S.; and Zolotow, M. "The Design of a Graphic to Convey Nutritional Information to Children: Pilot Studies." Council on Children, Media and Merchandising, October 1976.

Flavell, J.H. *The Development Psychology of Jean Piaget.* New York: D. Van Nostrand Co., 1963.

Fowles, Barbara R. Statement presented at Hearing before the Subcommittee on Communications of the Committee on Interstate and Foreign Commerce, House of Representatives (Serial No. 94-53). Washington, D.C.; Government Printing Office, 1975a.

_____ . "Moppets in the Marketplace: Evaluating Children's Responses to Television Advertising." Paper presented to the Association for Consumer Research, Cincinatti, Ohio, November 1, 1975b.

Fox, Renee C. "Illness." *International Encyclopedia of the Social Sciences,* vol. 7. New York: Macmillan, 1968, pp. 90-97.

Frideres, James S. "Advertising, Buying Patterns, and Children." *Journal of Advertising Research* 13 (February 1973): 34-36.

Friedlander, Bernard, and Wetstone, Harriet. "Effects of Informational and Cartoon Program Format, Musical Distractors and Age on Children's Listening to Television Soundtracks." New England Instructional Television Research Center, 1974.

Friedlander, Bernard; Wetstone, Harriet; and Scott, Christopher. "Suburban

Preschool Children's Comprehension of an Age-appropriate Informational Televison Program." *Child Development* 45 (1974): 561-565.

Friedrich, Lynette L. "Implications from Research on Prosocial Behavior for Programming and Advertising Directed to Children." Remarks to the Children's Advertising Review Unit Seminar, New York City, June 20, 1975.

Friedrich, Lynette, and Stein, Aletha. "Aggressive and Prosocial Television Programs and the Natural Behavior of Preschool Children." *Monographs of the Society for Research in Child Development* 38, no. 4 (1973).

Galst, JoAnn Paley, and White, Mary Alice. "The Unhealthy Persuader: The Reinforcing Value of Television and Children's Purchase Influence Attempts at the Supermarket." *Child Development* 47 (December 1976): 1089-1096.

Gardiner, M. "Mothers' Attitudes Toward Children's Advertising." *Sales Management* (July 1971).

Gardner, Robert K. "Replication of 'Children's Responses to Commercials: A Conjoint Analysis.'" Student paper, The Wharton School, University of Pennsylvania, 1975.

Gavian, Ruth. "Children's Experiences with Money." *Social Education* 2 (1938): 166-168.

Gerbner, George, and Gross, L. "Living with Television: The Violence Profile." *Journal of Communication* 26 (Spring 1976): 173-199.

Gertenbach, Robert. Address to Children's Review Unit Seminar, New York City, June 20, 1975.

Gianinno, Lawrence J., and Zuckerman, Paul A. "Measuring Children's Responses to Television Advertising." Unpublished paper with a summary version appearing in Clark Leavitt, ed., *Proceedings: American Pscyhological Association Division 23,* 85th Annual Convention, San Francisco, August 1977.

Gibbs, Mary. "Decision-Making Procedures by Young Consumers." *Journal of Home Economics* 55 (May 1963): 359-360.

Gilbert, Eugene. *Advertising and Marketing to Young People.* Pleasantville, N.Y.: Printers' Ink Books, 1957.

_____. "Why Today's Teenagers Seem So Different." *Harper's Magazine* 219 (November 1959): 76-79.

Gilkison, Paul. "What Influences the Buying Decision of Teenagers?" *Journal of Retailing* 41 (Fall 1965): 33-41.

Goldberg, Marvin E., and Gorn, Gerald J. "An Experimental Approach the Effects of Television Advertising on Children." In S.F. Divita, *Advertising and the Public Interest.* Chicago: American Marketing Association, 1974a, pp. 149-159.

Goldberg, Marvin E., and Gorn, Gerald J. "Children's Reactions to Television Advertising: An Experimental Approach." *Journal of Consumer Research* 1 (September 1974b): 69-75.

Goldberg, Marvin E., and Gorn, Gerald J. "Some Unintended Consequences of TV Advertising to Children." *Journal of Consumer Research* 5 (June 1978): 22-29.

Goldberg, Marvin E.; Gorn, Gerald J.; and Gibson, Wendy. "TV Messages for Snacks and Breakfast Foods: Do They Influence Children's Preferences?" *Journal of Consumer Research* 5 (1978): 73-81.

Goldblith, "Factors Which Will Influence the Future of the American Food Industry," Paper presented at the Industrial Liaison Program, Massachusetts Institute of Technology, 1976.

Gordon, Thomas F. "Mass Media and Socialization: Theoretical Approaches." Paper presented at the International Communication Association, New Orleans, April 1974.

Gorn, Gerald J., and Goldberg, Marvin E. "A Research Program Investigating the Effects of Television Commercials on Children in Canada." Working paper presented to the Standing Committee on Broadcasting, Films, and Assistance to the Arts, Ottawa, Ontario, Canada, June 12, 1973.

Gorn, Gerald J., and Goldberg, Marvin E. "Television Advertising and Lower Income Children." Unpublished paper, McGill University Faculty of Management, Montreal, 1976a.

Gorn, Gerald J., and Goldberg, Marvin E. "Children's TV Commercials and the Hierarchy of Effects Hypothesis." Unpublished paper, McGill University, Faculty of Management, Montreal, 1976b.

Gorn, Gerald J., and Goldberg, Marvin E. "Children's Television Commercials: Do Child Viewers Become Satiated, Too?" Unpublished working paper, June 1977a.

Gorn, Gerald J., and Goldberg, Marvin E. "The Impact of Television Advertising on Children from Low Income Families." *Journal of Consumer Research* 4, no. 2 (1977b): 86-88.

Gorn, Gerald J., and Goldberg, Marvin E. "Possible Moderating Influences of TV Advertising's Effects on Children: Repetitive Exposure and a Hierarchy of Effects." McGill University, Faculty of Management, Montreal. Submitted for publication, June 1978.

Goslin, David A. *Handbook of Socialization Theory and Research.* Chicago: Rand McNally and Co., 1971.

Goulart, Ron. *The Assault on Childhood.* Los Angeles: Sherbourne Press, Inc., 1969.

Green, Frederick C. Testimony before the Federal Trade Commission, November 12, 1971.

Greenberg, Bradley S.; Ericson, Philip M.; and Vlahos, Mantha. "Children's Television Behaviors as Perceived by Mother and Child." In Eli Rubinstein et al., eds. *Television and Social Behavior,* vol. 4. Washington, D.C.: U.S. Government Printing Office, 1972, pp. 395-409.

Greenberg, Bradley S., and Reeves, B. "Children and the Perceived Reality of Television." *Journal of Social Issues* 32, no. 4 (1976): 86-97.

Greyser, Stephen A. "Irritation in Advertising." *Journal of Advertising Research* 13 (February 1973): 1-8.

Griffin, Emilie. "The Children's Advertising Review Unit." Remarks before the National Association of Broadcasters, Children's Television Workshop, Washington, D.C., June 3, 1975.

_____ . "What's Fair to Children? The Policy Need for New Research on Children's Perceptions of Advertising Content." *Journal of Advertising* 5, no. 2 (1976).

Grojean, Patricia Jo. "Monetary Experiences and Consumer Practices of Your Children." Masters Thesis, Oklahoma State University, May 1972.

Grojean, Patricia Jo, and Johnston, A. "Children's Influence on Family Food Purchase Decision." Bulletin 671, Agricultural Experiment Station, Mississippi State College, Mississippi, September 1963.

Gronhaug, Mjell. "Advertising and Children in a Culture Without TV Commercials." Paper presented at the Third Annual Conference in Research in Marketing, Brussels, June 1974.

Gruenberg, Sidonie M., and Gruenberg, B.C. *Parents, Children, and Money.* New York: Viking Press, 1933.

Guest, Lester P. "The Genesis of Brand Awareness." *Journal of Applied Psychology* 26 (1942): 800-808.

_____ . "Brand Loyalty—Twelve Years Later." *Journal of Applied Psychology* 39 (1955): 405-408.

_____ . "A Longitudinal Study of Attitude Development and Some Correlates." *Child Development* 35 (1964): 770-784.

Gussow, Joan. "It Makes Even Milk a Dessert—A Report on the Counter Nutritional Messages of Children's Television Advertising." *Clinical Pediatrics* No. 12, pp. 68-71.

_____ . "Counternutritional Messages of TV Ads Aimed at Children." *Journal of Nutrition Education* 4, no. 2 (1972): 48-52.

_____ . "Children and Television: What Do We Know? What Do We Need to Know?" Paper prepared for the Ford Foundation Seminar, Dec. 17-19, 1973.

_____ . "The Empty Calories and Soft Drink Boom." *Madison Avenue* (March 1975).

Haefner, James E.; Leckenby, John B.; and Goldman, Steven L. "The Measurement of Advertising Impact on Children." Paper presented at the American Psychological Association, Chicago, August 1975.

Haefner, James E., and Permut, Steven E. "An Approach to the Evaluation of Deception in Television Advertising." *Journal of Advertising* 3, no. 4 (1974): 40-45.

Hagen, J.W. "The Effect of Distraction on Selective Attention." *Child Development* 38 (1967): 685-694.

Hagen, J.W., and Hall, C.A. "The Development of Attention in Children." In

A.D. Pick, ed., *Minnesota Symposium on Child Psychology*, vol. 7. Minneapolis: University of Minnesota Press, 1973.

Hanson, Rose L. "A Study of Children's Use of Money." *University of Iowa Studies in Child Welfare* 8 (1933): 221-247.

Hawkins, Del I., and Coney, C.A. "Peer Group Influences on Children's Product Preferences." *Journal of the Academy of Marketing Science* 2 (Spring 1974): 322-331.

Helitzer, Melvin L., and Heyel, Carl. *The Youth Market*. New York: Media Books, 1970.

Heller, Melvin S., and Polsky, Samuel. "Studies in Violence and Television." New York: American Broadcasting Company, 1976.

Hendon, Donald W. "The Effects of TV Commercials on 'Normal' and Mentally Retarded Children." Paper presented at American Academy of Advertising Conference, Tempe, Arizona, March 1973.

Hendon, Donald W.; McGann, Anthony F.; and Hendon, Brenda L. "Children's Age, Intelligence and Sex as Variables Mediating Reactions to TV Commercials: Repetition and Content Complexity; Implications for Advertisers." *Journal of Advertising* 17, no. 3 (1978): 4-12.

Hermann, Robert C., ed. *The Consumer Behavior of Children And Teenagers: An Annotated Bibliography*. Chicago: American Marketing Association, 1969.

Hershey Foods Corporation. *Annual Report*. Hershey, Penn., 1977.

Heslop, Louise. "The Effects of Premium Advertising on Cereal Choices by Parents and Children." Research supported in part by doctoral grant from Canadian Advertising Advisory Board.

Heslop, Louise, and Ryans, Adrian. "A Second Look at Children and Premiums: An Experimental Approach with Behavioral Measures." Unpublished working paper, 1978.

Hess, Robert D., and Goldman, H. "Parent's Views of the Effects of Television on Their Children." *Child Development* 33 (1962): 411-426.

Himmelweit, Hilde T. "The Social Cost of Advertising." A proposal to study the effects of TV commercials and children's programming on children, prepared for the Ford Foundation Seminar, December 1973.

Hobson, John. "Advertising in Today's Society." *Advertising Quarterly* (Winter 1977-78): 54.

Hollander, S.W., and Jacoby, J. "Recall of Crazy Mixed-Up Commercials." *Journal of Advertising Research* 13, no. 3 (1973): 39-42.

Horn, Thomas D., and Miller, L. "Children's Concepts Regarding Debt." *Elementary School Journal* 55 (March 1955): 406-412.

H.R. 8613. Bill introduced to House of Representatives to create a National Council on Children and Advertising by Representative Wirth (D-Colorado), July 14, 1975.

Howard, John A., and Hulbert, James. "Advertising and the Public Interest."

A staff report to the Federal Trade Commission, Washington, D.C., 1973.

Howard, John A.; Hulbert, James; and Lehmann, Donald R. "An Exploratory Analysis of the Effect of Television Advertising on Children." Working paper (n.d.).

Hulbert, James. "Applying Buyer Behavior Analysis to Social Problems: The Case of Drug Use." in Ronald C. Curhan, ed., *Proceedings of the American Marketing Association.* (1974), pp. 289-292.

Hulse, Stewart H.; Deese, James; and Egeth, Howard. *The Psychology of Learning*, 4th ed. New York: McGraw-Hill, 1975.

Hyams, Larry; Tanner, Shari; and Rossiter, John R. "Effects of Race Models on Children's Product Preferences." Paper presented at the 1975 Conference on Culture and Communications, Philadelphia, Temple University, March 1975.

Instructor. "Kids Don't Buy Ads." Vol. 82 (August-September 1972): 28.

Irwin, Mac. "Is Your Right to Communicate Being Threatened?" Speech presented to the Association of Canadian Advertisers, May 5, 1975.

Iskoe, Andrew. "Advertising Via Famous Personalities and the Effects on Children." Student paper, The Wharton School, University of Pennsylvania, March 1976.

Jacoby, J., and Kyner, D.B. "Experimentally Validating a Conceptualization of Brand Loyalty." Paper #115 in *Consumer Psychology*, Purdue University, 1972.

Jacoby, J., and Lymer, David B. "Brand Loyalty vs. Repeat Purchase Behavior." *Journal of Marketing Research* 10 (February 1973): 1-9.

Jacoby, J.; Olson, Jerry; Szybillo, George; and Hart, Edward. *Affirmative Nutritional Disclosure in Advertising and Selective Alternatives: The Likely Impact on Consumers.* Consumer Research Institute, Inc., 1975.

James, Don L. "Youth, Media, and Advertising." *Studies in Marketing*, no. 15. Bureau of Business Research, University of Texas at Austin, 1971.

Jennings, Ralph. "Programming and Advertising Practices in Television Directed to Children." Action for Children's Television, Newton, Mass., 1971.

Jennings, Ralph, and Jennings C. "Programming and Advertising Practices in Television Directed to Children—Another Look." Action for Children's Television, Newton, Mass., 1972.

Jerome, Norge W. "Children's Television Advertising: A Vehicle for Pro-Social Nutritional Messages." Remarks to the Children's Advertising Review Unit Seminar, New York, June 20, 1975.

Jerome, Norge W., and Frese, Donna J. "What Are the Relative Contributions of Family vs. Television to a Child's Food Preference?" Paper presented at the Sixth Annual Telecommunications Policy Research Conference, Airlee, Virginia, May 1978.

Johnson, Nicholas. "Bringing Home the Bacon in a Chlosterol-Conscious Age." Speech to the Grocery Manufacturers of America, Washington, D.C., September 17, 1971a.

_____. Testimony before Senate Subcommittee on the Effect of Promotion and Advertising of Over-the-Counter Drugs, September 22, 1971b.

_____. "Rx for Children's Television." Speech to second national Action for Children's Television Symposium on children and television, Chicago, October 1971c.

Kagen, J., and Moss, H.A. *Birth to Maturity: A Study in Psychological Development*. New York: John Wiley and Sons, Inc., 1962.

Kalman, Herbert C. "Compliance, Identification, and Internalization: Three Processes of Opinion Change." *Journal of Conflict Resolution* 2 (1958): 51-60.

Kane, Thomas R.; Joseph, Joanne M.; and Tedeschi, J.T. "Person Perception and the Berkowitz Paradigm for the Study of Aggression." *Journal of Personality and Social Psychology* 33 (1976): 666-673.

Kanter, Donald L. "Pharmaceutical Advertising and Youth." Unpublished paper, Coronado Unified School District, Coronado, California, 1970.

Katzman, Natan. "King Audience." Working paper, 1976.

Kay, Herbert. "Children's Responses to Advertising: Who's Really to Blame?" *Journal of Advertising* 3, no. 1 (1974).

Kaye, Evelyn. *The Family Guide to Children's Television*. New York: Panthenon, 1974.

Keiser, Stephen K. "Awareness of Brands and Slogans." *Journal of Advertising Research* 14 (August 1974): 37-43.

Keiser, Stephen K., and Kuehl P.G. "Social Class and Income Influences on External Search Processes of Adolescents." *Proceedings*, Third Annual Conference, Association for Consumer Research, 1973, pp. 602-631.

Keniston, K. "Youth: A 'New' Stage of Life." *American Scholar* 39 (Autumn 1970): 631-654.

Kenkel, W.F. "Family Interaction in Decision-Making on Spending." In N. Foote, ed., *Household Decision-Making*. New York: New York University Press, 1961.

King, Martha B. *Money Management: Children's Spending*. Chicago: Household Finance Corporation, 1946.

Klapper, Hope L. "Children's Perceptions of Television as A Function of Cognitive Stage: A Preliminary Inquiry." Unpublished paper, March 10, 1974.

Klemensberg, Peter. "Advertising to Children and Information Processing." MBA dissertation, McGill University, April 1974.

Knowles, William S. "The Effectiveness of Television Advertising on the Child Consumer." Unpublished paper, Southern Methodist University, Fall, 1971.

Kohlberg, L. "The Cognitive-Developmental Approach to Socialization." In D. Goslin, ed., *Handbook of Socialization Theory and Research*. Chicago: Rand McNally and Co., 1971.

Kolman, A.S. "Cereal Advertising: A Study in Family Policy." Paper presented at the meeting of the Midwest Sociological Society, Omaha, Neb., April 1974.

Krugman, Herbert. "The 'Draw a Super Market' Technique." *Public Opinion Quarterly* 24 (Spring 1960): 148-149.

_____. "The Impact of Television Advertising: Learning Without Involvement." *Public Opinion Quarterly* 29 (Fall 1965): 349-356.

_____. "Processes Underlying Exposure to Advertising." *American Psychologist* 23 (1968).

Kyner, David; Jacoby, Jacob; and Chestnut, Robert. "Dissonance Resolution by Grade School Consumer." Purdue University, 1974.

LaMothe, William E. Testimony of the Kellogg Company before the United States Senate Select Committee on Nutrition and Human Needs, March 12, 1973.

Laurendeau, M., and Pinard, A. *Causal Thinking in the Child*. New York: International University Press, 1962.

Laurie, Liz. "Measuring Commercial Impact." *Journal of Advertising Research* 15 (August 1975): 23-25.

Lehman, Donald R. "An Exploratory Analysis of the Effect of Television Advertising on Children." Working paper, Columbia University, Graduate School of Business, 1971.

Leifer, Aimee D. "An Examination of the Socializing Influence of Television in the United States." Paper presented to the Prix Jeunesse Seminar, "Television and Processes of Socialization Within the Family," Germany, June 1975.

Leifer, Aimee; Gordon, Neal J.; and Graves, Sherryl Browne. "Children's Television: More than Mere Entertainment." *Harvard Educational Review* 44 (1974): 213-245.

Lesser, Gerald. *Children and Television: Lessons from Sesame Street*. New York: Random House, 1974.

_____. "Nutrition in Children's Television Advertising." Remarks to the Children's Advertising Review Unit Seminar, New York, June 20, 1975.

Levin, Stephen, and Anderson, Daniel. "The Development of Attention." *Journal of Communication* 26 (Spring 1976): 126-135.

Lewis, Charles E., and Lewis, Mary Ann. "The Impact of Television Commercials on Health-Related Beliefs and Behaviors of Children." *Pediatrics* 53 (March 1974): 431-435.

Liebert, Diane E.; Sprafkin, Joyce N.; Liebert, Robert M.; and Rubinstein, Eli A. "Effects of Television Commercial Disclaimers on the Product Expectations of Children." *Journal of Communication* 27 (Winter 1977): 118-124.

Liebert, Robert M. Testimony before the subcommittee on Communications of the House Committee on Interstate and Foreign Commerce, July 16, 1975.

Liebert, Robert M.; Neale, J.M.; and Davidson, E.S. *The Early Window: Effects of Television on Children and Youth*. New York: Pergamon Press, Inc., 1973.

Liebert, Robert M., and Poulos R.W. "Television and Personality Development: The Socializing Effects of An Entertainment Medium." In A. Davids, ed., *Child Personality and Psychopathology: Current Topics*, vol. II. New York: Wiley, 1975.

Liebert, Robert; Schuetz, Stephen; and Sprafkin, Joyce. "Spot Messages Appearing Within Saturday Morning Television Programs: A Content Analysys." Written record presented at Hearings before the Subcommittee on Communications of the Committee on Interstate and Foreign Commerce, House of Representatives (Serial No. 94-53). Washington, D.C.: Government Printing Office, 1975.

Liebert, Robert M.; Sprafkin, J.N.; and Poulos, R.W. "Selling Cooperation to Children." In W. S. Hald, ed. *Proceedings of the 20th Annual Advertising Research Foundation Conference*. New York: Advertising Research Foundation, 1975, pp. 54-57.

Liefield, John P., and Norsworthy, F. "The Influence of Television Advertising on Children Compared to Peer and Parental Influence." Unpublished paper, University of Guelph, Ontario, Canada, 1974.

Liefield, John P., et al. "Television Advertising and Children: An Experimental Study." Working paper, University of Guelph, Ontario, Canada, 1974.

Lindquist, Jay. "Children's Attitudes Toward Advertising on Television and Radio and in Children's Magazines and Comic Books." Unpublished paper, 1978.

Littner, Ned. "Television Advertising and Its Psychological Effects on Children." Statement appended to Seymour Banks' statement before the Federal Trade Commission, October 28, 1971.

Locker, Aaron M. Statement to the House Communications Subcommittee from the Toy Manufacturers of America, Inc., July 16, 1975.

Lovett, Robert; Barker, E.; and Marcus, B. "The Effects of a Nutrition Education Program at the Second Grade Level." *Journal of Nutrition Education* 2 Supplement 1 (Fall 1970): 81-95.

Lubin, Joanne S. "From Bugs to Batman, Children's TV Shows Produce Adult Anxiety." *The Wall Street Journal* (October 19, 1976): 1, 37.

Lyle, Jack. "Research on Television Advertising and Children." Paper prepared for the Ford Foundation, August 1973.

Lyle, Jack, and Hoffman, Heidi R. "Children's Use of Television and Other Media." In Eli A. Rubinstein et al., eds., *Television and Social Behavior*, vol. 4. Washington, D.C.: Government Printing Office, 1972a, pp. 129-256.

Lyle, Jack, and Hoffman, Heidi R. "Explorations in Patterns of Television Viewing by Preschool-age Children." In Eli A. Rubinstein et al., eds., *Television and Social Behavior*, vol. 4. Washington, D.C.: U.S. Government Printing Office, 1972b, pp. 257-273.

Maccoby, Eleanor. "Role-Taking in Childhood and its Consequences for Social Learning." *Child Development* 30 (1959): 230-252.

_____. "The Effects of Television on Children." In W. Schramm, ed., *The Science of Human Communication*. New York: Basic Books, 1963, pp. 116-128.

Maccoby, E.E., and Hagen, J.W. "Effects of Distractions upon Central versus Incidental Recall: Developmental Trends." *Journal of Experimental Child Psychology* 2 (1965): 280-289.

Mandler, Jean, and Johnson, Nancy. "Remembrance of Things Passed: Story Structure and Recall." *Cognitive Psychology* 9 (1977): 111-151.

Marketing News. "Toy Marketing Isn't for Kids Even Though Santa Claus Doesn't Worry About it or its Public Policy Implications." (October 8, 1976): 6.

Marshall, Helen R. "Differences in Parent and Child Reports of the Child's Experience in the Use of Money." *Journal of Educational Psychology* 54 (1963): 132-137.

_____. "The Relation of Giving Children An Allowance to Children's Money Knowledge and Responsibility to Other Practices of Parents." *Journal of Genetic Psychology* 104 (1964): 35-51.

Marshall, Helen R., and Magruder, L. "Relations Between Parent Money Education Practices and Children's Knowledge and Use of Money." *Child Development* 31 (1960): 253-284.

Martin, Charles H. "The Berne Model and Advertising Messages: A Psychographic Study." Paper presented at Association for Education in Journalism convention in Ottawa, August 16-19, 1975.

Martin, Cora, and Benson, L. "Parental Perceptions of the Role of Television in Parent-Child Interaction." *Journal of Marriage and the Family* 32 (August 1970): 410-414.

Masters, John C.; Gordon, Robert F.; and Clark, Lawrence V. "Effects of Self-Dispensed and Externally Dispensed Model Consequences on Acquisition, Spontaneous and Oppositional Imitation, and Long-Term Retention." *Journal of Personality and Social Psychology* 33 (1976): 421-430.

Mauro, Frank J., and Feins, Roberta P. *Kids, Food and Television: The Compelling Case for State Action*. Report prepared by the Office of Research and Analysis, New York State Assembly, March 1977.

Mayer, Jean, ed. *U.S. Nutrition Policies in the Seventies*. San Francisco: W.H. Freeman and Co., 1973.

McArthur, Leslie Z., and Eisen, Susan V. "Television and Sex-Role Stereotyping." Unpublished paper, Brandeis University, Waltham, Mass. (n.d.).

McCarthy, Charlotte, J. "An Exploratory Study of the Monetary Concepts of Preschool Children." Unpublished Master's thesis, Oklahoma State University.

McCarthy, Elizabeth D.; Langner, Thomas S.; Gersten, Joanne C.; Eisenberg, Jeanne G.; and Orzack, Lida. "Violence and Behavior Disorders." *Journal of Communication* 25 (Autumn 1975): 71-85.

McGannon, Donald M. Statement before the Subcommittee on Communications, House Committee on Interstate and Foreign Commerce, July 14, 1975.

McGuire, William J. "Persuasion, Resistance, and Attitude Change." In I. S. Pool et al., eds., *Handbook of Communication*. Chicago: Rand-McNally, 1973, pp. 216-252.

McIntyre, Jennie J., and Teevan, James J., Jr. "Television Violence and Deviant Behavior." In George A. Comstock and Eli A. Rubinstein, eds. *Television and Social Behavior*, vol. 3. Washington, D.C.: U.S. Government Printing Office, 1972, pp. 383-435.

McLeod, Jack J., and Chaffee, Steven R. "The Construction of Social Reality." In J.T. Tedeschi, ed., *The Social Influence Process*. Chicago: Aldine Atherton Publishing, 1972, pp. 50-99.

McLuhan, Marshall. *Understanding Media: The Extensions of Man*. New York: McGraw-Hill Book Company, 1964.

McNeal, James U. "Children as Consumers." Bureau of Business Research, University of Texas at Austin, 1964.

_____. "The Child Consumer: A New Market." *Journal of Retailing* 40 (1969a): 15-22.

_____. "An Exploratory Study of the Consumer Behavior of Children." In McNeal, ed., *Dimensions of Consumer Behavior*. New York: Appleton-Century-Crofts, 1969b.

Media Decisions. "Children's TV; Calm Before the Storm?" (August 1974): 48.

Mehrotra, Sunil, and Torges, Sandra. "Determinants of Children's Influence on Mother's Buying Behavior." *Proceedings of the 1976 Annual Conference of the Association for Consumer Research*, vol. 4 (1976): 56-60.

Melody, William H. "Children's Television: Economics and Public Policy." Action for Children's Television, Newton, Mass., 1973a.

_____. *Children's TV: The Economics of Exploitation*. New Haven, Conn.: Yale University Press, 1973b.

Melody, William H., and Ehrlich, Wendy. "Children's TV Commercials: The Vanishing Policy Options." *Journal of Communication* 24 (Autumn 1974): 113-125.

Meringoff, Laurene K. "A Story A Story: The Influence of the Medium on Children's Apprehension of Stories." Unpublished doctoral dissertation, Harvard University, June 1978.

Meyer, Timothy P.; Donohue, Thomas R.; and Henke, Lucy L. "Black Children's Perceptions of TV Commercials: A Cognitive-Developmental Study." *Journal of Advertising Research*, (October 1978).

Milavsky, J. Ronald; Pekowsky, Berton; and Stipp, Horst. "TV Drug Advertising and Proprietary and Illicit Drug Use Among Teenage Boys." *Public Opinion Quarterly* 39 (Winter 1975-76): 457-481.

Milkovich, Mark, and Miller, M. "Effects of Television Advertising on Children—

Exploring the Relationship Between Television Viewing and Language Development." Report #3, Michigan State University, July 1975.

Miller, Donald. "Remarks Regarding Children's Advertising." Testimony before the Federal Trade Commission, November 10, 1971.

Mohr, Phillip J. "Television, Children and Parents." An unpublished report, Department of Speech Communication, Wichita State University, 1978.

Moleski, Leo. "Children's TV Advertisements: A Brief Review." Paper presented at the American Psychological Association, August 30, 1975.

Moore, Denise F. "Sharing in Family Financial Management by High School Students." *Marriage and Family Living* 15 (November 1953): 319-321.

Moore, Roy L. "A Cross-Sectional Analysis of Consumer Learning Among Younger vs. Older Adolescents." Unpublished Ph.D. dissertation, University of Wisconsin, 1974.

Moore, Roy L.; Moschis, G.P.; and Stephens, L.F. "An Exploratory Study of Consumer Role Perceptions in Adolescent Consumer Socialization." Paper presented to International Communication Association, Chicago, April 23-26, 1975.

Moore, Roy L., and Stephens, L.F. "Some Communication and Demographic Determinants of Consumer Learning Among Older and Younger Adolescents." Paper presented to the Mass Communications Division of the International Communication Association, New Orleans, April 1974.

Morris, Norman S. *Television's Child.* Toronto, Canada: Little, Brown, and Co., 1971.

Moschis, George P.; Lawton, Joseph T.; and Stampfl, Ronald W. "Children's Consumer Learning: An Experimental Comparison of Two Models." Unpublished paper, February 1968.

Moskin, Robert, ed. "The Case for Advertising: Highlights of the Industry Presentation to the Federal Trade Commission." American Association of Advertising Agencies, New York, 1973.

Munn, Mark. "The Effect of Parental Buying Habits on Children Exposed to Children's Television Programs." *Journal of Broadcasting* 2 (1958): 253-258.

Murray, John P. "Television in Inner-City Homes: Viewing Behavior of Young Boys." In E. A. Rubinstein et al., eds., *Television and Social Behavior*, vol. 4. Washington, D.C.: Government Printing Office, 1972, pp. 345-394.

Murray, John P.; Nayman, Oguz B.; and Atkin, Charles K. "Television and the Child: A Comprehensive Research Bibliography." *Journal of Broadcasting* 16 (Winter 1971-72).

Myers, John G. "Communication Models and Advertising Regulation." Berkeley: Institute of Business and Economic Research, University of California, May 1972.

_____. "Advertising and Socialization." Draft prepared for Russell Sage Foundation Social Science Frontiers Series, September 1973.

Myers, L., Jr. "Plan 12–Relation of Personality to Perception of Television Advertising Messages." In L. Arons and M. A. May, eds. *Television and Human Behavior: Tomorrow's Research in Mass Communications.* New York: Appleton-Century-Crofts, 1963, pp. 202-218.

National Advertising Division. *Children's Advertising Guidelines.* New York: Council of Better Business Bureaus, September 1977.

_____. *A Four Year Review of the Children's Advertising Review Unit, June 1974-June 1978.* New York: Council of Better Business Bureaus, 1978a.

_____. *Children and Advertising: A Bibliography.* New York: Council of Better Business Bureaus, June 1978b.

National Association of Broadcasters. "Children's TV Advertising Statement of Principles." *Code News* 7 (June 1974).

National Association of Broadcasters Code Authority. *Advertising Guidelines: Children's TV Advertising.* New York: National Association of Broadcasters, 1978a.

_____. *The Television Code*, 20th ed. Washington: National Association of Broadcasters, June 1978b.

National Clearinghouse for Poison Control Centers. *Tabulations of 1973 Reports.* Washington, D.C.: Food and Drug Administration, May-June 1974.

Nelson, Bardin H. "Role of Money in Rural Family Living." Bulletin 979, Texas Agricultural Experiment Station, Texas A&M College, College Station, Texas, June 1961.

Nelson, James E. "Children as Information Sources in the Family Decision to Eat Out." Unpublished manuscript, n.d.

Neville, G. "The Impact of Television Advertising on Children's Food Opinions and Practices: An Exploratory Study." Unpublished master's thesis, Cornell University, 1973.

A.C. Nielsen Co. "The Effects of Television Upon Children." Confidential report, 1974.

_____. *The Television Audience: 1979.* Chicago, A. C. Nielsen Company, 1979. (Series of annual volumes.)

Nissenson, Marilyn. "Report on the Seminar on Children and Television Advertising." Report to the Ford Foundation, February 1974.

Norman, D.A. *Memory and Attention: An Introduction to Human Information Processing.* New York: John Wiley and Sons, Inc., 1967.

O'Bryant, Shirley L., and Corder-Bolz, Charles R. "Black Children's Learning of Work Roles from Television Commercials." *Psychological Reports* 42 (1978): 227-230.

Odom, R.D. "Effects of Perceptual Salience on a Recall of Relevant and Incidental Dimensional Values: A Developmental Study." *Journal of Experimental Psychology* 92 (1972): 285-291.

Odom, R.D., and Corbin, D.W. "Perceptual Salience and Children's Multi-Dimensional Problem Solving." *Child Development* 44 (1973): 425-432.

Odom, R.D., and Guzman, R.D. "Development of Hierarchies of Dimensional Salience." *Developmental Psychology* 6 (1972): 271-287.

Odom, R.D., and Mumbauer, D.C. "Dimensional Salience and Identification of the Relevant Dimension in Problem Solving: A Developmental Study." *Developmental Psychology* 4 (1971): 135-140.

Ojemann, Ralph. "What Money Means to the Child." *University of Iowa Studies in Child Welfare* 25 (1933).

O'Kelly, Charlotte G. "Sexism in Children's Television." *Journalism Quarterly* (Winter 1974): 722-724.

Olien, C.N.; Tichenor, P.J.; and Donohue, G.A. "A Systems Evaluation of a Purposive Message: The 'Mulligan Stew' ETC Project." Report submitted to Agricultural Extension Service, Institute of Agriculture, Forestry, and Home Economics, University of Minnesota, March 1975.

Oppenheim, Irene G. "The Teen-Age Consumer." In *Educating the Teen-Ager in Human Relations and Management of Resources.* Washington, D.C.: American Home Economics Association, 1965, pp. 17-35.

_____. *The Family as Consumer.* New York: The Macmillan Co., 1969.

Oxtoby-Smith, Inc. "Why Do American Youth Use Illicit Drugs: A Review of Scientific Research." Report prepared for The Proprietary Association, New York, January 1971. (Supplements issued October 1971, April 1972, March 1973, August 1975.)

Palmer, Edward. "Formative Research in Educational Television Production: The Experience of the Children's Television Workshop." In W. Schramm, ed., *Quality in Instructional Television.* Honolulu: University Press of Hawaii, 1972.

_____. "Formative Research in the Production of Television for Children." In *Seventy-third Yearbook of the Society for the Study of Education,* 1974.

Parsons, Talcott, and Bales, R.F. *Family, Socialization, and Interaction Process.* Glencoe, Ill.: The Free Press, 1955.

Parsons, T.; Bales, R.F.; and Shils, E.A. *Working Paper in the Theory of Action.* Glencoe, Ill.: The Free Press, 1953.

Pearce, Alan. "The Economics of Network Children's Television Programming." Staff report submitted to Federal Communications Commission, July 1972.

_____. "The Economics of Children's Television: An Assessment of the Impact of a Reduction in the Amount of Advertising." Staff report for the Federal Communications Commission, June 1974.

Phelan, Gladys K., and Schuaneveldt, J. "Spending and Saving Patterns of Adolescent Siblings." *Journal of Home Economics* 61 (1969): 104-109.

Philip, J.M. *The Child's World and Television Advertising.* Toronto: AIM Ltd., 1971.

Piaget, Jean. *The Psychology of Intelligence.* London: Routledge and Kegan Paul Ltd., 1950.

_____. *The Origins of Intelligence in Children*. New York: International University Press, 1952.

_____. *The Child's Conception of the World*. Totowa, N.J.: Littlefield, Adams, and Co., 1965.

_____. *The Psychology of the Child*. New York: Basic Books, 1969.

Piaget, Jean, and Inhelder, B. *The Growth of Logical Thinking from Childhood to Adolescence*, translated by A. Parsons and S. Seagrin. New York: Basic Books, 1958.

Pick, Ann D.; Frankel, D.G.; and Hess, V.L. "Children's Attention: The Development of Selectivity." *Review of Child Development Research* 5 (1974): 82-89.

Pierce, F.N.; Hooper, L.J.; and Culley, J.D. "Perceptions of Television Advertising Directed at Children: An Investigation of the Views of an Entire Community." Paper presented at the meeting of the Association for Education in Journalism, San Diego, Calif., August 1974.

Pillemer, David B., and Ward, Scott. "Investigating the Effects of Television Advertising on Children: An Evaluation of the Empirical Studies." Unpublished manuscript, Harvard University, 1977.

Popper, Edward. "Structural and Situational Effects on Mothers' Responses to Children's Purchase Requests." Unpublished doctoral dissertation, Harvard University Graduate School of Business Administration, 1978.

Potter, David M. *People of Plenty; Economic Abundance and the American Character*. Chicago: University of Chicago Press, 1954.

Poulos, Rita Wicks. "Unintentional Negative Effects of Food Commercials on Children: A Case Study." Media Action Research Center, 1975.

Powell, Kathryn S., and Gover, D.A. "The Adolescent as a Consumer: Facts and Implications." *Marriage and Family Living* 25 (August 1963): 359-364.

Prasad, V. Kanti; Rao, T.R.; and Sheikh, Anees A. "Mother vs. Commercial." *Journal of Communication* 28 (Winter 1978): 91-96.

Preston, Ivan L. *The Great American Blow-Up: Puffery in Advertising and Selling*. Madison, Wisc.: University of Wisconsin Press, 1975.

Prevney, Esther E. "A Quantitative Study of Family Practices in Training Children in the Use of Money." *Journal of Educational Psychology* 36 (1945): 411-428.

Proprietary Association. "Comments of the Proprietary Association in Opposition to the Proposed Rule to Prohibit Advertising of Drugs on Television Before 9 P.M." Before the Federal Communications Commission, Washington, D.C., August 1975.

Rao, T. "Television Advertising and its Effects on Children." University of Wisconsin, Milwaukee, in progress.

Ray, Michael L. "Marketing Communication and the Hierarchy of Effects." In P. Clarke, ed. *New Models for Mass Communication Research*. Beverly Hills, Sage Publications, 1973.

Raymond, Charles. *Advertising Research: The State of the Art*. New York: Association of National Advertisers, 1976.

Reeves, Byron, and Greenberg, Bradley S. "Children's Perceptions of Television Characters." *Human Communication Research* 3 (Winter 1977): 113-127.

Reilly Group, Inc., The Gene. "Assumption by the Child of the Role of Consumer." *The Child* 1 (July 1973a).

_____. "Meals and Snacking: The Child and What He Eats." *The Child* 2 (December 1973b).

_____. "The Child, the Media, and the Message." *The Child* 3 (September 1974).

_____. "The Child's Private World of Leisure." *The Child* 4 (April 1975).

Reisman, David, and Roseborough, H. "Careers and Consumer Behavior." In L.H. Clark, ed., *Consumer Behavior, vol. II: The Life Cycle and Consumer Behavior*. New York: New York University Press, 1955, pp. 1-18.

Resnik, Alan, and Stern, Bruce L. "Children's Television Advertising and Brand Choice: A Laboratory Experiment." *Journal of Advertising* 6 (Summer 1977): 11-17.

Roberts, Donald F. "Communications and Children: A Developmental Approach." In I. de Sola Pool and W. Schram, eds., *Handbook of Communication*. Chicago: Rand-McNally College Publishing Co., 1973, pp. 174-215.

Roberts, Donald F.; Gibson, W.A.; Christianson, P.; and Mooser, L. "Immunizing Children Against Commercial Appeals." Paper presented to the American Psychological Association, Toronto, Canada, August 1978.

Robertson, Thomas S. "The Impact of Television Advertising on Children." *Wharton Quarterly* 7 (Fall 1972): 38-42.

Robertson, Thomas S., and Feldman, Shel. "Children as Consumers: The Need for Multitheoretical Perspectives." In Beverlee B. Anderson, ed., *Advances in Consumer Research, vol. III, Proceedings*, Association for Consumer Research, 1975, pp. 508-512.

Robertson, Thomas S., and Rossiter, John R. "Children and Commercial Persuasion: An Attribution Theory Analysis." *Journal of Consumer Research* 1 (June 1974a): 13-20.

Robertson, Thomas S., and Rossiter, John R. "The Impact of Advertising on Children: Long-Term and Campaign Effects." Draft July 16, 1974b.

Robertson, Thomas S., and Rossiter, John R. "The Effects of Concentrated Television Advertising on Children's Toy and Game Choices." Unpublished paper, February 1975a.

Robertson, Thomas S., and Rossiter, John R. "Children's Consumer Disappointment." Working paper, Center for Research on Media and Children, University of Pennsylvania, April 1975b.

Robertson, Thomas S., and Rossiter, John R. "Maturational and Social Factors in Children's Understanding of TV Commercials." Paper presented at the American Psychological Association, August 30, 1975c.

Robertson, Thomas S., and Rossiter, John R. "Attitude Theory and Children's Consumer Behavior." Draft for AMA Attitude Research Conference, Hilton Head, South Carolina, February 1976a.

Robertson, Thomas S., and Rossiter, John R. "Short-Run Advertising Effects on Children: A Field Study." *Journal of Marketing Research* 13 (February 1976b): 68, 70.

Robertson, Thomas S., and Rossiter, John R. "Children's Consumer Satisfaction." Working paper, Center for Research on Media and Children, University of Pennsylvania, 1976c.

Robertson, Thomas S., and Rossiter, John R. "Children's Responsiveness to Commercials." *Journal of Communication* 27 (Winter 1977): 101-106.

Robertson, Thomas S.; Rossiter, John R.; and Brenner, Deborah. "Children's Responses to Commercials: Conjoint Analysis." Working paper, Center for Research on Media and Children, University of Pennsylvania, 1975.

Robertson, Thomas S.; Rossiter, John R.; and Gleason, Terry C. *Televised Medicine Advertising and Children.* New York: Praeger Publishers, 1979.

Robinson, Helen F. "Money Concepts in the Kindergarten." *Journal of Nursery Education* 19 (1964): 73-77.

Rogerson, Lannie C., and Whitford, E.B. "Money Experience of Ninth-Grade Pupils." *Journal of Home Economics* 52 (1960): 44-45.

Roper Organization, Inc. "Trends in Public Attitudes Toward Television and Other Mass Media: 1959-1974." New York: Television Information Office, April 1975.

_____. "Changing Public Attitudes Toward Television and Other Mass Media: 1959-1976." New York: Television Information Office, 1977.

_____. "Public Perceptions of Television and Other Mass Media: A Twenty-Year Review, 1959-1978." New York: Television Information Office, 1979.

Rossiter, John R. "Children's Susceptibility to Television Advertising: A Behavioral Test of Cognition and Attitude." Doctoral dissertation, Annenberg School of Communications, University of Pennsylvania, 1974.

_____. "Visual and Verbal Memory in Children's Product Information Utilization." Paper presented at the Association for Consumer Research Conference, Cincinnati, Ohio, October 1975.

_____. "Reliability of a Short Test Measuring Children's Attitudes Toward TV Commercials." *Journal of Consumer Research* 3 (March 1977): 179-184.

Rossiter, John R., and Robertson, Thomas S. "The Reception—Yielding Paradigm in Children's Susceptibility to Television Advertising." Working paper, Center for Research on Media and Children, University of Pennsylvania, 1974a.

Rossiter, John R., and Robertson, Thomas S. "Children's TV Commercials: Testing the Defenses." *Journal of Communication* 24 (Autumn 1974b): 137-145.

Rossiter, John R., and Robertson, Thomas S. "Children's Television Viewing: An Examination of Parent-Child Consensus." *Sociometry* 38 (September 1975): 308-326.

Rossiter, John R., and Robertson, Thomas S. "Canonical Analysis of Developmental, Social, and Experimental Factors in Children's Comprehension of Television Advertising." *Journal of Genetic Psychology* 129 (1976): 317-327.

Rossiter, John R., and Robertson, Thomas S. "Attitude-Behavior Relationships in Children's Consumer Research." In Y. Wind and M.G. Greenberg, eds., *Moving A Head with Attitude Research*. Chicago: American Marketing Association, 1977, pp. 116-119.

Rubin, Ronald S. "An Exploratory Investigation of Children's Responses to Commercial Content of Television Advertising in Relation to their Stages of Cognitive Development." Unpublished doctoral dissertation submitted to the University of Massachusetts, 1972.

Rubinstein, Eli A. "Remarks on Pro-Social Research in Children's Television." Remarks to the Children's Advertising Review Unit Seminar, New York, June 20, 1975.

Rust, Langbourne, and Watkins, Thomas. "Children's Commercials: Creative Development." *Journal of Advertising Research* 15 (October 1975): 21-69.

Salomon, Gavriel. "Cognitive Skill Learning Across Cultures." *Journal of Communication* 26 (Spring 1976): 138-144.

Sarson, Evelyn, ed. *Action for Children's Television, The First National Symposium on the Effects of Television Programming and Advertising on Children*. New York: Avon Books, 1971.

Schneider, John A. Statement in behalf of the CBS Broadcast Group before the Subcommittee on Communications, House Interstate and Foreign Commerce Committee, July 17, 1975.

Schramm, Wilbur. "What the Research Says." In W. Schramm, ed., *Quality in Instructional Television* (Honolulu: University Press of Hawaii, 1972.

_____. *Big Media, Little Media*. Beverly Hills: Sage Publications, 1977.

Schramm, W.; Lyle, J.; and Parker, E.B. *Television in the Lives of Our Children*. Stanford, Calif.: Stanford University Press, 1961.

Schuetz, Stephen, and Sprafkin, Joyce N. "Spot Messages Appearing Within Saturday Morning Television Programs: A Content Analysis." Media Action Research Center, 1975.

Schuetz, Stephen, and Sprafkin, Joyce N. "The Effects of a Simulation Game on Children's Consumer Knowledge." Unpublished working paper, 1978.

Senate Select Committee. *Hearings on Nutrition and Human Needs: Television Advertising of Food to Children*, series 73/NE 3,4,5,8). Washington, D.C.: Government Printing Office, 1973.

Shaak, Bruce; Annes, Lori; and Rossiter, John R. "Effects of the Social Success Theme on Children's Product Preference." Paper presented at the 1975

Conference on Culture and Communications, Philadelphia, Temple University, March 1975.

Shaffer, Helen B. "Youth Market." *Editorial Research Reports* (August 25, 1965): 625-641.

Shapiro, Sydelle S.; Bale, R.L.; Scardino, V.; and Cerva, T. "An Evaluation of the Mulligan Stew 4-H Television Series," vol. I. Abt Associates, Inc., December 20, 1974.

Sharaga, S. "The Effects of Television Advertising on Children's Nutrition Knowledge, Nutrition Attitudes, and Eating Habits." Unpublished doctoral dissertation, Cornell University, 1974. (Ann Arbor, Mich.: University Microfilms Number 75-1451.)

Sheikh, Anees A., and Moleski, Martin L. "Conflict in the Family Over Commercials." *Journal of Communication* 27 (Winter 1977): 152-157.

Sheikh, Anees A.; Prasad, V.K.; and Rao, T.R. "Children's TV Commercials: A Review of the Research." *Journal of Communication* 24 (Autumn 1974): 126-136.

Sheth, Jagdish N. "A Theory of Family Buying Decisions." Paper presented to the American Psychological Association, Division of Consumer Psychology, September 5, 1970.

Shimp, Terence, and Dyer, Robert. "The Pain-Pill-Pleasure Model and Illicit Drug Consumption: Opportunities for Consumer Behavior Research." Unpublished manuscript, February 1978.

Shimp, Terence; Dyer, R.; and Divita, S. "Advertising of Children's Premiums on Television: An Experimental Evaluation of the F.T.C.'s Proposed Guide." 1975.

Shimp, Terence; Dyer, Robert; and Divita, S. "An Experimental Test of the Harmful Effects of Premium-Oriented Commercials on Children." *Journal of Consumer Research* 3 (June 1976): 1-11.

Singer, Jerome L. "Imaginative Play and Normal Child Development." Remarks to the Children's Advertising Review Unit Seminar, New York, June 20, 1975.

Smarden, Eddie. "The True Problem with Kids Television—and a No Nonsense Methodology for Improving the Medium." Paper written for Ogilvy and Mather, Inc., February 20, 1973.

Snow, Robert P. "How Children Interpret TV Violence in a Play Context." *Journalism Quarterly* 51 (1974): 13-21.

Snyder, Joyce. "New NAD Children's Unit Will Perform by Precedent, Not Push." *Television/Radio Age* (July 22, 1974).

Sobel, Gwenn, and Rossiter, John R. "Effects of Sex Stereotyping on Children's Product Preference and Advertising Recall." Paper presented at the 1975 Conference on Culture and Communications, Philadelphia, Temple University, March 1975.

Sorenson, Ann, and Hansen, R. Gaurth. "Index of Food Quality." *Journal of Nutrition Education* 7, no. 2 (1975).

Sponsor. "Always on Saturday and Occasionally on Sunday; Kids Don't Take Their Quarters Around the Corner to Loews Like They Used to: Admen are Learning." vol. 12 (January 23, 1967): 27-34.

Sprafkin, J.N.; Liebert, R.M.; and Poulos, R.W. "Effects of a Prosocial Televised Example on Children's Helping." *Journal of Experimental Child Psychology* (1975).

Stein, A.H. "Mass Media and Young Children's Development." *71st Yearbook of the National Society for the Study of Education*, 1972, pp. 191-202.

Stein, Aletha H., and Friedrich, Lynette K. "Television Content and Young Children's Behavior." In John P. Murray, Eli A. Rubinstein, and George A. Comstock, eds., *Television and Social Behavior, vol. 2.* Washington, D.C.: U.S. Government Printing Office, 1972, pp. 202-317.

Stein, G., and Bryan, J. "The Effect of a Television Model upon Rule Adoption Behavior of Children." *Child Development* 43 (1972): 268-273.

Steiner, Gary A. "The People Look at Commercials: A Study of Audience Behavior." *Journal of Business* 9 (April 1966): 272-304.

Steinfeld, J. Untitled testimony, U.S. Congress, Senate, hearings before the Subcommittee on Communications of the Commerce Committee, March 1972.

Stephens, Lowndes F., and Moore, R.L. "Consumer Socialization: A Communication Perspective." Paper presented to the International Communication Association Student Summer Conference, Athens, Ohio, 1973.

Stephens, Lowndes F., and Moore, Roy L. "Price Accuracy as a Consumer Skill Among Younger and Older Adolescents." Submitted to Association of Education in Journalism, August 1974.

Stephens, Lowndes F., and Moore, Roy L. "Price Accuracy As a Consumer Skill." *Journal of Advertising Research* 14 (August 1975): 27-34.

Stern, Bruce L., and Resnik, Alan J. "Children's Understanding of a Televised Commercial Disclaimer." Unpublished paper, Portland State University, 1978.

Strauss, Anselm L. "The Development and Transformation of Monetary Meanings in the Child." *American Sociological Review* 17 (1952): 275-286.

Streicher, Helen W., and Bonney, H.L. "Children Talk About Television." Paper presented to Eastern Sociological Society, 1973.

Streit, Fred; Halsted, Donald L.; and Pascale, Pietro J. "Differences among Youthful Users and Nonusers of Drugs Based on their Perceptions of Parental Behavior." *International Journal of the Addictions* 9 (1974): 749-755.

Suls, Jerry M., and Gutkin, Daniel C. "Children's Reactions to an Actor as a Function of Expectations and of the Consequence Received." *Journal of Personality* 44 (1976): 149-162.

Summers, John B. Statement of the National Association of Broadcasters before the Subcommittee on Communications of the House Interstate and Foreign Commerce Committee, July 15, 1975.

Surgeon-General's Scientific Advisory Committee on Television and Social Behavior, *Television and Growing Up: The Impact of Televised Violence.* Washington, D.C.: U.S. Government Printing Office, 1972.

Syzbillo, George J., and Sosanie, Arlene K. "Family Decision Making: Husband, Wife, and Children." *Advances in Consumer Research*, vol. 5.

Syzbillo, George; Sosanie, Arlene; and Tenebein, Aaron. "Should Children Be Seen But Not Heard?" *Journal of Advertising Research* 17 (December 1977): 7-13.

TV Guide Magazine. "TV and Your Child: In Search of an Answer." New York: TV Guide, 1969.

Television/Radio Age. "NARB and Kid Ads: New Code in Works?" (April 1, 1974): 21.

_____. "Advertising in a Restrictive Environment: New Codes Return Ad Concepts Back to Basics." (November 26, 1973): 39.

Teter, John W. "The Family, Peers, and Media Influences on Youth's Present and Future Consumption Preferences." Unpublished thesis, Oklahoma State University, Stillwater, Oklahoma, 1966.

Thompson, Glenn W. "Children's Acceptance of Television Advertising and the Reaction of Televiewing to School Achievement." *Journal of Education Research* 58 (December 1964): 171-174.

Treisman, A.M. "Verbal Cues, Language and Meaning in Selective Attention." *American Journal of Psychology* 77, (1964): 206-219.

Turner, Ralph H. *Family Interaction* New York: John Wiley and Sons, Inc., 1970.

Twomey, John E. "Some Views on TV Advertising to Children." Radio and Television Arts Department, Ryerson Polytechnic Institute, June 1973.

Ullrich, Helen, and Briggs, George. "The General Public." In J. Myer, ed., *U.S. Nutrition Policies in the Seventies*, San Francisco: W. H. Freeman and Co., 1973.

United States Congress. Hearing before Senate Select Committee on Nutrition and Human Needs. *Nutrition Education—1973*, parts 3-5. TV Advertising of Food to Children, 93rd Congress, 1st session, March 5-12, 1973. Washington, D.C.: Government Printing Office, 1973a.

_____. Hearings before Senate Select Committee on Nutrition and Human Needs. *Nutrition Education—1973*, part 8. Broadcast Industry's Response to TV Ads, 93rd Congress, 1st session, June 11, 1973. Washington, D.C.: Government Printing Office, 1973b.

_____. Hearing before House Subcommittee on Communications on Broadcast Advertising and Children, 94th Congress, 1st session, July 14-17, 1975. Washington, D.C.: Government Printing Office, 1975.

_____ . Hearings before House Subcommittee on Domestic Marketing, Consumer Relations and Nutrition. *Nutrition Education,* 95th Congress, 1st session, September-November 1977. Washington, D.C.: U.S. Government Printing Office, 1977.

U.S. Senate Select Committee on Nutrition and Human Needs. *Dietary Goals for the United States,* 2nd ed. Washington, D.C.: U.S. Government Printing Office, 1977.

Vaillancourt, Pauline Marie. "Stability of Children's Survey Responses." *Public Opinion Quarterly* 37, no. 3 (1973): 373-387.

Verna, Mary Ellen. "The Female Image in Children's TV Commercials." *Journal of Broadcasting* 19 (Summer 1975): 301-309.

Vogl, A.J. "The Changing Face of the Children's Market." *Sales Management* 93 (December 18, 1964): 35-36, 38.

Wackman, Daniel B. Statement to the Federal Trade Commission, November 11, 1971.

Wackman, Daniel B., and Ward, Scott. "Children's Information Processing of Television Commercial Messages." Manuscript based on a Symposium at the American Psychological Association Convention, Montreal, 1973.

Wackman, Daniel B., and Wartella, Ellen. "A Review of Research Related to Suggested Guidelines for Premium Advertising." April 1975.

Wackman, Daniel B., and Wartella, Ellen. "A Review of Cognitive Development Theory and Research and the Implications for Research on Children's Responses to Television." *Communication Research* 4 no. 2 (1977): 203-225.

Wackman, Daniel B.; Wartella, Ellen; and Ward, Scott. "Children's Information Processing of Television Advertising." Final report to the National Science Foundation, 1976.

Wackman, Daniel B.; Wartella, Ellen; and Ward, Scott. "Learning To Be Consumers: The Role of the Family." *Journal of Communication* 27 (Winter 1977): 138-151.

Walters, Richard H., and Parke, R.D. "Influences of Response Consequences to a Social Model on Resistance to Deviation." *Journal of Experimental Child Psychology* 1 (1964): 269-280.

Ward, Scott. "Effects of Television Advertising on Children and Adolescents." Research supported by National Institute for Mental Health and by the Marketing Science Institute, June 1971.

_____ . "Children and Television: Impressions, Impact, and Issues." Speech to Quaker Oats Management Conference, October 19, 1971.

_____ . "Advertising and Youth: Two Studies." *Sloan Management Review* 14 (1972a): 2-382.

_____ . "Children's Reactions to Commercials." *Journal of Advertising Research* 12 (April 1972b): 37-45.

_____. "Kids TV—Marketers on the Hot Seat." *Harvard Business Review* (July-August 1972c).

_____. "Consumer Socialization." *Journal of Consumer Research* 1 (September 1974): 1-14.

_____. "Can Pragmatic Marketing and Virtue March Together? Ask the Children!" Remarks to the Children's Advertising Review Unit Seminar, New York City, June 20, 1975.

Ward, Scott, and Faber, Ronald. "Validation of Mother-Child Purchase Influence Frequency Reports by the Multitrait-Multimethod Matrix." A working paper, Marketing Science Institute, 1975.

Ward, Scott; Levinson, D.; and Wackman, D. "Children's Attention to Television Advertising." In E.A. Rubinstein, et al., eds. *Television and Social Behavior,* vol. 4. Washington, D.C.: Government Printing Office, 1972, pp. 491-516.

Ward, Scott; Popper, Edward; and Wackman, Daniel B. "Parents Under Pressure: Influences on Mother's Responses to Children's Purchase Requests." Working paper no. 77-107, Marketing Science Institute, Cambridge, Mass. August 1977.

Ward, Scott; Reale, G.; and Levinson, D. "Children's Perceptions, Explanations, and Judgments of Television Advertising: A Further Exploration." In Eli A. Rubinstein et al., eds. *Television and Social Behavior,* vol. 4. Washington, D.C.: U.S. Government Printing Office, 1972, pp. 468-490.

Ward, Scott, and Robertson, T.S. "Family Influences on Adolescent Consumer Behavior." Paper presented to the First Annual Conference, Association of Consumer Research, Amherst, Mass., 1970.

Ward, Scott, and Robertson, T.S. "Adolescent Attitudes Toward Television Advertising: Preliminary Findings." In E.A. Rubinstein et al., eds., *Television and Social Behavior,* vol. 4. Washington, D.C.: Government Printing Office, 1972, pp. 526-542.

Ward, Scott; Robertson, T.S.; and Wackman, D.B. "Children's Attention to Television Advertising." In D.M. Gardner, ed., *Proceedings, Association for Consumer Research.* 1971, pp. 143-156.

Ward, Scott, and Wackman, Daniel. "Family and Media Influences on Adolescent Consumer Learning." *American Behavioral Scientist* 14 (January-February 1971): 415-427.

Ward, Scott, and Wackman, D.B. "Children's Purchase Influence Attempts and Parental Yielding." *Journal of Marketing Research* 9 (August 1972): 316-319.

Ward, Scott, and Wackman, D.B. "Effects of Television Advertising on Consumer Socialization." Marketing Science Institute, Cambridge, Mass., September 1973a.

Ward, Scott, and Wackman, D.B. "Children's Information Processing of Television Advertising." In P. Clarke, ed., *New Models for Mass Communication Research*. Beverly Hills, Calif.: Sage Publications, 1973b, pp. 119-146.

Ward, Scott; Wackman, D.B.; Faber, Ronald; and Lesser, Gerald. "Effects of Television Advertising on Consumer Socialization." Working paper, Marketing Science Institute, Cambridge, Mass.: 1974.

Ward, Scott; Wackman, D.B.; and Wartella, Ellen. "Contributions of Cognitive Development Theory to Consumer Socialization Research." Paper presented to the Association for Consumer Research, Cincinnati, Ohio, October 1975.

Ward, Scott; Wackman, Daniel B.; and Wartella, Ellen. *How Children Learn to Buy: The Development of Consumer Information-Processing Skills*. Beverly Hills: Sage Publications, 1977.

Wartella, Ellen. "A Research Model for Examining Consumer Socialization from a Cognitive Developmental Perspective." Paper presented at International Communications Association meeting, Chicago, April 1975.

Wartella, Ellen, and Ettema, James. "A Cognitive Developmental Study of Children's Attention to Television Commercials." *Communications Research* 1 (January 1974).

Weik, James L. "Advertising Recall as Influenced by the Number, Length, and Position of Commercials." In Ronald C. Curhan, ed., *1974 Proceedings: Series No. 36*. Chicago: American Marketing Association, 1974, pp. 406-410.

Weiss, Walter. "Mass Communication." *Annual Review of Psychology*. 22 (1971): 309-336.

——. "Effects of the Mass Media of Communication." In Gardner Lindzey and Elliot Aronson, eds., *The Handbook of Social Psychology*, 2nd ed., vol. 5. Reading, Mass: Addison-Wesley, 1969, pp. 77-195.

Wells, William D. "Children as Consumers." In J.W. Newman, ed., *On Knowing the Consumer*. New York: John Wiley and Sons, 1966.

——. "Communicating with Children." *Journal of Advertising Research* 5 (June 1965): 2-14.

——. "Television and Aggression: Replication of an Experimental Field Study." Unpublished manuscript, Graduate School of Business, University of Chicago, 1973.

Wells, William D., and LoScuito, Leonard A. "Direct Observation of Purchasing Behavior." *Journal of Marketing Research* 3 (August 1966): 227-233.

White House Conference on Food, Nutrition and Health—Final Report. Washington, D.C. Government Printing Office, 1970.

Wiley, Richard E. Statement on Children's Television Advertising before the Subcommittee on Communications. House Committee on Interstate and Foreign Commerce, July 17, 1975.

Wilkie, William L. "Assessment of Consumer Information Processing Research in Relation to Public Policy Needs." Washington, D.C.: Office of

Exploratory Research and Problem Assessment, National Science Foundation, 1974.

Williams, Joyce W. "A Gradient of the Economic Concepts of Elementary School Children and Factors Associated with Cognition." *Journal of Consumer Affairs* 4 (Winter 1970): 113-125.

Winick, Charles; Williamson, L.G.; Chuzmir, S.F.; and Winick, M.P. *Children's Television Commercials: A Content Analysis.* New York: Praeger Publishers, 1973.

Witryol, S.; Lowden, L.; and Fagan, J. "Incentive Effects upon Attention in Children's Discrimination Learning." *Journal of Experimental Child Psychology* 5 (1967): 94-108.

Wohlner, Grace. "How Children Learn to Handle Money." *Parents Magazine* 42 (1971): 84-86.

Wolf, T.M. "Effects of Televised Modeled Verbalizations on Resistance to Deviation." *Developmental Psychology* 8 (1973): 51-56.

Worchel, Stephen; Hardy, Thomas W.; and Hurley, Richard. "The Effects of Commercial Interruption of Violent and Nonviolent Films on Viewers' Subsequent Aggression." *Journal of Experimental Social Psychology* 12 (1976): 220-232.

Wrighter, Carl P. *I Can Sell You Anything.* New York: Ballantine Books, 1972.

Yankelovich, Daniel. *Mothers' Attitudes Toward Children's Programs and Commercials.* Newton, Mass: Action for Children's Television, 1970.

Zunich, Michael. "Teenagers Influence on Personal and Family Purchases." *Journal of Home Economics* 48 (June 1966): 483-484.

Index

About the Authors

Richard P. Adler is a visiting member of the Motion Picture/Television faculty in the Department of Theater Arts, University of California, Los Angeles. He was formerly director of the Aspen Institute Workshop on Television and assistant director of the Aspen Program on Communications and Society in Palo Alto. He received the B.A. from Harvard College and did graduate work in English at the University of California at Berkeley. He has taught at Berkeley, Oberlin College, and Stanford University, and served as a research associate at the Harvard Graduate School of Education.

Mr. Adler has edited a number of books on various aspects of television, including *All in the Family: A Critical Appraisal; The Electronic Box Office* (with Walter S. Baer); and *Television as a Social Force* and *Television as a Cultural Force* (with Douglass Cater). He has written a column of television criticism for *The Wall Street Journal* and contributed articles to many magazines. He is currently working on a book for parents about children and television.

Gerald S. Lesser is Bigelow Professor of Education and Developmental Psychology at Harvard University. He is also chairman of the Board of Advisers of the Children's Television Workshop.

Dr. Lesser received the B.S. and M.A. from Columbia University and the Ph.D. from Yale University, and taught at Adelphi College and Hunter College before going to Harvard. He is the author of *Children and Television: Lessons from Sesame Street* (1974), as well as many articles and several books on educational psychology and the effects of the visual media on children. In 1974, he was the recipient of the Distinguished Contribution Award for Applications in Psychology from the American Psychological Association.

Laurene Krasny Meringoff is currently a research associate at Harvard University's Project Zero, where she is codirecting a study of children's understanding of stories in television and other media. She received her academic training in child development and educational psychology at the Center for Research in Children's Television at the Harvard Graduate School of Education, where she received the doctorate. Dr. Meringoff has had considerable experience in testing television and print advertising with children for major advertisers, as a senior associate for the Gene Reilly Group, Inc. (a private research firm), and for the Children's Advertising Review Unit. She coordinated an industry-sponsored national survey of children's and mothers' consumer attitudes and behavior (*The Child*, 1973-1974). She has also served as a consultant to consumer groups and to the Federal Trade Commission in its Children's Advertising Rulemaking Proceeding. She has testified on the effects of television food advertising on children before a House subcommittee and before the Federal Trade Commission.

Thomas S. Robertson is professor and chairperson of the Marketing Department, The Wharton School, University of Pennsylvania, and is director of the Center for Research on Media and Children. He has taught previously at Harvard University, The University of California at Los Angeles, and Northwestern University. He received the Ph.D in marketing from Northwestern concurrently with the M.A. in sociology.

Publications by Dr. Robertson have appeared in many business and behavioral science journals. He is the author of *Innovative Behavior and Communications* (1971) and *Consumer Behavior* (1970); coeditor (with Harold H. Kassarjian) of *Perspectives in Consumer Behavior* (1980); coeditor (with Scott Ward) of *Consumer Behavior: Theoretical Sources* (1973); and coauthor of *Televised Medicine Advertising and Children* (1979).

John R. Rossiter is an associate professor at the Graduate School of Business, Columbia University. He was previously associated with the Center for Research on Media and Children, The Wharton School, University of Pennsylvania.

Dr. Rossiter received the Ph.D in communications from the University of Pennsylvania in 1974. He received the M.S. degree in marketing from the University of California at Los Angeles and an undergraduate honors degree in psychology from the University of Western Australia. Publications by Dr. Rossiter have appeared in several business journals, including the *Journal of Consumer Research* and the *Journal of Marketing Research*. He is coauthor (with Thomas S. Robertson and Terry C. Gleason) of *Televised Medicine Advertising and Children* (1979). He has also published in psychology, sociology, and communication research, and is coauthoring a book on communication models applied to advertising. He is a member of the American Marketing Association, Association for Consumer Research, International Communications Association, and the Australian, British, and American Psychological Associations.

Scott Ward is professor of marketing at The Wharton School, University of Pennsylvania, and a senior research associate at Marketing Science Institute, Cambridge, Massachusetts. Dr. Ward received the B.S., M.A., and Ph.D degrees from the University of Wisconsin. He worked in advertising and taught at the School of Communications at the University of Washington, and the Harvard Graduate School of Business Administration.

Dr. Ward has published articles in many professional journals, including *Public Opinion Quarterly, Harvard Business Review, Journal of Marketing Research,* and *American Behavioral Scientist.* He served as coeditor (with Michael Ray) of a special issue of *Communication Research,* and is coeditor of *Consumer Behavior: Theoretical Sources.* He has consulted with many firms and government agencies, and has testified before the Federal Trade Commission and the Federal Communications Commission.

About the Collaborators

Bernard Z. Friedlander is professor of psychology and director of the New England Television Research Center at the University of Hartford, where his principal research has been on topics concerned with child development. He is especially interested in the impact of television on children's lives.

Leslie Isler is a doctoral student in human development at the Harvard Graduate School of Education. She received the B.A. in communication and education from Clark University and the Ed.M. from the Harvard Graduate School of Education. Ms. Isler has worked as a research assistant at Marketing Science Institute, Cambridge, Massachusetts, where her research focused on the effects of television advertising on children and consumer socialization.

Ronald J. Faber is an assistant professor in the College of Communications at the University of Texas, Austin. He is preparing for the Ph.D. degree at the School of Journalism and Mass Communication of the University of Wisconsin, Madison. His research interests include life-span development and media use, cognitive development, and television advertising and children.

David B. Pillemer is an assistant professor of psychology at Wellesley College. His current interests include cognitive development in children and the relationships between social science and social policy.